£5.75

Macmillan Law Masters

Legal Method

D1353770

MACMILLAN LAW MASTERS

Series Editor: Marise Cremona

Legal Method

Second Edition

Ian McLeod
LLB, BA
Solicitor
London Guildhall University

Law series editor: Marise Cremona
Senior Fellow, Centre for Commercial Law Studies
Queen Mary and Westfield College, University of London

MACMILLAN

First edition 1993
Reprinted 1994
Second edition 1996

Published by
MACMILLAN PRESS LTD
Houndmills, Basingstoke, Hampshire RG21 6XS
and London.
Companies and representatives
throughout the world

ISBN 0–333–67696–3

A catalogue record for this book is available
from the British Library.

Copy-edited and typeset by Povey-Edmondson
Okehampton and Rochdale, England

10   9   8   7   6   5   4   3   2
05 04 03 02 01 00 99 98 97

Printed in Hong Kong

To Jacqui

Contents

Preface to the Second Edition

This book is intended to provide an introduction to the techniques of handling legal sources. Some comment on the nature of introductions may therefore be useful. Introductions may appear to be simple but they need not be simplistic: indeed good ones must not be: 'With all its surface simplicity, an introduction must cut as deep as its author has wit and strength to see the way. It must cut for that deepest simplicity which is true meaning' (Karl Llewellyn, *The Bramble Bush*, revised edn, 1950, p. 7).

Accordingly, I have tried to avoid the twin traps of oversimplification on the one hand, and unnecessary complexity on the other. However, I have been unable to avoid the fact that legal method is open-ended, even though on many occasions this has meant that I have been unable to offer the comfort of neat conclusions and reliable rules. As Hutchinson and Monahan said:

> 'Legal doctrine not only does not, but also cannot, generate determinant results in concrete cases. Law is not so much a rational enterprise as a vast exercise in rationalisation. Legal doctrine can be manipulated to justify an almost infinite spectrum of possible outcomes. Moreover, a plausible argument can be made that any such outcome has been derived from the dominant legal conceptions. Legal doctrine is nothing more than a sophisticated vocabulary and repertoire of manipulative techniques for categorising, describing, organising and comparing: it is *not* a methodology for reaching substantive outcomes'. (*Law, Politics and Critical Legal Scholars: The Unfolding Drama of American Legal Thought* (1984) 36 Stanford Law Rev, 199, at p. 206, original emphasis.)

Except when writing about the European Community and Union, in which context it often seems most natural to think in terms of 'Britain' or the 'United Kingdom', I have tended to write in terms of 'England' and 'English' law and practice. In doing so, I have intended to include 'Wales' and 'Welsh'. Some of what I have written may also apply in Scotland and Northern Ireland, but how much and to what extent is beyond my knowledge. It follows that readers in those jurisdictions should proceed with caution.

Authors commonly profess their indebtedness to others, and I am no exception. Many friends, colleagues and students have, in varying ways, had their impact on this book generally, and the improvements which have been incorporated into the second edition in particular. It would be futile to seek to name them all and invidious to name only some. Above all, however, I am indebted to my wife, Jacqui, not only for her word-processing and proofreading skills, but also for her patient good humour, the extent of which continues to amaze me.

As I finished writing the first edition of this book two quotations occurred to me. They are worth repeating here. The first was the much-quoted comment of Sir Walter Scott: 'A lawyer without history or literature is a mechanic, a mere working mason; if he possesses some knowledge of these, he may venture to call himself an architect' (*Guy Mannering*). The second was the old gibe that 'studying the law sharpens the mind by narrowing it'.

Reading these propositions together, it is reasonable to conclude that the better furnished the student's mind may be before embarking on a study of the law, the greater the chance that the narrowing process will leave something else besides the law. The desirability of this result was very succinctly expressed many years ago by Lord Goodman of Messrs Goodman Derrick & Co, the London solicitors, when he coined the dictum 'a lawyer who is only a lawyer isn't much of a lawyer'.

I have tried to make the body of the text up to date to 1 January 1996, although I have been able to accommodate a few later developments and, in the context of the suggestions for further reading, I have mentioned new editions which are scheduled for publication during 1996 where their publishers have made me aware of them. Additionally, it is worth noticing that in April 1996 the government abandoned the introduction of the transfer for trial procedure, which is mentioned at pp. 47–8. As a matter of human interest, the child who was at the centre of the *Cambridge Health Authority* case, which is discussed at p. 72, died in May 1996. Finally, in *Three Rivers District Council* v. *Bank of England* (No 2) [1996] 2 All ER 363, the High Court, having accepted the general proposition that statutes should be construed purposively, went on to say that it is particularly important that they should be so construed when the court is seeking to find a construction which is consistent with a Community obligation. The court said it followed that in these circumstances it is permissible to refer to ministerial statements in *Hansard* in order to identify the *purpose* of the domestic legislation, even though the criteria specified in *Pepper* v. *Hart* (see p. 296) may not be satisfied.

IAN MCLEOD.

Acknowledgements

The author and publishers wish to thank the following for permission to use copyright material: Institute of Advanced Legal Studies for extracts from *British and French Statutory Drafting* (1987); Oxford University Press for extracts from Engle, 'Bills are Made to Pass as Razors are Made to Sell', *Statute Law Review* (1983), pp. 7, 9, 12, 13–14, 15.

Every effort has been made to trace all the copyright-holders, but if any have been inadvertently overlooked the publishers will be pleased to make the necessary arrangement at the first opportunity.

Table of Cases

Ideas and Institutions

Having read this Part you should understand the nature of legal reasoning and have a basic knowledge of the structure of the English and European Community legal systems. You should also know how to find, cite and use the principal sources of law.

1 An Introduction to Law and Legal Reasoning

1.1 Introduction

It is obvious that lawyers think about law. It may seem to be equally obvious that the first question must be: *what is law*? In fact, as it happens, practising lawyers seldom if ever feel the need to ask themselves this question. They ask the much more specific question: *what is the law relating to this particular situation*? Nevertheless, the first and more general question is still worth asking, because it will lead you to consider some points of view which will inform your understanding of how law works, and of how lawyers handle their sources.

1.2 Distinguishing Law from Other Rules

If we begin by conjuring up some simple statements of law, we will immediately come up with examples such as 'parties to contracts who do not perform their obligations may have to pay damages to other parties', and 'people who commit theft may be punished'. In other words, the most straightforward definition of law might appear to be: *those rules which the courts will enforce*. This is useful because it excludes rules of a great many other kinds, such as the rules of clubs, the rules of sports, the requirements of religious observance, and so on. However, it is not a good definition, for three main reasons.

First, not all laws are prohibitory. Rather than imposing duties upon people many laws confer powers, and the law will not compel them to exercise those powers if they choose not to do so. For example, provided I am not already married, the law recognizes my power, or capacity, to get married. However, the courts cannot compel me to marry, and I may remain single for the rest of my life. Second, even where a clear legal prohibition is undoubtedly breached, the courts may have discretion to grant or withhold a remedy (see, for example, the discussion of equitable remedies at p. 28). Third, and most basically, the statement which we are considering is not really a definition of law at all, because it does not tell us whether a particular rule is one which the courts will enforce.

If we reformulate the question, and ask *which rules will the courts enforce*, it becomes apparent that the question is essentially political, because the answer involves giving an account of the relationships between various organs of the state, and between the state and the individual. The political nature of law may be self-evident, but it is nevertheless worth identifying. Moreover, its consequences for the nature of the judges' function in terms of law-making are worth consideration.

One widely held view is that a major part of the judges' role is to protect the established order of things. Griffith, a distinguished academic with avowedly left-wing sympathies, and formerly a professor of law at the London School of Economics, produced a typical statement of this view in a book which first appeared in 1977:

> 'Judges are concerned to preserve and to protect the existing order. This does not mean that no judges are capable of moving with the times, or adjusting to changed circumstances. But their function in our society is to do so belatedly. Law and order, the established distribution of power both public and private, the conventional and agreed view amongst those who exercise political and economic power, the fears and prejudices of the middle and upper classes, these are the forces which the judges are expected to uphold and do uphold . . . .
>
> 'That this is so is not a matter for recrimination. It is idle to criticize institutions for performing the task they were created to perform and have performed for centuries.' (*The Politics of the Judiciary*, 4th edn, 1991, p. 328.)

These assertions form part of the conclusion to an argument in which Griffith assembled a good deal of evidence from the cases to support his thesis that judges are not neutral players in the game of law but are 'politically . . . parasitic'.

Griffith's argument is not, of course, universally accepted. In particular Lee, arguing that Griffith's case underestimates the weight of contrary evidence and is logically fallacious, says:

> 'Griffith's book was immediately subjected to criticism by another LSE professor, Kenneth Minogue, who wrote in the *Times Literary Supplement*:
>
> > "The logic of Professor Griffith's argument is perfectly clear. It runs: if the courts were politically conservative, they would come down

against trade unions; they do come down against trade unions; therefore they are politically conservative. In logic, this is called the fallacy of affirming the consequent, and it is a fallacy because there are usually many different and possibly conflicting propositions from which the consequent might flow."

'In moments of realism, it seems obvious that there are explanations for trade unions losing cases in the courts, such as the fact that statutes might have been passed by a parliament elected on a platform of curbing trade union power, or the fact that trade unions *do* sometimes try to act above and beyond the law. It is also obvious that the courts do *not* always come down against the unions. But Griffith's fallacy of affirming the consequent nevertheless captures the imagination of some students and would survive any number of courses in logic from Professor Minogue. Some people want to believe that this is the key to judicial law-making.' (Original emphasis; *Judging Judges*, 1988, p. 13.)

Nevertheless, as we shall see in the rest of this book generally, and particularly in Chapter 15, English judges tend to be conscious of their own limitations in the context of law-making. Lord Devlin, a former Law Lord, writing long after his retirement, said:

'I am not one of those who believe that the only function of law is to preserve the status quo. Rather I should say that law is the gate-keeper of the status quo. There is always a host of new ideas galloping around the outskirts of a society's thoughts. All of them seek admission but each must first win its spurs; the law at first resists, but will submit to a conqueror and become his servant. In a changing society (and free societies that are composed of two or more generations are always changing because it is their nature to do so) the law acts as a valve. New policies must gather strength before they can force entry; when they are admitted and absorbed into the consensus, the legal system should expand to hold them, as also it should contract to squeeze out old policies which have lost the consensus they once obtained.' (*The Judge*, 1981, p. 1.)

Many people will have some instinctive sympathies on one side or the other of the difference of opinion between Griffith and Lee. However, many people, whichever side they favour, will also find it difficult to escape the conclusion that the debate itself is simply an endless game, representing little more than a variation on Shakespeare's proposition that 'the devil can cite Scripture for his purpose' (*The Merchant of Venice*, Act I, Sc. 3). Moreover, to play the game with any convincing degree of skill requires substantial knowledge of the law. Since the nature of this book is to be introductory, we will therefore now return to the technical question of which rules the courts will enforce, and where they will find them.

In practical terms the most important sources of law are Acts of Parliament (otherwise known as statutes), which are primary legislation; certain things done under the authority of Acts of Parliament, which are delegated (or subordinate) legislation; the decisions of the courts them-selves; and the system of European Community law. We will consider each of these at various stages of this book, but before doing so we can usefully consider a more theoretical matter, namely the concepts of *positivism* and *natural law*.

1.3 Positivism and Natural Law

Some lawyers are content to view law simply as a system of rules, leaving it to each legal system to decide for itself which rules its courts will recognize. This broad school of thought embraces many individual variations, but collectively it may be called *positivism*. The factor common to all types of positivism is that the legal validity of each rule is determined simply by reference to the question of whether it has been laid down, or *posited*, in accordance with whatever requirements are stipulated by the legal system in question.

Other lawyers are unhappy with positivism because it means that any law which satisfies the appropriate technical criteria is valid, whatever its moral quality may be. More particularly, positivism is absolutist in the sense that all the rules validated by a legal system must be law. This is an uncomfortable conclusion for many people, especially in the light of the Nazi experience in the second quarter of the twentieth century. Lon L. Fuller, a persuasive American critic of positivism, dealt with this problem thus:

'When we realize that order itself is something that must be worked for, it becomes apparent that the existence of a legal system, even a bad or evil legal system, is always a matter of degree. When we recogize this simple fact of everyday legal experience, it becomes impossible to dismiss the problems presented by the Nazi regime with a simple assertion: "Under the Nazis there was law, even if it was bad law." We have instead to inquire how much of a legal system survived the general debasement and perversion of all forms of social order that occurred under the Nazi rule . . . ' (See (1958) 71 Harv LR at p. 646.)

For reasons such as this, along with other considerations, many lawyers prefer to look outside the technical, definitional criteria of each legal system when seeking the distinguishing characteristic which marks out a rule as being *law*. Historically, many people who thought along these lines tended to speak in terms of *natural law*, against which laws made by humankind could be assessed for validity, and therefore the expression *natural law* is often used in contradistinction to *positivism*.

Many natural lawyers look to religious beliefs as sources of the criteria for identifying the validity of law. Others are content to derive their moral foundation from observable facts and logical inferences which may be drawn from them. Thus the Stoic school of philosophy in Ancient Greece taught that everything has it own nature, and that it is in the nature of humankind to be rational. Therefore, according to the Stoics, humankind ought to live according to reason, because to do otherwise would be going contrary to nature. One aspect of this argument is that the criteria for assessing the validity of human laws can be identified by the exercise of human reason.

Even those lawyers who are committed to a particular religious belief may express themselves in rationalistic terms. Thus St Thomas Aquinas, the eminent thirteenth-century Christian theologian, regarded natural law as 'the dictate of right reason'. But even appeals to reason as the basis of legal validity do not convince everyone. One of the most memorable dissenters was Jeremy Bentham, a leading English positivist whose life spanned the late eighteenth and early nineteenth centuries. Bentham regarded 'natural law' as being nothing more than a phrase, and the natural rights which are alleged to flow from it as being 'nonsense on stilts'.

Two points must be made about the differences between positivists and natural lawyers. First, it is important not to misrepresent positivism. Positivists do not ignore the question of whether a particular law is desirable on moral or other grounds. Their argument is simply that the question of identifying what the law is is a logical precondition to considering whether or not it is desirable. Second, it is not necessary to belong whole-heartedly to one camp or the other. Thus Hart, a leading twentieth-century positivist, was prepared to acknowledge what he called the 'minimum content of natural law' which validates certain basic laws such as those prohibiting murder, rape, theft and so on.

The arguments for and against various forms of natural law and positivism are fascinating, but they are complex and cannot be pursued in detail here. Nevertheless, a very brief consideration of two theorists, may give some flavour of the debate.

Oliver Wendell Holmes (1841–1935)

Oliver Wendell Holmes, the originator of the school of thought known as American Realism, produced a very straightforward definition of law:

> 'The prophecies of what the courts will do in fact, and nothing more pretentious, are what I mean by the law.' (*The Path of the Law* (1897) 10 Harv LR 457, abstracted in Freeman, *Lloyd's Introduction to Jurisprudence*, 6th edn, 1994, p. 670.)

Another reflection of Holmes' status as a Realist may be found in what is probably his most famous maxim: 'The life of the law has not been logic, it has been experience' (*The Common Law*, 1881, p. 1). He put the relationship between logic and experience thus:

> 'The training of lawyers is a training in logic . . . The language of judicial decision is mainly the language of logic. And the logical method and form flatter that longing for certainty and for repose which is in every human mind. But certainty generally is an illusion, and repose is not the destiny of man. Behind the logical form lies a judgment as to the relative worth and importance of competing legislative grounds, often an inarticulate and unconscious judgment it is true, and yet the very root and nerve of the whole proceeding. You can give any conclusion a logical form.' (*The Path of the Law* (1897) 10 Harv LR 61.)

In other words, behind any explicit formulation of judicial reasoning there lies an implicit attitude on the part of the judge. For reasons which will become apparent when you have read pp. 13–14, this implicit attitude may be called the 'inarticulate major premise'. The difficulty in identifying inarticulate major premises is, of course, simply that they are inarticulate, and therefore their precise formulation involves an element of guesswork by the reader. Nevertheless, there are cases in which the judges have obligingly articulated that which could easily have remained inarticulate, and it may be useful at this stage to consider a couple of examples.

In *Bourne* v. *Norwich Crematorium Ltd* [1967] 1 All ER 576, the issue was whether expenditure on a furnace chamber and chimney tower built by the crematorium company qualified for a tax allowance. This depended upon whether it was 'an industrial building or structure' for the purposes of the Income Tax Act 1952, and this in turn depended upon whether it was used 'for a trade which consists in the manufacture of goods or materials or the subjection of goods or materials to any process.'

Stamp J said:

'I would say at once that my mind recoils as much from the description of the bodies of the dead as "goods or materials" as it does from the idea that what is done in a crematorium can be described as "the subjection of" the human corpse to a "process". Nevertheless, the taxpayer so contends and I must examine that contention.'

Given this as the judge's starting point, it is not surprising that the taxpayer lost.

In *R* v. *West Dorset District Council ex parte Poupard* (1987) 19 HLR 254, Mr and Mrs Poupard had capital assets but they were meeting their weekly living expenses by drawing on an overdrawn bank account. They applied to the council for housing benefit. This benefit was subject to a means test, and therefore the question arose as to whether the drawings were 'income'. If they were, the amounts involved were sufficient to disqualify the applicants from receiving assistance under the relevant Regulations.

The council's Housing Review Board concluded that the drawings were income. The High Court held that in each case it was a question of fact whether specific sums of money were 'income', and that this question was to be decided on the basis of all that the council and their Review Board knew of the sources from which an applicant for benefit was maintaining himself and paying his bills. The conclusion was that on the present facts the local authority and their Review Board had made no error of law, and had acted reasonably in reaching their decision.

On his way to reaching his decision, Macpherson J, adopting an argument advanced by counsel for the local authority, said:

'The scheme [of Housing Benefit] is intended to help those who do not have the weekly resources to meet their bills, or their rent, and it is not intended to help comparatively better-off people (in capital terms) to venture into unsuccessful business and not to bring into account moneys which are regularly available for day-to-day spending, albeit that the use of moneys depletes their capital.'

Although the Court of Appeal upheld this decision (see (1988) 20 HLR 295), it will nevertheless be apparent that a court with different sympathies could have upheld, with equal or greater logic, the argument that the weekly drawings were outgo, rather than income, because each drawing increased the drawer's indebtedness to the bank. After all, it can be argued that if Parliament had intended to exclude people such as the applicants from eligibility for housing benefit it would have been a simple enough matter to enact an appropriate definition of what was meant by 'income' for the purposes of the means test.

Many people find that one of the most enduring pleasures of studying law is playing the game of 'hunt the inarticulate major premise', and you may often find that your reading of even the dullest of cases can be enlivened by trying to get behind the words and the doctrine in order to penetrate the mind of the judge as an individual human being.

Ronald Dworkin (b. 1931)

Returning to the natural law perspective, we have seen that the division between *what the law is* and *what the law ought to be* is not considered to be the stark dichotomy which is intrinsic in positivism. It is perhaps even less surprising, therefore, that natural lawyers should be influenced by factors other than the mere verbal formulation of the rule which falls to be applied. What those factors are, and where they are to be found, will vary widely.

Dworkin is a leading modern theorist whose arguments fall firmly within the natural law tradition. Briefly, Dworkin argues that the concept of rules provides an inadequate model of law as it really is. He proceeds to place great emphasis on what he calls 'standards'. Dworkin's 'standards' are ideas which exist independently of the rules which positivists regard as the totality of law, but which go into the melting pot together with those rules, when you are trying to identify the law which is to be applied to a given situation. More particularly, Dworkin calls these standards 'policies' and 'principles'.

> 'I call a "policy" that kind of standard that sets out a goal to be reached, generally an improvement in some economic, political or social feature of the community (though some goals are negative, in that they stipulate that some present feature is to be protected from adverse change). I call a "principle" a standard that is to be observed, not because it will advance or serve an economic, political or social situation deemed desirable, but because it is a requirement of justice or fairness or some other dimension of reality.' (*Is Law a System of Rules?* in *The Philosophy of Law*, 1977, p. 43.)

Expanding on the idea of principles and the way in which they work, Dworkin also says:

'All that is meant, when we say that a particular principle is a principle of our law, is that the principle is one which officials must take into account, if it is relevant, as a consideration inclining in one direction or another . . . Principles have a dimension that rules do not – the dimension of weight or importance. When principles intersect . . . one who must resolve the conflict has to take into account the relative weight of each. This cannot, of course, be an exact measurement, and the judgement that a particular principle or policy is more important than another will often be a controversial one. Nevertheless, it is an integral part of the concept of a principle that it has this dimension, that it makes sense to ask how important or how weighty it is.' (*Is Law a System of Rules?* in *The Philosophy of Law*, 1977, p. 47.)

One particularly controversial aspect of Dworkin's argument is his conclusion that there is always a 'right answer' to any legal question. The court may or may not find it, but it is always there.

Positivism and natural law compared

At a purely functional level it may be impossible to detect any real difference between the operation of Holmes' inarticulate major premise and Dworkin's policies and principles. For example, although the analysis of the housing benefit case has been presented in terms of an inarticulate major premise which was made articulate, it could equally convincingly have been presented as an example of the implementation of a policy of reducing homelessness, coupled with the application of a principle of fairness requiring that available resources should be made available to the most needy.

At a conceptual level, on the other hand, there remains a clear distinction between lawyers who think like Holmes and those who think like Dworkin. From the Holmesian point of view, the content of the inarticulate major premise is highly personalized. By way of contrast, the content of Dworkin's policies and principles can be be much more easily identified on an objective basis, because it is derived from material which is clearly within the public domain.

At this stage it is important to be absolutely clear what we are, and are not, saying. Quite clearly, even those judges who, in their academic moments, are inclined to be natural lawyers do not refuse to apply those rules which satisfy the formal criteria of validity. However, even those rules which are indisputably part of the law do not speak for themselves. The words in which they are expressed have to be interpreted, whether they are contained in previous decisions of the courts or in statutes, and the relevant statements of law have to be formulated and applied to the facts of the case in hand.

It is worth dwelling on this for a moment, because many people approach the study of the law on the basis that all they need do is identify and apply the plain meanings of the words in which the law is expressed. In fact, of course, this approach is based on the false assumption that words have plain, or literal, meanings in the first place.

'The literal meaning is a *potential meaning rather than an actual usage*; it is a conventional meaning within a system of such meanings (diction-ary) rather than an actual use of the word in combination with other words. The dictionary definition of a word is independent of any linguistic or empirical context . . . no word has a single simple literal meaning except in certain instances in the dictionary itself or more frequently in the mind of the judge.

'*A literal meaning is, at the end of the day, always an interpretative meaning.* A selection has to be made – consciously or unconsciously – to prefer *one of several possible literal meanings in the context of the phrase or clause or statutory rule to be interpreted.*' (Emphasis added. Good-rich, *Reading the Law*, 1986, p. 108.)

A couple of examples from non-legal situations will illustrate the point. First, consider two shops, one displaying a sign saying 'Pork Butcher', and the other displaying a sign saying 'Family Butcher'. You know, of course, that the first butcher specializes in pig meat, while the second does *not* butcher families. Yet *why* does one adjective qualify the activities of the butcher in terms of the meat sold, whilst the other does so in terms of the market served? The answer, as Goodrich says, is that the context is all-important.

Second, suppose that a university is worried about the possibility of being held liable for breaches of copyright by staff using photocopiers when they prepare teaching materials. Accordingly, every photocopier in the university bears a warning notice, which explains the relevant aspects of the law of copyright, and which is headed 'For the Attention of Every Single Member of Staff'. Are married members of staff entitled to ignore the notice? (You can provide your own answer to this one!)

We will return to the problem of *plain meaning* in Part III, but one thing is evident even at this stage. Once we accept that legal reasoning involves factors other than the apparently plain meaning of the words, it becomes an academic exercise to decide whether those factors are, strictly speaking, extra-legal, as positivists would say they are, or are part and parcel of the definition of law, as natural lawyers would say they are. At a purely practical level, the essential point is that the process of judicial decision-making requires the judge to go beyond the specific proposition of law which appears to govern the outcome of the case.

1.4 The Form of Legal Reasoning

The classic pattern of legal reasoning follows what is known technically as a syllogism. Syllogistic reasoning takes the following form:

$$\text{If} \quad A = B$$
$$\text{And} \quad B = C$$
$$\text{Then} \quad A = C$$

The first line is known as the *major premise*, the second as the *minor premise*, and the third as the *conclusion*. Taking a legal example, therefore, the pattern becomes:

> It is an offence to exceed the speed limit
> Exceeding the speed limit is what the defendant has done
> It is an offence to do what the defendant has done

or, expressing the conclusion more directly, the defendant is guilty of speeding.

Essentially, therefore, syllogistic reasoning is perfectly straightforward. However, syllogisms assume that the major and minor premises exist, without giving any assistance as to how they may be formulated. Returning to the speeding example, it is apparent that we have: a statement of law (the major premise) a statement of fact (the minor premise) a conclusion (applying the major premise to the minor premise). But it is equally apparent that we must establish both the premises before we can reach the conclusion. Taking the minor premise first, the facts of a case will either be proved to the satisfaction of the court, or agreed between the parties. In terms of professional practice, far more disputes involve questions of fact than involve questions of law. Therefore all competent practitioners need a good grasp of the law of evidence, so that they know how to go about trying to prove the facts on which they rely, and how to try to prevent their opponents from proving other facts. For the moment, however, we need say no more about the minor premise, although at the end of Chapter 2 we will return to some of the problems surrounding the distinction between 'law' and 'fact'.

The major premise will be formulated from those sources which the legal system accepts as being authoritative. In English terms, and for almost all practical purposes, this means Acts of Parliament and delegated legislation (see pp. 64 and 69); case-law (see Part II); and European Community law (see Chapters 6, 7, 8, 16 and 23). The ability to handle those sources, in such a way that you are able to produce a convincing formulation of the law, is a highly developed intellectual skill, which cannot be acquired quickly, easily or painlessly. However, one of the major purposes of this book is to provide a critical foundation on which you can seek to develop that skill.

In passing you will notice that you are now in a position fully to understand the Holmesian concept of the *inarticulate major premise* (see p. 8). What Holmes was asserting is that the formal syllogism is all very well as far as it goes, but that what really matters is the judge's personal starting-point – the inarticulate major premise – since it is this which will usually govern the final outcome of the case.

At this stage it will be useful to examine some more generalized aspects of intellectual argument, so that legal method can be seen within the context of the broader field of intellectual endeavour, rather than as a thing apart.

1.5   Propositions and Processes: Truth and Validity

It is useful to observe and to maintain the key distinction between the *truth of a proposition or conclusion* on the one hand, and the *validity of the process of argument* on the other. Some examples will illustrate the point. These examples will use incontrovertible scientific facts, simply because no-one can feel strongly about such subject-matter, and therefore no-one will be distracted by considerations of what they think the position *ought* to be.

Speaking in round figures, it is true to say that the sun is 93 000 000 miles from the earth, and that light travels at 186 000 miles a second. It is also logically valid to say that if we know the distance between two points, and the speed at which something is travelling, we can work out the time taken for the journey by dividing the distance by the speed. Thus if A and B are 100 miles apart, something travelling at 100 miles an hour will take one hour to make the journey. Applying this to the figures given at the start of this paragraph, we can say that dividing 93 000 000 by 186 000 will give us the number of seconds which light takes to travel from the sun to the earth, namely 500. In this example we have applied a process of reasoning which is valid to facts which are true, and therefore we have inevitably come to a conclusion which is true.

However, it is also possible to produce a conclusion which happens to be true by applying valid reasoning to premises which are untrue. If I tell you that the sun is 1 000 000 miles from the earth, and that light travels at

2 000 miles a second, dividing 1 000 000 by 2 000 still produces the figure of 500 seconds. In this example the propositions which form the premises are false, but the process of reasoning (dividing one figure by the other) is valid. *Quite by chance* the conclusion happens to be true.

A third example will take the matter one stage further by showing that applying invalid logic to false premises may also produce a conclusion which happens to be true. Suppose I tell you not only that the sun is 5 000 miles from the earth, and that the speed of light is 0.1 miles a second, but also that the way to do the calculation is to multiply one figure by the other, rather than by dividing one by the other. This calculation will still produce the figure of 500 seconds. As we know, this happens to be true. However, it remains perfectly obvious both that the premises are false and that the argument is invalid.

In practical terms, the second and third examples illustrate a very common danger. If you see a valid argument which ends with a conclusion which you either know to be true or want to be true, it is easy to fall into the trap of assuming that the premises are true and that the argument is valid. Falling into this trap is particularly easy if the premises are drawn from a field in which you lack expertise, and if you are less than skilled in identifying invalid arguments. In the vast majority of cases, of course, there will be no problem. Premises which are true will be used as the basis of arguments which are valid, and the conclusions which are reached will, therefore, also be true. However, good lawyers are constantly on the look-out for cases which embody false premises or invalid arguments, or both. We must now consider three common methods of reasoning.

1.6 Methods of Reasoning: Induction, Deduction and Analogy

Reasoning by induction, deduction and analogy are all methods which are commonly employed in a variety of contexts. We will look at each method in turn, and then place them in a legal context.

Inductive reasoning

The process known as *inductive reasoning* involves making a number of observations and then proceeding to formulate a principle which will be of general application. This form of reasoning is typified by the methods of experimental science, where if the same thing happens repeatedly it is assumed that there is a principle which ensures that it will always do so. So, if I drop a heavy object and a light object from the same height at the same time, and they reach the ground together, *and this happens on a large number of occasions*, I can conclude that the acceleration due to gravity is a constant, and does not depend on the weight of the objects concerned. The potential weakness of inductive reasoning is that, however many observations support the conclusion, there remains the possibility that some other observations may refute it. In terms of legal method, this weakness is represented by the doctrine of *per incuriam*, which deals with the situation where a relevant legal authority is overlooked. This doctrine is discussed at p. 147.

Deductive reasoning

The process known as *deductive reasoning* involves stating one or more propositions and then reasoning your way to a conclusion by applying established principles of logic. Deductive reasoning is typified by mathematical method where propositions are asserted and then used as the basis of reasoning. Thus, if $A = B$ it follows that $2A = 2B$, and that $A - B = 0$, and so on. There are two potential weakness of deductive reasoning: the premises may be false and the reasoning itself may be invalid, as illustrated in the examples previously given, based on the speed of light. A specifically legal example of invalid deductive reasoning may be found in *Ward* v. *James* [1965] 1 All ER 563, which is discussed at p. 20.

Reasoning by analogy

The process of *reasoning by analogy* involves saying that, if a number of different things are similar to each other in a number of different specific ways, they are, or should be, similar to each other in other ways as well. This process may be seen operating in the doctrine of precedent, which requires that cases with similar facts should be treated as being similar in law. The problem with reasoning by analogy is to identify which points need to be similar, and how similar they need to be. This is pursued at some length in Chapter 10 in the context of identifying the ratio of a case.

Judges seldom use technical vocabulary such as *induction* and *deduction*, but a notable exception may be found in the speech of Lord Diplock in *Home Office* v. *Dorset Yacht Co Ltd* [1970] 2 All ER 294. The case raised the question of whether one party owed a duty of care to another in the law of negligence, which explains some of Lord Diplock's precise observations. However, the general tone of the passage is clearly of more general application.

'The justification of the courts' role in giving the effect of law to the judges' conception of the public interest in the field of negligence is based on the cumulative experience of the judiciary of the actual consequences of lack of care in particular instances. And the judicial development of the law of negligence rightly proceeds by seeking first to identify the relevant characteristics that are common to the kinds of conduct and relationships which have been held in previous decisions of the courts to give rise to a duty of care.

'The method adopted at this stage of the process is analytical and inductive. It starts with an analysis of the characteristics of the conduct and relationships involved in each of the decided cases. But the analyst must know what he is looking for; and this involves his approaching his analysis with some general conception of conduct and relationships which *ought* to give rise to a duty of care. This analysis leads to a proposition which can be stated in the form: "In all the decisions that have been analysed a duty of care has been held to exist wherever the conduct and the relationship possessed each of the characteristics A, B, C, D, etc., and has not been found to exist when any of these characteristics were absent."

'For the second stage, which is deductive and analytical, that proposition is converted to: "In all cases where the conduct and relationship possess each of the characteristics A, B, C, D, etc., a duty of care arises." The conduct and relationship involved in the case for decision is then analysed to ascertain whether they possess each of these characteristics. If they do the conclusion follows that a duty of care does arise in the case for decision.

'But since *ex hypothesi* the kind of case which we are now considering offers a choice whether or not to extend the kinds of conduct or relationships which give rise to a duty of care, the conduct or relationship which is involved in it will lack at least one of the characteristics A, B, C, D, etc. And the choice is exercised by making a policy decision whether or not a duty of care ought to exist if the characteristic which is lacking were absent or redefined in terms broad enough to include the case under consideration. The policy decision will be influenced by the same general conception of what ought to give rise to a duty of care as was used in approaching the analysis. The choice to extend is given effect to by redefining the characteristics in more general terms so as to exclude the necessity to conform to limitations imposed by the former definition which are considered to be inessential. The cases which are landmarks in the common law . . . are cases where the cumulative experience of the judges has led to a restatement in wide general terms of characteristics of conduct and relationships which give rise to legal liability.

'Inherent in this methodology, however, is a practical limitation which is imposed by the sheer volume of reported cases. The initial selection of previous cases to be analysed will itself eliminate from the analysis those in which the conduct or relationship involved possessed characteristics which are obviously absent in the case for decision. The proposition used in the deductive stage is not a true universal. It needs to be qualified so as to read: "In all cases where the conduct and relationship possess each of the characteristics A, B, C and D, etc., *but do not possess any of the characteristics Z, Y or X, etc. . . . which were present in the cases eliminated from the analysis*, a duty of care arises." But this qualification, being irrelevant to the decision of the particular case, is generally left unexpressed.' (Original emphasis.)

1.7   Legal Practice and Legal Scholarship

Legal practice

In practical terms the legal enterprise consists of advising clients how they may best use the law to achieve their objectives. These objectives vary widely, but it is worth identifying some of the more common possibilities, spanning a range from the wholly non-contentious, in the sense that they are highly unlikely ever to go to court, to the wholly contentious, in the sense that they are already the subject of legal proceedings in court. Matters such as making a will are almost always non-contentious, as are straightforward conveyancing transactions. Even matters such as these, however, are potentially contentious, in the sense that the court may have to adjudicate upon the validity or effect of the will, or on the rights and obligations of the parties to the conveyancing transaction; and, of course, they become contentious when disputes actually do develop and court proceedings are either threatened or instituted. Nevertheless, even matters which have become contentious are commonly then settled by agreement, and it is commonly to the advantage of the parties that this should be so. As Jesus said in the Sermon on the Mount:

'If someone sues you, come to terms with him promptly while you are both on your way to court; otherwise he may hand you over to the judge, and the judge to the constable, and you will be put in jail. I tell you, once you are there you will not be let out till you have paid the last farthing.' (*The Gospel according to St. Matthew*, ch. 5, verses 25–6.)

Although this passage does not reflect the English distinction between civil and criminal law (see p. 34), the sentiment remains clearly applicable. More recently, and more authoritatively from a legal point of view, Lord Mackay LC said: 'The interests of justice are, in my opinion, served by the promotion of early settlements' (*O'Sullivan* v. *Herdmans Ltd* [1987] 3 All ER 129).

Of course, if you are cynical, you may recall the famous *Punch* cartoon of two farmers arguing over ownership of a cow. One farmer was pulling at the head and the other was pulling at the tail, while the lawyer was sitting happily in the middle, milking the cow. On the basis of this you may concede that early settlements may be in the interests of the parties and even in the interests of justice, but still harbour a lurking suspicion that they may not be in the interests of the lawyers. However, there are two reasons why virtually all practising lawyers would agree that this would be taking cynicism too far. First, the outcome of litigation is never cut and dried (for reasons which will become apparent throughout this book), so clients are usually grateful if a reasonable settlement can be reached by negotiation, since this eliminates the element of chance. Second, competent lawyers offering the sort of expertise which the market demands should never be short of work, and a case which is settled represents an opportunity for the lawyers to devote time and energy to other clients' affairs.

In practice, therefore, many lawyers spend much of their time on work which neither the lawyers nor their clients think will ever go anywhere near a court, or on work which is directed at resolving disputes without the necessity of court proceedings. Bearing this in mind, you may well wonder why this book, along with the vast majority of other legal textbooks, places so much emphasis on what the courts will and will not do. The answer is straightforward.

One element which contributes to the advice which any lawyer gives to any client is the lawyer's perception of how, *if it ever comes to it*, the court will look at the legality of the client's position. This comment is not intended in any way to underestimate the importance of the many other elements, such as identifying the client's objectives and relating them to relevant legal possibilities, which go to make up good lawyering in practice, but it is intended to recognize the harsh fact of life that where the law is involved the courts are always at least potentially involved as well. And it follows that a good grounding in the techniques which the judges use is an invaluable foundation on which to build the habit of thinking like a lawyer.

Legal scholarship

There are many different models of legal scholarship, reflecting substantial variations in the degree of emphasis placed on sociological, economic and political factors. However, Feldman provides a useful version of a traditional model of scholarship in general:

'It is the attempt to understand something, by a person who is guided by certain ideals, which distinguishes scholarship both from the single-minded pursuit of an end and from dilettantism.

The ideals include: (1) a commitment to employing methods of investigation and analysis best suited to satisfying that curiosity; (2) self-conscious and reflective open-mindedness, so that one does not assume the desired result and adopt a procedure designed to verify it, or even pervert one's material to support a chosen conclusion; and (3) the desire to publish the work for the illumination of students, fellow scholars or the general public and to enable others to evaluate and criticise it.' (*The Nature of Legal Scholarship* (1989) 52 MLR 498.)

While it is important to recognize that a willingness to indulge in self-criticism is part and parcel of scholarship, it is equally essential to emphasize the need for self-confidence. More particularly, it is important to be willing to criticize received wisdom where its foundations are, and can be demonstrated to be, defective. The judgement of the Court of Appeal in *Ward* v. *James* [1965] 1 All ER 563 is a case in point.

The background to the case was a general feeling among lawyers that juries were not making a very good job of assessing damages in personal injuries cases. This led Lord Denning MR, with the full agreement of the other members of the court, to two conclusions. First, juries should not normally hear personal injuries cases. Second, where there are special circumstances which justify the participation of a jury in such a case, the jury's role should be restricted to determining the facts, rather than extending to the assessment of damages. The conclusion that juries should not assess damages may well be eminently sensible in purely practical terms, but there is a difficulty in terms of the relationship between this conclusion and the premise from which it purports to flow.

If juries are not very good at assessing damages in personal injuries cases, the only conclusion we can validly draw is that they should not assess damages in such cases: not that they should normally have no role at all. For example, in a typical case arising from a road traffic accident, a jury composed of ordinary motorists may be particularly well-equipped to decide whether the quality of the defendant's driving was up to the standard required of the reasonable driver. Admittedly, in cases where the defendant is found liable it may well be preferable for the judge to quantify the damages, but this is a long way from saying that juries should not normally have any role in such cases. In other words, *on the basis of the premise from which the court started*, the situation of juries dealing with the issue of liability, and judges dealing with the assessment of any damages which might be appropriate, should be the norm, and not the exception.

1.8 Law and Justice

Introduction

Having seen that there are wide variations of approach to the question of the nature of law, you will not be surprised to discover that there are also wide variations to the question of the nature of justice. Taking two comments from opposite ends of the spectrum: Ross, a member of the Scandinavian Realist school of jurisprudence, says: 'To invoke justice is the same thing as banging on the table: an emotional expression which turns one's demand into an absolute postulate' (*On Law and Justice*, 1958, p. 274). More optimistically, Tenzin Gyatso, the fourteenth Dalai Lama of Tibet, regards it as an inescapable truth that: 'In the end, the innate desire of all people for truth, justice and human understanding must triumph over ignorance and despair' (emphasis added, *Freedom in Exile*, pp. 88–9). The heart of the matter, of course, is that most people would acknowledge that defining justice and applying its requirements in a concrete situation are both very largely matters of subjective judgement.

Suppose, for example, that a thief steals my property and sells it to you. Suppose also that you acted in good faith, with no suspicion that the property was stolen. Does justice require that you return the property to me, on the basis that the act of theft cannot have destroyed my legal title to it? Or should you be allowed to keep the property, on the basis that you paid for it? Theoretically, the parties who lose out in such cases will be able to sue the thieves, but this is only realistic if the thieves are found and they have enough money to enable them to pay damages. Both these conditions will seldom be satisfied, and typically neither of them will be. It follows, therefore, that the law has to choose who stands the loss, and that the facts present no self-evident conception of justice to assist in the making of that choice.

Nevertheless, judges do commonly speak of justice, even if only in Ross's table-banging, justificatory sense. This leads us to the question: *what is the relationship between law and justice?*

Law and justice: context and content

As a starting-point it may be tempting to say that law involves the application of the abstract concept of justice to real situations. As Lord Donaldson MR said in *R* v. *Secretary of State for the Home Department ex parte Cheblak* [1991] 2 All ER 319:

'And it is the law and the rule of law which governs all. Judges take a judicial oath "to do right by all manner of people after the laws and usages of this Realm without fear or favour, affection or ill will" . . . Justice is not an abstract concept. It has to have a context and a content. The context is provided by the facts underlying particular disputes. The content is the law.

'In individual cases injustice can arise from two quite different sources – human fallibility on the part of the judges or tribunal members and defects in the law. Human fallibility can never be eliminated, but its effects can be and are reduced by dedicated professionalism and by the system making provision for appeals. Defects in the law can be remedied by changing the law, but not by departing from it, an approach which would end by producing far more injustices than it cured. Judges are exhorted by commentators to be "robust". If what is meant is that judges should be very ready to re-examine the law in novel or changed circumstances, I agree that judges should indeed be "robust" and I hope that we are. But if what is meant is that in cases which arouse their sympathy, of which the present could well be one, they should depart from the law, I must disagree.'

The doctrine of the rule of law is outlined at p. 62, and its significance is a major theme implicit throughout this book. However, for the moment we must put Lord Donaldson's comments in *Cheblak* into perspective by considering some of the complexities arising from the seemingly straightforward word *justice*. The central problem is that although it may be desirable to give judges an element of discretion in individual cases, it is also true that the predictability of legal outcomes plays an important part in any legal system which claims to be just. Yet it is obvious that any significant element of predictability reduces the potential scope for the exercise of discretion in individual cases. This simple truth needs to be fully understood, because it underlies many of the problems which arise in legal method.

If I ask you whether the law should be rigid, or whether the courts should have the power to do what they think is right in the circumstances of each case, most of you will probably opt for the courts doing what they think is right in the circumstances of each case. (You may find yourself in some difficulty if I then ask you how the courts are to decide what they think is right in the circumstances of each case, but for the moment we will let that pass.) However, if I ask you whether people should be able to predict the legal consequences of their conduct in advance, so that they may modify their conduct accordingly, or should they have to wait until after the court has decided the case arising from their conduct, most of you will probably opt for being able to predict the legal outcome in advance. However, a moment's thought shows that the two answers which I have indicated as being probable are in fact self-contradictory.

If each answer considered individually appears to be right, but both cannot co-exist, the only alternative is to seek a compromise in terms of finding a balance which combines an acceptable degree of predictability with an acceptable degree of flexibility to deal with individual cases. The focus, therefore, is simply on what 'acceptable' means in this context. There is, of course, no definitive answer to this question, since it involves matters of judgement and, as Alexander Pope said, albeit in a different context and before the substantially levelling effects of quartz technology:

> ' 'Tis with our watches as our judgements, none
> Go just alike, yet each believes his own.'
> *(An Essay on Criticism.)*

Nevertheless, what we can do is to explore how the courts seek to strike the balance, and indeed, this is the major theme of this book. However, it is important to approach the task of striking the balance in the right spirit. More particularly, we must understand that striking a balance does not result from a failure to grasp the nettle. Rather, it results from grasping the nettle firmly, in the sense of accepting the reality of the situation, which is that, where legitimate interests are competing but incompatible, both cannot be fully satisfied.

The need for a real dispute

You will recall (from p. 21) that, in *R* v. *Secretary of State for the Home Department ex parte Cheblak* [1991] 2 All ER 319, Lord Donaldson MR said that 'the facts underlying particular disputes' provide a context for the administration of justice. This comment is important not only for itself, but also because it reflects a very deep-seated idea of English law.

The courts are not happy unless they are dealing with real disputes, based on real facts, where the outcome will actually matter to someone in real terms. Two kinds of case are likely to fall foul of this attitude. First, there are cases which involve purely hypothetical points. This category is of little significance in practice because, even if anyone tried to start proceedings, it is extremely unlikely that the court would allow the matter to proceed to a hearing. Second, and more importantly in practice, there are those cases where there has been a real dispute but the parties have been overtaken by events in such a way that the dispute has effectively evaporated.

The dispute in *Ainsbury* v. *Millington* [1987] 1 All ER 929 involved rights of access to a council house. After the proceedings had started, the council terminated the tenancy, and so there ceased to be any real substance to the dispute. Lord Bridge cited with approval the words of

Viscount Simon LC in *Sun Life Assurance Co of Canada* v. *Jervis* [1944] 1 All ER 469:

'I do not think that it would be a proper exercise of the authority which this House possesses to hear appeals if it occupies time in this case in deciding an academic question, the answer to which cannot affect the respondent in any way. If the House undertook to do so, it would not be deciding an existing *lis* [i.e. a piece of litigation] between the parties who are before it, but would merely be expressing its view on a legal conundrum which the appellant hopes to get decided in his favour without in any way affecting the position between the parties . . . I think it is an essential quality of an appeal fit to be disposed of by this House that there should exist between the parties a matter in actual controversy which the House undertakes to decide as a living issue.'

Lord Bridge went on to say:

'It has always been a fundamental feature of our judicial system that the courts decide disputes between the parties before them; they do not pronounce on abstract questions of law when there is no dispute to be resolved

'Different considerations may arise in relation to what are called "friendly actions" and conceivably in relation to proceedings instituted as a test case . . . Again litigation may sometimes be properly continued for the sole purpose of resolving an issue as to costs when all other matters in dispute have been resolved.'

Summary

1   In practice lawyers seldom think about the nature of law, but the topic is worth considering as an introduction to the study of law and legal method.
2   In general terms law may be described as those rules which the courts will enforce, but this is not a true definition because some laws confer powers rather than imposing duties. Placing the emphasis on the courts is useful because it automatically emphasizes the importance of the judges' role. There is disagreement about how judges do, and ought to, function.
3   Positivists consider the question of what the law is as being distinct from the question of what the law ought to be. Natural lawyers consider the two questions to be inextricably intertwined.
4   Legal reasoning is syllogistic in form.
5   Propositions and conclusions may be true or false. Reasoning may be valid or invalid. In general, valid reasoning will produce a conclusion which is true, and invalid reasoning will produce a conclusion which is

false. However, a conclusion which is true may appear to result from reasoning which is invalid; and a conclusion which is false may appear to result from reasoning which is valid.

6 The process of *inductive reasoning* involves making a number of observations and then proceeding to formulate a principle which will be of general application. The process of *deductive reasoning* involves stating one or more propositions and then reasoning your way to a conclusion by applying established principles of logic. The process of *reasoning by analogy* involves saying that if a number of different things are similar to each other in a number of different specific ways, they are, or should be, similar to each other in other ways as well.

7 Seeking to achieve the clients' objectives is the principal aim of *legal practice*. However, in *legal scholarship* the emphasis falls on developing a critical understanding of legal principles.

8 There are many views of *justice* as a concept. In practical terms, however, justice needs both a *context* and a *content*. The *context* is the factual situation giving rise to the case, and the *content* is the law which is applicable.

Exercises

1 What is Griffith's view of the way judges function? Contrast this with Lord Devlin's view.
2 Distinguish between *positivism* and *natural law?*
3 What is meant by an *inarticulate major premise?*
4 What does Dworkin mean by *standards?*
5 Distinguish between *truth* and *validity.*
6 What does each of the following mean: *syllogism; induction; deduction?*
7 According to Lord Donaldson MR, what is the relationship between *law* and *justice?*
8 Will English courts pronounce on abstract questions of law?

2 The Classifications of English Law

2.1 Introduction

You will rapidly discover that when lawyers have analysed their material
they proceed to classify it in various ways. Unfortunately, some of the
most basic terms used by lawyers in the classifying process have a variety
of meanings, depending on the context in which they are used. However,
this chapter will outline most of the major variations, at least to the extent
of sketching an overall context within which specific topics may be placed,
and introducing some of the technical terminology which will soon
become familiar to you. The chapter concludes with a discussion of the
distinction between matters which are regarded as being issues of fact and
those which are regarded as being issues of law.

2.2 The Possible Meanings of Common Law

The phrase *common law* may be contrasted with *statute law*, *equity* and
civil law. We will consider each of these contrasts in turn.

Common law and statute law

When *common law* is contrasted with *statute law*, it means that part of the
law which is contained in the decisions of the courts, rather than having
been enacted by Parliament. The explanation of the use of the word
common in this context is historical. In the centuries after the Norman
Conquest, the King's judges travelled round the country deciding cases in
various places. This meant that the judges built up an overall picture of the
law in various areas, and by extending the area of operation of sensible
principles and allowing less sensible ones to lapse, they were able to unify
the law of the entire country. Another way of saying that the law was
unified was to say that it was common to the whole country, and so it
became known as the *common law*.

Common law and equity

The origins and nature of equity

The heart of the common law was originally the writ system. Writs were – and still are – documents issued in order to start an action in the courts. The court office which issued writs was called the chancery, and its head was the Lord Chancellor. In the early stages, the common law was flexible and responded to new situations as they arose by issuing new forms of writ. In the fourteenth century the common law became more rigid. The attitude of the office of chancery came to be that, if a potential litigant asked for a writ, and there was no existing form to cover the facts which were alleged, this could only be because there was no right capable of legal protection.

Even in those cases where the common law was willing to provide an appropriate writ, an additional problem could arise. If a case was proved by evidence, the courts would regard themselves as being bound to make the order for which the proceedings had been brought. Normally this would be unobjectionable, but sometimes it would cause injustice. Take, for example, a case where there was written evidence of a debt, but the debtor repaid the money without ensuring that the documentary evidence was cancelled by the creditor. In these circumstances, if the creditor sued the debtor alleging non-payment, the courts would say, 'what better evidence could we have that the debt remains outstanding than the uncancelled document which the creditor has produced to us?' Accordingly the courts would order the debtor to repay the money for a second time. To be fair to the courts, it must be emphasized that they were not saying that double repayment was just. What they were saying was that the overriding principle was that disputes should be decided according to the best evidence which could be produced, and in this case the best evidence was the uncancelled document.

This combination of general stagnation and individual injustice gave rise to the emergence of equity. What happened was that litigants who were unable to obtain satisfaction from the King's courts developed the practice of petitioning the King himself, asking for an exception from the general rules to be made in their cases. Before deciding what to do about individual petitions, the King would take advice. One of his principal advisers was the Lord Chancellor, who not only had expert knowledge of the common law through his headship of the office of chancery, but also, at this stage of legal history, was perceived as having the additional advantage of being a clergyman. This latter qualification meant that he could be presumed to have an informed conscience as to what ought to be done. It was for this reason that the Lord Chancellor was often called 'the keeper of the King's conscience'.

Although the King originally made his own decisions in the light of advice which he received, he soon developed the practice of delegating to the Lord Chancellor the whole of the task of making decisions on individual petitions. As this practice became established, litigants began to present petitions directly to the Lord Chancellor, by-passing the King altogether. In the initial stages the Lord Chancellor issued decrees in the King's name. By the end of the fifteenth century he was issuing them in his own name. Thus the *office* of chancery had evolved into the *court* of chancery.

The existence of the court of chancery alongside the courts of common law had real advantages for the development of the law and the working of justice in individual cases, but it also gave rise to the possibility of conflict when two courts – one of chancery and one of common law – made conflicting orders in relation to the same facts. The details of the way in which this conflict was resolved are a fascinating piece of legal history. Briefly, however, in the early part of the seventeenth century it became established that, where equity and the law conflict, equity prevails. Furthermore, the enactment of the Judicature Acts 1873–75 merged the administration of the systems of law and equity, laying the foundations of the present arrangement whereby both systems are applied by the same courts. Nevertheless, the historical origins of the two systems remain relevant, especially as an aid to understanding the differences between legal and equitable remedies.

Remedies at common law and in equity

A discussion of the principles governing the granting of remedies at common law and in equity is a particularly useful way of emphasizing some of the distinctions between the two ways of thinking. Where there has been an infringement of the civil law, such as a breach of contract, the victim may well think of claiming damages. Damages are a common law remedy, and the basic principle, sometimes called the *compensation principle* is:

'[Damages] should as nearly as possible . . . put the party who has suffered in the same position as he would have been in if he had not sustained the wrong for which he is . . . getting . . . compensation.' (*Livingstone* v. *Rawyards Coal Co* (1880) 5 App Cas 25.)

Of course, the court may experience real difficulty in putting a financial value on the plaintiff's loss but, unless the extent of the loss is a matter of pure speculation, the court must do its best to quantify it.

Many cases are relatively routine. For example, the courts have developed a set of financial values for various kinds of physical harm, and these values are routinely used as the basis for assessing damages in personal injury cases. The courts keep these values under constant review and they are varied from time to time. The effect of this is that in most cases, once liability has been established or admitted, the area of dispute between the parties can be narrowed down to such variables as loss of future earning capacity. Other cases may be more challenging. In *Chaplin* v. *Hicks* [1911–13] All ER Rep 224, the court put a financial value on the loss of an opportunity to take part in a beauty contest, even though the plaintiff may not have won anything anyway. The court took the view that the chance itself had a value.

In some cases the courts will deviate from the compensation principle and award a sum other than that which a genuine quantification of the loss requires. These are cases involving *contemptuous, nominal* and *punitive* – also known as *exemplary* – damages. Damages quantified according to the compensation principle are known as *substantial* damages, but this merely means that they are more than nominal, and not that a large sum is necessarily involved.

An award of *contemptuous damages* is the court's way of showing that it regards the plaintiff with contempt for having brought the action, even though it has been successful. A typical case for contemptuous damages would be a libel action where the plaintiff has not actually suffered harm, and the bringing of the case has generated more publicity for the libel than its original publication had achieved. Traditionally, they are the smallest coin of the realm, so currently they are one penny. Bearing in mind how contemptuous damages work, it may seem somewhat artificial to call them a remedy at all. However, they are still damages, even though only of a trifling amount. The point of principle which they illustrate is that, as you will remember from the origins of equity, the common law has no discretion to refuse a remedy to a successful litigant.

Nominal damages are essentially different from contemptuous damages, even though they too are awarded where the plaintiff cannot prove actual loss. The difference is that by awarding nominal damages the court accepts that the plaintiff was acting reasonably in bringing the case. For example, in *Hanfstaengl* v. *W. H. Smith & Sons* (1905) 92 LT 676, the defendants had infringed the plaintiff's copyright. Even though he proved no loss, the plaintiff was awarded nominal damages to mark the fact that his rights had been infringed and to discourage others from undertaking more serious infringements in the future. Traditionally, nominal damages are £2, although both smaller and larger sums have been known. If there appears to be little difference between nominal and contemptuous damages the appearance is deceptive. The real significance of the distinction lies in the parties' liability in costs.

The basic principle is that the court always has a discretion as to the award of costs. However, this discretion is exercised according to well-established principles. Normally an unsuccessful party will be ordered to pay the legal costs of the successful party, and this will be applied in the case of nominal damages. In the event of contemptuous damages, however, there is a refinement to the usual practice, which results in the plaintiff paying the defendant's costs, even though the plaintiff has won. The plaintiff's victory, therefore, is Pyrrhic.

Liability for costs is not, however, always limited to the parties. Since the amendment of s.51 of the Supreme Court Act 1981 by s.4 of the Courts and Legal Services Act 1990, the court has power to make a *wasted costs order* against a legal or other representative whose 'improper, unreasonable or negligent act or omission' has resulted in costs being incurred.

Punitive or *exemplary* damages are the third exception to the compensation principle. Here the court is deviating from the compensation principle by self-consciously awarding more than the plaintiff has lost, in order to punish the defendant and make an example of him. As the House of Lords made clear in *Cassell & Co Ltd* v. *Broome* [1972] 1 All ER 801, punitive damages are available in three situations only. The first situation where punitive damages may be appropriate is where the defendant calculated to make more from the wrongdoing than the plaintiff would lose, and therefore more than the plaintiff could recover on a purely compensatory basis. The second situation is oppressive, arbitrary or unconstitutional action by servants of the government. In this context it is worth noticing that in *Cassell* Lord Diplock emphasized that the phrase 'servants of the government' should be interpreted widely, and it clearly includes, among others, local government employees and police officers. The third situation in which punitive damages are available is where they are authorized by statute, but this is extremely rare, and of no real significance.

Despite the exceptions, it is important to remember that the usual basis for damages is compensatory. We have seen that there may be cases where damages are difficult to quantify, but these cases must be carefully distinguished from cases where damages are wholly inappropriate. In the latter type of case equity will recall its origins as an exceptional jurisdiction, created to fill the gaps left by the law, and will try to make a distinctively equitable contribution to the righting of wrongs . The entire range of equitable remedies cannot be covered here, but it is possible to give an indication of how they work.

The equitable remedy of specific performance is the order of the court which compels the defendant actually to perform the contract, rather than paying damages for failing to do so. For example, where there is a contract for the sale of a second-hand example of a popular car, if the seller fails to perform the contract, the purchaser can easily buy a similar car elsewhere. The measure of the purchaser's damages will be the difference (if any) between the price originally agreed and the price actually paid. Because any loss will be capable of being compensated by money, damages will be an adequate remedy. On the other hand, if there is a contract for the sale of an 'old master' painting, and the seller fails to perform the contract, no amount of money will enable the purchaser to acquire the practical equivalent of that painting elsewhere, simply because it has no practical equivalent. Therefore the court may decide to compel the seller to perform his contract.

Similarly, a neighbour who erects a garden shed partly on my garden commits the tort of trespass. If the court allows the shed to remain in position on payment of damages, the effect would be the same as compelling me to sell my land to my neighbour. Since this would clearly be an unjust outcome, it follows that damages would be an inadequate remedy, and therefore the court could grant me the equitable remedy of an injunction to restrain my neighbour from continuing the trespass. However, one of the maxims of equity is that 'equity like nature does nothing in vain', and therefore the court will not grant a remedy which it would be unwilling or unable to enforce.

In *Paton* v. *British Pregnancy Advisory Service* [1978] 2 All ER 987, the facts were that a woman wanted to have an abortion. Her husband, who was the father of the child in the womb, did not agree. He asked the court for an injunction to prevent his wife from having the abortion. An injunction is an order of the court which, if breached, is enforceable by means of committal to prison for contempt of court. Sir George Baker P decided that the case really came down to whether the father had a legal right in the matter, in which context he said:

'I ask the question, "If an injunction were ordered, what could be the remedy?" and I do not think I need say any more than that no judge could even consider sending a husband or wife to prison for breaking such an order. That, of itself, seems to me to cover the application here; this husband cannot by law stop his wife by injunction from having what is . . . a lawful abortion.'

We have already noted that equity began as a court of conscience, attempting to work justice where it thought the common law had failed to do so. This tradition still endures. One aspect of this is that equity does not bestow its favours indiscriminately, but may well find relevance in the conduct of those who are seeking its aid. As one of the equitable maxims puts it, 'he who comes to equity must come with clean hands'. The operation of this principle can be illustrated by the case of *Gill* v. *Lewis* [1956] 1 All ER 844. The defendant was the tenant of a house. He fell behind with the rent, and the landlord obtained an order for possession. The tenant then found the money to pay the arrears. As the debt could now be paid, the tenant asked equity to prevent the landlord from enforcing the possession order. While in the house, however, the tenant had indecently assaulted two boys. As a result, the landlord argued that the tenant had not come with clean hands. The court rejected this argument because the indecent assaults were unconnected with the rent arrears.

In other words, the fact that the modern court exercising the equitable jurisdiction is the direct descendant of a court which came into being as a court of conscience does not entitle it to act as a general arbiter of morals, as distinct from the morality of the individuals concerned in the case in relation to each other. However, all equitable remedies remain discretionary.

Equity and trusts

It would be wrong to discuss equity as if it dealt only with remedies. One of the most important aspects of equitable doctrine deals with the law of trusts. A trust may be described as the situation which exists when one person (a trustee) holds property on behalf of another person (a beneficiary). There is a very substantial body of law dealing with the way in which such relationships can be created and terminated, and the rights and duties of the parties while the relationship exists.

Common law and civil law

Another way in which the phrase *common law* is used is by way of contrast to *civil law*. In this context, the distinction which is being drawn is basically between the English legal system (together with those countries whose legal systems are derived from it, such as Australia, New Zealand and the United States of America) on the one hand and the legal systems of most of the states of Western Europe on the other.

The historical origin of this distinction is that continental Europe was heavily influenced by Roman law, and the modern European systems still show this heritage to a marked degree. In England, on the other hand, Roman law and its concepts have had no lasting impact. One of the most important aspects of the distinction is that the basic principles of law in a civil law country will be found in an enactment, or a series of enactments, called a *code*, whereas in the common law countries the basic principles have evolved through the decisions of the courts.

Admittedly, as the rate of social change has accelerated from the time of the Industrial Revolution onwards, statute law has overtaken the common law as the main vehicle of legal change even in common law countries, but the historical perspective continues to influence the way in which lawyers from different traditions approach what are basically similar problems. An unfortunate terminological confusion also arises when dealing with codification, because even in the English legal system some comprehensive statutes are referred to as being codes, but all this means is that, when enacted, they contained all the English law on the topic concerned. The fundamental point remains that much of the basis of English law emerged piecemeal over the centuries as and when suitable cases came before the courts, rather than being formulated as a coherent whole.

It is worth noting that the early political union between England and Wales has resulted in the latter being part of the English legal system, and generally the same law applies throughout England and Wales. By way of contrast, Scotland, having retained its political independence for rather longer, and having previously been a civil law country, now finds itself with a curiously hybrid system. Many Scots lawyers regard themselves as enjoying the best of both the common law and civil law worlds, but English lawyers are sometimes less convinced. For example, Evershed LJ recorded Lord Maugham as having spoken of 'those interesting relics of barbarism, tempered by a few importations from Rome, known to the world as Scots law' (cited in Megarry, *Miscellany-at-Law*, 1955, revised impression 1958, p. 323). Northern Ireland is basically a common law jurisdiction, but for a variety of reasons it is not unusual to find that some statutes apply only to that Province, and that others do not apply there.

2.3   The Possible Meanings of Civil Law

Quite apart from its use in contradistinction to *common law*, the phrase *civil law* has a variety of distinct and proper usages even within the English legal system. Here, the alternatives to *civil law* are variously *criminal law*, *ecclesiatical* (or *canon*) *law* and *military law*. Only the distinction between *civil law* and *criminal law* need be considered here, since the legal affairs of neither the Church nor the armed forces are likely to concern most law students.

Civil law and criminal law

The essence of the distinction between civil law and criminal law is that in civil law (which involves matters such as breach of contract, and torts such as trespass, libel, slander, negligence and many others) the focus is on compensating the victim, whereas in criminal law (which involves matters such as theft, murder, motoring offences, and so on) the focus is on punishing the offender.

Closer examination of the relevant law shows that this version of the distinction, although a useful starting-point, is something of an over-statement. This is so partly because, in modern times, the range of powers available to the courts exercising criminal jurisdiction has increased substantially, with some possible options (such as probation) being intended to help the offender rather than to punish him. Furthermore, quite apart from such rehabilitative possibilities, there are circumstances in which a court can use the Powers of Criminal Courts Act 1963 to compensate the victim of crime at the same time as it sentences the offender.

Similarly, as we saw at p. 29, there are circumstances in which the court in a civil case can punish the wrongdoer by awarding damages over and above the sum required for compensation. Nevertheless, the basic point remains that in a criminal case, once guilt has been proved, the fundamental question for the court is 'what should be done with the offender?' whereas in a civil case the corresponding question, on proof of liability, is 'what should be done for the victim?'

One of the most immediately apparent distinctions between *civil law* and *criminal law* lies in the basic terminology. A typical civil case will be concerned with proof of *liability*, and will be called an *action*, although there are other terminological possibilities, including an *application* and a *petition*. A criminal case will be concerned with proof of *guilt*, and will be called a *prosecution*. The legal descriptions of the parties also varies. In a typical civil case a *plaintiff* will *sue* a *defendant*. In a criminal case a *prosecutor* will *prosecute* the other party, who may be called either the *defendant* or the *accused*. The only context in which it is proper to use the term *prosecution* in a civil context is where the plaintiff has started, but failed to pursue, an action, in which case the defendant may apply to the court to have the action 'struck out for want of prosecution'.

Second, the standard of proof will usually differ between civil and criminal cases. Superficially, it is often said that the facts necessary to establish civil liability need be proved only *on the balance of probabilities*, but the facts on which the prosecution relies must be established *beyond reasonable doubt*. This topic is pursued further at p. 43.

Finally, there are various other distinctions between civil and criminal cases, including detailed matters of procedure and evidence, liability as to costs and the availability of legal aid.

2.4 Public Law and Private Law

The distinction between *public law* and *private law* came to prominence with *O'Reilly* v. *Mackman* [1982] 3 All ER 1124, where the House of Lords decided that, generally speaking, matters of *public law* can be raised only in the High Court and only by using a special procedure known as an *application for judicial review*. It is impossible to be absolutely precise as to where the line between public law and private law is drawn, but a useful perspective can be derived from the fact that some areas of law involve public bodies or public officials doing things which, by their very nature, could not be done by private individuals. It seems that these cases, at least, involve matters of public law.

For example, if a local authority trespasses on land owned by someone else, the landowner can sue the local authority just as any other landowner could sue any other trespasser. However, the position is different if, for example, a local authority issues an enforcement notice in respect of development which has been undertaken without planning permission. In this case, the local authority has power to take action only because it is a local authority: no private individual could have taken the enforcement action. In other words, the trespass example falls within the sphere of private law, and the planning example falls within the sphere of public law.

Wherever the courts draw the line between public and private law, it is possible to make two general points arising from the distinction. First, a court which is dealing with judicial review will be supervising the way in which the decision which is being challenged was made; and the separation of powers (see p. 71) means the court cannot substitute its own decision. In other words, the court acknowledges that some kinds of decision – such as whether a local authority wishes to take enforcement action against unauthorized development, for example – are properly within the discretion of the public decision-makers themselves, because such decisions are inextricably linked with questions of policy and subjective assessments of the merits of the situation. In cases such as these, the court will compel the public decision-maker to consider each matter individually and in a fair way, having regard to all legally relevant factors. However, provided the *decision-making process* complies with the law, the *actual decision* is not something with which the court will interfere.

Second, certain aspects of procedure apply only to public law cases. These are thought to be necessary to protect public decision-makers from the constant risk of petty, vexatious and frivolous challenges made by people wanting to use the judicial process as a means of making political points. One of the most important of these safeguards is that no private individual has the right to challenge a matter of public law without first making a preliminary application to the court, asking for leave to make the full application. One factor which must be established is that the challenger has 'a sufficient interest' in the matter, and is not merely a busybody. This is known technically as the requirement of *locus standi*.

2.5   Substantive Law and Procedural Law

Some rules of law deal with substantive rights and duties, whilst others deal with the procedural aspects of enforcing the substantive rules. Procedural law is sometimes known by the alternative name of adjectival law. When a judge draws a distinction between matters of substance and matters of procedure, he will usually say why, in the context in question, the distinction is relevant. No exhaustive catalogue can be given here, but by way of example it can be said that time limits are often – though not always – procedural. The significance of a time limit being held to be procedural is well illustrated by the case of *Kammins Ballrooms Co Ltd* v. *Zenith Investments Ltd* [1970] 2 All ER 871, which is considered in detail in the context of statutory interpretation at p. 259. An example of a substantive time limit will be found in s.21(2) of the Firearms Act 1968, under which it is an offence for any person to possess a firearm or ammunition within five years of being released from certain types of custodial sentences. Here the time limit is clearly part of the substance of the offence.

2.6   Classification by Subject-Matter

The classifications which have been outlined are all basic, in the sense that they are part of the conceptual structure of the legal system. However, the classifications which are referred to most frequently are those which are formulated according to the subject-matter under consideration. As a matter of convenience, lawyers often refer to identifiable bodies of law, such as those dealing with contract, tort, crime and so on. These usages may be convenient shorthand, but in reality one set of facts may give rise to many different legal relationships, and in any event the legal concepts themselves do not occupy watertight compartments. Attempts to force legal material to fit such predetermined schemes will often result in a seriously blinkered approach, and lead to misunderstanding.

2.7 The Distinction between Matters of Fact and Matters of Law

One of the most vexed questions in the whole topic of legal classification is the distinction between matters of law and matters of fact. The distinction arises in many contexts, and even within a single context there may well be competing policy motives, each supporting the drawing of the line in different places.

As you will see in Part II, the doctrine of binding precedent deals only with propositions of law, therefore one motive for classifying certain matters as being matters of fact may be the purely practical desire to avoid a multiplicity of authorities: otherwise 'the precedent system will die from a surfeit of authorities' and the judges might be 'crushed under the weight of [their] own reports' (Lord Somervell and Lord Denning respectively, in *Qualcast (Wolverhampton) Ltd* v. *Haynes* [1959] 2 All ER 38).

Looking at it more positively, classifying a question as being a matter of law, and therefore as being subject to the doctrine of binding precedent, is one way of seeking to establish uniformity of decision-making across a large number of similar cases. (How far such uniformity is actually achieved, rather than merely desired, is something you may wish to think about when you have digested Part II.) On the other hand, there may be situations in which open flexibility of decision-making is seen to be desirable. For example, in *Brutus* v. *Cozens* [1972] 2 All ER 1297, the facts were that anti-apartheid activists disrupted the Wimbledon tennis tournament with a political demonstration. The magistrates acquitted them of 'insulting behaviour whereby a breach of the peace was likely to be occasioned'. In due course the House of Lords took the view that the question of whether specific conduct was 'insulting' was a matter of fact to be determined by the tribunal of fact, and was not a question of law to be taken on appeal. Lord Reid said: 'The meaning of an ordinary word of the English language is not a question of law'.

Brutus v. *Cozens* may be defensible on the basis that the magistrates would know their own area and the climate of opinion within it, and could make their decisions accordingly, but the flexibility which this attitude promotes may undermine the rule of law (see p. 62 for a discussion of the meaning of *the rule of law*) by making it very difficult for the individual to predict the legal outcome of proposed conduct. This consideration led the House of Lords to adopt a staunchly constitutionalist stand in the patents case of *Energy Conversion Devices Incorporated's Applications*

[1982] FSR 544, where Lord Diplock, expressing the unanimous opinion of the House, said:

> 'Your Lordships should, however, in my view take this opportunity of stating once again the important constitutional principle that questions of construction of all legislation, primary or secondary, are questions of law to be determined authoritatively by courts of law; that errors in construing primary or secondary legislation made by inferior tribunals that are not courts of law, however specialized and prestigious they may be, are subject to correction by judicial review; no tribunal and no court of law has any discretion to vary the meaning of the words of primary or secondary legislation from case to case in order to meet what the tribunal or court happens to think is the justice of the particular case. Tempting though it might sound, to do so is the negation of the rule of law. If there are cases in which the application of the Patents Rules leads to injustice, the cure is for the Secretary of State to amend the Rules. If what is thought to be the injustice results from the terms of the Act itself, the remedy is for Parliament to amend the Act.'

Although the importance of the rule of law cannot be doubted, the fact remains that in practice the dividing line between *law* and *fact* can be difficult to draw.

In *R* v. *Spens* [1991] 4 All ER 421, the Court of Appeal held that the construction of the City Code on Take-overs and Mergers was a matter of law for the trial judge, rather than a matter of fact for the jury. Watkins LJ, giving the judgement of the Court, acknowledged that generally speaking the construction of documents raises questions of fact. However, the court asserted that contractual and legislative documents constitute exceptions to this general principle, with the need for consistency between cases being asserted as an 'almost overriding' consideration to justify the conclusion. In the result therefore it was for the judge to decide what the Code meant, and then for the jury to decide whether the defendant's conduct fell within the requirements of the Code.

Although Watkins LJ in *R* v. *Spens* expressed himself to be perfectly well satisfied that that decision was consistent with *Brutus* v. *Cozens*, observers possessing a greater degree of detachment may feel less certain. In particular, it may be thought that the application of the principle in *R* v. *Spens* to the situation which arose in *Brutus* v. *Cozens* would require the concept of 'insult' to be defined as a matter of law, before determining, as a matter of fact, whether the conduct alleged in the case fell within that concept.

The distinction between fact and law has also prompted judicial comment in Administrative Law, where a decision-maker's errors of law are often more easily challengeable than errors of fact. Here again the courts are unable to offer definitive guidance as to the nature of the distinction, but the following extract from the judgement of Denning LJ, in *British Launderers' Research Association* v. *Central Middlesex Assessment Committee and Borough of Hendon Rating Authority* [1949] 1 All ER 21, provides some framework within which the question can be considered:

'It is important to distinguish between primary facts and the conclusions from them. *Primary facts are facts which are observed by witnesses and proved by oral testimony or facts proved by the production of a thing itself, such as original documents.* Their determination is essentially a question of fact for the tribunal of fact, and the only question of law that can arise on them is whether there was any evidence to support the finding. *The conclusions from primary facts are, however, inferences deduced by a process of reasoning from them. If, and in so far as, those conclusions can as well be drawn by a layman (properly instructed on the law) as a lawyer, they are conclusions of fact for the tribunal of fact*: and the only questions of law which can arise on them are whether there was a proper direction in point of law; and whether the conclusion is one which could reasonably be drawn from the primary facts: see *Bracegirdle* v. *Oxley* [1947] 1 All ER 126. *If, and in so far, however, as the correct conclusion to be drawn from primary facts requires, for its correctness, determination by a trained lawyer – as for instance, because it involves the interpretation of documents or because the law on the point cannot properly be understood or applied except by a trained lawyer – the conclusion is a conclusion of law.*' (Emphasis added.)

In *Edwards* v. *Bairstow* [1955] 3 All ER 48, the Inland Revenue had assessed the taxpayers to income tax on profit made from the purchase and sale of certain machinery, on the basis that the transaction was an 'adventure in the nature of trade'. The taxpayers succeeded on appeal to the General Commissioners, but both the High Court and the Court of Appeal held that the matter was one of fact, which meant that the General Commissioners' finding could not be overturned. Finally, however, the House of Lords decided that the meaning of 'adventure in the nature of trade' for the purposes of the income tax legislation was a question of law. More particularly, Lord Radcliffe said:

'The law does not supply a precise definition of the word "trade" . . . In effect it lays down the limits within which it would be permissible to say that a "trade" . . . does or does not exist. But the field so marked out is a wide one and there are many combinations of circumstances in which it could not be said to be wrong to arrive at a conclusion one way or the other. If the facts of any particular case are fairly capable of being so described, it seems to me that it necessarily follows that the determination . . . that "trade" does not exist is not "erroneous in point of law" . . . All these cases in which the facts warrant a determination either way can be described as questions of degree and therefore as questions of fact.'

On the other hand:

'If the Case [that is as stated by the General Commissioners] contains anything *ex facie* which is bad law and which bears on the determination, it is, obviously, erroneous in point of law. But without any such misconception appearing *ex facie* it may be that the facts found are such that *no person acting judicially and properly instructed as to the relevant law could have come to the determination under appeal.* In these circumstances, too, the court must intervene. It has no option but to assume that there has been some misconception of the law, and that this has been responsible for the determination. So, there, too, there has been an error in point of law. I do not think it much matters whether this state of affairs is described as one in which there is no evidence to support the determination, or as one in which the evidence is inconsistent with, and contradictory of, the determination, or as one in which the true and only reasonable conclusion contradicts the determination. Rightly understood, each phrase propounds the same test. For my part, I prefer the last of the three.' (Emphasis added.)

On the central question in the instant case, Lord Radcliffe asked:

'What detail does [this purchase and sale] lack that prevents it from being an adventure in the nature of trade, or what element is present in it that makes it capable of being aptly described as anything else?'

Comparing *Brutus* v. *Cozens* with *Edwards* v. *Bairstow*, however, it is difficult to see any distinction in principle between having to decide whether the factual conduct of demonstrating amounts to 'insulting behaviour' for the purposes of one statute, and having to decide whether the factual conduct of buying and selling amounts to 'an adventure in the nature of trade' for the purposes of another statute.

It is not altogether surprising, therefore, that academic commentators tend to unite in scepticism as to whether the law-fact distinction has any practical utility as a basis for predicting judicial outcomes. Thus Craig says: 'The case law on judicial review provides little in the way of guidance on the question of whether a certain issue is one of law or fact' (*Admin-*

istrative Law, 3rd edn, 1994, p. 347). Wade and Forsyth are even more forthright:

> 'The truth is . . . that there can hardly be a subject on which the courts act with such total lack of consistency as the difference between fact and law . . . It may be that judges instinctively agree with an American comment:[*]
>
>> "No two terms of legal science have rendered better service than 'law' and 'fact' . . . They are the creations of centuries. What judge has not found refuge in them? The man who could succeed in defining them would be a public enemy." [*]Leon Green, *Judge and Jury*, p. 270.'
>
> (*Administrative Law*, 7th edn, 1994, p. 948.)

The distinction between matters of law and matters of fact is further complicated by judicial references to questions of 'mixed law and fact'. Turning again to material drawn from Administrative Law for elucidation, the following comment of Laws J, writing extra-judicially, are instructive:

> 'The judges have frequently had recourse to the notion of "a mixed question of law and fact" in dealing with cases where an issue arises whether a particular set of facts falls within a particular category. However, taken literally, no such notion can exist. There can be no *single* question which is both a question of law and a question of fact: elementarily, factual propositions are proved by evidence, and legal propositions are established by reference to statutory provisions or common law principles; thus anything that is apparently a mixed question of law and fact will always on analysis prove to involve at least two questions, viz. what are the facts and what is the law. The difficulty arises where, these questions having received answers, there still remains a further question whether in the end the facts lie within the legal category identified. This happens where the category . . . is elastic; as for instance when the issue is whether or not a particular person is a servant or an independent contractor . . . In principle, therefore . . . there is . . . on analysis no such legal construct as a mixed question of law and fact; rather . . . the assignment of the facts to their correct legal category depends not only on the tribunal's ascertainment of the *primary* facts, but also – and critically - on its judgment as to what weight should be given to one aspect of the facts over another: and this latter exercise will be treated by the court as within the tribunal's fact-finding sphere [and not as a matter of law].' (Original emphasis. *Judicial Review*, 1992, edited by Supperstone and Goudie, pp. 74–5.)

All in all, therefore, it may seem that we can do little more than note the difficulty of drawing the distinction between matters of law and matters of fact. However, it may be appropriate at this point to develop one matter which Laws J mentioned when discussing mixed questions of law and fact, namely the question of how the parties can establish each kind of matter to the satisfaction of the court.

Establishing matters of law is, of course, the major theme of the whole of this book in general, and of Parts II and III in particular. Before moving on to those matters, however, some practical aspects of establishing matters of fact will be dealt with here in outline. Broadly speaking, there are three major possibilities: the facts may be agreed; the court may take judicial notice of the facts; and the facts may be proved by evidence. We will consider each of these in turn.

First, where the parties to a dispute agree some or all of the facts between themselves, these facts can then be either formally admitted or proved without challenge in subsequent legal proceedings. Second, the court may take judicial notice of matters of fact. The basic idea underlying the doctrine of judicial notice is that some matters are so well-known that a requirement of proof would be superfluous. For example, in *Nye* v. *Niblett* [1918] 1 KB 23, the court took judicial notice of the fact that cats are kept for domestic purposes. In *Bridlington Relay Ltd* v. *Yorkshire Electricity Board* [1965] 1 All ER 264, the court took judicial notice of the fact that the reception of television broadcasts is a common feature of English domestic life.

Sometimes, however, the court may seek advice before taking judicial notice of a particular fact. A common example would be whether or not Her Majesty's Government recognizes a foreign state (see, for example, *Duff Development Co* v. *Government of Kelantan* [1924] AC 797, where the advice of the Secretary of State for the Colonies was obtained). What is happening in cases such as this may look more like the reception of evidence than the taking of judicial notice, and indeed the judges do not always agree on the nature of what is happening. In the *Kelantan* case, Lord Finlay thought that judicial notice was being taken, but Lord Sumner thought the best evidence was being received. The point is important, for three reasons. First, if judicial notice is being taken the court will not allow the parties to dispute the accuracy of the advice which it receives. Second, facts which are judicially noticed constitute binding precedents, whereas facts decided in the light of evidence do not. Third, in a jury trial it is for the judge to take judicial notice, but for the jury to consider the evidence. However, all we can do here is to note the difficulty, and recognize it as merely one of many areas in which the courts effectively reserve to themselves a very substantial degree of discretion.

The third possibility in relation to determining the facts of a case is that, as we have seen from the comment of Denning LJ in the *British Launderers'* case (see p. 39), the court will receive evidence on disputed matters before deciding matters of fact. The law of evidence determines what can and cannot be put before the court in order to prove various allegations, and on whom the burden of proof rests. Nothing can usefully be said here by way of attempting to summarize such a large and complex body of law as that relating to evidence at large, but one specific point is worth pursuing.

It is often said that there are different standards of proof in *criminal* cases (*proof beyond reasonable doubt*) and *civil* cases (*proof on the balance of probabilities*). For example, in *Miller* v. *Minister of Pensions* [1947] 2 All ER 372, Denning LJ said, in relation to criminal cases:

'That degree is well settled. It need not reach certainty, but it must carry a high degree of probability. Proof beyond a reasonable doubt does not mean proof beyond the shadow of a doubt. The law would fail to protect the community if it admitted fanciful possibilities to deflect the course of justice. If the evidence is so strong . . . as to leave only a remote possibility . . . which can be dismissed with the sentence "of course it is possible but not in the least probable" the case is proved beyond reasonable doubt, but nothing short of that will suffice.'

Contrasting this with the civil standard of proof, he said:

'That degree is well settled. It must carry a reasonable degree of probability, but not so high as is required in a criminal case. If the evidence is such that the tribunal can say: "we think it more probable than not", the burden is discharged, but if the probabilities are equal it is not.'

However, the comments of the same judge in *Bater* v. *Bater* [1951] P 35, are also important:

'It is . . . true that . . . a higher standard of proof is required in criminal cases than in civil cases. But . . . there is no absolute standard in either case. In criminal cases the charge must be proved beyond reasonable doubt, but there may be degrees of proof within that standard . . . So also in civil cases the case must be proved by a preponderance of probability, but there may be degrees of probability within that standard. The degree depends on the subject-matter. A civil court, when considering a charge of fraud, will naturally require . . . a higher degree of probability than that which it would require when asking if negligence is established. It does not adopt so high a degree as a criminal court, even when considering a charge of a criminal nature; but still it does require a degree of probability which is commensurate with the occasion.'

Experience shows that even this statement of principle is a little over-cautious. There have been civil cases where the criminal standard of proof has been explicitly applied. For example, *Halford* v. *Brookes* [1991] *The Independent*, 1 October, involved a claim for damages arising out of an alleged murder. Because a conclusion that the defendant was liable in damages would amount to a finding that he was guilty of murder, the court specifically required that the plaintiff should satisfy it on the criminal standard. Similarly in *R* v. *Commissioner Rowe QC (Mr) ex parte Mainwaring* [1992] 4 All ER 821, the Court of Appeal said that the criminal standard of proof must be satisfied in order to establish allegations of malpractice during an election campaign, even though the proceedings were civil.

Even courts which have been unwilling to go as far as those in *Halford* v. *Brookes* and *R* v. *Commissioner Rowe QC (Mr) ex parte Mainwaring* will still remind themselves of the variable standard of proof. In the immigration case of *R* v. *Secretary of State for the Home Department ex parte Khawaja* [1983] 1 All ER 765, where the issue was whether facts existed which would justify restraining the liberty of the individual, Lord Scarman said:

'The reviewing court will . . . require to be satisfied that the facts which are required for the justification of the restraint put on liberty do exist. The flexibility of the civil standard of proof suffices to ensure that the court will require the high degree of probability which is appropriate to what is at stake.'

Exceptionally, the court may even explicitly decline to classify the proceedings as being either civil or criminal, preferring to place the sole emphasis on the question of the relevant standard of proof. In *Percy* v. *Director of Public Prosecutions* [1995] 1 WLR 1382, the High Court allowed an appeal against a decision of a magistrates' court to commit a woman to prison for refusing to be bound over to keep the peace. The jursidiction to bind people over is ancient, going back to at least the Justices of the Peace Act 1361, but even after the passage of six centuries the character of the proceedings remains in some doubt. Collins J, giving the judgement of the court, said:

'There are pointers either way to whether the proceedings should be labelled criminal or civil. We do not need to decide which is appropriate, although we would incline to criminal, largely for the reasons given in *R. v. Bolton JJ ex parte Graeme* (1986) 150 JP 190. In our judgement, the consequences and circumstances of the proceedings require proof to a high standard. Accordingly, whatever the nature of the proceedings, we consider that the proper standard to be applied is the criminal standard, namely proof beyond reasonable doubt.'

As an all-embracing summary of the law on standards of proof, there is much to be said for the test suggested by Ormrod LJ in *Re J S (A Minor)* [1980] 1 All ER 1061:

'The plaintiff (or the party on whom the burden rests) must satisfy the court that it is *reasonably safe* in all the circumstances of the case *to act on the evidence* before the court, *bearing in mind the consequences which will follow.*' (Emphasis added.)

Summary

1 Lawyers classify their material in various ways. The terms they use may have a variety of meanings, depending on the context in which they are used.
2 *Common law* may be contrasted with *statute law, equity* and *civil law.*
3 *Civil law* may be contrasted not only with *common law*, but also with *criminal law, ecclesiastical law* and *military law.*
4 *Public law* may be contrasted with *private law.*
5 *Substantive law* may be contrasted with *procedural* (or *adjectival*) *law.*
6 Law may be classified by reference to its subject-matter.
7 There is an important distinction between matters of *law* and matters of *fact*. However, there is very little in the way of principle offering reliable guidance as to how this distinction should be drawn. When facts have to be proved, the degree of proof which is required varies according to the circumstances of the case.

Exercises

1 How and why did equity come into existence?
2 What does *specific performance* mean and when may it be ordered?
3 What does *civil law* mean when used in contradistinction to (a) *criminal law;* (b) *common law?*
4 Why may it be important to know whether an issue is one of *fact* or *law?*
5 'The civil law standard of proof is *on the balance of probabilities;* the criminal law standard of proof is *beyond reasonable doubt.*' Explain the inadequacy of this statement.

3 The Jurisdictions of the Principal English Courts

3.1 Introduction

This chapter outlines the jurisdictions of the principal English courts, and the correct way to refer to their judicial personnel. All law students should know this material well enough to be able to feel confident when using the technical terminology which it involves. The principal statutes governing the jurisdictions of the English courts are the Magistrates' Courts Act 1980, the Supreme Court Act 1981, the County Courts Act 1984 and the Courts and Legal Services Act 1990. The mass of detail contained in these statutes need not be pursued here, but the most important points are summarized in the remaining paragraphs of this chapter. (The jurisdiction of the European Court of Justice is covered in Chapter 5.)

The first point to notice is that there are two principal types of jurisdiction, namely jurisdiction at *first instance*, which means that the court will be finding the facts and trying the issue between the parties, and *appellate* jurisdiction, which means that another court has already heard the case and the decision of that court is being appealed.

Second, the summary begins with a diagrammatic representation in which arrows indicate the principal avenues of appeal, and continues with textual explanation. Before turning to the summary, however, there is one matter which requires emphasis. As the arrows in the diagram show, there are often two avenues of appeal. It is essential to grasp that these avenues do not simply present aspiring appellants with a choice in each case: the availability of one avenue rather than another will depend on the circumstances, with the *avenue* of appeal being generally dictated by the *ground* of appeal. You will need to read the textual explanation carefully if you are to understand how this works in practice, although the final paragraph of this chapter attempts to provide a brief overview of rights of appeal. Finally, the arrows on the diagram deal only with avenues of *appeal*. Therefore they do not indicate the possibility of *reference* to the European Court of Justice (see p. 81), nor the possibility of *judicial review* (see p. 35), both of which are conceptually quite distinct from *appeal* (see p. 55).

3.2 The Hierarchy of the Courts as a Diagram

It cannot be emphasised too strongly that this diagram shows only the *possible* avenues of appeal. You must read the rest of the chapter in order to understand when each avenue of appeal will *actually* be available.

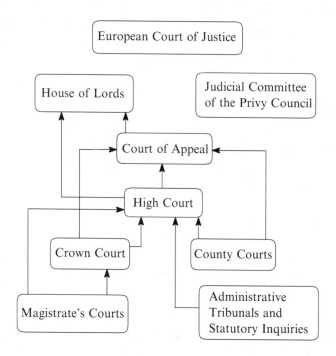

3.3 Magistrates' Courts

The magistrates' courts' jurisdiction has both civil and criminal elements, and is exercisable both at first instance and on appeal.

Magistrates' Courts as courts of first instance

Criminal jurisdiction

Virtually all criminal cases begin in magistrates' courts, and well over 90 per cent also end there. Where the magistrates do not dispose of the case entirely, they will commit the defendant to the Crown Court, either for trial or for sentence. Committal for trial will be replaced by a new procedure, to be known as 'transfer for trial', on the coming into force of the Part I of Schedule IV to the Criminal Justice and Public Order Act 1994. Under the transfer procedure, where the magistrates' court is not going to hear the case itself, the prosecution will serve, on both the defendant and the magistrates' court, a set of papers containing its case. The case will then be automatically transferred to the Crown court, as a purely administrative process, unless the defence applies for the case to be dismissed. It is envisaged that applications for dismissal will normally be dealt with on the basis of written representations, but there is provision for oral hearings in cases of 'complexity or difficulty'.

Magistrates sitting as *Youth Courts* exercise criminal jurisdiction over those between 10 and 18 years of age. It is interesting to notice in passing that 10 is the age of criminal responsibility. In other words, a child under the age of 10 is *conclusively* presumed not to be guilty of any offence, and is therefore not subject to the criminal law. The position of children between the ages of 10 and 14 was considered by the House of Lords in *C (A Minor)* v. *DPP* [1995] 2 All ER 43, which is discussed at p. 208.

Civil jurisdiction

Magistrates have an enormously wide-ranging civil jurisdiction. Much of it relates to local government aspects of Administrative Law, including certain aspects of the law of highways and public health and licensing. This jurisdiction represents the residue of those functions which the magistracy exercised before the creation of elected local authorities in the nineteenth century. Other civil matters within the jurisdiction of the magistrates include, by way of examples from a vast range of possibilities, the power to make orders for the destruction of dangerous dogs and for the disposal of property which is in the hands of the police and the ownership of which is disputed.

The civil jurisdiction of youth courts includes care proceedings in respect of children and young persons. Magistrates sitting as family proceedings courts have extensive jurisdiction in family law, but this does not extend to divorce.

Magistrates' Courts as appeal courts

The magistrates' appellate jurisdiction, which is principally civil, is very diverse but of little practical significance. To take only two examples, the magistrates can hear appeals against refusals to issue driving licences, and can also hear appeals in certain cases arising out of the making of compulsory purchase orders by public authorities.

Judicial personnel in Magistrates' Courts

Magistrates are technically known as *justices of the peace*. The expressions *the magistrates* and *the justices* are interchangeable. Most magistrates are lay, in the sense of not being qualified lawyers, and will therefore rely heavily on their clerks. Some magistrates, however, are qualified lawyers. These are known as *stipendiaries* because they are salaried. Stipendiary magistrates generally sit in the busiest courts, because their legal expertise enables them to dispose of the courts' business more efficiently.

3.4 The Crown Court

The Crown Court's jurisdiction has both civil and criminal elements, and is exercisable both at first instance and on appeal.

The Crown Court as a court of first instance

Criminal jurisdiction

The Crown Court has exclusive jurisdiction with respect to criminal trials on indictment, which is the next stage in the procedure where the magistrates have committed defendants for trial (and will continue to be so when the transfer for trial procedure, outlined on p. 48, comes into operation), and where the magistrates have committed defendants for sentence. Strictly speaking, it may be argued that the prior involvement of the magistrates means that these jurisdictions are not at first instance, but on the other hand neither are they appellate. They are best regarded as being effectively a stage in the first instance procedure.

Civil jurisdiction

It would be misleading to give the impression that the Crown Court has any generally significant civil jurisdiction at first instance, but, for example, the Highways Act 1980 does confer upon it jurisdiction to adjudicate in certain disputes as to the status of highways and whether they are in disrepair.

The Crown Court as an appeal court

Criminal jurisdiction

The defendant has a right of appeal to the Crown Court against conviction or sentence or both in magistrates' courts. An appeal to the Crown Court against conviction is an appeal on the facts. The prosecution has no corresponding right of appeal against an acquittal, nor against a sentence which it considers to be too lenient. An appeal against conviction is a full re-hearing, which means that the witnesses are called again, and their evidence is assessed afresh. Where there is an appeal against sentence only, no witnesses are called, but the prosecution will present an outline of the facts.

If the defendant is appealing from the magistrates on a point of law, the appropriate route is to the High Court, using a procedure known as 'appeal by way of case stated' (see, p. 53). In this situation the defence loses the advantage which it has in relation to appeals on the facts and appeals against sentence, because here the prosecution does have a corresponding right of appeal.

In addition to its genuinely appellate jurisdiction, the Crown Court has a quasi-appellate jurisdiction under s.11 of the Criminal Appeal Act 1995. Section 11 of the Act enables the Criminal Cases Review Commission, which was created by s.8 of the Act, to refer to the Crown Court cases where there has been a conviction in a magistrates' court. The reference may be in respect of conviction or sentence or both, and the proceedings will be treated as if they were by way of appeal. Strictly speaking, however, the proceedings are not appellate because they are instituted by someone other than the person who is affected by the original decision. Although the Act does not say so, the procedure is intended to enable cases to be reopened where it is thought that there has been a miscarriage of justice. As we shall see, at p. 56, the Criminal Cases Review Commission has an equivalent power to refer cases to the Court of Appeal following conviction on indictment.

Civil jurisdiction

The Crown Court has a very wide-ranging appellate jurisdiction in respect of decisions of magistrates' courts in civil cases, but unlike the position in relation to criminal cases, no general distinction is drawn between the parties in terms of their rights of appeal. As with criminal cases, however, if the appeal is on a point of law, the appropriate route is to the High Court by way of case stated.

Judicial personnel in the Crown Court

Cases in the Crown Court are presided over by either a High Court judge, a circuit judge, a deputy circuit judge, a recorder, or an assistant recorder, the last three of which hold office on a part-time basis. Additionally, in trials there will be a jury. In committals for sentence and appeals of any kind, there will be no jury but the bench will include a number of magistrates.

The matter of the correct description of judicial personnel in the Crown Court is dealt with by a *Practice Direction (Judges: Mode of Address)*, issued by Lord Lane CJ and reported at [1982] 1 WLR 101. A circuit judge is referred to as 'His (or Her) Honour Judge A', which may be abbreviated in writing to 'H. H. Judge A'. A deputy circuit judge is referred to as 'His (or Her) Honour BC sitting as a deputy circuit judge'. Recorders are referred to as 'Mr (or Mrs) Recorder D'. Assistant recorders are referred to as 'Mr (or Mrs or Miss or Ms) EF sitting as an assistant recorder'.

3.5 County Courts

The County Courts' jurisdiction is entirely civil, and is exercisable both at first instance and on appeal.

County Courts as courts of first instance

To a very large extent the jurisdiction of the County Courts makes them into a sort of mini-High Court. They have jurisdiction in respect of contractual disputes and almost all torts. They also have jurisdiction in relation to probate and divorce, and may have an Admiralty jurisdiction. The provisions governing exclusion from the County Courts' jurisdiction and the precise interrelationship between the County Court and the High Court is very complex, with detailed procedures for transferring cases from one to the other. In most cases the basis of the distinction between the courts' jurisdictions will be the sum of money claimed, or the value of the property involved, but the complexity and importance of the case may also be relevant. The financial criteria may be varied from time to time by the Lord Chancellor.

County Courts also have a jurisdiction in arbitration, which is a relatively informal procedure for use in small claims.

County Courts as appeal courts

The appellate jurisdiction of the County Courts is very limited, but one notable field of activity is in relation to appeals arising out of certain types of action taken by local authorities, under the Housing Act 1985, in relation to sub-standard housing. It is impossible to discern any basis of principle underlying the statutes which allocate such cases to the County

Court rather than to Magistrates' Courts. Historical accident appears to have been the major determining factor.

Judicial personnel in County Courts

The principal judges in the County Court are circuit judges from the Crown Court, but the Courts and Legal Services Act 1990 recognized the status of the officials who were formerly known as *registrars* by redesignating them as *district judges*. A district judge is referred to as 'Mr (or Mrs) District Judge A'.

3.6   The High Court

The High Court's jurisdiction has both civil and criminal elements, and is exercisable both at first instance and on appeal. It also has a supervisory jurisdiction. Although the High Court is nominally one court, for administrative purposes it is split into three units, namely the *Queen's Bench Division*, the *Chancery Division* and the *Family Division*.

The High Court as a court of first instance

Criminal jurisdiction

None of the Divisions has a criminal jurisdiction at first instance, other than the power to deal with criminal contempts of court.

Civil jurisdiction

The *Queen's Bench Division* deals with civil matters such as claims in contract and tort without any limit as to value, and judges who are asssigned to the Crown Office list hear applications for judicial review and similar cases. In addition to this mainstream work, it also has two specialist sub-divisions, namely the *Admiralty Court* and the *Commercial Court*. The latter is designed to be particularly closely attuned to the needs of the commercial community. In practice, this means that the procedure is speedy, which is achieved by placing greater reliance on documentary evidence, and by giving the judge the more active role of an arbitrator, rather than the more passive one of an adjudicator. The *Chancery Division* deals with matters such as land law, trusts, the administration of estates, bankruptcy, partnerships, companies, revenue cases and contentious probate, without limit as to value. The *Family Division* deals with matters such as defended divorces, as well as some matters relating to children, and some probate cases.

The High Court as an appeal court

Two or more judges, sitting together, may constitute a *Divisional Court of the Queen's Bench Division.* The Divisional Court has both appellate and supervisory functions. (The concept of *supervisory* jurisdiction is discussed at p. 55.) A minor terminological complication arises because the modern practice is for a single-judge court to exercise the supervisory jurisdiction in many civil cases, with multi-judge courts tending to be reserved for criminal cases. Although as a matter of definition a single-judge court cannot be a Divisional Court, in practice that phrase is not uncommonly applied to such courts. The other Divisions of the High Court also have Divisional Courts, but since those Divisions have no appellate jurisdiction in criminal matters, it follows that the split between their single-judge courts and Divisional Courts (using the latter phrase strictly), cannot be as straightforward as it is in the Queen's Bench Division. Accordingly, there are detailed provisions as to the jurisdiction of a single judge in the other Divisions.

Criminal Jurisdiction

Queen's Bench Division

The Queen's Bench Division has an important appellate jurisdiction relating to *appeals by way of case stated* from magistrates' courts, and from the Crown court sitting without a jury (for example, when hearing an appeal from a magistrates' court). These appeals are available only on points of law, and not on questions of fact. Appeal by way of case stated is a procedure whereby the court whose decision is being challenged prepares a document ('states a case') asking for the opinion of the High Court. The 'case' will contain an account of the facts which the court found to have been proved, a statement of the relevant law as the court understood it, and an application of that law to those facts. The court stating the case then formally asks the High Court whether it was right on the law and on the application of the law to the facts.

If the High Court disagrees with the lower court, it *may* remit the case to the lower court, but it does not always do so. A typical reason for refusing to remit a case would be lapse of time since the facts giving rise to the case or since the hearing in the lower court, especially when the case is relatively trivial and the appeal has been brought principally to clarify the law for the future. In these cases the delivery of the court's judgement alone will be thought to be sufficient to serve the real purpose of the appeal. In the more usual situation where the case is remitted, the High Court may direct either that the lower court must find the case proved or not proved, or that the hearing should continue in the light of the law as stated by the High Court.

Appeal by way of case stated is somewhat anomalous, being an appeal in name, but having some of the characteristics of the court's supervisory jurisdiction (see p. 55), at least to the extent that the court may be unable to dispose of the matter fully, but may have to remit it to the lower court. The explanation for this is historical and need not be explored here.

Appeal by way of case stated is generally available to any party to any proceedings in magistrates' courts. It is also generally available in the Crown Court except in respect of matters relating to trials on indictment. This exception is, of course, very common in practice, and appeals by way of case stated from the Crown Court are rare. However, they may be brought against, for example, a decision made on appeal from a magistrates' court.

Chancery Division and Family Division

Neither the Chancery Division nor the Family Division has any appellate jurisdiction in criminal cases.

Civil Jurisdiction

Queen's Bench Division

The Queen's Bench Division deals with appeals by way of case stated in civil matters, just as it does in criminal matters.

Chancery Division

The Chancery Division deals with a variety of appeals from County Courts, including those in insolvency cases.

Family Division

The Family Division deals with appeals in domestic cases from magistrates' courts and the Crown Court, the latter being by way of case stated.

The High Court as a supervisory court

The Queen's Bench Division has a supervisory jurisdiction, which is exercisable by way of the procedure known as an *application for judicial review*. As we shall see in Chapter 14 when we are considering the doctrine of precedent in the High Court, there is room for disagreement in that context as to whether the supervisory jurisdiction is genuinely discrete or is simply one aspect of the jurisdiction at first instance, but in the present context its is useful to treat the two as being separate and distinct.

The concept of review originated at common law where there were, and still are, no rights of appeal. The procedure, as distinct from the grounds, is now governed by Order 53 of the Rules of the Supreme Court, and s.31 of the Supreme Court Act 1981. The distinction between appellate and supervisory jurisdictions is that in the former the court is concerned with challenges to the *correctness of decisions*, or, adopting Lord Diplock's phraseology in *Megarity* v. *Law Society* [1981] 1 All ER 641, an appellant is 'having a second bite at the legal cherry'. By contrast, a court exercising a supervisory role is concerned only with challenges to the *legality of decision-making processes*, and is not called upon to assess the correctness of the decisions themselves. One consequence of this is that, except where the appeal is by way of case stated (see p. 53) a court which allows an appeal will usually substitute its own decision for that of the original court, whereas a court which allows an application for review will be limited to remitting the case to the decision-maker for the decision to be remade properly.

Applications for judicial review in civil cases are usually heard by a single judge of the Queen's Bench Division, while those arising from criminal cases are usually heard by a two, or sometimes three, judge Divisional Court. There appears to be no magic in the distinction between a single judge and a Divisional Court. In *R.* v. *Secretary of State for the Home Department ex parte Chinoy* (1992) 4 Admin LR 457, Bingham LJ, sitting in a two member Divisional Court, said: 'We exercise, for all practical purposes, the same jurisdiction as a single judge.'

Judicial personnel in the High Court

The head of the Queen's Bench Division is the Lord Chief Justice, who is referred to in writing as, for example, Lord Black CJ, or Lord Black LCJ. The effective head of the Chancery Division is the Vice-Chancellor although, as a result of the historical process outlined at pp. 27–8, the Lord Chancellor may still be regarded as its nominal head. The Vice-Chancellor is referred to in writing as, for example, Sir John Brown V-C, or merely as Brown V-C. The head of the Family Division is known as the President, and is referred to in writing as, for example, Sir David White P. Ordinary judges of the High Court, who are technically termed *puisne judges* (*puisne* is pronounced *puny* and merely means *junior*), are referred to orally as, for example, Mr (or Mrs) Justice Green. The written form of the title – Green J – is sexually non-specific. Judges of the Court of Appeal may sit in the High Court, but they will usually do so only where that court is exercising its appellate and supervisory jurisdictions.

3.7   The Court of Appeal

Although the Court of Appeal is nominally one court, it is divided into the Criminal Division and the Civil Division. The principal jurisdiction of both Divisions is appellate, but the Criminal Division also has a limited quasi-appellate jurisdiction.

Court of Appeal (Criminal Division)

Appellate jurisdiction

The appellate jurisdiction of the Court of Appeal (Criminal Division) relates to appeals against conviction, sentence or both from the Crown Court. (As we shall see at p. 58, criminal appeals from the High Court go directly to the House of Lords.) In the case of an appeal against conviction, the Court of Appeal has power to hear witnesses, but seldom does so because most appeals against conviction turn on an analysis of the quality of the trial judge's summing-up to the jury. A major function of the Criminal Division is the issuing of guidelines on sentencing for the assistance of lower courts.

Quasi-appellate jurisdiction

In addition to the genuinely appellate jurisdiction outlined above, there are three provisions which enable cases to be referred to the Court of Appeal (Criminal Division), namely s.9 of the Criminal Appeal Act 1995, s.36 of the Criminal Justice Act 1972, and s.36 of the Criminal Justice Act 1988.

Section 9 of the Criminal Appeal Act 1995, which is intended to provide a mechanism for correcting miscarriages of justice, enables the Criminal Cases Review Commission, which was created by s.8 of the Act, to refer to the Court of Appeal cases where there has been a conviction on indictment.The reference may be in respect of either conviction or sentence or both, and the proceedings will be treated as if they were by way of appeal. Strictly speaking, however, the proceedings are not appellate because they are instituted by someone other than the person who is affected by the original decision. The procedure under s.9 replaces the Home Secretary's power to refer cases to the Court of Appeal, under s.17 of the Criminal Appeal Act 1968.

Section 36 of the Criminal Justice Act 1972 provides that where there has been an acquittal on indictment (in which case, as we saw above, the prosecution has no avenue of appeal), the Attorney-General can refer a point of law to the Court of Appeal. This procedure does not amount to an appeal by the prosecution, because the result of the Court of Appeal's deliberations has no effect on the defendant, who remains acquitted.

Under *s.36 of the Criminal Justice Act 1988* the Attorney-General can refer a case to the Court of Appeal if he considers that a sentence imposed by the Crown court is too lenient. Although this provision is cast in terms of a reference by the Attorney-General, rather than an appeal by the prosecution, the court can vary the actual sentence, either upwards or downwards. This is, of course, in clear contradistinction to the Attorney-General's Reference procedure under s.36 of the Criminal Justice Act 1972 following an acquittal, where the opinion of the Court of Appeal does not affect the outcome of the individual case.

Court of Appeal (Civil Division)

The Court of Appeal (Civil Division) deals almost entirely with appeals from County Courts and the High Court. Appeals are said to be by way of re-hearing, but in the vast majority of cases only documentary evidence, supported by the oral arguments of counsel, is received in practice. The procedure, therefore, is not the same as the full re-hearing which takes place on an appeal from a magistrates' court to the Crown Court (see p. 51).

Judicial personnel in the Court of Appeal

The Lord Chief Justice is not only the head of the Queen's Bench Division of the High Court (see p. 55), but also of the Court of Appeal (Criminal Division). The head of the Court of Appeal (Civil Division) is the Master of the Rolls, who is referred to in writing as, for example, Sir John Pink MR. An ordinary judge of the Court of Appeal will have the title of Lord Justice of Appeal, and it seems to be the practice to use this term irrespective of the sex of the individual concerned. The written form of the style is, of course, sexually non-specific, and appears as, for example, Grey LJ. On retirement from the Court of Appeal, judges sometimes return to judicial work on a part-time basis to help out with heavy workloads. Under these circumstances they will simply be referred to, both orally and in writing, by reference to the knighthood (or damehood) which they already possessed before retirement, for example Dame Jane Grey.

Circuit judges may also sit in the Criminal Division of the Court of Appeal, where their day-to-day experience of conducting criminal trials can be useful.

3.8   The House of Lords

The House of Lords, or more accurately the Appellate Committee of the House of Lords, has jurisdiction in both civil and criminal cases. In practice, as its title suggests, the jurisdiction is almost entirely appellate, although there is a residual and very limited jurisdiction at first instance. As a minor point of terminology, it is worth noticing that the *Appeals* Committee (as distinct from the *Appellate* Committee) of the House of Lords is the body which deals with applications for leave to appeal to the House.

The House of Lords as a court of first instance

The House of Lords' jurisdiction at first instance is very limited, but it includes disputes between claimants of peerages.

The House of Lords as an appeal court

The House of Lords has appellate jurisdiction in both criminal and civil cases.

Criminal jurisdiction

The criminal jurisdiction of the House of Lords relates to appeals by either the prosecution or the defence from the Court of Appeal (Criminal Division) and the High Court.

Civil jurisdiction

This jurisdiction covers, principally, appeals from the Court of Appeal (Civil Division), but additionally there is the leapfrog procedure, governed by ss.12 and 13 of the Administration of Justice Act 1969, under which cases may progress directly from the High Court to the House of Lords. In other words, they 'leapfrog' over the Court of Appeal. This procedure, which is considered in more detail at p. 189, is intended to save time and money in certain cases which are likely to end up in the House of Lords anyway.

Judicial personnel in the House of Lords

In practice virtually all members who sit in the Appellate Committee of the House of Lords are appointed specifically to do so. Commonly known as 'Law Lords', they are technically known as 'Lords of Appeal in Ordinary'. Law Lords are simply referred to by their titles, for example Lord

Bounderby, either with or without the appropriate geographical designation (e.g. Lord Bounderby *of Coketown*). The Lord Chancellor, who is a member of the Government, but who can and does sit in the Appellate Committee of the House of Lords, is referred to in writing as, for example, Lord Henchard LC. As with other Law Lords, the use of the geographical designation (e.g. Lord Henchard *of Casterbridge*) is optional.

3.9 The Judicial Committee of the Privy Council

The constitutional function of the Privy Council as a whole is to advise the Crown, and therefore, theoretically at least, its Judicial Committee does not actually determine cases but merely offers advice. In practice, however, the advice is always accepted, so it is not uncommon to speak of decisions of the Judicial Committee of the Privy Council, or simply of the Privy Council.

The jurisdiction of the Judicial Committee of the Privy Council

The Judicial Committee is principally concerned with both civil and criminal appeals from certain Commonwealth countries, although the number of countries preserving this avenue of appeal has diminished over the years. Additionally, it has jurisdiction over a wide range of appeals relating to disciplinary proceedings brought by various professions, such as doctors, dentists and opticians, as well as dealing with a variety of Admiralty and ecclesiastical matters.

Judicial personnel of the Judicial Committee of the Privy Council

The Committee's membership overlaps to a large extent with the membership of the Appellate Committee of the House of Lords sitting judicially, although members from overseas may sometimes sit as well.

3.10 Administrative Tribunals and Statutory Inquiries

As their names suggest, administrative tribunals and statutory inquiries are not courts and therefore cannot be part of the hierarchy of the courts. Nevertheless, they are generally subject to control by the courts, by way of either appeal, where statute so provides, or supervisory review. A major difference between tribunals and courts is that the members of a tribunal will usually have extensive, practical knowledge of the type of cases which come before them. Additionally, tribunals tend to be less formal, cheaper and generally more accessible than courts. Examples of tribunals include Industrial Tribunals, dealing with certain types of disputes between employers and employees, and Social Security Appeal Tribunals, whose jurisdiction is self-evident.

Inquiries are also usually conducted by people with technical expertise. Examples of inquiries include appeals to the Secretary of State for the Environment against refusals of planning permission by local authorities. Inquiries tend to be less formal, cheaper and more accessible than the courts. Nevertheless, they are essentially different from tribunals, as indicated by the following comment from the Council on Tribunals Annual Report for 1960:

'Tribunals, generally speaking, exercise an independent jurisdiction: they decide particular cases by applying rules and regulations and sometimes by using their own discretion. Inquiries, on the other hand, form part of the process by which a Minister exercises his discretion – discretion for which he is answerable to Parliament.'

There will often be the possibility of an appeal to the High Court on a *point of law only* (i.e. *not on the merits* of the case), but whether this is so in any particular case will depend upon the relevant statutory provision.

3.11 Rights of Appeal and Leave to Appeal

There have been various references throughout this chapter to *rights of appeal*. Whether there is any right of appeal in a given situation will always depend on the relevant statutory provisions. However, as a very general proposition, where there is a right of appeal there will often be one appeal on the facts and the law, but with the possibility of further appeal on the law only. It is also worth noticing that some rights of appeal are conditional, in the sense that leave to appeal must be obtained before the right is exercised. Depending on the detailed statutory provisions in question, leave may be obtainable either from the court whose decision is being challenged or from the court which will deal with the appeal if it proceeds.

Summary

1 You need to be confident that you understand what each court does.
2 The structure of the courts' system within the English legal system is hierarchical.

3 The magistrates' courts' jurisdiction has both civil and criminal elements, and is exercisable both at first instance and on appeal.

4 The Crown Court's jurisdiction has both civil and criminal elements, and is exercisable both at first instance and on appeal.

5 The County Courts' jurisdiction is entirely civil, and is exercisable both at first instance and on appeal.

6 Although the High Court is nominally one court, for administrative purposes it is split into three parts, namely the Queen's Bench Division, the Chancery Division and the Family Division. As a whole, the High Court's jurisdiction comprises both civil and criminal matters, and is exercisable both at first instance and on appeal. It also has a supervisory jurisdiction.

7 Although the Court of Appeal is nominally one court, it is divided into the Criminal Division and the Civil Division. The principal jurisdiction of both Divisions is appellate, but the Criminal Division also has a limited quasi-appellate jurisdiction.

8 The Appellate Committee of the House of Lords has jurisdiction in both civil and criminal cases. In practice the jurisdiction is almost entirely appellate, although there is a residual and very limited jurisdiction at first instance.

9 The Judicial Committee of the Privy Council, which has jurisdiction in both civil and criminal cases, is principally concerned with appeals from certain Commonwealth countries. Additionally, it has jurisdiction over a wide range of appeals relating to disciplinary proceedings brought by various professions, such as doctors, dentists and opticians, as well as dealing with a variety of Admiralty and ecclesiastical matters.

10 Administrative tribunals and statutory inquiries are not courts and therefore cannot be part of the hierarchy of the courts. Nevertheless, they are generally subject to control by the courts, by way of either appeal or supervisory review.

11 The system of appeals is governed entirely by statute, which means that in each case the existence and extent of any right of appeal depends on the relevant statute. However, it is common to find a more extensive right to appeal against rulings of law than against findings of fact.

Exercises

1 Apart from the Court of Appeal (Civil Division), which court has only civil jurisdiction?

2 Distinguish between *appeal* and *review*.

3 In what sense can it be said that the Judicial Committee of the Privy Council does not give *judgements*?

4 Distinguish between *tribunals* and *inquiries*.

5 Generally speaking, are the rights of appeal more extensive in relation to matters of *fact* or matters of *law*?

4 The Constitutional Context of Legal Method

4.1 Introduction

As we shall see throughout this book, a major part of legal method involves identifying the scope of the power of the courts to apply and develop the law. It follows from this that, although the study of constitutional law is a substantial exercise in its own right, the study of legal method must include at least an overview of the legal basis of the constitution as the foundation of any real understanding. This chapter will therefore consider the legal framework of the British constitution generally, while the next three chapters will consider the European Community context.

Although the British constitution is usually described as being unwritten, there are some underlying ideas which are of enduring influence. These include the rule of law, the legislative supremacy of Parliament and the separation of powers. We will consider each of these in turn.

4.2 The Rule of Law

The rule of law contains a number of elements. First, it

'is a principle of institutional morality. As such it guides all forms of law-making and law-enforcement. In particular, it suggests that legal certainty and procedural protections are . . . fundamental requirements of good governance. These requirements are not . . . unqualified. But they are qualified only by the fact that they may be overridden in the interest of other administrative virtues (such as responsive decision-making).' (Jowell, *The Rule of Law Today*, in Jowell and Oliver, *The Changing Constitution*, 3rd edn, 1994, p. 72.)

The tension, which this quotation discloses, between the requirements of 'legal certainty' and 'responsive decision-making' will be an all-pervading theme of this book, but you have already encountered it in the context of the questions, and hypothetical answers, which are discussed at p. 22.

Second, the rule of law requires the provision of a system for identifying rights and liabilities and for redressing grievances, and thus helps to dissuade people from resorting to self-help. The rule of law is, therefore, a vital factor in promoting social cohesion.

4.3 The Legislative Supremacy of Parliament

A statement of the doctrine

According to Dicey, whose influential book *The Law of the Constitution* was first published in 1885, 'the very keystone of the law of the Constitution' is that:

> 'Parliament . . . has . . . the right to make or unmake any law whatever; and further, that no person or body is recognised by the law of England as having a right to override or set aside the legislation of Parliament.'

It is clear that Parliament may set aside, or repeal, its own legislation either expressly or impliedly. Express repeal will be obvious. Implied repeal will occur where a later statute is inconsistent with an earlier one, because the court will conclude that Parliament knew what it was doing, and therefore it must have intended the later statute to prevail.

There is, however, a logical conundrum lurking within the concept of the legislative supremacy of Parliament, namely the question of whether one Parliament can enact legislation in such a way that a later Parliament cannot repeal it, even by an express provision purporting to do so. The classic reply to this is that such unrepealable provisions are impossible, because their effect would be to destroy the supremacy of later Parliaments. As Sir Robert Megarry said, in *Manuel* v. *Attorney-General* [1982] 3 All ER 822: 'As a matter of law the courts of England recognise Parliament as being omnipotent in all save the power to destroy its own omnipotence.' We will return to this question of whether one Parliament can prevail over its successors when we consider the impact of Community law on English law and national sovereignty in Chapter 7. For the moment, however, it will be useful to consider the origins of Parliament as a basis for understanding the doctrine of legislative supremacy generally.

The origins and evolution of Parliament

The details of the origins of Parliament are shrouded in a good deal of historical uncertainty. Nevertheless, in broad outline, the period between the Norman Conquest and the so-called Glorious Revolution of 1688 clearly witnessed a transition from absolute monarchy to constitutional monarchy. Even in the early days of absolute monarchy, however, the Kings of England kept in touch with political reality through the *Curia Regis* (or *King's Council*), which consisted of advisers who helped the king to govern the country. At this stage, Parliament was, as the Norman–French root of the word indicates, merely a talking-shop.

In time, however, Parliament came to be a legislative body. In other words, statutes, having been made originally by the King, started to be made by Parliament. Thus it was that statutes changed from being Acts of the King into being Acts of Parliament. Similarly, the constitutionally correct form of words to describe the legislature is the King (or Queen) in Parliament, as reflected in the standard form of words used at the beginning of statutes:

> '*Be it enacted by the Queen's most Excellent Majesty, by and with the advice and consent of the Lords Spiritual and Temporal, and Commons, in this present Parliament assembled, and by the authority of the same, as follows: . . .*'

Admittedly the final stage of the legislative process was, and indeed still is, the giving of the Royal Assent, but this is now merely a formality, and is certainly not a mark of Royal initiative.

The problem of the royal prerogative

As we have seen, the power of making statutes devolved from the King alone to the King in Parliament. However, there remained two questions. First, did the process of devolution to Parliament totally extinguish the King's personal legislative power? Second, if the King did retain any personal power, what were its limits? In other words, rolling both questions into one: what, if anything, remained of the *royal prerogative*? In order to answer this question we must survey, albeit briefly, the political history of the seventeenth century.

The starting-point is that at the beginning of the seventeenth century Parliamentary legislation enjoyed much lower status than it does now. For example, in *Bonham's Case* (1610) 8 Co. Rep. 114, Coke cj said: 'When an Act of Parliament is against common right and reason, or repugnant, or impossible to be performed, the common law will control it, and adjudge such Act to be void.' In this context, therefore, it is not altogether surprising that the courts were willing to listen to arguments presented on behalf of the King and against Parliament. A classic example is to be found in *R* v. *Hampden* (1637) 3 St Tr 825 (also known as the *Shipmoney Case*). Charles I claimed to have the right to raise a tax to pay for ships for the defence of the realm, without the consent of Parliament, even though the Petition of Right 1628 required such consent. Sir John Hampden refused to pay, although he conceded that he would have had no choice if there had been an actual emergency, rather than merely a threatened one. The court decided against Hampden, holding not only that in the case of an emergency the King had the power he claimed, but also that the King was the sole judge of whether there was a sufficient emergency to justify such a tax. The King was also held to be the sole judge of how much the tax should be. In passing it is interesting to note that, whatever constitutional significance *R* v. *Hampden* may have, Sir John's lasting fame is probably due more to Thomas Gray, who, in his *Elegy Written in a Country Churchyard*, wrote:

> 'Some village Hampden that with dauntless breast
> The little tyrant of his fields withstood;
> Some mute, inglorious Milton here may rest;
> Some Cromwell, guiltless of his country's blood.'

Despite some of the cases concerning the royal prerogative in the early part of the seventeenth century, it would be a mistake to conclude that the courts were simply an agency to enforce royal whims: they certainly did control the power of the King where they thought it appropriate to do so. For example, in the *Case of Proclamations* (1611) 12 Co Rep 74, the court said:

> '1. The King by his proclamation cannot create any offence which was not one before; for then he might alter the law of the land in a high point; for if he may create an offence where none is, upon that ensues fine and imprisonment.
> 2. The King hath no prerogative but what the law of the land allows him.'

R v. *Hampden* was, of course, decided before the civil war. Even after the restoration of the monarchy, however, the new King claimed rights which seemed to be out of line with the spirit of the age. The classic case here is *Godden* v. *Hales* (1686) 11 St Tr 1165. Hales, a Roman Catholic, was appointed as a colonel in the army. Contrary to the law, he refused to take holy communion in the Anglican church and to take the usual form of oath of allegiance. King James II, also a Roman Catholic, claimed to have the power to dispense with the ordinary legal requirements, so that Hales would suffer no adverse consequences as a result of his refusal to obey the law. The court accepted that the King did have the power which he claimed.

The revolution and its outcome

The departure of King James II in 1688 caused a fundamental break in the legitimacy of constitutional power, which was resolved as follows. First, in 1688 an informal group, consisting of peers, former members of the House of Commons (which had not met since 1685) and leading citizens of the City of London, invited William of Orange to summon a Convention. Second, the Convention met, declared the throne to be vacant, and invited William and Mary to occupy it jointly. The offer was, however, conditional on William and Mary accepting the terms of a document which was drawn up and called the Declaration of Right. Third, William and Mary accepted the offer of the throne, on the terms indicated. (In passing, it is interesting to note that, despite Shelley's view that poets are 'the unacknowledged legislators of mankind', Dryden was dismissed from the post of Poet Laureate for refusing to take an oath of allegiance to William and Mary.) Finally, the Convention passed the Crown and Parliament Act 1689, declaring itself to be a properly constituted Parliament, and it then enacted the Bill of Rights 1689, which restated the terms of the Declaration of Right.

The most important terms of the Bill of Rights (in modernized spelling) are:

'(1)   That the pretended power of suspending* of laws or the execution of laws by regal authority without consent of Parliament is illegal.
'(2)   That the pretended power of dispensing* with laws or the execution of laws by regal authority as it hath been assumed and exercised of late is illegal.

. . .

'(4)   That the levying of money for or to the use of the crown by pretence of prerogative without grant of Parliament for longer time or in other manner than the same is or shall be granted is illegal.

. . .

'(6)   That the raising or keeping of a standing army within the kingdom in time of peace unless it be with the consent of Parliament is against the law

. . .

'(8) That election of members of Parliament ought to be free.

'(9) That the freedom of speech and debates or proceedings in Parliament ought not to be impeached or questioned in any court or place out of Parliament.

'(10) That excessive bail ought not be required nor excessive fines imposed nor cruel and unusual punishments inflicted.

'(11) That jurors ought to be duly impannelled and returned . . .

. . .

'(13) And that for redress of all grievances and for the amending, strengthening and preserving of the laws Parliaments ought to be held frequently.'

(* The distinction between *suspending* and *dispensing* is that the former had the effect of preventing the operation of a law generally, whereas the latter was personalized, as in *Godden* v. *Hales*.)

Although the intrinsic legitimacy of this process involved the Convention in nothing more sophisticated than lifting itself up by its own bootstraps, two points are basic. First, the idea of the legislative supremacy of Parliament was fundamental to the intentions of the drafters of the Bill of Rights. Second, and bootstrapping notwithstanding, the courts accepted not only the legitimacy of statutes passed by the post-1689 Parliaments, but also the implication of their own newly-defined status as being subordinate to Parliament. Although the revolution established the basis of constitutional monarchy, the newly-established structure still lacked anything which could, in modern terms, be regarded as democratic legitimacy. Indeed, Chesterton, in his poem *The Secret People*, expresses a more cynical view of the revolution:

'We saw the King as they killed him and his face was proud and pale; And a few men talked of freedom, while England talked of ale.'

It was not until the passing of the Great Reform Act in 1832 that the House of Commons started to become genuinely representative, and this process was not completed until 1928, with the extension of the franchise to women on equal terms with men. Historically, therefore, the question of the royal prerogative cannot accurately be seen in terms of exemption from democratic control, but simply as a straightforward power struggle between two legislative institutions: the King on the one hand and Parliament on the other.

The significance of the role of the courts after the revolution

Although we have just seen that an integral part of the post-Revolution settlement was the courts' acceptance of their own subordinate position, it is worth reflecting on the significance of this. For example, if A claims a particular right, and B agrees *when it is open to B to disagree and B's disagreement would have the practical consequence of preventing A from enforcing the right*, it can be argued that in reality B is exercising the greater power, because B could frustrate A's alleged right. Thus, if the courts had withheld their recognition of post-Revolution statutes, on the basis that they were the invalid acts of an illegitimate Parliament, the Revolution would not have been resolved in the way that it was. (What would have happened instead must, of course, remain speculative.)

This leads to the somewhat paradoxical statement that the legislative supremacy of Parliament, which is the most fundamental constitutional doctrine of English law, is effectively the creation of the courts, rather than of Parliament itself. Two consequences flow from this. First, and in the abstract, supremacy which is held on sufferance is clearly a peculiar kind of supremacy. Second, and more practically, arguments sometimes arise as to the extent to which, if at all, one Parliament can bind future Parliaments. However, as we have seen, a technically more accurate way of expressing this problem would be to ask to what extent the courts will recognize the power of one Parliament to bind future Parliaments.

Of course, the sudden rejection by the courts of the idea of the legislative supremacy of Parliament would itself be so fundamental that it could reasonably be characterized as revolutionary, and therefore it is unlikely to be undertaken lightly, if at all. However, the question of how far one Parliament can bind its successors has arisen in the very real context of the relationship between English law and Community law. This is examined in some detail in Chapter 7.

A modern example of the legislative supremacy of Parliament

In *Burmah Oil Ltd* v. *Lord Advocate* [1964] 2 All ER 348, the House of Lords held that the Crown was liable to compensate the oil company for certain losses sustained during the Second World War. Parliament promptly passed the War Damage Act 1965, saying that the Crown was not, and never had been, under any such liability. In *British Railways Board* v. *Pickin* [1974] 1 All ER 609, Pickin wished to advance a challenge to the validity of the British Railways Act 1968 on the basis that the Board had obtained the passing of the Act by misleading Parliament. The House of Lords held that the courts had no jurisdiction to entertain such challenges.

The nature and status of delegated legislation

Statutes, which are *primary* legislation, must be rigorously distinguished from *delegated* (or *subordinate*) legislation. Delegated legislation is made by people such as Ministers of the Crown, local authorities and others, under authority conferred by statute. In each case, the relevant statute will prescribe the procedure which must be followed when making the delegated legislation. The procedure may, or may not, require Parliamentary approval of each piece of delegated legislation, but, in any case, as a matter of Constitutional doctrine, delegated legislation may be quashed by the courts if its maker has exceeded the relevant statutory power, or has failed to follow the prescribed procedure. Statutory instruments and byelaws are among the most common forms of delegated legislation. Statutory instruments are typically, but not always, made by Secretaries of State. Byelaws are typically, but not always, made by local authorities.

Challenging delegated legislation

Delegated legislation may be challenged *directly* or *collaterally*. Direct challenge will be by means of an application for judicial review (which is discussed at p. 55). Collateral challenge may arise in a variety of ways, but typically it will involve some public authority taking legal proceedings for an alleged contravention of some specific delegated legislation, in response to which the defence will argue that the delegated legislation is itself unlawful, and that therefore no legal consequences flow from its contravention.

Where a direct challenge is successful the court has a range of available options. Although, strictly speaking, all the remedies in Administrative Law are discretionary, the court will usually hold that the delegated legislation is totally void, has no legal effect whatsoever, and should be quashed. Exceptionally, however, the court may hold that the delegated legislation is basically valid, but that it has no effect as against the challenger. For example, in *Agricultural, Horticultural and Forestry Training Board* v. *Aylesbury Mushrooms Ltd* [1972] 1 All ER 280, the Minister of Labour had power to create industrial training boards, which then had power to raise a levy from employers within the industry in order to finance training schemes. Although there was an obligation to consult relevant employers before a board was created, in this case the Mushroom Growers' Association was not consulted, and therefore the question arose as to whether its members could be compelled to pay the levy. The court held that the levy was basically lawful, but only as against those people who had been consulted. However, cases such as this, involving what may be called relative invalidity, are very much the exception.

Successful collateral challenge, on the other hand, does not involve the quashing of the delegated legislation whose validity is being impugned. Therefore, although of course the individual challenger will escape liability, there is nothing to prevent another court, faced with an identical defence, from forming a different opinion as to the legality of the delegated legislation. *R* v. *Wood* (1885) 119 ER 400, is a classic example of collateral challenge. The relevant statute provided that byelaws could be made requiring occupiers of premises to remove 'dust, ashes, rubbish, filth, manure, dung and soil' from footpaths outside their premises. A byelaw was made requiring the removal of snow and the defendant was prosecuted for failing to comply with it. The court held that the byelaw itself was unlawful, and that therefore the defendant had not committed an offence.

Whether delegated legislation is being challenged directly or collaterally, a problem will arise if the court thinks that part of the legislation is good, and part bad. Clearly, it becomes necessary to know whether the defective part can be severed, leaving the good part valid and effective, or must the whole of the delegated legislation be quashed or ignored?

The leading case of *Director of Public Prosecutions* v. *Hutchinson and Another* [1990] 3 WLR 196, involved s.14(1) of the Military Lands Act 1892, under which the Secretary of State for Defence had power to make byelaws regulating the use of land which had been appropriated for military purposes, provided that the byelaws did not 'take away or prejudicially affect any right of common'. In purported exercise of that power, the Secretary of State made the RAF Greenham Common Byelaws 1985, which, despite the statutory proviso, prejudicially affected rights of common. A magistrates' court convicted the appellants of entering RAF Greenham Common, contrary to byelaw 2(b) of the 1985 Byelaws. Neither of the appellants had rights of common, but the Crown Court allowed their appeals on the basis that the Secretary of State had exceeded his powers when he made the byelaw. The Divisional Court allowed an appeal by the prosecutor, on the basis that, where a byelaw is drawn more widely than permitted by its enabling Act, a defendant could still be convicted of an offence contrary to the byelaw, provided that the conduct alleged to constitute the offence would still have been criminal even if the byelaw had been properly drawn. The House of Lords allowed the defendants' appeals. More particularly, Lord Bridge, with the concurrence of three of his colleagues, recognized that there are two types of severability:

'A legislative instrument is *textually severable* if a clause, a sentence, a phrase or a single word may be disregarded, as exceeding the law-maker's power, and what remains of the text is still grammatical and coherent. A legislative instrument is *substantially severable* if the substance of what remains after severance is essentially unchanged in its legislative purpose, operation and effect.' (Emphasis added.)

Lord Bridge's overall conclusion was that although both types of severability would normally need to be possible, substantial severability was the more important:

'A rigid insistence that the test of textual severability must always be satisfied . . . will in some cases . . . have the unreasonable consequence of defeating subordinate legislation of which the substantial purpose and effect was clearly within the lawmaker's power when, by some oversight or misapprehension of the scope of that power, the text, as written, has a range of application which exceeds that scope. It is important, however, that in all cases an appropriate test of substantial severability should be applied.'

On the facts of the case, the House concluded that byelaws which preserved the rights of common would be of a totally different character from the byelaws which were actually made, and therefore byelaw 2(b) could not be cured by severance. (It is interesting to observe, in passing, that Lord Bridge commented that the outcome of *Aylesbury Mushrooms* (see p. 69) might have been different if the issue of severance had been argued.)

4.4 The Separation of Powers

The doctrine of the separation of powers is usually traced back to *L'Ésprit des Lois*, in which Montesquieu maintained that the doctrine played a vital part in ensuring the political stability of Britain. At its simplest, the doctrine states that political power is of three types (*legislative, executive* and *judicial*) and that these should be separated from each other so that no one person or institution exercises more than one type of power.

It must be said immediately that Montesquieu was wrong: the strict doctrine of the separation of powers does not characterize the British Constitution, nor has it ever done so. For example, the members of the executive form part of the legislature. Furthermore, as we shall see in Part II of this book, the courts have substantial practical power to develop the law through the doctrine of precedent. It is plain, therefore, that Montesquieu's view of the significance of the separation of powers in the British context involved substantial overstatement. Nevertheless, the doctrine is not without importance, and at various stages it will become apparent that the doctrine does exercise the minds of the judges when they are seeking to identify the constitutionally legitimate scope of the judicial role.

For example in *R. v. Cambridge Health Authority ex parte B* [1995] 2 All ER 129, the health authority had decided not to provide medical treatment for a child suffering from leukaemia. When the child's father applied for judicial review, the health authority sought to justify its decision on both medical and resource grounds. The first stage, which would cost about £15 000 was estimated to have a 10 per cent to 20 per cent chance of success. If this stage was successful, the child would then progress to the second stage, which would cost about £60 000, and which would again have a 10 per cent to 20 per cent chance of success. At best, therefore the overall chances of success were estimated at 20 per cent of 20 per cent, and at worst they were 10 per cent of 10 per cent. The High Court refused to order the health authority to proceed with the treatment, but did order it to reconsider the matter. The Court of Appeal felt that it was inappropriate even to order reconsideration. Sir Thomas Bingham MR dealt with the medical aspect of the case thus:

> 'Were we to express opinions as to the likelihood of the effectiveness of medical treatment, or as to the merits of medical judgement, then we would be straying far from the sphere which under our constitution is accorded to us.'

He was equally unwilling to interfere with the health authority's decision as to how it should allocate its resources:

> 'I have no doubt that in a perfect world any treatment which a patient, or a patient's family, sought would be provided if doctors were willing to give it, no matter how much it cost, particularly when a life was potentially at stake. It would however, in my view, be shutting one's eyes to the real world if the court were to proceed on the basis that we do live in such a world. It is common knowledge that health authorities of all kinds are constantly pressed to make ends meet . . . Difficult and agonizing judgements have to be made as to how a limited budget is best allocated to the maximum advantage of the maximum number of patients. That is not a judgement which the court can make.'

4.5   Balancing the Constitutional Doctrines

It will be apparent at various stages throughout this book that the three constitutional doctrines may create conflicts which the courts must resolve. Although the doctrine of the legislative supremacy of Parliament will always receive at least lip-service, it can scarcely be denied that the courts play a genuinely creative role. The practical difficulty is to identify in advance how far the courts will be willing to go. Two cases, decided within a few years of each other, will illustrate the problem. The particular context is that which arises where an Act has been passed but is not yet in force.

In *R* v. *Walsall Justices ex parte W* [1989] 3 All ER 460, a juvenile was charged with assault occasioning grievous bodily harm to a 12–year-old boy. The defendant pleaded not guilty, whereupon the case was adjourned for a hearing. On the day fixed for the hearing the parties attended court but the prosecution informed the court that there was no independent evidence to corroborate the victim's allegation against the defendant. It followed that, if the magistrates took the view that the victim was of insufficient understanding to take the oath, the inevitable consequence in accordance with s.38(1) of the Children and Young Persons Act 1933 would be that the prosecution would fail. The prosecution also pointed out that the following day, when s.34 of the Criminal Justice Act 1988 came into effect, the need for corroboration would be abolished. On this basis the prosecution applied for an adjournment, which the court granted on the basis of 'the interests of justice'.

The defence applied for judicial review of the decision. Granting the application, the High Court said that what the magistrates had done was to pass a qualitative judgement on the existing law. This approach was inconsistent with the principle that it is the function of the courts to apply the law, and amounted to taking an illegitimate consideration into account when deciding to grant the adjournment. In passing, it is interesting, and not a little curious, to note that the court indicated that the position might be different if the imminent change in the law had related only to procedural matters. This is, therefore, an example of the fact that the courts sometimes approach substantive and procedural provisions differently. (The distinction between substantive and procedural provisions is discussed at p. 36.)

An instructive comparison with the Walsall case may be found in *R* v. *Parole Board and Another ex parte Wilson* (1992) 4 Admin LR 525, where the Parole Board had repeatedly refused to recommend the release of a prisoner. He claimed the right to see the reports on himself which had been considered by the Parole Board. The European Court of Human Rights had said that there should be such a right, and Parliament had responded obediently by including appropriate provisions in the Criminal Justice Act 1991. These provisions had not, however, been brought into force. The Court of Appeal felt able to extend the common law in such a way as to give the prisoner the right which he claimed, since it would have been unfair to have made him wait until the 1991 provisions came into force.

Cases such as these involve the judges in making decisions without any clear and explicit legal authority to guide them. In reality, therefore, they will fall back on their perceptions of the scope of the judicial role, in the light of their own understanding of the nature and purpose of the law. Holmes (see p. 8) would say that they are relying on their inarticulate major premises. Dworkin (see p. 10) would invite them to apply policies and principles. Whichever approach is preferred – and the Holmesian and Dworkinian options are only two of many – the theoretical perspectives do in fact help to explain the apparent judicial inconsistency between the *Walsall* and *Wilson* cases. More particularly, there is a strong argument that the decisions are in fact mutually consistent, on the basis that both favoured the liberty of the subject over the interests of the authorities.

Summary

1   Legal method is an aspect of Constitutional law.
2   The doctrine of the rule of law requires that the subject is entitled to be ruled according to law, and that the law should be predictable.
3   The doctrine of the legislative supremacy of Parliament means that Parliament can make or unmake any law, and that (subject to European Community law) nobody else may override or set aside the law which Parliament has made. However, the courts do have power to quash delegated legislation, either in whole or in part.
4   The doctrine of the separation of powers states that political power is of three types (*legislative*, *executive* and *judicial*) and that these should be separated from each other so that no one person or institution should exercise more than one type of power.
5   The three principal constitutional doctrines may create conflicts which the courts will have to resolve.

Exercises

1   Explain what each of the following means: (a) the rule of law; (b) the legislative supremacy of parliament; (c) the separation of powers.
2   How did the revolution of 1688 clarify the relationship between the Crown and Parliament?
3   What does *severability* mean in the context of delegated legislation?
4   Give one example of a case involving a conflict between constitutional doctrines.

5 The Legal Structure of the European Community

5.1 Introduction

This chapter will outline both the creation and the institutional structure of the European Community. Other aspects of Community law and its impact on English law will be dealt with in Chapters 6, 7 and 8. Aspects of precedent within the European Court of Justice, and the interpretation of Community legislation, are dealt with in Chapters 16 and 23, respectively.

5.2 The European Communities

The Treaty of Rome 1957 created what was then known as the *European Economic Community*, with the initial members being France, Germany, Italy, Belgium, the Netherlands and Luxembourg. The United Kingdom, Ireland, Denmark, Greece, Portugal, Spain, Austria, Finland and Sweden have become members at a variety of later dates. Since the Treaty on European Union 1992, which is sometimes known as the TEU or Maastricht Treaty, it has been technically correct to refer simply to the *European Community*, and in practice it is commonly called simply the *Community*.

For the avoidance of confusion, however, it is important to note that there was another Treaty of Rome, also signed in 1957, which created the separate community known as *Euratom*. Euratom had the same membership as the European Economic Community, but its objectives were different, namely to develop nuclear energy, to distribute it throughout the community, and to sell the surplus to the outside world. Because there were two Treaties of Rome, both signed in 1957, it is usual to refer to the *EC Treaty* (which was, of course, the *EEC Treaty* before 1992), and the *Euratom Treaty*, as appropriate. In passing, it may be noted that the Treaty of Paris 1951 had already established the European Coal and Steel Community, whose objectives are self-evident from its name.

Despite the fact that the treaty on *union* renamed the *community*, the union and the community are not interchangeable concepts.

'The European Union established by the Maastricht Treaty is a composite organization not itself having legal personality or legal capacities. It is likened to a temple supported by three pillars. The central pillar which is, in a mixture of metaphors, the foundation of the Union, is constituted by the three European Communities, each of them having an independent legal personality and functioning under its founding treaty (as subsequently amended). The other pillars are the Common Foreign and Security Policy (CFSP) and Co-operation in Justice and Home Affairs (CJHA) (e.g. immigration policy and police co-operation). The CFSP and the CJHA are intergovernmental pillars, action under these heads having generally to be taken by agreement of all 15 member states. (The European Court of Justice . . . has no jurisdiction in respect of these pillars.) Such intergovernmental decisions may be implemented by co-ordinated or joint action of the member states or, if necessary, by "borrowing" the institutions and procedures of the Communities. The European Council . . . gives impetus and direction to the European Union.' (Turpin, *British Government and the Constitution: Text Cases and Materials*, 3rd edn, 1995, p. 263.)

In essence, therefore, the union is a *political* entity, and the community is a *legal* entity, although the interface between the two concepts is by no means always straightforward. For example, art.8 of the EC Treaty, which was inserted by the TEU, provides that anyone holding the nationality of a member state is automatically also a citizen of the *Union*, and accordingly have certain rights as a matter of *Community* law.

Even though the origins of each community were, and their continued existences are, distinct, all three communities now share the same institutions, and have done so since the Merger Treaty 1965. Similarly, all three communities are subject to the same basic legal principles. However, in order to maintain clarity and relevance, only the Economic Community will be dealt with here.

Under the EC Treaty, the principal institutions of the community are the European Commission, the Council of the European Union, the European Parliament, the Court of Justice of the European Communities, the Court of First Instance and the Court of Auditors. A committee known as COREPER and a body known as the European Council must also be mentioned.

5.3   The European Commission

Members of the Commission hold office for renewable periods of four years. They are appointed by the common accord of the member states, and are chosen on the grounds of their general competence (art.157, EC Treaty). Each member state provides at least one, but not more than two, Commissioners. The present practice is for the United Kingdom, France, Germany, Italy (the so-called 'big four') and Spain to provide two Commissioners each, whilst the other member states each provide one. The United Kingdom practice is for the Labour and Conservative parties each to provide one Commissioner.

Despite the national, and party-political, character of the Commission's membership, it is a fundamental principle that Commissioners 'shall, in the general interest of the Community, be completely independent in the performance of their duties' (art.157(2), EC Treaty). Each Commissioner is allocated a specific area of responsibility, and may be called upon to answer questions on that topic in the European Parliament. However, the Commission as a whole accepts collective responsibility for all its activities.

Although the Commission does issue legislation, its main task is the formulation of policy. This policy must, of course, be consistent with the framework of the Treaty, and any policy which is formulated must then be submitted to the Council, which is the Community's principal legislative body. The Commission makes its decisions on the basis of a simple majority vote.

5.4 The Council of the European Union

The Council of the European Union, which was known as the *Council of Ministers* before the Treaty on European Union, is commonly known in both incarnations simply as the *Council*. It is the principal legislative organ of the Community. In one sense, the Council is a smaller body than the Commission, with each member state having one member only. However, this membership is constantly fluctuating, because the Council's composition at any particular meeting will depend entirely on the subject-matter under discussion. Thus, for example, if the business of the day involves agricultural policy, there will be a meeting of the *Agricultural Council*, attended by Agriculture Ministers. A meeting of the *General Council*, consisting of Foreign Ministers, has the widest remit.

By way of contrast with the Commission, members of the Council, who must be 'at Ministerial level, authorized to commit the government of [their] member state' (art.146, EC Treaty), are present as national representatives. However, the significance of this should not be overstated, since they also have a responsibility for helping to achieve the Community's objectives. Generally speaking, the Council can act only on a proposal from the Commission, and can amend such proposals only by a unanimous vote, although where unanimity is not forthcoming the Council can send proposals back to the Commission for reconsideration. In practice, this process can result in proposals going through many drafts, as they pass repeatedly from the Commission to the Council and back again, until a formulation emerges which is acceptable to both bodies. The Council normally proceeds according to a system known as *qualified majority voting*, although there are exceptions, such as the harmonization of taxation, where unanimity is required. Essentially, qualified majority voting means that the member states have varying numbers of votes, according to their size, although there is an additional requirement that a specified number of states must be part of the majority when certain types of subject-matter are involved.

The office of President of the Council rotates around the member states at six-monthly intervals.

5.5   The European Parliament

The European Parliament, which began life as the European Assembly, has been known by its current name since 1962, and this usage was confirmed by the Single European Act 1986. The Parliament has more than 600 members. Originally its members were nominated by the Parliaments of member states, but since 1979 its members have been elected directly, for a period of five years. In the nature of the Community there is no division between 'government' and 'opposition', and the members sit in international groupings formed in accordance with party-political sympathies. The Parliament is organized into specialist committees, through which a great deal of its business is transacted.

Historically, national Parliaments tended to originate as discussion chambers, with the emergence of the legislative function being an evolutionary development. This pattern is being followed by the European Parliament, which is developing from a situation in which its primary functions were discussion and debate coupled with a supervisory function in respect of the Commission, towards becoming a fully-fledged part of the legislative process.

In its supervisory capacity, the Parliament approves the appointment of Commissioners, as well as receiving and debating an annual General Report from the Commission. It can ask questions of both the Commission and the Council, as well as having the power to pass a motion of censure on the Commission. If such a motion were carried by a two-thirds majority, the Commission would be required to resign. This has never happened, and is unlikely to do so, bearing in mind that the Parliament and the Commission share a pro-European outlook. Nevertheless, the possibility of censure could emerge as a potentially useful long-stop control if the Commission ever became too detached from political reality as perceived by democratically elected politicians.

In addition to its supervisory role, the Parliament has become increasingly involved in the legislative process in a number of ways. First, the Commission commonly consults the Parliament when formulating its legislative proposals. Second, there are cases in which the Council has a Treaty obligation to consult the Parliament, and although the Council is not bound by the outcome of such consultation, there is a conciliation procedure which operates where the Council wishes to depart from the Parliament's views in respect of certain Community acts of general application which have appreciable financial consequences. The essence of the process is that a three-month period comes into play, during which there will be an attempt to resolve the conflict. Third, there is the *co-operation procedure*, which requires that in certain cases, including matters relating to transport and environmental protection, the Parliament joins the Commission and the Council as a partner in the legislative process. Admittedly, the procedure works in such a way that the Council retains the last word, but only a unanimous vote of the Council can override the views of the Parliament. Finally, the Treaty on European Union created a *co-decision* procedure for action in respect of certain matters, including free movement of workers, freedom of establishment, public health, consumer protection and the single market. The details of this procedure are complex, but essentially the Parliament becomes a genuine co-decision-maker with the Council, to the extent that it can veto proposals which it finds unacceptable, although its positive assent is not normally necessary. However, there are areas of decision-making, including the accession of new member states, where the positive assent of the Parliament is required.

5.6 The Court of Justice of the European Communities

Composition

The Court of Justice of the European Communities, which is commonly called the *European Court of Justice*, consists of one judge from each member state, together with nine Advocates-General. Judges and Advocates-General, who are appointed by common accord of the governments of the member states for a period of six years, must be

'persons whose independence is beyond doubt and who possess the qualifications required for appointment to the highest judicial offices in their respective countries or who are jurisconsults of recognized competence.' (Art.167, EC Treaty.)

The judges elect one of their number to be President of the court, for a renewable period of three years.

The role of the Advocate-General is one aspect of procedure in the Court which often appears to be a trifle odd to observers who are more familiar with the English legal system. The office of Advocate-General is based on the French *Commissaire du Gouvernement* in the *Conseil d'État* (the French constitutional court), who is sometimes described as being the 'disembodied conscience of the court'.

'It shall be the duty of the Advocate-General, acting with complete impartiality and independence, to make, in open court, reasoned submissions on cases brought before the Court of Justice, in order to assist the Court in the performance of the task assigned to it . . .' (Art.166, EC Treaty.)

To some extent the role of the Advocate-General may suggest a parallel with the English concept of the *amicus curiae*, who will typically be called upon by the court to present whatever opposing arguments are possible in difficult cases where only one party appears. However, this parallel is misleading.

First, there will be an Advocate-General in every case before the Court, whereas cases involving an *amicus curiae* are distinctly unusual. Second, his responsibility is to give a reasoned opinion as to what he thinks Community law is on the point which is being litigated. This is particularly important because the Court, in common with continental courts generally, tends to give rather short judgements. Thus, where the Court agrees with the Advocate-General, it will usually be necessary to read his argument in order to identify the reasoning behind the decision. The Court is, of course, under no obligation to agree with the Advocate-General. If it does not do so, his opinion will take on something approximating to the status of a dissenting judgement in English law. However, in accordance with continental legal tradition, the Court itself always delivers a judgement of the Court, without the possibility of dissenting judgements.

Jurisdiction

For many years, the Court of Justice was the Communities' only court apart from the Court of Auditors, which is a court in name only, rather than being a judicial body. Subsequently, the Single European Act 1986 provided for the creation of a new *Court of First Instance* (see p. 82), which began operation in September 1989, and which has acquired a very large part of the original jurisdiction of the Court of Justice. Briefly, the remaining jurisdiction of the Court of Justice may be said to relate to certain actions for annulment and failure to act, certain actions for damages arising from the Communities' liability in non-contractual matters, all references under art.177, EC Treaty, and appeals on points of law from the Court of First Instance.

Actions for annulment and for failure to act

Actions for annulment and for failure to act, which equate with judicial review in English law, may be brought in order to determine the legality of an act of, or a failure to act by, a Community institution. (Arts.173 and 175, EC Treaty.) An institution which is found to have acted illegally 'shall be required to take the necessary measures to comply with the judgement of the Court of Justice' (art.176, EC Treaty). Additionally, art.184, EC Treaty creates the possibility of raising a plea of illegality by way of defence to proceedings in the Court. (This is clearly similar to the possibility of raising a collateral challenge to the validity of delegated legislation in the English legal system, which is discussed at p. 69).

The Court deals only with those cases which are brought by either a Community institution or a member state, leaving the Court of First Instance to deal with cases brought by any other parties, who are technically known as 'non-privileged parties'.

Actions for damages

Article 215(2) of the EC Treaty provides that:

'In the case of non-contractual liability, the Community shall, in accordance with the general principles common to the laws of member states, make good any damage caused by its institutions or by its servants in the performance of their duties.'

As with actions for annulment and for failure to act, the Court deals only with cases brought by either a Community institution or a member state.

Article 177 references

References to the Court in order to obtain a preliminary ruling on a point of Community law, are governed by art.177 of the EC Treaty, which provides:

'The Court of Justice shall have jurisdiction to give preliminary rulings concerning:

(a) the interpretation of this Treaty;

(b) the validity and interpretation of acts of the institutions of the Community and of the European Central Bank;

(c) the interpretation of the statutes of bodies established by an act of the Council, where those statutes so provide.

'Where such a question is raised before *any* court or tribunal of a Member State, that court or tribunal *may*, if it considers that a decision on the question is necessary to enable it to give judgement, request the Court of Justice to give a ruling thereon.

'Where any such question is raised in a case pending before *a court or tribunal of a member State, against whose decision there is no judicial remedy under national law*, that court or tribunal *shall* bring the matter before the Court of Justice.' (Emphasis added.)

It is apparent from the emphasized parts of the text of art.177 that the *power* to refer, which is enjoyed by all courts and tribunals, becomes a *duty* to refer where the court or tribunal in question is not subject to appeal. This gives rise to an apparent difficulty where, for example, the Court of Appeal decides a case and refuses leave to appeal to the House of Lords. The House of Lords itself may, of course, subsequently grant leave, but at the conclusion of the proceedings in the Court of Appeal nobody can know whether or not this will happen. The answer is that the Court of Appeal has no duty to refer, even though a refusal of leave will have the effect of making the Court of Appeal into 'a court . . . against whose decision there is no judicial remedy'. (*Chiron Corporation* v. *Murex Diagnostics Ltd* [1995] All ER (EC) 88.)

The Court's jurisdiction under art.177 may appear to give natural or legal persons a right of access to the Court, and therefore, to this extent, it may appear to be fundamentally different from the jurisdictions relating to actions for annulment and failure to act and actions for damages, but the appearance is deceptive. The decision to refer a case to the European Court of Justice lies with the national court, not with the individual litigant, who can do no more than ask that a reference shall be made.

5.7 The Court of First Instance

Composition

Judges of the Court of First Instance are, in common with judges of the Court of Justice, appointed by common accord of the governments of the member states for a period of six years, but the level of qualification required is slightly less rigorous, with appointment being limited to 'persons whose independence is beyond doubt and who possess the ability required for appointment to judicial office' (art.168a, EC Treaty). There are no Advocates-General in the Court of First Instance, but the judges may agree that one of their number shall perform that role in a particular case if they so wish. The Court of First Instance generally sits in chambers of three or five judges.

Jurisdiction

Initially, the scope of the Court of First Instance was rather limited, but the Council, acting on the request of the Court of Justice and after consultation with the Commission and the Parliament has power to extend its jurisdiction and has done so. Perhaps the most important point to make is the negative one that the Court of First Instance does not deal with art.177 references. More positively, however, its jurisdiction does extend to all other actions brought by non-privileged parties (i.e. parties other than member states and Community institutions).

5.8 The Court of Auditors

The Court of Auditors was established in 1977 but did not formally become an institution of the Communities until the Treaty on European Union 1992. As its name suggests, it is concerned with financial management and control. It has one member from each member state, with appointments being made by the Council for a period of six years.

5.9 COREPER and the European Council

Two other bodies must be mentioned at this stage, namely COREPER and the European Council.

COREPER

COREPER is an acronym made up from the French title of the committee, namely *Comité des Représentants Permanents*. It is a committee consisting of officials, having ambassadorial rank, which in effect undertakes much of the routine work of the Council, with the Council itself then simply endorsing what has been done. Bearing in mind the loose-knit nature of the Council, which is an inevitable consequence of a fluctuating membership, COREPER performs a particularly vital function, although it would be comforting to be able to regard as an overstatement the account given by Alan Clark (a former Conservative Cabinet Minister):

'Not, really, that it makes the slightest difference to the conclusions of a meeting [of the Council] what Ministers say at it. Everything is decided, horse-traded off, by officials at COREPER, the Council [*sic*] of Permanent Representatives. The Ministers arrive on the scene at the last minute, hot, tired, ill or drunk (sometimes all of these together) read out their piece, and depart.' (*Diaries*, 1994, p. 139.)

The European Council

The European Council originated as an unofficial body consisting of the heads of government of the member states. However, it was recognized by the Single European Act 1986, which required it to meet at least twice a year and gave it special responsibility for encouraging European political co-operation. It was further recognized by art.D of the TEU, which provides, *inter alia*:

'The European Council shall provide the Union with the necessary impetus for its development and shall define the general political guidelines thereof.

'The European Council shall bring together the Heads of State or of Government of the Member States and the President of the Commission.'

Additionally, art.J3 of the TEU provides that the European Council shall provide general guidelines within which the Council of the European Union shall decide whether a matter should be the subject of joint action, which will commit the member states, as part of the Common Foreign and Security Policy.

It is important not to confuse the European Council with the Council of Europe. The latter is a totally distinct legal entity from the European Communities, whose responsibilities include the European Court of Human Rights. The European Court of Human Rights, which sits in Strasbourg, must in turn be rigorously distinguished from the Court of Justice of the European Communities, more familiarly known as the European Court of Justice, which sits in Luxembourg.

Summary

1 European Community law is part of English law.

2 The European Economic Community was created by the Treaty of Rome, 1957, but since the Treaty on European Union, 1992, it has become known simply as 'the European Community'.

3 The European Commission has legislative power, but its main function is to formulate policy.

4 The Council of the European Union is the Community's principal legislative body, but generally speaking it can act only on proposals from the Commission.

5 The European Parliament is not a legislative body in the same way as national parliaments are. Nevertheless, its influence on the legislative process of the Community is steadily growing.

6 The principal work of the European Court of Justice involves (a) judicial review; (b) enforcement proceedings; (c) plenary jurisdiction; and (d) art.177 references. Since 1989 there has also been a Court of First Instance.

7 The *Comite des Representants Permanents* (COREPER) is a committee consisting of officials having ambassadorial rank, which undertakes much of the routine work of the Council of the European Union, with the Council itself then simply endorsing what has been done.

8 The European Council, which must not be confused with the Council of Europe, began as an entirely unofficial body, consisting of the heads of government of the member states, but it has since been incorporated into the structure of the Community. It has special responsibility for encouraging European political co-operation and the development of the Common Foreign and Security Policy.

Exercises

1 Which of the three European Communities is most important to English law?

2 Explain the role of: (a) the European Commission; (b) the Council of the European Union; and (c) the European Parliament; .

3 Distinguish between the *European Council* and the *Council of Europe*.

4 What are the main aspects of the European Court of Justice's work?

6 The Enforceability of European Community Law in the United Kingdom

6.1 Introduction

Having considered the institutional structure of the Community in the previous chapter, we can now consider some of the more interesting questions which arise from the way the system of Community law actually works. More particularly, this chapter will examine the extent to which Community law enters into the legal systems of member states and becomes enforceable in their courts. The English perspective will be taken as the primary focus, but the system of Community law is an integrated whole, and therefore cases involving other member states will also be relevant. Since Community law ultimately derives from the treaties, a good starting point is the status of treaties in English law.

6.2 The Status of Treaties in English Law

According to English law any treaty operates only at the international level, and therefore treaty provisions do not automatically become part of the English legal system. The practical solution is that, in those situations where it is thought to be desirable or essential that the provisions of a treaty should be incorporated into English law, Parliament passes a statute to achieve that result. In the present context, the key provision is s.2(1) of the European Communities Act 1972:

'All . . . rights, powers, liabilities, obligations and restrictions from time to time created or arising by or under the Treaties, and all such remedies and procedures from time to time provided for by or under the Treaties, as in accordance with the Treaties are without further enactment to be given legal effect or used in the United Kingdom shall be recognised and available in law, and be enforced, allowed and followed accordingly;

and the expression "enforceable Community right" and similar expressions shall be read as referring to one to which this subsection applies.'

This provision is reinforced by s.2(4) of the Act:

'Any enactment passed or to be passed . . . shall be construed and have effect subject to the foregoing provisions of this section.'

Section 2(2) provides that the Queen by Order in Council, or a Minister by Regulation, may make provision for implementing Community obligations, or deal with matters arising or related to such obligations. However, the second schedule to the Act excludes four types of provision from this power, namely provisions which impose or increase taxation; give retrospective effect to any provision; confer power to make delegated legislation (other than rules of procedure for courts and tribunals); and create new criminal offences punishable beyond certain specified limits. It is important to note that what the Act is saying here is simply that in these cases delegated legislation will be insufficient, and Parliament itself must act: it is not saying that there can be no Community obligations in these cases.

Discussion of the enforceability of Community law requires an analysis of the various forms of law, namely the Treaty provisions themselves, Regulations, Directives and Decisions. However, before the discussion can proceed further, we must consider the distinction between the concepts of the direct applicability and the direct effect of Community law within the legal systems of member states.

6.3 Direct Applicability and Direct Effect of Community Law

The distinction between direct applicability and direct effect

The distinction between *direct applicability* and *direct effect* is essentially quite straightforward, although an element of confusion arises from time to time because some commentators – and even some courts, including the European Court of Justice itself – have been known to use both terms loosely, and even interchangeably.

The essence of the distinction is that a provision of Community law will be *directly applicable* if it becomes part of the law of a member state automatically. Thus, not only is there no need for member states to do anything to incorporate directly applicable provisions into their legal systems, but also there is no possibility of member states countermanding such provisions. On the other hand, a provision of Community law will be *directly effective* if, and only if, it creates rights which are enforceable by the courts of a member state at the instance of people who are aggrieved by breaches of the provision. In other words the concept of *direct applicability* is concerned solely with the *reception* of Community law into the legal system of a member state. The concept of *direct effect* deals with the more essentially practical question of the *enforceability* of Community law once reception has occurred.

At first sight, the proposition that something can be part of the law without being enforceable by the courts may seem difficult to grasp. In reality, however, the idea of law without enforceability is not uncommon. For example, in public law, a decision may be illegal, without anyone possessing the necessary *locus standi* (see p. 36) to bring the matter before the court to seek an order establishing the illegality. Furthermore, some areas of law are power-conferring rather than duty-imposing, and therefore in their nature do not give rise to rights at all. For example, local authorities have a statutory power to adopt a scheme of licensing in respect of sex shops, but they are under no duty to do so. It follows, therefore, that a local authority which chooses not to adopt the scheme is not infringing anybody's legal rights. Turning specifically to Community law for an example of direct applicability without direct effect, it is necessary to look no further than art.177 of the EC Treaty (see p. 81).

Returning to the main theme, however, whilst it would seem logical to say that *direct applicability* is a necessary precondition to *direct effect*, the cases on Directives and Decisions (see pp. 90–4) show that the European Court of Justice will not withhold direct effect from these measures simply because the Treaty does not declare them to be directly applicable. Indeed, it can be said that the European Court of Justice has shown a marked tendency to regard direct effect as the norm rather than the exception. However, this is subject to the purely practical consideration that a court cannot enforce something unless it knows precisely what it is being asked to enforce. Therefore a provision of Community law cannot be directly effective unless it is both clear and precise in its expression (so that national courts can know what it is they are being asked to enforce) and self-contained (in the sense that its implementation must not depend on the exercise of discretion by the public authorities of member states). These two qualities can conveniently be called the *criteria for direct effect*. However, one indication of the European Court of Justice's enthusiasm for promoting the effectiveness of Community law is that the whole of the provision in question does not need to satisfy the criteria for direct effect. Provided a national court could apply the relevant part of the provision to the facts of the case which it is considering, it will be irrelevant that other cases could arise to which the court could not apply the same provision.

This may be illustrated by reference to *Defrenne* v. *Sabena No 2* [1976] 2 CMLR 98, which is discussed at p. 90.

Vertical and horizontal direct effect

Where a provision of Community law is enforceable against the member state in its own courts, the direct effect is said to be *vertical*, in the sense that the member state is politically superior to its subjects. Where a provision of Community law is enforceable against other people in the courts of the member state, the direct effect is said to be *horizontal*, in the sense that the subjects of a member state are all on the same level as between themselves.

6.4   Direct Applicability and Direct Effect of Different Types of Community Legislation

Treaty articles

The position in relation to treaty articles has been clear since the early days of the Community. In the leading case of *van Gend en Loos* v. *Nederlandse Administratie der Belastingen* [1963] CMLR 105, a Dutch company was aggrieved by a contravention of art.12 of the EC Treaty, which prohibits member states from 'introducing between themselves any new customs duties'. The question was whether the company could bring an action in the Dutch courts, in order to enforce art.12 against the Dutch customs authorities. The European Court of Justice said:

> 'The wording of art.12 contains a clear and unconditional prohibition which is not a positive but a negative obligation. This obligation, moreover, is not qualified by any reservation on the part of states which would make its implementation conditional upon a positive legislative measure enacted under national law. The very nature of this prohibition makes it ideally adapted to produce direct effects in the legal relationship between the member states and their subjects . . .
> 'It follows . . . that . . . art.12 must be interpreted as producing direct effects and creating individual rights which national courts must protect.'

In *van Gend en Loos* the direct effect was vertical, but *Defrenne* v. *Sabena No 2* [1976] 2 CMLR 98 established that treaty provisions may also have horizontal direct effect.

Defrenne arose from the Belgian airline's practice of paying female flight attendants less than their male colleagues, despite the fact that both were doing identical jobs. Article 119 of the EC Treaty required member states to ensure 'the application of the principle that men and women should receive equal pay for work of equal value'. Clearly, there could be cases where it would be very difficult to establish whether different types of work were nevertheless of equal value, and in these cases it may be that art.119 would lack sufficient precision to enable national courts to enforce it. In *Defrenne*, however, it was obvious – and the airline did not dispute – that the work was identical and that the sex of the employees was the only reason for the differential rates of pay. The Court of Justice saw no reason why the inability of other employees to rely on the direct effect of art.119 in more complicated cases should be used as a ground for denying Defrenne the right to do so:

'18. For the purposes of the implementation of these provisions a distinction must be drawn within the whole area of application of art.119 between, first, direct and overt discrimination which may be identified solely with the aid of the criteria based on equal work and equal pay referred to by the article in question; and secondly, indirect and disguised discrimination which can only be identified by reference to more explicit implementing provisions of a Community or national character.'

Regulations

Article 189 of the EC Treaty expressly provides that a Regulation 'shall have general application [and] . . . shall be binding in its entirety and directly applicable in all member states'. In practice, provided they satisfy the criteria for direct effect, Regulations will also give rise to rights which are enforceable in the courts of member states. Moreover, as with Treaty articles, their direct effect may be both vertical and horizontal.

Directives

Article 189 makes it plain that Directives are generically different from Regulations. A Directive is 'binding, as to the result to be achieved, upon each member state to which it is addressed, but shall leave to the national authorities the choice of form and methods'. It is clear, therefore, that the drafter of the Treaty envisaged Directives as being catalysts which would produce changes in the national legal systems of member states, rather than being themselves the vehicles of such changes. Two points arise from this. First, art.189 does *not* make Directives *directly applicable*. Second, as

Directives are not stated to be directly applicable, it would appear that they lack the necessary precondition for direct effect. However, the European Court of Justice has approached this aspect of Directives in a singularly creative way.

The starting point is that it is obviously in the nature of Directives that a period of time must be allowed for implementation by the member states. The question then arises as to the consequences which should flow from a member state's failure to implement a Directive. The answer to this question depends on the identity of the defendant.

The German case of *Grad* [1971] CMLR 1 dealt mainly with a Decision (see p. 94) but the European Court of Justice indicated that, once the time for compliance had expired, a Directive which satisfied the criteria for direct effect could actually become directly effective against the member state which had failed to implement it. The Court took the view that any other result would amount to allowing member states to take advantage from their own wrongdoing in failing to implement Directives. (For the presumption against deriving advantage from wrongdoing as a principle of English statutory interpretation, see p. 316.) The Court further took the view that this consideration outweighed the counter-argument that the Treaty did not make Directives directly applicable, and that therefore the necessary precondition to direct effect was lacking. It is important to emphasize that the justification for holding that there are circumstances in which Directives can be directly effective is no more than an application of the commonsense principle that people (in this case the member states who are in default) should not be allowed to gain an advantage from their own wrongdoing. Clearly this argument cannot be used where the defendant is a private individual or organization, who would have had no power to introduce legislation to implement the Directive anyway, and who cannot therefore be regarded as being at fault.

The consequence of this, as the Court of Justice recognized in *Marshall v. Southampton & South West Hampshire Area Health Authority* [1986] 1 CMLR 688, where a female employee had been forced to retire at 62 when her male colleagues were able to continue working until they were 65, is that the direct effect of Directives can only ever be vertical, and never horizontal. Obviously, therefore, it becomes essential to know where Community law draws the line between defendants who count as being part of the member state for the present purposes, and those who are treated simply as private individuals and organizations.

The test which emerges from *Foster* v. *British Gas plc* [1991] 2 WLR 258 is whether the member state has made the defendant responsible for providing a public service under the control of the state, as a result of which the defendant has acquired special powers beyond those resulting from the normal rules applicable in relationships between individuals. In

Foster itself, British Gas plc was held to come within this category, as were health authorities in *Marshall* and local authorities in *R* v. *London Boroughs Transport Committee ex parte Freight Transport Association Ltd and Others* [1991] 3 All ER 916. On the other hand, in *Doughty* v. *Rolls-Royce plc* [1992] IRLR 126, a nationalized industry, which had not been made responsible for providing a public service under the control of the state, was held not to be within the category.

Despite the apparent attractiveness of the concept of vertical direct effect as a means of imposing liability on those member states who have defaulted on their Community obligations, it will be apparent that the distinction between vertical and horizontal direct effect can create injustice in two ways. First, from the point of view of potential plaintiffs, it is unfair that the availability of a remedy should depend upon the public or private status of the potential defendant. Second, from the point of view of potential defendants, the fundamental argument that vertical direct effect is necessary to prevent states from gaining advantage from their own wrongful inaction is not strictly relevant to other public bodies within the state, yet such bodies are clearly at risk from the vertical version of direct effect. In *Marshall* itself, the Court of Justice responded to criticisms based on the unjust consequences of the distinction by saying that any injustice could easily be avoided 'if the member state concerned has correctly implemented the Directive in national law'. Whether this response is convincing, or merely glib, may be open to debate, but it is a clear indication of the Court's commitment to the effective enforcement of Community law. This commitment may be further illustrated by the case of *Marshall* v. *Southampton and South West Hampshire Area Health Authority (No 2)* [1993] 3 CMLR 293, which was the sequel to the earlier *Marshall* case.

Following Marshall's success in establishing the direct effect of the Directive, the case went back to an Industrial Tribunal for compensation to be assessed. The difficulty then arose that she was claiming £18 404, including a sum of £7710 in respect of interest, whereas the Sex Discrimination Act 1975 limited compensation, at the relevant time, to a maximim of £6250, and it was unclear whether the Tribunal could award interest. Accordingly, the case returned to the Court of Justice, as *Marshall (No 2)*, where Marshall was once again successful. The court said:

'24 . . . the objective is to arrive at real equality of opportunity . . .
'26 When financial compensation is the measure adopted in order to achieve the objective . . . it must be adequate . . .
'30 . . . the fixing of an upper limit of the kind at issue in the main proceedings cannot, by definition, constitute proper implementation [of the relevant article of the Directive] . . .

'31 With regard to . . . the award of interest, suffice it to say that full compensation . . . cannot leave out of account factors, such as effluxion of time, which may in fact reduce its value . . . The award of interest . . . must therefore be regarded as an essential component of compensation for the purposes of restoring real equality of treatment.'

Additionally, reflecting the court's attitude in *Defrenne* v. *Sabena No 2* [1976] 2 CMLR 98 (see p. 90) that direct effect should not be denied to a treaty article in a clear case simply because there may be other, less clear cases in which it would be impossible to uphold direct effect, the court in *Marshall (No 2)* said:

'36 The fact that member states may choose among different solutions in order to achieve the objective pursued by the Directive depending on the situations which may arise, cannot result in an individual's being prevented from relying on [the relevant article of the Directive] in a situation such as that in the main proceedings where the national authorities have no discretion in applying the chosen solution.'

In the case of both Treaty articles and Directives, therefore, the court may be able to distil a minimum content of Community law, which exists independently of implementation by member states, and which may be capable of having direct effect.

However, returning to the mainstream of the discussion of the vertical and horizontal direct effect of Directives, it becomes necessary to consider the Italian case of *Francovich* v. *Italian State* [1991] IRLR 84, where a group of employees were seeking compensation from the Italian state for its failure to implement a Directive which was intended to ensure payment of arrears of wages on the insolvency of employers. The Court of Justice found that all the criteria for direct effect were not satisfied, but then turned to art.5 of the EC Treaty, which requires member states to 'take all appropriate measures' to ensure compliance with their Community obligations. The Court then interpreted art.5 as requiring member states to pay compensation where they had failed to implement a Directive, provided that three conditions were satisfied, namely the Directive must confer rights on individuals, the content of those rights must be identifiable from the Directive, and there must be a causal link between the member state's failure and the claimant's loss. The Court justified this conclusion on the basis that it was inherent in the scheme of the Treaty.

The fact that the *Francovich* doctrine applies only where the rights which are conferred on individuals can be identified from the Directive is no more than a variation on the criterion for direct effect which requires a provision to be clear and precise in its expression (see p. 88), but both requirements merely reflect the reality that courts must know what they are being asked to enforce, rather than having any deep doctrinal significance.

It seems likely that, in the longer term, the *Francovich* doctrine will replace the doctrine of direct effect, by giving a right of action in damages in respect of a member state's failure to implement Community obligations. For example, in *Faccini Dori* v. *Recreb srl* [1995] All ER (EC) 1, which arose from Italy's failure to implement a consumer protection Directive. The Court of Justice rejected the Advocate-General's argument that the Directive should be given horizontal direct effect, but drew attention to the possibility of a *Francovich* claim in damages.

Decisions

For completeness, it is necessary to note the position in relation to Decisions. Article 189 of the EC Treaty provides that a Decision is 'binding in its entirety upon those to whom it is addressed'. Although art.189 does not make Decisions directly applicable, the Court of Justice held in the *Grad* case (see p. 91) that they were capable of direct effect. Here the discussion of vertical and horizontal direct effect is irrelevant, because the person to whom a Decision is addressed is the only possible defendant in the event of non-compliance.

6.5   Indirect Effect of Community Law

Finally, it should be noted that, even where Community law lacks direct effect, it may still have an *indirect effect* on the laws of member states, in the sense that a relevant provision of Community law may influence the interpretation of existing national laws of member states. This proposition, which is sometimes known as the *von Colson principle*, has the potential to render redundant all the technicalities surrounding direct applicability and direct effect, but it is best considered in more detail in the next chapter, which deals with Community law and national sovereignty.

Summary

1   When examining the reception of Community law into English law we must also consider some cases involving other member states, because Community law is an integrated whole.
2   Treaties do not become part of English law unless they are incorporated by statute. The European Communities Act 1972 incorporated the EC Treaty into English law.

3 A provision of Community law is *directly applicable* if it enters the legal systems of member states automatically. A provision of Community law is *directly effective* if it creates rights which are enforceable by the courts of a member state at the instance of people who are aggrieved by breaches of the provision. Direct effect is *vertical* where a provision of Community law is enforceable against the member state in its own courts. Direct effect is *horizontal* where a provision of Community law is enforceable against other people in the courts of the member state.

4 Treaty articles and Regulations may have *both* vertical and horizontal direct effect. Directives may have vertical direct effect *only*. The discussion of vertical and horizontal direct effect is irrelevant in relation to Decisions.

5 In the longer term, the *Francovich* doctrine, under which member states may be liable in damages in respect of their failure to implement Community obligations, may replace the doctrine of direct effect.

6 A provision of Community law which lacks direct effect may nevertheless have *indirect effect*, in accordance with the *von Colson principle*.

Exercises

1 What is the status of treaties in English law?

2 Distinguish between *direct applicability* and *direct effect* of Community law.

3 What are the *criteria for direct effect*?

4 Distinguish between *vertical* and *horizontal* direct effect.

5 Can a Directive have direct effect, and if so, can it be *vertical* or *horizontal* or both?

6 What does *indirect effect* mean? Give another expression which means the same as indirect effect.

7 European Community Law and National Sovereignty

7.1 Introduction

The reception of Community law into the domestic legal systems of member states raises the crucial question of national sovereignty. At its simplest, the issue is: does Community law prevail over inconsistent provisions of the national legal systems of member states?

7.2 The Community Law View of National Sovereignty

From the point of view of the Community there can be no doubt that Community law does prevail over national law. In the seminal case of *van Gend en Loos* [1963] CMLR 105 (see p. 89), the Court said: 'The Community constitutes a new legal order . . . for whose benefit the states have limited their sovereign rights.' Similarly, in *Costa* v. *ENEL* [1964] CMLR 425, the Court said:

'The reception within the laws of each member State, of provisions having a Community source, and more particularly of the terms and of the spirit of the Treaty, has as a corollary the impossibility, for the member State, to give preference to a unilateral and *subsequent* measure against a legal order accepted by them on the basis of reciprocity . . .

'The transfer, by member States, from their national orders in favour of the Community order of the rights and obligations arising from the Treaty, carries with it a clear limitation of their sovereign right upon which a *subsequent* unilateral law, incompatible with the aims of the Community, cannot prevail.' (Emphasis added.)

Additionally, it is clear from *Internationale Handelsgessellschaft mbH* [1974] 2 CMLR 540 that Community law prevails even in the face of the most fundamental constitutional doctrines of member states. The facts were that a German company claimed that a Community Regulation was invalid on the basis that it infringed the principle of proportionality (see Chapter 16), which was a fundamental principle of the German Constitution. There was nothing in the Constitution to give primacy to Community law. On the merits of the case the European Court of Justice decided that there had been no breach of the principle of proportionality, but the significance of the case for the present purposes is the force with which the Court of Justice stated that the validity of Community law cannot be judged by reference to national law.

'The law born from the Treaty [cannot] have the courts opposing to it rules of national law *of any nature whatsoever* . . . the validity of a Community instrument or its effect within a member state cannot be affected by allegations that it strikes at either the fundamental rights as formulated in that state's constitution or the principles of a national constitutional structure.' (Emphasis added.)

Even more specifically, the Court of Justice justifies the primacy of Community law over national law on the basis that the Community's legal order must apply equally throughout all the member states. As the Court said in *Italian Finance Administration* v. *Simmenthal* [1978] ECR 629:

'In accordance with the principle of the precedence of Community law, the relationship between provisions of the Treaty and direct applicable measures of the institutions on the one hand and the national law of the member states on the other is such that those provisions and measures not only by their entry into force render automatically inapplicable any conflicting provision of current national law but – in so far as they are an integral part of, and take precedence in, the legal order applicable in the territory of each of the member states – also preclude the valid adoption of new national legislative measures to the extent to which they would be incompatible with Community provisions.

'Indeed any recognition that national legislative measures which encroach upon the field within which the Community exercises its legislative power or which are otherwise incompatible with the provisions of Community law had any legal effect would amount to a corresponding denial of the effectiveness of obligations undertaken unconditionally and irrevocably by member states pursuant to the Treaty and would thus imperil the very foundations of the Community.'

7.3 The English View of Sovereignty in the Community Context

From the point of view of English law, the question can be very precisely stated: what does the doctrine of the legislative supremacy of Parliament amount to in the light of Community membership?

The European Communities Act 1972

As we saw, at p. 86, s.2(1) of the European Communities Act 1972 provides:

> 'All . . . rights, powers, liabilities, obligations and restrictions from time to time *created or arising by or under the Treaties*, and all such remedies and procedures from time to time *provided for by or under the Treaties*, as in accordance with the Treaties are without further enactment to be given legal effect or used in the United Kingdom shall be recognised and available in law, and be enforced, allowed and followed accordingly . . .' (Emphasis added.)

As we also saw, s.2(4) of the Act provides, *inter alia*:

> 'Any enactment passed or to be passed . . . shall be construed and have effect subject to the foregoing provisions of this section.'

The view of the English courts generally

From the English point of view, there is no difficulty in relation to statutes whose enactment pre-dates the 1972 Act, since the doctrine of implied repeal (which is discussed at p. 63) can cope perfectly adequately with the need to give primacy to Community law over inconsistent English law. However, in relation to statutes whose enactment post-dates the 1972 Act, an old problem arises: can one Parliament bind its successors? If the answer to this is *No* – and there is no doubt that this was the conventional wisdom before the Community era dawned (see p. 63) – it must follow that Parliament can legislate in a way which is contrary to Community law. Clearly, therefore, the possibility of conflict between Community law and English law needs to be examined more closely.

From the start the English courts have recognized the potential difficulty inherent in this situation. In *McCarthys* v. *Smith* [1979] 3 All ER 32, Lord Denning MR asserted the traditional view whilst conceding that, as a matter of practical politics, it was unlikely that direct conflict would arise:

'If the time should come when our Parliament deliberately passes an Act – with the intention of repudiating the Treaty or any provision of it – or intentionally of acting inconsistently with it – *and says so in express terms* – then I should have thought that it would be the duty of our courts to follow the statute of our Parliament. I do not, however, envisage any such situation.' (Emphasis added.)

Although Parliament may well avoid explicit conflicts between Community law and English law, the conceptual and linguistic ingenuity of lawyers in seeking to detect implicit conflicts should never be underrated. Nevertheless, the English courts have generally managed, by means of sympathetic interpretation, to avoid such conflicts. As Lord Diplock put it in *Garland* v. *British Rail Engineering Ltd* [1982] 2 All ER 402:

'It is a principle of construction of United Kingdom statutes . . . that the words of a statute passed after the Treaty has been signed and dealing with the subject matter of the international obligations of the United Kingdom, are to be construed, if they are reasonably capable of bearing such a meaning, as intended to carry out the obligation, and not to be inconsistent with it.'

This statement draws no distinction between those cases where the English provision was introduced in pursuance of an obligation under Community law and those where there is no causal link between the two systems. On the other hand, it can be argued that, at one stage, the Court of Justice did identify such a distinction. In *von Colson* v. *Land Nordrhein-Westfalen* [1986] 2 CMLR 702, the court said:

'In applying the national law *and in particular the provision of a national law specifically introduced in order to implement [a Directive]*, national courts are required to interpret their national law in the light of the wording and the purpose of the Directive in order to achieve the result referred to in [the Treaty].' (Emphasis added.)

Although this version of the *von Colson* principle emphasizes those provisions which are specifically introduced to implement Community obligations, if it is read as a whole the quotation clearly applies to all national provisions. However, in the same case the Court went on to say:

'It is for the national court to interpret and apply *the legislation adopted for the implementation of the Directive* in conformity with the requirements of Community law, in so far as it is given discretion to do so under national law.' (Emphasis added.)

It will be apparent not only that this is a narrower version of the principle, but also that it represents a profoundly uncharacteristic departure from the Court's usual and uncompromising assertion of the unconditional primacy of Community law. This latter factor alone is sufficient to suggest that the wider version is to be preferred, and both Court of Justice and the House of Lords have accepted this. It is clear, therefore, that earlier English legislation must be construed in accordance with later provisions of Community law, wherever this is possible. The leading cases are *Pickstone* v. *Freemans plc* [1988] 2 All ER 803, *Litster* v. *Forth Dry Docks Ltd* [1989] 1 All ER 1194 and *Webb* v. *EMO (Air Cargo) Ltd (No 2)* [1995] 4 All ER 577, although the wayward decision of *Duke* v. *GEC Reliance Ltd* [1988] 1 All ER 626 must also be mentioned.

Pickstone v. *Freemans plc* involved the Equal Pay (Amendment) Regulations 1983, which were introduced as a consequence of a decision by the European Court of Justice in 1981 to the effect that the United Kingdom had failed to comply with a specific requirement of Community law. The House decided to read the instrument as if it contained certain words which were not actually there. Lord Templeman said:

'The draft of the 1983 regulations was not subject to any process of amendment by Parliament. In these circumstances the explanations of the government and the criticisms voiced by members of Parliament in the debates which led to approval of the draft regulations provide some indications of the intentions of Parliament.'

Lord Templeman continued his speech, and included a passage from *Hansard*, which at that time was not generally available for the purposes of statutory interpretation. (For the current position regarding the use of *Hansard*, see pp. 293–9.) Lord Oliver acknowledged that the decision involved departing from some well-established rules of construction:

'The intention of Parliament has, it is said, to be ascertained from the words which it has used and those words are to be construed according to their plain and ordinary meaning. The fact that a statute is passed to give effect to an international treaty does not, of itself, enable the treaty to be referred to in order to construe the words used in other than their plain and unambiguous sense. Moreover, even in the case of ambiguity, what is said in Parliament in the course of the passage of a Bill, cannot ordinarily be referred to to assist in construction. I think, however, that it has also to be recognised that a statute which is passed in order to give effect to the United Kingdom's obligations under the EEC Treaty falls into a special category and it does so because, unlike other treaty obligations, those obligations have, in effect, been incorporated into English Law by the European Communities Act 1972.'

In *Duke* v. *GEC Reliance Ltd* [1988] 1 All ER 626, the House of Lords had to construe the Sex Discrimination Act 1975, which had been amended in order to bring English law into line with the Equal Treatment Directive 76/207 as a result of the decision in *Marshall* v. *Southampton & South West Hampshire Area Health Authority* (see p. 91). The specific problem was that the amendment had not been made retrospective, and yet the plaintiff was seeking a remedy in respect of a period before the amendment was effected. The House of Lords took the view that the failure to make the amendment retrospective was a clear indication that Parliament had intended English law to have been inconsistent with Community law between the 1975 Act and the date of the amendment. In a statement of principle which is out of line with the mainstream of authority, Lord Templeman said:

'Section 2(4) of the European Communities Act 1972 does not in my opinion enable or constrain a British court to distort the meaning of a British statute in order to enforce against an individual a Community Directive which has no direct effect between individuals. Section 2(4) applies and only applies where Community provisions are directly applicable.'

The deviation in *Duke* was short-lived, and in *Litster* v. *Forth Dry Docks Ltd* [1989] 1 All ER 1194, the House of Lords returned to the mainstream. The case involved certain United Kingdom regulations *which had been made specifically to implement an EC Directive*. The House cited and approved *Pickstone*, saying that where English legislation had been introduced in pursuance of a Community obligation, the English courts must interpret that legislation accordingly, even if that means 'supplying the necessary words by implication'. The House did not refer to *Duke*, nor to the fact that the Directive in question was not directly effective.

At this stage, therefore, the position was clear in relation to the interpretation of national measures which had been implemented in pursuance of Community obligations, but the two versions of the *von Colson* principle meant that an element of doubt remained in other cases. In *Marleasing SA* v. *La Comercial Internacional de Alimentacion SA* [1992] 1 CMLR 305, the Court of Justice resolved the doubt by holding that the *von Colson* principle requires national courts to interpret national law in accordance with Community law wherever this is possible, *even if no national legislation has been enacted specifically to comply with Community law*. This must include the situation in which the relevant national law consists of *prior* legislation, because this plainly cannot have been enacted to comply with something which did not exist at the time of its enactment.

The House of Lords clearly accepted *Marleasing*, albeit without referring to it, in *Webb* v. *EMO (Air Cargo) (UK) Ltd (No 2)* [1994] 4 All ER 115, which once again involved the interpretation of the Sex Discrimination Act 1975 in the light of the Equal Treatment Directive of 1976. The relevant provisions of the Sex Discrimination Act 1975 state that 'a person discriminates against a woman . . . if . . . on the ground of her sex he treats her less favourably than . . . a man . . .' and 'a comparison of the cases of persons of different sex . . . must be such that the relevant circumstances in the one case are the same, or not materially different, in the other . . .' [*sic*]. The Equal Treatment Directive of 1976 prohibits discrimination on the ground of sex. The question which arose was whether it was unlawful for an employer to dismiss a female employee who had been recruited for an unlimited period, on the ground that pregnancy prevented her from performing the duties for which she had been employed, when a male employee who required similar leave of absence for medical or other reasons would also have been dismissed.

On an art.177 reference, the Court of Justice held that pregnancy is not comparable with illness, and that even an illness arising from pregnancy should not be treated differently from any other illness. Furthermore, denying a pregnant woman the protection of the law in the circumstances of the present case would effectively nullify the Equal Treatment Directive.

When the case returned to the House of Lords (see [1995] 4 All ER 577), Lord Keith, with whom all his colleagues agreed, acknowledged that the 1975 Act fell to be interpreted in the light of the Directive. He proceeded to hold that the woman's pregnancy was a 'circumstance relevant to her case, being a circumstance which could not be present in the case of the hypothetical man', and that, therefore, her unfavourable treatment on the ground of pregnancy was discrimination on the ground of her sex. (The House of Lords noted that the Court of Justice seemed to have treated the indefinite duration of the employment as a relevant factor, and concluded that the same result would not necessarily follow where the employment was temporary and the employee had to be absent for the whole of the period for which she had been recruited.)

Webb may be taken to have confirmed the marginal status of the decision in *Duke*, to which Lord Keith did not even refer, and which now appears to have been an aberration in the course of an otherwise coherent line of authority.

In purely practical terms, conflicts between English law and Community law should be very few and far between, although one such conflict did arise under the Merchant Shipping Act 1988, and a series of cases ensued.

Before considering those cases, which may be called collectively the *Factortame litigation* because a company called Factortame Ltd was one of the major protagonists, it is essential to emphasize that there was no express statement of an intention to create the conflict.

7.4 The House of Lords Accepts the Community View: The *Factortame* Litigation

Part II of the Merchant Shipping Act 1988 was passed to deal with the problem of 'quota-hopping', which is the name given to the practice whereby foreign-owned fishing boats would become registered in Britain simply in order to gain access to fishing quotas which the EC had allocated to Britain. The purpose of the Act was to ensure that British-registered boats, fishing for British quotas, were also British-owned and British-managed.

On an application for a declaration that the provision contravened certain provisions of the Treaty prohibiting discrimination on the grounds of nationality, the High Court referred the question to the Court of Justice under art.177 of the Treaty, and made an interim order disapplying the provision until the substantive question had been resolved. On appeal against the interim order only, the Court of Appeal held that the British courts had no power to disapply a statute. On further appeal, the House of Lords decided to make another art.177 reference: this time in respect of the question of the power to grant interim relief. In addition to these art.177 references, the matter came before the Court of Justice in proceedings brought against the United Kingdom by the Commission. In these proceedings, the court held, in October 1989, that the British statute did contravene the Treaty, and issued an interim order requiring the suspension of the nationality requirement, pending a full trial of the issue. (*Re Nationality of Fishermen: EC Commission* v. *United Kingdom (Ireland Intervening)* [1989] 3 CMLR 601.) The United Kingdom responded to this by enacting the Merchant Shipping Act 1988 (Amendment) Order 1989, which suspended the British citizenship requirements of s.14, but only so far as they related to vessels which were fishing under the British flag up to 31 March 1989 and which were owned by nationals of a member state of the Communities.

In June 1990, the Court of Justice determined the House of Lords' art.177 reference, holding that, where there is an application to a national court for interim relief in a case where there is alleged to be a conflict between Community law and national law, and the national court holds that the only obstacle to the grant of interim relief is some rule of national law, the national court could set aside that rule of national law, and grant the interim relief accordingly. In other words, Community law prevailed. In consequence of this decision, the House of Lords granted interim relief (*Factortame Ltd* v. *Secretary of State for Transport (No 2)* [1991] 1 All ER 70.) The following comments of Lord Bridge deal with the heart of the matter:

'Some public comments on the decision of the Court of Justice, affirming the jurisdiction of the courts of member States to override national legislation if necessary to enable interim relief to be granted in protection of rights under Community law, have suggested that this was a novel and dangerous invasion by a Community institution of the sovereignty of the United Kingdom Parliament. But such comments are based on a misconception. If the supremacy within the European Community of Community law over the national law of member States was not always inherent in the EEC Treaty, it was certainly well established in the jurisprudence of the Court of Justice long before the United Kingdom joined the Community. Thus, whatever limitation of its sovereignty Parliament accepted when it enacted the European Communities Act 1972 was entirely voluntary. Under the terms of the 1972 Act it has always been clear that it was the duty of a United Kingdom court, when delivering final judgement, to override any rule of national law found to be in conflict with any directly enforceable rule of Community law. Similarly, when decisions of the Court of Justice have exposed areas of United Kingdom law which failed to implement Council Directives, Parliament has always loyally accepted the obligation to make appropriate and prompt amendments. Thus there is nothing in any way novel in according supremacy to rules of Community law.'

On the High Court's art.177 reference, the European Court of Justice decided that the legislation was contrary to Community law (see *R* v. *Secretary of State for Transport ex parte Factortame Ltd* [1991] 3 All ER 769.) Finally, in *R* v. *Secretary of State for Transport ex parte Factortame Ltd (No. 4)* [1996] *The Times*, March 7, the court held that the United Kingdom could be liable in damages to the parties who suffered loss, on the basis that a member state is liable for loss suffered as a result of a breach of a Community law by a national legislature, provided that the relevant provision of Community law was intended to confer rights on individuals, the breach was sufficiently serious, and there was a direct causal link between the breach and the loss. Moreover, exemplary damages could be payable if they would be available under the law of the member state. (The concept of exemplary damages in English law is explained at p. 30.) During the lifetime of this edition of this book, therefore, the English courts are likely to have to hear, and quantify, claims for damages, which will no doubt involve very substantial sums of money, even if no exemplary damages are awarded.

The *Equal Opportunities Commission* case

In *Equal Opportunities Commission* v. *Secretary of State for Employment* [1994] 1 All ER 910, the House of Lords granted declarations that the provisions of the Employment Protection (Consolidation) Act 1978 which restricted redundancy rights and unfair dismissal rights to those working at least 16 hours a week, were incompatible with art.119 of the EC Treaty and the Equal Pay Directive, and with the Equal Treatment Directive respectively.

The future

The only problem which remains is whether the House of Lords would uphold a statute containing an *express* intention to contravene Community law. This is almost certainly entirely academic, since the tension within the Community which would give rise to this situation would be likely to be resolved by political means.

Summary

1   The reception of Community law into the domestic legal systems of member states raises the crucial question of national sovereignty: does Community law prevail over inconsistent provisions of the national legal systems of member states?
2   From the point of view of the Community there can be no doubt that Community law prevails over national law.
3   The House of Lords has held that Community law prevails over an English statute, but the situation in which a statute expresses an intention to contravene Community law has not yet arisen. It is unlikely that such a statute will ever be passed, because the conflict leading up to it would almost certainly be resolved by political means before the legislative stage was reached.

Exercises

1   Explain the Community law view of member states' national sovereignty.
2   Explain the importance of the *Factortame* litigation from the point of view of the British constitution.

8 Finding, Citing and Using the Sources of Law

8.1 Introduction

When you are looking for the law you will usually use textbooks and journals, law reports and statutes. This chapter will examine each of these in turn, before concluding with a brief overview of some of the more readily accessible sources of Community law.

One point of general application may, however, usefully be made at the outset. When you see references to law reports you will notice that sometimes the date is in square brackets, and sometimes it is in round ones, as in [1973] 2 All ER 97 and (1989) 155 JP 494. The difference is vitally important. A date in square brackets is an essential part of the reference: there has been a volume 2 of the *All England Law Reports* every year since the series started in 1936, and each of those volumes has had a page 97. It follows that the bare reference 2 All ER 97 is useless. On the other hand, a date in round brackets is not an essential element of the reference. For example, the *Justice of the Peace Reports* first appeared in 1837 and have been numbered annually, on a serial basis, ever since. It follows that 155 JP 494 is a perfectly adequate reference to enable you to find the report. In practice, however, it is common to use the date as well, because it may be useful to know at a glance whether the case is old, middle-aged or recent, as well as being able to identify its chronological relationship with other decisions on the same subject-matter.

As a rule of thumb, the square bracket style is the more modern, but occasionally new series start on a serially numbered basis (see, for example, *Administrative Law Reports*, which first appeared in 1989). Also as a rule of thumb, the square bracket style will apply if the volume number is 1, 2, 3 or 4. It will be obvious, however, that this principle is not infallible, because even the serially numbered volumes started somewhere, and therefore have volume numbers of 1 to 4.

The same distinction between square and round brackets applies to references to journals. For example, the annual volumes of the *Law Quarterly Review* are serially numbered, but those of *Public Law* are not.

8.2 Textbooks and Journals

The first instinct of most people who want to look up the law on a particular point will probably be to consult a textbook, or perhaps an article in a journal. This inevitably raises the question of whether statements made by authors can be treated as being authoritative pronouncements of what the law actually is. The traditional answer to this question falls fairly neatly into two parts, which may conveniently be labelled ancient and modern.

Starting with the ancient authors, there is a select band from Glanvill in the twelfth century to Blackstone in the eighteenth century, and including Bracton, Fitzherbert, Littleton, Coke, Hale, Hawkins and Foster on the way. Historically, the courts were willing to treat these authors' statements of law as being authentic and therefore binding. Even in modern times, when the works of these authors are all very old, the courts may speak in terms which seem to indicate that the writings of certain authors are authoritative sources of law. For example, the case of *Reid v. Metropolitan Police Commissioner* [1973] 2 All ER 97 raised a nice point of law concerning the ownership of stolen goods which had subsequently been sold to a third party. Lord Denning MR commented: 'To solve this question we have to go back to the works of Sir Edward Coke'.

Two points must be made here. First, the ancient authors do not always agree with each other, thus leaving the court with the task of choosing between them. To find an example of this in practice it is necessary to do no more than return to the decision in *Reid* where Lord Denning MR concluded, for various reasons, that the court 'should follow the words of Sir Edward Coke rather than those of Sir William Blackstone'. Second, it will be very infrequent that works which are anything from two hundred to eight hundred years old will be found to contain statements of law which are relevant to modern conditions, and yet have escaped entering the more formally established canon of legal sources, namely case-law and statute.

The most balanced view of the status of the ancient authors, therefore, is that, although their works were originally treated as being authoritative, and may still be treated with considerable respect, they will certainly not be binding on a modern court. On the other hand, a modern court may treat their works as being excellent evidence of what the law was at the time when they were writing, and the court may (or may not) choose to infer that the law is still the same today.

In explaining the change from the old practice to the new one, it is important to notice that during the nineteenth century, as the rate of social and economic change accelerated, statutes became increasingly important as a source of law. At the same time the common law, while of declining importance as a source of law, became increasingly accessible as the reliability of the system of law reporting improved. In other words, as the major primary sources of law became more readily and reliably available, the courts no longer needed to place such great reliance on the works of authors, whose works were increasingly out of touch with the needs of modern society. Thus textbooks came to be seen as having no more than persuasive value in the task of identifying the law.

The reasons why the classic authors lost their authoritative status were, of course, largely applicable to their more modern successors, apart from the matter of being increasingly out of touch with modern society. Additionally, however, the courts found another reason for being cautious in their use of some modern authors, namely that they were still alive. In *Greenlands (Limited)* v. *Wilmshurst and Others* (1913) 29 TLR 685, Vaughan Williams LJ said:

'No doubt Mr. Odger's book [on the law of libel] is a most admirable work, which we all use, but I think we ought in this Court still to maintain the old idea that counsel are not entitled to quote living authors as authorities for a proposition they are putting forward, but they may adopt the author's statements as part of their argument.'

Two points may be made. First, in practical terms the distinction between citing a statement as authority and incorporating it into an argument may involve the finest of distinctions. Second, the view that simply being alive intrinsically disqualifies authors from being authoritative, rests on the fact that living authors can change their minds as to what they think the law is, whereas dead ones clearly cannot do so. The transparently unconvincing nature of this argument becomes obvious if we compare authors with judges. Judicial pronouncements are clearly treated as being sources of law, despite the fact that individual judges can – and do – change their minds, as we shall shortly see in the context of *R* v. *Shivpuri* [1986] 2 All ER 334 (see p. 111). Perhaps Megarry, beneath the characteristic lightness of his turn of phrase, identifies the true reason for some judges' scepticism of some authors:

'The passage of years and the activities of those who edit the books of the departed tend to produce criticism and sometimes the elimination of frailties, and so give greater confidence in what remains. Further, many books by dead authors represent mature views after a lifetime of studying and, often, practising in the particular branch of the law concerned, whereas all too many books by the living are written by those who, laudably enough, have merely hoped to learn the rudiments of a subject by writing a book about it. Finally, it must be admitted that there are a number of living authors whose appearance and demeanour do something to sap any confidence in their omniscience which the printed page may have instilled; the dead, on the other hand, so often leave little clue to what manner of men they were save the majestic skill with which they have arrayed the learning of centuries and exposed the failings of the bench.' (*Miscellany-at-Law*, 1955, revised impression 1958, p. 328.)

Returning to the mainstream of the discussion, it may be thought that particular difficulties will arise in the case of individuals who are both judges and authors, which brings us again to Megarry as a leading example of this phenomenon. Not unnaturally, this dual role led to counsel citing Megarry's own works to him while he was performing his judicial function. In turn this led Megarry to draw a distinction between the functions of authors and of judges:

> 'The process of authorship is entirely different from that of judicial decision. The author . . . has the benefit of a broad and comprehensive study of his chosen subject . . . But he is exposed to the perils of yielding to preconceptions and he lacks the . . . sharpening of focus which the detailed facts of a particular case bring to the judge. Above all, he has to form his ideas without the aid of the purifying ordeal of skilled argument on the specific facts of a contested case . . . and I would, therefore, give credit to the words of any reputable author . . . as expressing tenable and arguable ideas, as fertilisers of thought, and as conveniently expressing the fruits of research in print . . . But I would expose those views to the testing and refining process of argument.' (*Cordell* v. *Second Clanfield Properties* [1968] 3 All ER 746.)

A rather more fulsome view of the value of legal authors, again formulated by a distinguished judge, may be found in a book review by Denning J at (1947) 63 LQR 516:

> '[Textbooks] are not digests of cases but repositories of principles. They are written by men who have studied the law as a science with more detachment than is possible to men engaged in busy practice.'

One of the most succinct statement of the utility of textbooks is to be found in the words of Sir George Jessell MR in *Henty* v. *Wrey* (1882) 21 ChD 332: 'Although textbooks do not make law, they show more or less whether a principle has been generally accepted'. Nevertheless, it is important to emphasize the point made by Lord Goddard CJ in *Bastin* v. *Davies* [1950] 1 All ER 1095, when speaking of *Bell's Sale of Food and Drugs*: '[A court] would never hesitate to disagree with a statement in a textbook . . . if it thought fit'. However:

> 'If a statement has appeared in a well-known textbook for a great number of years and has never been dissented from by a judicial decision, it would be most unfortunate to throw doubt on it after it had been acted on . . . for so long.'

Some textbooks, such as the massively multi-volumed *Halsbury's Laws of England*, are encyclopaedic in nature, and some, such as the *Encyclopaedia of Planning Law and Practice*, are even so by name. Useful though such works are, they are no more infallible than any other books. Examples of cases where the courts have commented adversely on individual textbooks include *Watson* v. *Thomas S. Witney & Co Ltd* [1966] 1 All ER 122, where the Court of Appeal refused to accept the accuracy of a clear statement in *Halsbury's Laws of England*. Similarly, in *R* v. *Oxford Crown Court and Another ex parte Smith* (1990) 2 Admin LR 395, the High Court gave short shrift to one aspect of the case, with Simon Brown J explaining the matter thus:

> 'The reason why I can deal with this argument comparatively briefly is because it flies in the face of clear Court of Appeal authority directly and indistinguishably in point – *Britt* v. *Buckinghamshire County Council* [1964] 1 QB 77. This case alas did not feature in [counsel for the applicant's] arguments save in reply. That, it emerged, was because he was unaware of it until [counsel for the respondent's] submissions . . . he candidly admitted to sitting transfixed when it came to be cited. One wonders whether any of this litigation would have occurred had it been earlier discovered by the applicant's advisers. It is certainly unfortunate that it finds no mention in the *Planning Encyclopaedia*.'

In *Shenton* v. *Tyler* [1939] 1 All ER 827, Sir Wilfrid Greene MR referred to a wide range of textbooks on the law of evidence, only to conclude that they were all wrong on the point in issue. In *R* v. *Keriwala* [1991] *The Times*, January 4, the court pointed out that the *Current Law Statutes* version of s.58(1) of the Police and Criminal Evidence Act 1984, read: 'A person who is in police detention shall be entitled if he so requests to consult a solicitor privately at any time', whereas the Queen's Printer's version read: 'A person arrested and held in custody in a police station or other premises shall be entitled, if he so requests, to consult a solicitor privately at any time.' Moreover, the first and second editions of Professor

Zander's book entitled *Police and Criminal Evidence Act 1984* shared the erroneous version of the statute with the *Current Law* series.

No doubt many authors have had cause to be relieved that more judges do not share the attitude which Staughton LJ expressed in *Holmes and Bradbury* v. *Bradford Metropolitan City Council*, which is reported at (1995) 158 LG Rev 561, and noted briefly at (1994) 158 JPN 438. The case brought to light an inaccurate statement of law in the *Encyclopaedia of Planning Law and Practice*. Perusal of that part of the transcript of the judgement which, in accordance with the usual practice is not reported, shows that when the question of costs came to be discussed, Staughton LJ said: 'We cannot really make the editor [of the *Encyclopaedia*] pay the costs.' When counsel replied: 'Sadly, no', Staughton LJ responded with: 'We would rather like to.' In fact, no order as to costs was made against anyone.

Although authors and editors, being only human, may make mistakes, there can be no doubt that the legal profession and the courts would both find life practically impossible if they were left only with the primary sources of law, and judges not infrequently acknowledge their indebtedness to legal authors. In this context Lord Bridge, in the case of *R* v. *Shivpuri* [1986] 2 All ER 334, deserves full marks for judicial candour. The background to *Shivpuri* was that in *Anderton* v. *Ryan* [1985] 2 All ER 355, the House of Lords had formulated a principle, the details of which need not be explored here, which had aroused the almost universal wrath of academic criminal lawyers. The House had the opportunity of returning to the point in *Shivpuri*, when it decided to overrule its previous decision. Lord Bridge, who was in the unenviable position of being a member of the House on both occasions, concluded the substance of his speech with the following words:

> 'I have had the advantage, since the conclusion of argument in this appeal, of reading an article by Professor Glanville Williams . . . The language in which he criticizes the decision in *Anderton* v. *Ryan* is not conspicuous for its moderation, but it would be foolish, on that account, not to recognise the force of the criticism and churlish not to acknowledge the assistance I have derived from it.'

The cases of *Anderton* v. *Ryan* and *R* v. *Shivpuri* are discussed further, in the context of the doctrine of precedent, at pp. 176–7.

One particularly useful publication for anyone undertaking serious research is *The Digest*, formerly entitled *The English and Empire Digest*, which is literally a massive digest of case-law, arranged by subject-matter. However, its scope goes far beyond the needs of most law students.

8.3   Law Reports

Introduction

Since the English legal system depends so heavily on the doctrine of precedent, there is an obvious need for accessible, accurate and reliable reports of what the courts have decided. It is not surprising, therefore, that there are many series of law reports, although it may be thought more surprising that there is no such thing as 'official' law reports. The closest to 'official' law reports are those published by the Incorporated Council of Law Reporting for England and Wales, which is a non-profit-making body, created and run by the legal profession.

The range of law reports

Although any series of reports of the decisions of the courts may be, and often are, referred to as 'law reports', the phrase is sometimes used in a somewhat stricter sense, in which case it refers to the principal products of the Incorporated Council. Using the phrase in this strict sense for the moment, the *Law Reports* currently contain sub-series entitled *Appeal Cases*, which abbreviates to AC, and which covers the House of Lords; *Chancery Division*, which abbreviates to Ch, *Family Division*, which abbreviates to Fam, and *Queen's Bench Division*, which abbreviates to QB. The Chancery, Family and Queen's Bench reports cover not only the decisions of the respective divisions of the High Court, but also the decisions of the Court of Appeal arising from them. Somewhat oddly, in view of their title, the *Law Reports* also contain an annual volume containing statutes, but the topic of the citation of statutes will be left until p. 118.

The Incorporated Council also publishes the *Weekly Law Reports*, which abbreviates to WLR. As their title implies, these are published in weekly parts, although they are also available annually in three bound volumes. Each weekly part is divided into cases destined for volume one on the one hand or volumes two or three on the other. The cases appearing in volumes two and three also appear again, after some delay, in the appropriate volume of the *Law Reports*, while those published in volume one will not do so. The later version is more valuable when it appears because it contains summaries of the arguments which were presented to the court. The production of the *Weekly Law Reports* is nevertheless justified by their earlier publication.

Unlike the products of the Incorporated Council, however, the majority of series of law reports are published as purely commercial ventures. The leading series of general law reports produced on a commercial basis is the

All England Law Reports (All ER) which appears in weekly parts. Since the beginning of 1995, there has also been an *All England Law Reports European Cases* series (All ER (EC)), which appears ten times a year. Additionally, there are many specialized series, such as *Administrative Law Reports* (Admin LR), *Building Law Reports* (BLR), and *Road Traffic Reports* (RTR), to name only three. The frequency of appearance of the specialist series varies, but their content will be self-evident from their titles. (A list of the most frequently encountered law reports and their abbreviations is provided in Appendix 1.)

Several newspapers publish law reports, as do many periodicals. In the case of the latter, the reports will, naturally, relate to the periodical's subject-matter, which will generally be apparent from its title: for example, *Criminal Law Review* (Crim LR) and the *Journal of Planning and Environmental Law* (JPL or JPEL).

The value of the specialized series of free-standing reports, and of the reports incorporated into periodicals, is that their editors may well include cases which lack sufficient general or lasting interest to justify inclusion in the more mainstream series, and yet are of topical or specialized interest. Such reports may also be accompanied by useful academic commentaries, as exemplified by the *Criminal Law Review* and the *Journal of Planning and Environmental Law*. However, it is important to remember that, unlike the free-standing series of reports, reports in newspapers and perioicals are shortened versions of the judgement, which means that they are merely the reporter's version of what the judge has said. It will be obvious that there will always be a question-mark over the accuracy and reliability of any short report. In *Export Credits Guarantee Department* v. *Universal Oil Products Co* [1983] 2 All ER 205, Lord Roskill described a case reported only in the *Solicitors' Journal* as being 'virtually unreported'. Even more pointedly, in *Brentnall & Cleland Limited* v. *London County Council* [1945] 1 KB 115, Humphreys J, speaking of a report of one of his own previous decisions, said:

'These short reports . . . ought to be accepted with a good deal of care. If I am correctly reported in *The Law Times* . . . I can only say, first that that was an *obiter dictum*, and secondly that I think it was wrong. I have no recollection of saying anything of the sort, and I cannot believe that I said it.' (The meaning of *obiter dictum* is discussed in Chapter 10.)

The unreliability of short reports does not mean that the whole of a full-transcript report should be read uncritically. In particular it is important to distinguish between the headnote and the judgement itself. The headnote, which is the introductory summary of the decision, is written by the reporter rather than by the judge, and therefore it is not authoritative.

Many headnotes are of a very high standard, but, to adopt the words of Megarry: 'The composition of a . . . headnote to a law report is generally recognized as calling for a high degree of skill' (*Miscellany-at-Law*, 1955, revised impression 1958, p. 289). It is not altogether surprising, therefore, that headnotes vary in their clarity or accuracy, or both.

The proper utility of the headnote is limited to telling readers what the case is about, so that they can decide whether to invest further time and energy in reading the judgement itself.

The citability of law reports in court

Initially law reports are used by practitioners and others for guidance as to what the law is. In this context, reports may be very useful when giving advice to clients and in achieving negotiated settlements. However, many matters do go to court, so it will be apparent that the ultimate utility of a law report would be seriously diminished if the courts were not willing to look at it if occasion demanded. An important question, therefore, becomes: 'which law reports are citable in court?' The traditional view is: 'A "law report" means any account of a case vouched for by a barrister who was present at the hearing' (Dias, *Jurisprudence*, 5th edn, p. 134, relying on Pollock's *Essays in the Law*, p. 243). The Court of Appeal reflected this view in *Birtwistle* v. *Tweedale* [1953] 2 All ER 1598, where Somervell LJ, speaking of an *Estates Gazette* report, said that he did not wish to have cases cited if they were not reported by barristers, since such reports 'might mislead rather than assist the court'. Denning LJ said that there were sufficient cases that could be cited apart from those in the *Estates Gazette*. Romer LJ agreed with both his colleagues.

The proposition that reporters must not only be barristers but must also be present at the hearing appears to be deeply ingrained in the academic consciousness. For example, in *The Limits of Citation Determined* (1983) 80 LS Gaz 1337, Roderick Munday said: 'Anyone today is entitled to publish law reports, *provided that the judgements are attested to by a member of the Bar present at the decision*' (emphasis added). However, the fact that a proposition is deeply ingrained does not make it correct, or even defensible, and in the present context the lack of justification for the traditional view is apparent when the nature of a law report in analysed.

A full-transcript report consists of a copy of the judgement of the court (which is publicly available anyway), together with any apparatus by way of headnote, cross-references to textbooks, and so on, which the reporter considers to be appropriate. Since headnotes are never authoritative anyway, there can be no basis for challenging the accuracy of a report merely because the headnote-writer is not a barrister and worked from a transcript of the judgement, rather than being present in court. Furthermore, the modern practice in many cases is for the court to announce its decision and then to hand down the judgement, without occupying court time by reading it out. In such cases, therefore, any reporter will have no option but to work from the transcript.

Since it is obviously in the best interests of the administration of justice that the courts should be able to refer to the widest possible range of legal sources, it is fortunate that current judicial practice does not reflect the traditional view of the citability of law reports. Among many others, the *Justice of the Peace Reports* are frequently cited. For example, in *Wellingborough Borough Council* v. *Gordon* (1991) 155 JP 494, the High Court relied on the report of *Cooke* v. *Adatia and Others* (1989) 153 JP 129, which was prepared by a solicitor, who was not present at the hearing. The court made no comment whatsoever as to the provenance of the earlier report.

In passing, it is interesting to note that those instructing the drafter of s.115 of the Courts and Legal Services Act 1990 appear to have shared the common misconception as to the citability of law reports. The section provides that a law report prepared by a solicitor, or anyone else who has acquired the right of advocacy in the higher courts, 'shall have the same authority as if it had been made by a barrister'. This provision is clearly superfluous.

In the final analysis, each court must be the master of its own practice in relation to the citation of reports. However, the fact that, as we have seen, all law reports may be cited does not mean that courts have no preferences in the matter. In a *Practice Note* [1995] 3 All ER 256, Sir Thomas Bingham MR said:

> 'If a case is reported in the official Law Reports published by the Incorporated Council of Law Reporting for England and Wales, that report should be cited. These are the most authoritative reports; they contain a summary of the argument; and they are most readily available.
>
> 'If a case is not (or not yet) reported in the official Law Reports, but is reported in the Weekly Law Reports or the All England Law Reports, that report should be cited.
>
> 'If a case is not reported in any of these series of reports, a report in any of the authoritative specialist series of reports may be cited . . .
>
> 'It is recognized that occasions arise when one report is fuller than another, or when there are discrepancies between reports. On such occasions, the practice outlined above need not be followed.'

Whether the *Law Reports* are necessarily more accurate than any other series is open to question. In *Re C* [1937] 3 All ER 783, Luxmoore J is reported as having read two extracts from the Parliamentary proceedings which produced the Adoption of Children Act 1926. At that time judicial references to Parliamentary proceedings were not allowed, although this rule has since been relaxed (see pp. 293–9). When the case came to be reported in the *Law Reports* (at [1938] Ch 131), the offending section of the judgement was omitted, presumably as a result of the judge's intervention, or at least to avoid causing him embarrassment.

Editorial discretion in law reporting

With the possible exception of a series of law reports dealing with a very small and specialized area of law, it would be impossible for any series to include all the cases falling within its scope. The question therefore arises as to how the editors of the various series of law reports decide which cases to include. The answer, which may seem less than satisfactory, is that it is simply a matter of editorial judgement.

If the series is a general one, such as the *All England Law Reports*, the editor will have regard to the perceived needs of the general practitioner. More particularly, the publishing director of Butterworths, the proprietors of the *All England Law Reports*, said that the series' editors exercise their discretion according to the following criteria: does the case make new law or contain a modern restatement of an existing principle; does it clarify conflicting decisions of lower courts or interpret legislation which is likely to be of wide application; does it interpret a common clause in documents such as wills or contracts, or clarify an important point of practice or procedure? (See Brown, *Law Reporting: the Inside Story* (1989) 20 *The Law Librarian*, 15.)

Naturally, in addition to any explicit statement of editorial policy, any commercial enterprise must always bear in mind that the level of sub-scription income will determine the upper limit on the number of pages which can be produced in each year, and even the Incorporated Council prefers to have paid its way at the end of the year. The editors of the more specialized series will use their judgement in a similar fashion, but having regard to their perceptions of the needs of their subscribers.

Obviously, a specialized series can justify the inclusion of cases which would not be appropriate in a general series. Particularly in the case of specialist series, subscribers themselves may sometimes draw the editors' attention to cases in which they have been involved, and which they believe may be of interest to other specialists.

The problem of delay in law reporting

The process of preparing, printing and distributing law reports clearly takes some time. In the case of a newspaper report this may only be a day or so, but in the case of the free-standing series it may often be several months, or even a year or more. This is simply one of the less happy facts of legal life, and in no way detracts from the validity of the proposition that the bindingness of precedent operates immediately, as illustrated by the cases of *Re Schweppes Ltd's Agreement* and *Re Automatic Telephone and Electric Co Ltd's Agreement.*

Some instances of late reporting are explicable on the basis that an elderly but unreported case has been cited in a more recent case which attracts an editor's attention. The case of *Scherer* v. *Counting Instruments Ltd* was decided in 1977, but not then reported. Subsequently it was cited in *Aden Refinery Co Ltd* v. *Ugland Management Co*, which was reported at [1986] 3 All ER 737. The editor of the reports took the opportunity to report the earlier case, which appears at [1986] 2 All ER 529.

Sometimes there may be prompt reporting in one series and less prompt reporting in another, with the specialist series often gaining a substantial march on their more mainstream contemporaries. For example, the case of *City of London Corporation* v. *Bovis* was reported at (1988) 153 LG Rev 166, but not until [1992] 3 All ER 697. Similarly, when the House of Lords decided *Cremin* v. *Thomson* it was promptly reported at (1941) 71 Ll Rep 1. The *All England Law Reports* did not include the case until [1953] 2 All ER 1185, where it appears as *Thomson* v. *Cremin.*

Computer databases

No discussion of law reporting would be complete without mentioning the availability and use of computer databases, such as *Lexis*. In *Stanley* v. *International Harvester Co Ltd* [1983] *The Times*, 7 February, the Court of Appeal urged counsel to practise 'proper discretion' in citing cases which have not appeared in any series of law reports. A few days later, in *Roberts Petroleum Ltd* v. *Bernard Kenny Ltd* [1983] 1 All ER 564, the House of Lords rather more forthrightly said that it did not wish to receive unreported cases unless counsel stated that the case dealt with a principle which was not only binding on the Court of Appeal, but which additionally was not covered by a case contained in the recognized reports.

Conventions in case names

The usual convention is that the name of the party who is initiating the current stage of the proceedings will be placed first. So if Smith is suing Jones for breach of contract, the case will be *Smith* v. *Jones*. If Smith loses and appeals, the case will still be *Smith* v. *Jones* on appeal. However, if Jones loses and appeals, the case will become *Jones* v. *Smith* on appeal. However, there are two principal exceptions to the usual convention.

First, the modern practice in the House of Lords is for the case name to revert to whatever form it had at first instance, irrespective of who is the appellant. Second, in criminal law case names are usually given in the form of e.g. *R* v. *Smith*, whether at first instance or on appeal. (The *R* stands for either *Rex* or *Regina*, depending upon the sex of the reigning monarch at the time of the case.)

Additionally, cases of some types are usually given names in a special form. One of the most common examples is in judicial review, where historically the application to the court was made by the Crown on behalf of the real applicant. Although this is now pure fiction, the case names still reflect the original practice, as in *R* v. *Secretary of State for Whatever ex parte Smith*. Other exceptional usages include cases involving ships, which are sometimes given the ship's name, as in *The Skylark*. Similarly, cases involving the estate of someone who has died are often given the name of the deceased, preceded by the word *Re*, which means 'in the matter of'. So if Smith has died, a case dealing with the estate may be reported as *Re Smith*. A similar form is often used when cases deal with the welfare of children, except that that the convention here is to use only an initial (as in *Re S*) in order to preserve anonymity.

Despite the existence of broadly understood conventions, the naming of cases is neither a precise science nor a highly developed art. Accordingly, it is not uncommon to find the editors of different series of law reports giving different names to the same case. References to such a case may indicate what has happened by using the abbreviation *sub nom* (meaning *sub nomine*, or 'under the name of'). For example, you may encounter the following: *Ellerman Lines Ltd* v. *Murray* [1930] All ER Rep 503, *sub nom The Croxteth Hall, The Celtic* 47 TLR 147.

8.4 Statutes

The usual way of citing a statute is by its short title – for example, the Local Government Act 1972. The short title is usually found towards the end of the body of the text, but before the schedules (if any). To pursue the example of the Local Government Act 1972, the relevant provision is s.274.

The convenience of being able to refer to a statute by its short title may seem to be obvious, but it becomes even clearer when the alternatives are considered. First, there is the long title, which is found at the beginning of the statute. To give an indication of the unwieldy nature of the long title, it is necessary to do no more than return to the example of the Local Government Act 1972:

'An Act to make provision with respect to local government and the functions of local authorities in England and Wales; to amend Part II of the Transport Act 1968; to confer rights of appeal in respect of decisions relating to licences under the Home Counties (Music and Dancing) Licensing Act 1926; to make further provision with respect to magistrates' courts committees; to abolish certain inferior courts of record; and for connected purposes.'

A technical way of referring to a statute, and one which is hardly ever encountered in practice, is by its year and chapter number – thus the Local Government Act 1972 may be cited as '1972, c.70', meaning that it was the seventieth statute to receive the Royal Assent in 1972. Whilst this form of citation enables the statute to be identified, it has the clear drawback of conveying nothing of any real meaning on the face of the reference. Furthermore, this method of citation, in the form of the example which has been taken, dates only from 1962. Before that date the convention was to cite a statute according to the session of the Parliament in which it was passed, and a session of Parliament usually spans two calendar years, running from the autumn of one year to the summer of the next. To make matters worse, the session of Parliament was identified by reference to the monarch's regnal year or years, rather than the calendar years.

Each regnal year begins with the anniversary of the monarch's accession, which means that the regnal year of Queen Elizabeth the Second runs from 6 February of one year to 5 February of the next. The fact that this regnal year does not correspond with the Parliamentary year causes complications because of the impossibility of foretelling the future. The difficulty is that the Queen may die or abdicate at any time and – perhaps more probably – Parliament may be dissolved at any time. This means that, where a statute was passed during the first regnal year of a session of Parliament, only that regnal year could be allocated to it, in case either the monarch or the Parliament did not survive into the next regnal year. For example, the Tanganyika Independence Act 1961 is cited as 10 Eliz. 2 c.1, although in reality the session of Parliament extended into the next regnal year as well, so with the benefit of hindsight the Act could have been cited as 10 & 11 Eliz. 2 c.1. Later statutes from that session are referred to by both regnal years – for example, the Local Government (Records) Act 1962 is 10 & 11 Eliz. 2 c.56.

Finally, there is the question of what is the best source for finding the actual wording of a statute. The textbook answer must be that the most authoritative version which is readily available is the text of the Queen's Printer's copy as published by Her Majesty's Stationery Office. However, in this, as in so many other things, the textbook answer overlooks a whole dimension of pure practicality. The principal deficiencies of the Queen's

Printer's version are that it contains no editorial matter by way of commentary, explanation or even cross-reference and – even more seriously – of necessity it represents the text of the Act as it was at the date of the Royal Assent, without the incorporation of subsequent amendments. As well as being published by the Stationery Office as individual statutes, and in bound volumes as Public and General Acts and Measures, the Queen's Printer's version of the text is also reproduced in the *Statutes* volume of the Incorporated Council's *Law Reports*.

The commercially published series, *Current Law Statutes Annotated*, supplements the Queen's Printer's text with very full annotations, section by section. The format usually includes a useful introductory essay commenting on the background and purposes of the statute. The editorial process inevitably involves some delay between the Royal Assent and publication of the annotated version of the statute. Perhaps the most useful version overall, however, is *Halsbury's Statutes of England*, which is another commercial publication. *Halsbury's Statutes* has the advantage that the text is supported, not only by full annotations, but also by an updating service which makes it relatively easy to keep track of repeals and amendments as they take place.

Two caveats must be entered in relation to anything other than the Queen's Printer's versions of statutes. First, there is always the possibility that the text is inaccurate in some way (see, for example, *R* v. *Keriwala*, p. 110). Second, although editorial commentaries may be useful, they are never as authoritative as judicial interpretations of the words of the statute itself.

8.5   European Community Law

Since Community law is a whole legal order in itself, you will not be surprised to learn that it enjoys an enormous range of sources. Apart from the *European Court Reports* (ECR) the *Common Market Law Reports* (CMLR) and the treaties themselves, the most useful official sources are probably the *Official Journal* and the bulletin called the *Proceedings of the Court of Justice and the Court of First Instance of the European Communities*.

The *Official Journal* is published in several parts. The three most generally useful parts are the L series (containing the text of agreed legislation), the C series (containing draft legislation, official announcements and information on Community activities) and the Annexe (containing the full text of debates in the European Parliament). The Court of Justice's *Bulletin* contains digested versions of recent decisions. Inevitably, these are not as authoritative as full reports, but they do become available a great deal more quickly.

There are also various commercial publications, including a number of loose-leaf encyclopaedias. A particularly accessible text may be found in volumes 51 and 52 of *Halsbury's Laws of England*, although of course these must be read with the aid of the updating service.

8.6 Keeping Up-to-Date

Keeping up-to-date is a life-long (not to say life-shortening) nightmare for many lawyers. Students are perhaps more fortunate, since they can generally delegate this task to their lecturers. Nevertheless, it is worth commenting that the monthly parts of *Current Law*, with their annual cumulation into the *Current Law Year Books*, provide a generally reliable guide to recent developments, including the publication of textbooks and articles.

The *Current Law* family of publications includes case and statute citators, which enable you to trace cases in which earlier cases and statutes have been cited, as well as delegated legislation and amendments to statutes.

Halsbury's Laws and *Halsbury's Statutes* both have loose-leaf current service volumes, and specialist encyclopaedias are also usually loose-leaf. Once you have enough basic knowledge to be able to understand and assess recent developments, one of the best ways of keeping up-to-date in a broadly-based way is to skim one or more of the generalist weekly journals (the *Law Society's Gazette*, the *Solicitors' Journal* and the *New Law Journal*). Specialists will, of course, probably read the relevant journals more closely. Experienced lawyers often find that they retain the knowledge that they have known something long after the content of that specific knowledge has gone. It is then simply a case of retracing the source.

Summary

1 When you are looking for the law you will usually use textbooks and journals, law reports and statutes. Where a reference contains a date in square brackets, the date is an essential part of the reference. Where a date is in round brackets it is not an essential element of the reference.
2 Textbooks and journals are very useful but they are not authoritative in the way that statutes and judicial decisions are.
3 There are many series of law reports. The superior courts prefer to receive the Incorporated Council for Law Reporting's *Law Reports*, but

any court may receive any report. There is no longer any force in the old rule that only a barrister present at the hearing can produce an authoritative law report.

4   There are various ways of citing statutes, but the use of the short title is the most usual and convenient method.

5   Keeping up-to-date with legal developments requires mastery of a law library.

Exercises

1   What is the distinction between round brackets and square brackets in the citation of legal references?

2   Are textbooks and journals authoritative sources of English law?

3   Which law reports do the superior courts prefer to have cited to them? Why?

4   What is the most common and convenient way of citing a statute?

5   What does the *Official Journal* of the European Communities contain?

Case-Law and Precedent

Having read this Part you should understand the basic concepts of the English doctrine of binding precedent and appreciate how those concepts are applied in practice. More particularly, you should be able to understand how the doctrine attempts to balance the interests of flexibility and predictability. You will also gain a comparative insight from considering the practice of the European Court of Justice.

9 An Introduction to the Doctrine of Binding Precedent

9.1 Introduction

Briefly, the doctrine of binding precedent states that all courts bind all lower courts, and some courts also bind themselves. The hierarchy of the courts, which was outlined in Chapter 3, clearly becomes relevant in the present context. In this Part we will examine the operation of the doctrine of precedent in some detail, both in conceptual terms and through each of the superior courts.

9.2 Bindingness, Flexibility and the Rule of Law

First, and without wishing in any way to bypass the discussion which follows, it is worth commenting that a proper understanding of the doctrine of precedent will lead you to the conclusion that in many cases the bindingness, which is alleged to be the basis of the doctrine, is more apparent than real. As Carleton Kemp Allen said:

'Whatever merits precedent may possess (and they are many) certainty is the very last quality which can be attributed to it . . . Nobody knows, until a case has come to trial, what will emerge from all the "authorities" . . . Every lawyer is aware of points on which the authorities are conflicting and obscure, and as precedents multiply, so do the conflicts and obscurities.' (*Case Law: An Unwarrantable Intervention* (1935) 51 LQR 333.)

Second, it follows that a central task facing any discussion of the doctrine of binding precedent is to identify as precisely as possible the extent of the discretion available to the judges in each case. More particularly, it will be apparent that there is a constant tension between the separation of powers (see p. 71), which allows judges sufficient independent discretion to interpret and apply the law on a case-by-case basis, and the rule of law (see p. 62), which requires that people should be able to predict the legal consequences of their conduct with some degree of certainty. Although the attainment of both these objectives may be thought to be desirable, it is nevertheless obvious that there is a significant extent to which they are mutually inconsistent. In other words, a balance must be struck.

Third, this Part will conclude by considering the practice of the European Court of Justice with regard to precedent. This material is useful not only as a necessary foundation on which to study Community law in its own right, but also because a comparative perspective possesses its own value in leading English lawyers to question some of their most basic assumptions as to the operation and desirability of their own traditional doctrine of binding precedent.

9.3   A Wide View of Precedent

The idea of precedent may be formulated in a relatively broad way, by simply saying that it is desirable that similar cases should be decided in a similar manner. This broad view of precedent is based partly on the proposition that consistency is an important element of justice, and partly on the fact that the practice of following previous decisions results in improved efficiency, because points of law which have once been decided can simply be applied subsequently, without being subject to repeated re-argument.

It is not surprising, therefore, that the courts in any developed legal system are likely to follow precedent to a significant extent. Certainly there is nothing peculiarly English about such a practice. However, the idea of precedent may also develop in a rather narrower sense, with the result that courts may regard themselves as being actually bound to follow earlier decisions. The use of precedent in this narrow sense is largely peculiar to English law, although it is also evident to some extent in the other common law jurisdictions which derive from English law.

9.4   A Narrow View of Precedent: the Doctrine of *Stare Decisis*

Those who feel that using Latin tags adds a veneer of learning to what might otherwise sound commonplace sometimes refer to the doctrine of binding precedent as the doctrine of stare decisis. This phrase translates as *to stand by decisions*, and therefore in itself it adds nothing to an understanding of the concept.

Taking a more functional view, at its simplest the doctrine of binding precedent states that all courts bind all lower courts, and some courts may also bind themselves. The two halves of this proposition may respectively be labelled the *vertical* and the *horizontal* dimensions of precedent. We will consider both these dimensions in due course, but before doing so it will be useful to draw a distinction between the doctrine of binding precedent and the doctrine of *res judicata*.

9.5 The Distinction between Binding Precedent and *Res Judicata*

The practical administration of justice in any legal system plainly requires that once a case has been decided the parties should be bound by the decision, because endless reopening of cases is wasteful of resources, as well as creating injustice to those who have to defend themselves repeatedly in respect of the same matter. The point at which finality will be imposed will depend on the detail of any appeal system which may be available, but at some stage the appeals must run out and finality must be imposed. This requirement of finality is provided by the doctrine of res judicata. There is no convenient English equivalent for this phrase, but it may be translated as *the matter has been decided*. The conceptual difference between binding precedent and *res judicata* is simply that the former deals with matters of *law*, while the latter deals with matters of *fact*.

The relationship between the two doctrines is well illustrated by a short series of cases decided during, and shortly after, the Second World War. In order to understand these cases, however, it is necessary to understand something of the law relating to the taxation of certain kinds of legacies.

It is common for testators, when drawing up their wills, to make provision for beneficiaries to receive annual incomes out of the estate. Furthermore, a testator may decide that such an annuity should be 'free of tax', thus ensuring that the beneficiary will continue to receive the same income even if the rate of income tax changes. Of course, a testator has no legal power to dispense exemption from income tax, so, in order to illustrate how these tax-free annuities actually work in practice, it will be useful to look at a hypothetical set of facts. Suppose:

– I leave an annuity of £5000 to X, payable for the rest of his life, and I state it to be free of tax;
– I leave all the other income from my estate to Y for the rest of her life; and
– Five years after my death, income tax is increased.

Because I stated X's annuity to be free of tax, he will continue to receive the benefit of £5000 a year. Nevertheless, the tax has to be paid. In fact, therefore, the loss falls on Y because the increased tax which must be paid on X's £5000 means that the amount of income left for Y is reduced. Since this is what the testator intended, Y will have no legitimate grounds for complaint. Moreover, any decreases in the rate of tax will effectively increase Y's income, so there is a swings-and-roundabouts argument.

However, if unforeseeable circumstances cause a very large increase in the rate of taxation, you could argue that the testator might not have wished the arrangement to continue. This is exactly what happened during the Second World War, when income tax rose from 5s. 6d. in the £ to 10s. in the £ (that is, from 27.5p to 50p). As a result, Parliament included a provision in the Finance Act 1941 to the effect that where this type of 'provision . . . was made before 3 September 1939' the beneficiary would get the annuity free from the first 5s. 6d. of tax, but would have to bear the burden of the increase.

The statutory provision may seem clear enough, but careful consideration of it reveals a problem. What would be the position where the will was made before 3 September 1939, but the death occurred after that date? In other words, when was the provision made in a case such as this? On the one hand it can be argued that a testator who makes a will would probably regard himself as having made provision for the beneficiaries. On the other hand, if a testator wishes to change his will for any reason, he may do so at any time before his death, and therefore it is not until the death that anyone can say with certainty what provision has been made and for whom.

This problem came before the courts on a number of occasions. In *Re Waring, Westminster Bank* v. *Awdrey and Others* [1942] 1 Ch 425, the will had been made before 3 September 1939, but the death did not occur until after that date. There were two annuitants, but only one of them was able to be a party to the case, the other one being in German-occupied Belgium. The Court of Appeal held that the 1941 Act applied, and that therefore the annuities were subject to the top slice of income tax. Another case, involving the same point of law but arising out of a totally separate set of facts, came before the courts in *Berkeley* v. *Berkeley* [1946] AC 555. The House of Lords held that the 1941 Act did not apply, on the basis that provision was not made until the death occurred. In other words the annuitant was protected and the rest of the estate had to bear the whole of the income tax liability.

This decision led to the case of *Re Waring, Westminster Bank* v. *Burton-Butler* [1948] 1 Ch 221, which involved the same will as the previous *Re Waring* case, but this time, the war having ended, both the annuitants were parties. The court held that the annuitant who had been a party to the earlier case was not entitled to the benefit of the House of Lord's decision in *Berkeley*, because the matter was *res judicata* as a result of the earlier case. However, the position of the other annuitant was different because she had not been involved in the earlier case. As far as she was concerned, therefore, the doctrine of binding precedent operated in the ordinary way, so she was entitled to the benefit of the decision in *Berkeley*. Accordingly she received the annuity completely free of tax.

9.6 The Immediacy of Binding Precedent

One thing which might strike you as being rather odd about the *Waring-Berkeley-Waring* saga is that the *Berkeley* decision affected the outcome of the second *Waring* – at least as far as one of the beneficiaries was concerned – even though all the facts of the *Waring* case had occurred before the *Berkeley* decision was made. The retrospective effect of precedent in this kind of situation gives rise to one of the most unattractive aspects of the whole doctrine.

Three judges of the Court of Appeal heard the cases of *Re Schweppes Ltd's Agreement* [1965] 1 All ER 195, and *Re Automatic Telephone and Electric Co Ltd's Agreement* [1965] 1 All ER 206 on the same day. The cases involved different sets of facts, but the point of law was the same in each case. In the first case Willmer LJ dissented, but in the second case he accepted that under the doctrine of binding precedent he was bound by the decision in the first case. In other words, the doctrine of binding precedent operates in such a way that the outcome of a case may depend on the court's statement of the law, even though that statement had not been made when the facts of the case arose.

Precedent operates retrospectively even in criminal cases, as illustrated by the cases of *R* v. *R (Rape: Marital Exemption)* [1991] 4 All ER 481, and *R* v. *W* (Crown Court, unreported). In the first case, R had been charged with attempting to rape his wife. He had argued that English law did not recognize the possibility of a man raping his wife, and therefore he could not be convicted of doing something which was not an offence. The basis of his argument was Sir Matthew Hale's statement, dating from 1736, that

'the husband cannot be guilty of rape committed by himself upon his lawful wife, for by their mutual matrimonial consent and contract the wife hath given herself up in this kind unto her husband which she cannot retract.'

Furthermore, s.1 of the Sexual Offences (Amendment) Act 1976 provides: 'A man commits rape if (a) he has *unlawful* sexual intercourse with a woman who at the time of the intercourse does not consent to it' (emphasis added). Could it be argued that the statutory use of the word 'unlawful' indicated the need for an additional element over and above the lack of consent; and if so, was that additional element the unmarried status of the parties?

When the trial judge ruled against him, the defendant pleaded guilty and was convicted in July 1990. He then pursued the matter by way of appeal. The Court of Appeal (in March 1991) and the House of Lords (in October 1991) both held that the husband could be convicted. They noted that there were already several exceptions to the rule, and concluded that the modern view of the nature of marriage, and of equality within marriage, meant that the old rule had become offensive to the point where it could no longer be sustained. According to Lord Keith, with whom all the other Law Lords agreed, the word 'unlawful' in the 1976 Act is mere surplusage: 'The fact is that it is clearly unlawful to have sexual intercourse with any woman without her consent, and that the use of the word in the subsection adds nothing' He went on to quote, and endorse, the words of Lord Lane CJ at the Court of Appeal stage of the case:

> 'The remaining and no less difficult question is whether . . . this is an area where the court should step aside to leave the matter to the parliamentary process. This is not the creation of a new offence, it is the removal of a common law fiction which has become anachronistic and offensive and we consider that it is our duty having reached that conclusion to act upon it.'

The difficulty with this comment is that, while the outcome of the case may represent a wholly welcome development of the law, from the point of view of the defendant there can surely be no difference between the removal of a pre-existing defence and the imposition of substantive liability. Additionally, of course, the decision affected other cases, notably *R* v. *W*, where the facts alleged to constitute the offence had occurred in February 1989. As in *R* v. *R*, the defendant had pleaded guilty to attempted rape of his wife following a ruling by the trial judge, in April 1991 (i.e. one month after the Court of Appeal's decision in *R* v. *R*) that the traditional doctrine no longer applied. The defendant then lodged an appeal against conviction, but he withdrew his appeal when the House of Lords decided *R* v. *R*.

On the face of it, the retrospectivity contained within this sequence of events could be said to contravene art.7 of the European Convention on Human Rights, which provides:

> '1. No one shall be held guilty of any criminal offence on account of any act or omission which did not constitute a criminal offence under national or international law at the time when it was committed. Nor

shall a heavier penalty be imposed than the one that was applicable at the time the criminal offence was committed.

'2. This Article shall not prejudice the trial and punishment of any person for any act or omission which, at the time when it was committed, was criminal according to the general principles of law recognized by civilized nations.'

However, the European Court of Human Rights found that there was no breach of the Convention, because the defendants could reasonably have foreseen (had they taken legal advice) that the elements of the offence of rape would be changed. Moreover, the

'debasing character of rape was so manifest that . . . [the decisions of the English courts] . . . could not be said to be at variance with the object and purpose of art.7, namely to ensure that no-one should be subjected to arbitrary prosecution, conviction or punishment',

and additionally the rejection of the former doctrine

'was in conformity not only with a civilized concept of marriage, but also, and above all, with the fundamental objectives of the Convention, the very essence of which was respect for human dignity and human freedom.' (*S W* v. *United Kingdom* and *C R* v. *United Kingdom* [1995] *The Times*, December 12.)

Sometimes, however, the retrospective operation of the doctrine of precedent will inhibit the courts from making what would otherwise be a highly desirable decision. In *Prudential Assurance Co Ltd* v. *London Residuary Body* [1992] 3 All ER 504, the House of Lords followed a body of case law concerning a technical aspect of the law relating to leases, but one aspect of Lord Browne-Wilkinson's speech, which both Lord Griffiths and Lord Mustill endorsed, is significant.

'[The] bizarre outcome [of this case] results from the application of an ancient and technical rule of law which requires the maximum duration of a term of years [i.e. a lease] to be ascertainable from the outset. No one has produced any satisfactory rationale for the genesis of this rule. No one has been able to point to any useful purpose that it serves in the present day. If, by overruling the existing authorities, this House were able to change only the law for the future I would have urged your Lordships to do so. But for this House to depart from a rule relating to land law which has been established for many centuries might upset long-established titles [to land]. I must therefore confine myself to

expressing the hope that the Law Commission might look at the subject
to see whether there is in fact any good reason now for maintaining a rule
which operates to defeat contractually agreed arrangements between the
parties (of which all successors in title are aware) and which is capable
of producing such an extraordinary result as that in the present case.'

The case-law makes it clear, therefore, that the retrospective operation of
the doctrine of precedent may or may not inhibit the courts from changing
the law, but leaves unclear which option will be pursued in an individual
case. As Lord Russell said, a party may have 'all the law on his side, but [be]
(in effect) facing the prophets'. (*Sudbrook* v. *Eggleston* [1982] 3 All ER 1.)

In passing, it is worth noticing that the problem typified by the
Prudential Assurance case would vanish if the courts had the power of
prospective overruling, which is discussed at p. 203.

An uncommon, but nevertheless real, difficulty arising from the immediately binding nature of precedent was illustrated in *Hedger* v. *Shutler*
(1942) 139 EG 369. The case turned on the notoriously labyrinthine
provisions of the Rent Acts. A Court of Appeal consisting of MacKinnon
and Goddard LJJ and Lord Clauson dismissed an appeal on 24 April 1942.
On 30 April the case came before the court for a second time, and on this
occasion the appeal was allowed.

'What had happened, it seems, was that after the first decision Goddard
LJ had gone away with an uneasy feeling that the point in question had
been before him on a previous occasion. On looking into it, he found
that only two years earlier in *Tibber* v. *Upcott*, which had not been cited
in *Hedger* v. *Shutler*, a Court of Appeal consisting of Slesser, Luxmoore
and Goddard LJJ had reached a decision which was indistinguishable,
and to the contrary effect. As the order in *Hedger* v. *Shutler* had not
been drawn up, "it was possible for the court to correct the error into
which they fell".' (Megarry, *Miscellany-at-Law*, 1955 revised impression
1958, p. 313.)

It must remain a matter for speculation what the legal position would have
been if someone present in court on 24 April had acted immediately on the
decision.

9.7   Are the Decisions of the Courts Actually Law or Merely Evidence of the Law?

At one level it seems to be obvious that the decisions of the courts do
actually make the law, and there is no shortage of judicial comment to this

effect. For example, in *Attorney-General* v. *Butterworth* [1962] 3 All ER 326, Lord Denning MR said:

'It may be that there is no authority to be found in the books, but, if this be so, all I can say is that the sooner we make one the better . . . I have no hesitation in declaring that the victimisation of a witness is a contempt of court, whether done while the proceedings are still pending or after they have finished.'

Similarly, although in an extra-judicial context, Lord Edmund-Davies said:

'But, like it or not, the fact remains that judges will continue to make law as long as our present system of determining disputes remains . . . The simple and certain fact is that judges inevitably act as legislators.' (*Judicial Activism* in *Current Legal Problems*, 1975, p. 1.)

Inevitability and desirability are, of course, not the same thing, but we will adjourn discussion of the desirability of judicial legislation until Chapter 15. At this stage we will simply ask: if it is abundantly clear that the judges make law, how can anybody raise any doubt in the matter?

The problem is largely constitutional. First, if you cast your mind back to Chapter 4, you will recall the doctrine of the separation of powers, which suggests that the legislative, judicial and executive branches of state power should be exercised by separate agencies. It follows, therefore, that if the courts make law there is a clear breach of the doctrine. Second, the retrospective operation of the doctrine of precedent, as illustrated by the decisions in *Re Schweppes Ltd's Agreement*, and *Re Automatic Telephone and Electric Co Ltd's Agreement* (see p. 129) appears to be a contravention of the rule of law, in the sense that people cannot know, in advance, the legal consequences of their conduct. A final constitutional argument is simply this: if the decisions of the courts are law, why are only some other courts, namely those in the appropriate hierarchical relationship to the deciding courts, bound by those decisions? In other words, if an earlier decision contains the law, those courts which are not bound by it are being placed above the law.

Historically, arguments such as these were generally accepted, and the so-called *declaratory theory* held sway. In his *History of the Common Law*, originally published in 1713, Sir Matthew Hale said:

'[The decisions of the courts cannot] make a law properly so-called, for that only the King and Parliament can do; yet they have great weight and authority in expounding, declaring and pubishing what the law of this Kingdom is, especially when such decisions hold a consonancy and congruity with resolutions and decisions of former times, and though several such decisions are less than a law, yet they are a greater evidence thereof than the opinion of any private persons.' (6th edn, p. 90.)

Subsequently, some commentators began to doubt the validity of the declaratory theory. Probably the most famous dissenting comment came from Austin, who spoke of:

'The childish fiction employed by our judges that judiciary or common law is not made by them, but is a miraculous something, made by nobody, existing, I suppose, from eternity, and merely declared from time to time by the judges.' (*Jurisprudence*, 5th edn, ii, p. 655.)

Nevertheless, even at the end of the nineteenth century, Lord Esher MR said:

'There is in fact no such thing as judge-made law, for the judges do not make the law though they frequently have to apply existing law to circumstances as to which it has not previously been authoritatively laid down that such law is applicable.' (*Willis* v. *Baddeley* [1892] 2 QB 324.)

The argument that the decisions of the courts do not actually make law, but are merely evidence of the law, proceeds by way of an analogy with evidence as to matters of fact, where several witnesses to a factual occurrence may find that their evidence differs depending on their perceptions of what happened.

According to this argument, if the decisions of the courts do actually contain the law the judges should have no difficulty in identifying the law and applying it. Yet dissenting judgements, and judgements which are reversed on appeal, are both commonly encountered. Are these judgements simply wrong, because they are inconsistent with the majority judgements and the appellate judgements respectively? If so, the incidence of incompetence among the judges is remarkably high, especially in the context of a group of people who have reached the pinnacle of their profession.

However, the problem vanishes if the relationship between the judges and the law is equated with the relationship between witnesses and the facts which they observe. Just as different witnesses who all see the same incident may nevertheless give different versions of what happened, so different judges who all use the same legal sources, and who all hear the same arguments, may nevertheless give different versions of what the law is. The differences between the judges, therefore, become matters of perception, rather than of competence. The difficulty with the argument that the decisions of the courts are only evidence of the law are twofold. First, at a purely practical level, there is no doubt that earlier decisions of the courts may govern the decisions of later courts, as we have already seen (at p. 129) in relation to the decisions in *Re Schweppes Ltd's Agreement* and *Re Automatic Telephone and Electric Co Ltd's Agreement.* Although ultimately the question may depend on what we mean by 'law', there is nevertheless clearly at least one sense in which a statement of legal principle which determines the outcome of a case can itself be called 'law'. Second, and more theoretically, in what sense can it be said that the common law exists other than in the decisions of the courts? There is no difficulty is saying that factual events occur, and that witnesses observe them. Variations between the evidence of different witnesses may stem from a variety of factors, including their perception of what happened, without altering the historical facts which they observed.

However, if the parallel between witnesses and judges is to be maintained, it is necessary to show that the rules of common law possess a separate existence, independently of their being articulated by judges, just as historical facts possess a separate existence, independently of their being observed by witnesses. Additionally, any credible argument which is constructed to meet this criticism must also be able to explain how the law, in whatever separate existence it may have, is capable of changing to meet the changing needs of society.

Is it possible to come to a conclusion on the question of whether judges make law, or must the issue simply be left open as a matter for academic speculation? As the arguments outlined in the previous paragraphs have shown, the obvious and practical solution gives rise to some constitutional problems. Yet the alternative solution cannot be said to be without its difficulties. The most promising answer may lie in borrowing a technique from the natural scientists.

More particularly, when physicists are explaining the nature of light, they often find the best explanation involves thinking of light as a wave formation, just like the waves in a pond which result from the throwing of a stone into the water. However, the explanation of light in terms of a wave formation has its limitations. The waves in the pond are a disturbance of the water through which they travel, rather than having any substantial existence themselves. But if light waves have no existence independently of the medium through which they travel, how can physics explain the passage of light across the empty vastness of interplanetary and interstellar space, where there is no matter through which the waves may travel? The answer is that *in order to explain this aspect of light* the model changes, and light is regarded as being a stream of particles rather than a wave formation.

If we adopt and adapt this technique of analysis when seeking to answer the question of whether the decisions of the courts actually are law, or are merely evidence of the law, we find that it is no longer necessary to range the arguments on each side against each other in order to determine which side wins. In fact, as we have seen, even if we do this, we do not emerge with a clear answer. The most useful analysis is simply to say that the answer we give depends on the question we ask. Questions couched in practical terms receive practical answers and those couched in theoretical terms receive theoretical ones.

Summary

1   The doctrine of binding precedent states that all courts bind all lower courts, and some courts also bind themselves.
2   However, in many cases the bindingness is more apparent than real. It follows that we must identify as precisely as possible the extent of the discretion available to the judges in each case.
3   The idea of precedent may be formulated in a relatively broad way, by simply saying that it is desirable that similar cases should be decided in a similar manner.
4   The idea of precedent may also be formulated more narrowly, by saying that similar cases must be decided in a similar way.
5   The practical administration of justice in any legal system plainly requires that once a case has been decided the parties should be bound by the decision. This is achieved by the doctrine of *res judicata*.
6   Binding precedent operates immediately a decision is made, which means that it is effectively retrospective in relation to facts occurring before that time.
7   There is disagreement over whether the decisions of the courts are actually law, or merely evidence of the law. It may be best simply to give practical answers to practical questions and theoretical answers to theoretical questions.

Exercises

1   What is meant by 'precedent' in (a) a broad sense; (b) a narrow sense?
2   Distinguish between binding precedent and *res judicata*.
3   What is meant by saying that the doctrine of binding precedent operates retrospectively?
4   What difficulties are involved in saying that the decisions of the courts make law?

10 *Ratio Decidendi* and *Obiter Dictum*

10.1 Introduction

Although the doctrine of binding precedent states that all courts bind all lower courts and some courts also bind themselves, it would be wrong to conclude that everything contained in a decision is of equal weight. The traditional view is that we have to differentiate between the *ratio decidendi* of a judgement, which will be the binding part, and the *obiter dicta*, which will be the non-binding part. In order to make sense of this statement we must not only analyse what we mean by *ratio decidendi* and *obiter dictum* (which is the singular of *obiter dicta*), but must also consider more precisely what we mean in the present context by *bindingness*. Before doing so, however, we must identify a trap in order to avoid falling into it.

When speaking of the *ratio decidendi* of a case it is tempting to think in terms of a fixed and single entity with an objective and continuing existence, which merely needs to be located and identified, just as a treasure hunter may seek to locate and identify a sunken wreck within a given area of the seabed. As we shall see in the remainder of this chapter, however, this model is seriously misleading. The reality of the situation is that a ratio is a dynamic entity, whose relationship with the cases has been described in literally graphic terms: 'If we think of the rule of law as a line on a graph, then the case itself is like a point through which that line is drawn' (*Salmond on Jurisprudence*, 12th edn, 1966, p. 170). As we shall see in the remainder of this Part, formulating the ratio of a case is a creative enterprise, and one which will often involve choosing between various competing possibilities.

10.2 The Meaning of *Ratio Decidendi*

The phrase *ratio decidendi* may be translated as *the reason for the decision*. Obviously, however, merely attaching a label to a concept, whether the label is expressed in English or Latin, is of little practical utility: *what matters is, how are we to identify the ratio of a case?*

Goodhart's view

One of the most influential commentators on the concept of ratio was Goodhart, whose essay *The Ratio Decidendi of a Case* first appeared in (1930) 40 Yale LJ 161, and was reprinted in 1931 in *Essays in Jurisprudence and the Common Law*, p. 1.

The essence of Goodhart's argument is that the ratio can be discovered by taking into account *the material facts* and *the decision based on those facts*. Furthermore, facts as to *person, time, place, kind* and *amount* are all presumed to be *not material* unless there is good reason to the contrary. Identifying the ratio by reference to the material facts is explicable on the basis that it is reasonable to suppose that both the judge and the advocates were concentrating on the law as it related to those facts, and therefore the quality of those parts of the judgement which relate to the material facts is likely to be higher than the quality of anything else which the judge says. One particular consequence of this is that if a case is decided on a preliminary point of law, before the facts have been established, the weight of the judgement in terms of precedent may be reduced. In *Murphy* v. *Brentwood District Council* [1990] 2 All ER 908, the House of Lords decided that its own previous decision in *Anns* v. *Merton London Borough Council* [1977] 2 All ER 492 had been wrongly decided and should no longer be followed. Lord Mackay LC pointed out that, even though the earlier decision 'was taken after very full consideration by a committee consisting of most eminent members of this House', it was nevertheless

> 'taken as a preliminary issue of law and accordingly the facts had not at that stage been examined in detail and the House proceeded upon the basis of the facts stated in the pleadings supplemented by such further facts and documents as had been agreed between the parties . . . When one attempts to apply the proposition established by the decision to detailed factual situations, difficulties arise.'

The importance of the court receiving full argument was emphasized in *Re Hetherington* [1989] 2 All ER 129, where Sir Nicolas Browne-Wilkinson v-c had to consider whether the High Court was bound by a particular aspect of the decision of the House of Lords in *Bourne* v. *Keane* [1919] AC 815. The House had assumed the point in question to be the law without having had the benefit of any argument on the matter. Having surveyed the case-law generally, the Vice-Chancellor said:

> 'In my judgement the authorities . . . clearly establish that, even where a decision of a point of law in a particular sense was essential to an earlier decision of a superior court, but that superior court merely assumed the

correctness of the law on a particular issue, a judge in a later case is not bound to hold that the law is decided in that sense'.

The importance of the materiality of the facts may, therefore, be thought to be clear enough, but one crucial question remains: *who decides which facts are material – the earlier judge or the later one?* No satisfactory answer to this question can be given without recognizing that the phrase *ratio decidendi* is capable of being used in two distinct ways: *descriptively* and *prescriptively*.

Descriptive and prescriptive ratios

In its *descriptive* sense the phrase *ratio decidendi* is used to *describe the way in which the earlier judge reached the decision*. Clearly, therefore, in this context a later judge must acknowledge the materiality of the facts which the earlier judge treated as being material. However, the crucial question arising from the doctrine of binding precedent in practice is the extent to which later courts are bound by earlier ones. The essential question, therefore, is not *how did the earlier judge come to the decision*, but *what is it in the earlier case which is binding on the later judge?*

The answer to this question lies in identifying the *prescriptive ratio* of the earlier case or, in other words, the statement of law derived from the earlier case which that case *prescribes as being the law for later courts to follow*. Julius Stone's version of the distinction is as succinct as any.

'Should we not . . . try scrupulously to respect the distinction between that use of the term *ratio decidendi* which describes the process of reasoning by which decision was reached (the "descriptive" *ratio decidendi*), and that which identifies and delimits the reasoning which a later court is bound to follow (the "prescriptive" or "binding" *ratio decidendi*)?' (*The Ratio of the Ratio Decidendi* (1959) 22 MLR 597.)

This is not to say that the idea of material facts has become unimportant. As Lord Halsbury LC said in *Quinn* v. *Leathem* [1901] AC 495: 'The generality of the expressions which may be found . . . are not intended to be expositions of the whole law, but govern and are qualified by the particular facts of the case.' But it is to say that the later judge has a vital role in interpreting earlier cases in order to formulate the rule which will then become binding in the present case.

'The truth of the matter is a truth so obvious and trite that it is somewhat regularly overlooked by students. *That no case can have a*

meaning by itself! Standing alone it gives you no guidance. It can give
you no guidance as to how far it carries, as to how much of its language
will hold water later. What counts, what gives you leads, what gives you
sureness, *that is the background of the other cases* in relation to which
you must read this one. They colour the language, the technical terms
used in the opinion. But above all they give you the wherewithal to find
which of the facts are significant, and in what aspect they are significant,
and how far the rules laid down are to be trusted.' (Original emphasis,
Karl Llewellyn, *The Bramble Bush*, 1950, pp. 48–9.)

Similarly, in *Osborne to Rowlett* (1880) 13 ChD 774, Lord Jessel MR said:

'Now, I have often said, and I repeat it, that the only thing in a judge's
decision binding as an authority upon a subsequent judge is the
principle upon which the case was decided: but it is not sufficient that
the case should have been decided on a principle if that principle is not
itself a right principle, or one not applicable to the case; *and it is for a
subsequent judge to say whether or not it is a right principle, and, if not, he
may himself lay down the true principle*. In that case the prior decision
ceases to be a binding authority or guide for any subsequent judge.'
(Emphasis added.)

However, in *Elliott* v. *C (A Minor)* [1983] 2 All ER 1005, Robert Goff LJ,
while acknowledging the legitimacy of subsequent judicial interpretation,
emphasized that the process nevertheless has its limits.

'I feel . . . that I would be lacking in candour if I were to conceal my
unhappiness about the conclusion which I feel compelled to reach. In
my opinion, although of course the courts of this country are bound by
the doctrine of precedent, sensibly interpreted, nevertheless it would be
irresponsible for judges to act as automata, rigidly applying authorities
without regard to consequences. Where, therefore, it appears at first
sight that authority compels a judge to reach a conclusion which he
senses to be unjust or inappropriate, he is, I consider, under a positive
duty to examine the relevant authorities with scrupulous care to
ascertain whether he can, within the limits imposed by the doctrine of
precedent (always sensibly interpreted), *legitimately interpret or qualify
the principle expressed in the authorities to achieve the result which he
perceives to be just or appropriate in the particular case*. I do not disguise
the fact that I have sought to perform this function in the present case.'
(Emphasis added.)

Identifying the appropriate level of generality of the facts

Part and parcel of the process of identifying the material facts of a case is the identification of the appropriate *level of generality*, or *abstraction*. Returning to Llewellyn:

'Each concrete fact of the case arranges itself, I say, as a representative of a much wider abstract category of facts and it is not in itself but as a member of the category that you attribute significance to it. But what is to tell you whether to make your category "Buicks" or "motor cars" or "vehicles"? What is there to make your category "road" or "public highway"? The court may tell you. But the precise point that you have up for study is how far it is safe to trust what the court says. The precise issue which you are attempting to solve is whether the court's language can be taken as it stands, or must be amplified, or whittled down.' (*The Bramble Bush*, 1950, p. 48.)

The more general, or abstract, the statement of the facts is, the greater the number of subsequent cases which will fall within the principle which is being formulated, and therefore the wider the ratio will be. For example, in *Donoghue* v. *Stevenson* [1932] AC 562, the House of Lords held that a manufacturer of ginger beer could be liable to the ultimate consumer of the ginger beer if the ginger beer became contaminated during the manufacturing/bottling process by the presence of a dead snail, and the consumer became ill as a result of drinking the ginger beer. At one extreme, this could be approached on a very specific basis, as a result of which it could be argued that the case is binding only where precisely similar facts recur. On this basis the earlier case would not be binding in a later case where the drink was lemonade. However, it is impossible to see why, as a matter of law, there should be any distinction between ginger beer and lemonade, and therefore any degree of sensitivity to the concerns of the legal process will make it apparent that it would be hopelessly unrealistic to seek to rely on such a distinction. At the very least, the principle of the case must be capable of applying to all items of food and drink.

Putting it another way, formulating the principle in terms of *ginger beer* will produce a very *narrow ratio*, whereas formulating it in terms of *food and drink* will produce a relatively *wide ratio*. Going one stage further and formulating the principle in terms of *manufactured goods* will produce a still *wider ratio*. In fact, shortly after the decision in *Donoghue* v. *Stevenson*, the *manufactured goods approach* was applied by the Privy Council in *Grant* v. *Australian Knitting Mills* [1936] AC 85, so that a manufacturer of woollen underwear was held liable when the garments contained chemicals which caused dermatitis. A yet further extension, beyond the realm of both manufactured goods and physical illness, can be seen in the case of *Hedley Byrne & Co Ltd* v. *Heller & Partners Ltd* [1963] 2 All ER 575, which is discussed more fully at p. 150.

It will be apparent that it is difficult to overstate the importance of identifying the appropriate level of generality when seeking to identify the material facts. In practical terms, the outcome of a case may well depend on the level of generality which the court can be persuaded to accept as being appropriate. In *Scruttons Ltd* v. *Midland Silicones Ltd* [1962] 1 All ER 1, Lord Reid, while attempting to identify the ratio of an earlier case, said: 'If I had to try, the result might depend on whether or not I was striving to obtain a narrow ratio.'

Sometimes the comments of subsequent judges may result in the ratio of a case becoming so narrow that it is effectively confined to its own facts, which is a way of saying that unless absolutely identical facts were to recur – and this, of course, is unlikely to the point of impossibility – the case should never be binding on anyone. (The process of confining a decision to its own facts is also discussed at p. 146.)

The possibility of multiple ratios

So far we have been assuming that a case has a single ratio, but in practice multiple ratios may occur. There are two possibilities. First, a judge may base the decision on more than one line of reasoning. In this situation it is clear from the judgement of Devlin J in *Behrens* v. *Bertram Mills Circus Ltd* [1957] 1 All ER 583 that both ratios will be binding, and that a later court cannot simply pick and choose between them. Second, it is common for there to be more than one judge in an appellate court, and each judge may deliver a fully reasoned judgement. Even if each judgement contains only one ratio, therefore, the case as a whole will contain more than one ratio – unless, of course, all the judges agree fully with each other, which is unlikely if they have all taken the trouble to prepare full judgements. Logically, you might well think that the *Behrens* principle should apply equally in cases of disagreement, and that such a case should simply be treated as having multiple ratios. The reality, however, is that in this situation a later court will take the view that wherever possible one or more of the judgements must be identified as containing the ratio of the case, with the *Behrens* principle being used only as a last resort.

There are two principal possibilities, namely that there will be disagreement on the reasoning, but there will nevertheless be agreement on the result; or there will be disagreement on both the reasoning and the result. Taking these in turn, where there is agreement on the result and a majority agreement as to the reasoning, it is clear that this reasoning should be the ratio of the case as a whole. If there is agreement as to the result, but no majority agreement as to the reasoning, and the individual ratios vary in their width, the decision of the Court of Appeal in *Gold* v. *Essex County Council* [1942] 1 KB 293 establishes that the ratio of the whole case will be the *narrowest* of the individual ratios. If there is agreement as to the result, and the various ratios are simply different – rather than some being wider and some being narrower – logic requires that the case should be treated as having more than one ratio, and the *Behrens* principle reasserts itself.

In the situations mentioned above, it is immaterial which court is involved. However, where there is equal division as to the result, the identity of the court does become relevant, although unfortunately the matter remains less than clear-cut.

Where the House of Lords is equally divided the case of *Beamish* v. *Beamish* (1861) 11 ER 735 established that the decision which is the subject of the appeal is confirmed, and then becomes binding on a subsequent House of Lords. (In practice, of course, an equal division is unlikely to occur, because the Appellate Committee usually consists of an odd number of Law Lords, but death or illness may occur part of the way through a hearing.)

Where the Court of Appeal is equally divided *The Vera Cruz* (1880) 9 PD 96 established that, although the appeal fails, the decision does not then become binding on a subsequent Court of Appeal. The difference between the Court of Appeal and the House of Lords in this respect was said to turn on the greater need for certainty in the latter, because it was the court of last resort. On the other hand, in *Hart* v. *Riversdale Mill Ltd* [1928] 1 KB 176, the Court of Appeal came to the conclusion that the House of Lords' practice in *Beamish* also applied to itself. Unfortunately, however, the authority of *Hart* is open to question, because *The Vera Cruz* was not cited to the court. In *Galloway* v. *Galloway* [1954] P 312, the court resumed its original position, holding that the later court could choose between the ratios of the earlier, equally divided, court. Once again, however, the status of this authority is open to question, since neither *The Vera Cruz* nor *Hart* was cited. Admittedly, as with the House of Lords, it will be rare for the Court of Appeal to be equally divided, since it is usual for an odd number of judges to sit, but it is interesting to note, in passing, that s.54 of the Supreme Court Act 1981 makes provision for appeals against sentence in the Criminal Division of the Court of Appeal to be heard by two judges rather than three. However, the section specifically provides that, in the event of an equal division, the appeal shall be reheard before an odd number of judges, which in practice is usually three. Appeals against sentence are usually the shortest kind of appeals, therefore the time which s.54 could potentially waste is kept to a minimum. In the context of the Divisional Court, *Grocock* v. *Grocock*

[1920] 1 KB 1, establishes that the later court is free to choose between the ratios of an equally divided, earlier one.

In view of the confusing situation revealed in the previous paragraphs, it is tempting to argue that, even where a court has a number of judges, there should be only one judgement. Indeed, this is sometimes effectively the position where there is one leading judgement, with the others being simply short statements of concurrence. In some cases even the short statements of concurrence are omitted, with the leading judgement stated to be 'the judgement of the court'.

Some judges may have a temperamental reluctance to dissent. As the American judge R. H. Jackson J said:

> 'Each dissenting opinion is a confession of failure to convince the writer's colleagues, and the true test of a judge is his influence in leading, not in opposing, his court.' (*The Supreme Court in the American System of Government*, p. 18, quoted by Megarry, *A Second Miscellany-at-Law*, 1973, p. 149.)

However, judges from the Common Law tradition do not generally welcome the idea of single judgements on a compulsory basis. (The continental tradition is different, with single judgements being standard. Not surprisingly, this practice has been adopted by the European Court of Justice and the Court of First Instance: see pp. 79–83.) The Common Law tradition stems partly from the judges' fear that single judgements would often be compromises, and may therefore be lacking in the desired clarity; and partly from the feeling that dissenting judgements can usefully sow the seeds of future legal developments. In the law, as in other subjects, it is not unknown for yesterday's heterodoxy to become tomorrow's orthodoxy. Moreover, Lord Reid saw a particular advantage in multiple judgements:

> 'I think that it is desirable to try to extract from the authorities the principles on which most of them are based. When we are trying to do so, my experience has been that there are dangers in there being only one speech in this House. The statements in it have often tended to be treated as definitions and it is not the function of a court or of this House to frame definitions: some latitude should be left for future developments. The true ratio of a decision generally appears more clearly from a comparison of two or more statements in different words which are intended to supplement each other.' (*Saunders* v. *Anglia Building Society* [1970] 3 All ER 961.)

Occasionally, a case will contain a judgement which dissents in substance but concurs in form. For example, in *R* v. *Mandair* [1994] 2 All ER 715,

Lord Mustill concluded his speech by saying, 'for my part . . . I would have dismissed the appeal, but since your Lordships are of a different opinion I agree with the order proposed.' Applying the usual principle that substance prevails over form it would seem that such a judgement should be regarded as a dissent for academic purposes.

Does every case have a ratio?

In view of the difficulties that can arise in identifying the ratio of a case, it is sometimes tempting to give up, and to simply conclude that a particular case has no ratio. Although such a conclusion will be strictly exceptional, there is some authority to suggest that it is possible. In *The Mostyn* [1928] AC 57, Lord Dunedin said: 'If it is not clear, then I do not think it is part of a tribunal's duty to spell out with great difficulty a *ratio decidendi* in order to be bound by it.' On the other hand, Lord Reid took a more conventional view in *Nash* v. *Tamplin & Sons Brewery (Brighton) Ltd* [1951] 2 All ER 869: 'It matters not how difficult it is to find the *ratio decidendi* of a previous case, that ratio must be found.' Given the enormous flexibility of precedent, this particular difference of opinion is of little practical significance.

10.3   Techniques Used in Handling Ratios

A number of terms have acquired relatively well-defined meanings in the context of describing the way courts handle ratios.

Following, approving and applying

An earlier decision is said to be *followed* in a later case where the facts of the two cases are sufficiently similar for the judge in the later case to be persuaded that the same principle of law should be used. Any court may follow a decision of any other court, but where the later court is higher than the earlier one, the principle may be said not simply to have been *followed* but to have been *approved*. If a later court finds an earlier decision attractive, and the facts of the cases fall short of being substantially the same but can be said to be not dissimilar, the later court may *apply* the earlier decision.

Not following, doubting, disapproving and overruling

An earlier case may not seem attractive to a later court, even though the facts of both cases are substantially the same. Where this happens, and the hierarchical relationship of the courts concerned is such that the later court is not bound by the earlier decision, the later court may *not follow* it. *Not following* may result in the earlier case being said to have been *doubted* or even *disapproved*. If the later court is hierarchically superior to the earlier one, and is satisfied not only that the earlier decision is wrong, but also that it should no longer be followed, the later court may *overrule* the earlier decision, thus depriving it of any power to bind any court in the future.

Distinguishing

In practical terms, however, perhaps the most significant technique of all is *distinguishing*. This takes us back to the idea of material facts. If the material facts of the earlier case, having been formulated at the appropriate level of generality, are not the same as the material facts of the later one, the later court may simply distinguish the earlier one. For example, in *Bridges* v. *Hawkesworth* (1851) LJ 21 QB 75, a customer was held to be entitled to keep money which he had found on the floor of a shop. By way of contrast, in *South Staffordshire Water Company* v. *Sharwood* [1896] 2 QB 44, the finder of two gold rings in the mud at the bottom of a reservoir was held to be not entitled to retain them, because the site of the finding had not been open to the public.

Distinguishing an earlier case is simply a way of saying that it is irrelevant to the later case. Therefore distinguishing does not usually imply any criticism of the correctness of the earlier decision in relation to its own facts, nor does it undermine that decision's bindingness in other cases. However, it is worth noticing that there is one special form of distinguishing which may be taken as implying doubt as to the correctness of the earlier decision. This arises where the later court expresses the view that the earlier decision should be *confined to its own facts*. For example, in *Jobling* v. *Associated Dairies Ltd* [1981] 2 All ER 752, the House of Lords chose not to follow its own earlier decision in *Baker* v. *Willoughby* [1970] AC 467, on a point concerning damages for personal injuries. The House expressed some doubts as to whether the earlier case had been justified by the state of the authorities at the time of that decision, and could therefore have chosen to depart from the decision in exercise of the power conferred upon it by the *Practice Statement (Judicial Precedent)* [1966] 3 All ER 77. However, the decision actually proceeded on the basis that the earlier case should be confined to the status of a decision on its own facts.

Confining cases to the status of being decisions on their own facts is rare and, cases such as *Jobling* notwithstanding, it is likely to occur only where the later court would otherwise be bound to follow a decision which it really cannot tolerate, but from which it can see no other way of escaping within the generally recognized limits of the doctrine of precedent. Such cases may perhaps be most accurately regarded as involving the formulation of a prescriptive ratio in particularly narrow terms. Whether a judge will confine an earlier decision to its own facts, or follow it with great reluctance, is a matter which does not lend itself to easy and accurate prediction.

In addition to the basic terminology which is explained in the preceding paragraphs, two rather more substantial matters must be mentioned, namely the *per incuriam* rule and the *changed circumstances* rule. Both of these rules – or it may be better to think of them as being *doctrines* to avoid implying a degree of rigidity which they do not possess – can be used to justify a decision to ignore a previous, and apparently binding, precedent. We will consider each of them in turn.

The *per incuriam* doctrine

A literal translation of *per incuriam* is simply 'through lack of care'. However, the way the rule works indicates that rather more than mere carelessness is required, as shown by the judgement of Sir John Donaldson MR in *Duke* v. *Reliance Systems Ltd* [1987] 2 All ER 858:

'I have always understood that the doctrine of *per incuriam* only applies where [a court] has reached a decision in the absence of knowledge of a decision binding on it or a statute, and that in either case it has to be shown that, had the court had this material, it must have reached a contrary decision . . . I do not understand the doctrine to extend to a case where, if different arguments had been placed before it, it might have reached a different conclusion.'

More particularly, a decision is not *per incuriam* merely because the judgement does not refer to a statute or a case which the later courts thinks is relevant, because the later court will assume that the earlier court, being aware of all the facts, had good reason for deciding that the statute or case was not relevant. Neither will a decision be *per incuriam* simply because the case was not fully argued. In *Miliangos* v. *George Frank (Textiles) Ltd* [1975] 3 All ER 801, which is discussed more fully at pp. 149 and 171, Lord Simon emphasized that the *per incuriam* doctrine should be 'modestly invoked'.

One complication which can arise in connection with the *per incuriam* doctrine is illustrated by *Rakhit* v. *Carty* [1990] 2 All ER 202. The case concerned a tenancy of a flat, which was let on a furnished basis at a rent of £450 per month. The tenancy was created in 1987, but unknown to either party a fair rent of £550 per year had been registered in 1974, on the basis that the premises were unfurnished. In a dispute over security of tenure one question which arose, therefore, was whether the tenant had been overpaying rent by a substantial amount. The County Court held itself bound by Court of Appeal authorities, dating from 1982 and 1988, to hold, *inter alia*, that the transition from unfurnished to furnished status meant that the fair rent was no longer binding, and that therefore the tenant could not recover the allegedly excess rent. However, under s.67(3) of the Rent Act 1977, the true position was that in these circumstances either party could apply for a re-registration. In the 1988 case, the Court of Appeal had assumed the 1982 decision to be correct, and had therefore followed it, albeit with some reluctance because the court was unhappy with the result. In the present case it was not until the Court of Appeal stage of the proceedings that the 1982 case was shown to have been decided *per incuriam*. Clearly the court was not bound by the first decision, but what about the second one? Lord Donaldson MR said:

> 'The decision in [the 1982 case] was indeed given *per incuriam* . . . However, the same cannot be said of [the 1988 decision]. If, therefore, that court having had all the relevant authorities before it, had concluded that [the 1982 case] was rightly decided, I would have felt bound to follow it, leaving it to the House of Lords to rectify the error. However, I do not think that this court is bound in all cases to follow a previous decision which is based solely on the authority of an earlier decision which was itself given *per incuriam*. In this case we are concerned not only with the rights of the immediate parties, but, indirectly, with those of thousands of landlords and tenants throughout the country. In these exceptional circumstances I think that we are entitled, and should, decline to follow [the 1988 decision].'

It is also significant that Russell LJ felt that departing from the earlier authorities would not work injustice, because the landlord, or at least the landlord's advisers, could have inspected the public register of fair rents and then applied for re-registration.

The changed circumstances doctrine

A useful starting-point when considering the *changed circumstances* doctrine is that it is sometimes identified by the Latin tag *cessante ratione, cessat ipsa lex*. This may be translated as *with the ceasing of the reason for the existence of a legal rule, the legal rule itself ceases to exist*.

This doctrine has acquired particular significance in relation to the practice of the House of Lords when deciding whether to follow or depart from one of their own previous decisions (see Chapter 12). Although it is not limited to this context, it was in such a case that Lord Simon gave the best modern explanation of the rule:

'(1) The maxim in the form *cessante ratione cessat ipsa lex* reflects one of the considerations which your Lordships will weigh in deciding whether to overrule, by virtue of the 1966 declaration, a previous decision of your Lordships' House; (2) in relation to courts bound by the rule of precedent the maxim . . . in its literal and widest sense is misleading and erroneous; (3) specifically, courts which are bound by the rule of precedent are not free to disregard an otherwise binding precedent on the ground that the reason which led to the formulation of the rule embodied in such precedent seems to the court to have lost cogency; (4) the maxim in reality reflects the process of legal reasoning whereby a previous authority is judicially distinguished or an exception is made to a principal legal rule; (5) an otherwise binding precedent or rule may, on proper analysis, be held to have been impliedly overruled by a subsequent decision of a higher court or impliedly abrogated by an Act of Parliament; but this doctrine is not accurately reflected by the citation of the maxim *cessante ratione cessat ipsa lex*.' (*Miliangos* v. *George Frank (Textiles) Ltd* [1975] 3 All ER 801.)

In reality, therefore, it is best to regard the changed circumstances doctrine as a special form of distinguishing. However, unlike ordinary distinguishing which is available to any court, the doctrine does not itself confer a power to depart from a previous decision. All it does is to justify the exercise of the power to depart, provided that the hierarchical aspects of the case are such that that power already exists.

Having considered at some length what is meant by *ratio decidendi*, and how ratios are identified and handled by the courts, we must now move on to a corresponding consideration of the complementary concept of *obiter dictum* (or *obiter dicta* in the plural), which is often referred to simply as *dictum* (or *dicta*).

10.4   The Meaning of *Obiter Dictum*

The distinction between ratio and dictum

The starting-point is that the concept of *obiter dictum* is defined negatively, in the sense that it embraces all those parts of a judgement which are capable of being statements of law but which do not fall within the definition of *ratio decidendi*. The functional distinction, as opposed to the definitional one, is, of course, that *obiter dicta* are not binding. This is explicable on the bases not only that the court may not have heard full argument on the points covered by the dicta, but also that, even where full argument has been received, it is likely that the court will have delivered the dicta without giving them the same careful consideration which would be appropriate to the more central aspects of the case. Although dicta are not binding, it does not follow that they are worthless in terms of the doctrine of precedent. Indeed, it is quite clear that dicta may be persuasive, and that their degree of persuasiveness will vary from virtually nothing to something which in practice is virtually indistinguishable from ratio.

One form of terminology which some commentators employ in an attempt to convey the possible variations in the weight of dicta is *gratis dicta* and *judicial dicta*, although it must be said immediately that this terminology is seldom if ever encountered in the judgements of the courts themselves. *Gratis dicta* are mere throwaways (sayings which are given away, as it were, free) and so of very little, if any, value or persuasive force. It is likely, therefore, that *gratis dicta* will not have been the product of much thought by the judge. *Judicial dicta*, on the other hand, will have been preceded, not only by a great deal of careful thought, but also by extensive argument on the point in question. In reality, therefore, *judicial dicta* may be so strongly persuasive as to be practically indistinguishable from ratio. An example will make the matter clear.

In *Hedley Byrne & Co Ltd* v. *Heller & Partners Ltd* [1963] 2 All ER 575, the facts were that A gave B a banker's reference about C. The reference was stated to have been given 'without responsibility', but B nevertheless relied on it and extended credit to C. The reference was inaccurate and B suffered financial loss as a result. The House of Lords decided that, in principle, there could be liability in negligence for a misstatement resulting in financial loss. However, on the present facts, all the House of Lords needed to do was to say that, even if liability existed in principle, the disclaimer would be effective to prevent B from succeeding against A. Therefore, on the material facts of the case, there was no need to decide whether the liability did actually exist in principle, and it follows that the statement to this effect could be regarded as *obiter*.

Nevertheless, the House of Lords actually examined the issue of principle in great detail, even though on the present facts the disclaimer operated to negative any liability there may have been. It follows that it would be wholly artificial to discount the statement that such liability exists in principle, simply because that statement was not strictly necessary to the actual outcome of the case. As Cairns J said, in *Anderson (W.B.) & Sons Ltd* v. *Rhodes* [1967] 2 All ER 850:

'When five members of the House of Lords have all said after close examination of the authorities that a certain type of tort exists, I think that a judge of first instance should proceed on the basis that it does exist, without pausing to embark on an investigation whether what was said was necessary to the ultimate decision.'

Further support for the artificiality of any strict dichotomy between ratio and dictum may be derived from the Attorney-General's reference procedure under s.36 of the Criminal Justice Act, 1972 (see p. 56). In the present context the difficulty arising from the s.36 reference procedure is that juries simply give a verdict, without identifying their findings of fact or their reasoning based on those facts. Therefore it may well be almost impossible for the Court of Appeal to identify the jury's view of the facts with any degree of precision or certainty.

According to a strict application of the definition of ratio which depends on material facts, therefore, it would seem possible to mount a credible argument to the effect that decisions in s.36 cases cannot have any ratios. On the other hand, however, the creation of the procedure in the first place was clearly based on the assumption that it would produce authoritative rulings, and there is no doubt that in practice the main thrust of a judgement resulting from a s.36 reference is accorded equal status with any other decision of the Court of Appeal.

Is a dissenting ratio a dictum?

As a final point in the discussion of the concept of dictum, we must consider the situation where there is a majority ratio and a dissenting ratio. In terms of the doctrine of precedent, what is the status of the dissent? On the basis of the definition of dictum as being everything which is capable of being a statement of law but which is not ratio, it would appear to follow that a dissenting ratio must be a dictum, since it clearly cannot be the ratio *of the case*. A paradoxical consequence of this conclusion would be that a subsequent court could follow the dissenting ratio. However, this immediately raises the difficulty that the hierarchical relationship between the courts may be such that the subsequent court is bound to follow the majority ratio, and therefore must be unable to follow the minority ratio.

The problem here really arises from being enslaved by the concepts and the words used to express them, rather than dealing with the practical reality. The position is that a later court, whose status in the hierarchy of the courts is such that it is not bound by the decision containing the dissenting judgement, may choose to follow the dissent, if the later court feels the dissent to be more cogent than the majority judgement. However, where the hierarchical relationship is such that the later court is bound by the earlier decision, the later court has no choice but to reject the dissent and accept the majority judgement. From the viewpoint of the subsequent court, therefore, any attempt to analyse this situation in terms of ratio and dictum is at best unhelpful, and may at worst be positively misleading.

Summary

1   Any judgement can be analysed into *ratio decidendi*, which may be said to be the binding part, and *obiter dicta*, which are not binding.
2   More particularly, the *ratio decidendi* is found in the central legal issue of the case. There is a *descriptive ratio*, which is a description of the reasoning adopted by the judge in reaching his conclusion. There is also a *prescriptive ratio*, which is the interpretation which a later judge places on an earlier judgement when deciding whether or not it is binding. It is the *prescriptive ratio* which is *binding*. When formulating the *prescriptive ratio* of a case the judge must identify the *appropriate level of generality* (or *abstraction*) at which the facts of the earlier case should be viewed.
3   There are various techniques which may be used when handling ratios. The ability to *distinguish on the facts* is particularly powerful.
4   *Obiter dicta* are those parts of a judgement which are capable of being statements of law but which are not *ratio*. Although *obiter dicta* are never strictly binding, they may be so strongly persuasive that they are practically binding.

Exercises

1   Distinguish between *ratio decidendi* and *obiter dictum*. Discuss the bindingness of each.
2   Distinguish between *descriptive ratios* and *prescriptive ratios*. Why may they differ? Which one is binding on the later court? Who identifies the *prescriptive ratio*?
3   What is meant by *distinguishing on the facts*?

11 Vertical and Horizontal Dimensions of Precedent

11.1 Introduction

Chapter 3 contains a diagram of the hierarchy of the courts (see p. 47), and Chapter 9 contains the general proposition that all courts bind all lower courts, and that some courts also bind themselves. The first half of this proposition can conveniently be described as the *vertical* dimension of precedent, and the second half as the *horizontal* dimension.

The next three chapters will be devoted to exploring the horizontal dimension in some detail on a court-by-court basis. Although the vertical dimension is much more straightforward, and may appear to involve no more than learning the hierarchy of the courts, it is not wholly without interest, as the remainder of this chapter will demonstrate.

11.2 The Vertical Dimension of Precedent

The House of Lords and the Court of Appeal

In practical terms there is seldom any doubt that the Court of Appeal will hold itself bound by decisions of the House of Lords. Occasionally, however, some challenges to this proposition have emerged, as the following cases show.

In *Conway* v. *Rimmer* [1967] 2 All ER 1260, the issue was whether the Crown could refuse to produce certain evidence which would have been useful to the plaintiff. According to the decision of the House of Lords in *Duncan* v. *Cammell Laird & Co Ltd* [1942] 1 All ER 587, the Crown had an absolute right to withhold the evidence. However, when *Conway* v. *Rimmer* reached the Court of Appeal, Lord Denning MR, albeit in a dissenting judgement, indicated that he thought *Duncan* v. *Cammell Laird & Co Ltd* should not be followed. He was particularly influenced by the fact that the Supreme Courts of many other Commonwealth countries had considered, and rejected, the law contained in that decision, and also by the House of Lords' *Practice Statement on Judicial Precedent* of 1966 (see

p. 161), which at that time had only recently been issued. According to Lord Denning MR: 'The doctrine of precedent has been transformed by the recent statement of Lord Gardiner LC. This is the very case in which to throw off the fetters'.

In fact, as we shall see when we consider the House of Lords' *Practice Statement* in the next chapter, this comment was entirely illegitimate, and was not surprisingly rejected by the House of Lords when *Conway* v. *Rimmer* reached the end of the appellate process. Nevertheless, as an example of an attempt to loosen the formal constraints of the doctrine of binding precedent, the comment is worth noticing.

Another example of wayward decision-making in the Court of Appeal, although on this occasion all three judges concurred, arose in *Broome* v. *Cassell & Co Ltd* [1971] 2 All ER 187. The problem arose out of the court's application of the *per incuriam* doctrine (which is discussed at p. 147) in relation to the House of Lords' decision in *Rookes* v. *Barnard* [1964] 1 All ER 367. The substantive issue involved the availability of exemplary or punitive damages (which are discussed at p. 30), but for the present purposes the point is simply that the Court of Appeal unanimously concluded that the decision of the House of Lords in *Rookes* v. *Barnard* was *per incuriam* because the House had not taken account of two of its own previous decisions. Since a decision which has been validly characterized as being *per incuriam* need not be followed by any subsequent court, it follows that, if this statement by the Court of Appeal was legitimate, the somewhat startling result would be that the lower court had deprived the House of Lords' decision of its authority. When the case went to the House of Lords, as *Cassell & Co Ltd* v. *Broome* [1972] 1 All ER 801, all the Law Lords agreed that it was not open to the Court of Appeal to say that a decision of the House of Lords was *per incuriam*. Viewing the matter in disciplinary terms, Lord Hailsham said:

'It is not open to the Court of Appeal to give gratuitous advice to judges of first instance to ignore decisions of the House of Lords . . . The fact is, and I hope it will never be necessary to say so again, that, in the hierarchical system of courts which exists in this country, it is necessary for each lower tier, including the Court of Appeal, to accept loyally the decisions of the higher tiers.'

The Court of Appeal again found itself in difficulty with the House of Lords in relation to the form in which judgement should be given in a dispute arising from a contract which was expressed in foreign currency. In *Re United Railways of Havana and Regla Warehouses Ltd* [1960] 2 All ER 332, the House of Lords had held that an English court giving judgement in damages must express the amount in sterling, and not in the foreign currency which the parties had specified as the means of payment for the goods under the contract.

The point arose in the Court of Appeal in *Schorsh Meier GmbH* v. *Henning* [1975] 1 All ER 152, where Lord Denning MR and Foster LJ relied on the maxim *cessante ratione cessat ipsa lex* (which is discussed at p. 148), to justify holding that judgements expressed in foreign currency had become permissible. The crucial arguments justifying this conclusion were that sterling was no longer a stable currency; that British membership of the European Economic Community, and more particularly the terms of art.106 of the Treaty of Rome, required the change; and that changes in the standard wording of English judgements meant that the change would not be objectionable on technical grounds. Lawton LJ, however, refused to join his colleagues, preferring to say: 'I stand in awe of the House of Lords . . . It is my duty to apply the law, not to reform it.'

The *Schorsh Meier* case did not go to the House of Lords, but precisely the same point arose very shortly afterwards in *Miliangos* v. *George Frank (Textiles) Ltd* [1975] 3 All ER 801. At first instance, Bristow J, faced with choosing between the House of Lords in *Havana Railways* and the Court of Appeal in *Schorsh Meier*, chose to follow the House of Lords. When the case reached the Court of Appeal, the court, which included Lord Denning MR, unanimously held itself bound by its own decision in *Schorsh Meier*. (When you have considered Lord Denning's record in relation to the self-bindingness of the Court of Appeal, which is discussed in Chapter 13, you may find something odd in his enthusiasm to be bound in this case.) In due course, the House of Lords, with Lord Simon dissenting, upheld the decision of the Court of Appeal as to the result. In other words, the House departed from its earlier decision. However, for the present purposes the main interest of the case lies in some of Lord Simon's observations on the precedent aspects of the case. (The fact that he was dissenting on the merits of the case in relation to the foreign currency point need not detract from the weight of those observations in relation to the precedent point.)

In the first place, Lord Simon criticized the trial judge for following the House of Lords, saying that this meant the trial judge was passing judgement on, and finding fault with, the Court of Appeal:

'It is the duty of a subordinate court to give credence to the decision of the immediately higher court, notwithstanding that it may appear to conflict with the decision of a still higher court. The decision of the still higher court must be assumed to have been correctly distinguished (or otherwise interpreted) in the decision of the immediately higher court.'

Second, however, Lord Simon did say that, once the Court of Appeal had erred in *Schorsh Meier*, it had been right to follow that decision in the present case because the pursuit of self-bindingness in this context would give at least some measure of certainty. Lord Cross agreed with Lord Simon in part, saying that 'it is not for any inferior court . . . to review decisions of this House'. However, he went on to say that 'it was wrong for the Court of Appeal in this case to follow the *Schorsh Meier* decision'.

In passing, it is worth noticing that the *Miliangos* case is also important as the source of Lord Simon's explanation of the operation of the maxim *cessante ratione cessat ipsa lex*. (This aspect of the case is discussed at p. 149.)

Before leaving the topic of the relationship between the Court of Appeal and the House of Lords, it will be instructive to consider the case of *Pittalis* v. *Grant* [1989] 2 All ER 622. The background to the case was that originally the only right of appeal from the County Court to the Court of Appeal was on a point of law. Furthermore, in *Smith* v. *Baker & Sons* [1891–94] All ER Rep 69, the House of Lords had held that a point of law could not be raised on appeal unless it had already been raised at the trial, although a more relaxed view was taken in the case of appeals on points of law from other courts. Section 77(1) of the County Courts Act 1984 amended the law, so that issues of fact could also form the basis of appeals from the County Court to the Court of Appeal. Quite apart from the 1984 reform, however, the common law had itself developed a number of exceptions over the years, up to and including the decision of the Court of Appeal in *Jones* v. *Department of Employment* [1988] 1 All ER 725, where Glidewell LJ, whilst limiting himself to the creation of another exception, indicated that, in the light of the 1984 reform, the basic rule 'may be open to future consideration'. In *Pittalis* v. *Grant* the Court of Appeal took the bull by the horns when Nourse LJ, giving the judgement of the court, said:

'The rule in *Smith* v. *Baker & Sons* ought no longer to be applied. We are conscious that it may seem a strong thing for this court to hold thus of a rule established by the House of Lords, albeit one enfeebled by exceptions, the statutory support which gave it life at last turned off. *But, where it can see that the decision of the higher court has become obsolete, the lower court, if it is not to deny justice to the parties in the suit, is bound to say so and to act accordingly.*' (Emphasis added.)

At a technical level, it must be noted that *Miliangos* was not cited in *Pittalis*, and therefore it is possible to argue that the latter is *per incuriam*. However, it may also be that the decision in *Pittalis*, irrespective of the manner in which it was reached, represents an element of flexibility which is inherent – if strictly exceptional – within the doctrine of precedent.

Additional support for the existence of such flexibility may be derived from the decision of the High Court in *Derby & Co Ltd* v. *Weldon (No 3)* [1989] 3 All ER 118. This case involved a defendant's application to strike out a claim, on the basis that the facts which were alleged (and which of course at that stage must have been hypothetical in the sense that they had not yet been proved) did not disclose a cause of action. Vinelott J held that, where such an application is made on the basis of a recent decision of the Court of Appeal which might be reversed by the House of Lords, the High Court's decision need not be governed by the decision of the Court of Appeal, but may take into account the possibility of that decision's future reversal.

The Court of Appeal and Divisional Courts

There are some ways in which Divisional Courts and the Court of Appeal appear to enjoy approximately equal status. For example, criminal appeals from Divisional Courts go directly to the House of Lords, and there is a substantial overlap of judges who sit in both courts. Nevertheless, it is clear that decisions of the Court of Appeal bind Divisional Courts in both criminal and civil cases (see *Ruse* v. *Read* [1949] 1 KB 370 and *Read* v. *Joannon* (1890) 25 QBD 300 respectively).

Divisional Courts and the Crown Court

The starting point is that the Crown Court is clearly part of the Supreme Court (the current authority being s.1 of the Supreme Court Act 1981). Moreover, in *R* v. *Colyer* [1974] Crim LR 243, the Crown Court held that this gives it equal status with the High Court, which in turn means that it is not bound by a Divisional Court decision. This decision is problematic.

First, the premise is suspect. Section 1 of the1981 Acts provides that 'the Supreme Court of England and Wales shall consist of the Court of Appeal, the High Court of Justice and the Crown Court . . .'. Since the Court of Appeal and the High Court are clearly not co-equals, it is less than self-evident that the statute is conferrring equal status on the High Court and the Crown Court. Second, it is difficult to see why a single judge, whether in the High Court or the Crown Court, should be free to depart from a decision which, in accordance with *Watson*, would be binding on a three-judge High Court. Third, the application of *R.* v. *Colyer* could produce the following, less than logical situation.

Suppose a magistrates' court, which is clearly bound by an appellate decision of the Divisional Court, convicts a defendant, who then appeals to the Crown Court. Such an appeal would be essentially on the facts (see p. 50) but the Crown Court would obviously need to have regard to the law as well, and, according to *Colyer*, it would be free to make a decision at odds with that of the Divisional Court in a previous case. However, if it did so, and the prosecution made the point of law the basis of an appeal to the Divisional Court, the Divisional Court would have to treat its own earlier decision as being binding, thus making the Crown Court stage a waste of time and money. If this genuinely is the way in which the doctrine of precedent operates, it would be reasonable to expect a leapfrog procedure from the Crown Court to the Court of Appeal in civil cases and to the House of Lords in criminal cases. This procedure would, therefore, by-pass the Divisional Court in the same way as the Court of Appeal may be by-passed in civil cases by virtue of the leapfrog procedure contained in s.12 of the Administration of Justice 1969, which is discussed at p. 58. Such a procedure does not exist. The only sensible conclusion seems to be that *R.* v. *Colyer* was wrongly decided and that the Crown Court should accept that it is hierarchically subordinate to the Divisional Court.

11.3   The Horizontal Dimension of Precedent

If a legal system is going to have a doctrine of binding precedent at all it may seem to be reasonably obvious that higher courts will bind lower ones. Furthermore, as we have seen, this *vertical* dimension of precedent raises relatively few difficulties in practice. Unfortunately, the question of whether courts also bind themselves, and if so which courts and to what extent – which we have labelled the *horizontal* dimension of precedent – produces answers which are both less obvious and less straightforward, as the next three chapters will show. However, before progressing to a detailed consideration of the horizontal dimension, it will be convenient to comment on the position of the Judicial Committee of the Privy Council in relation to precedent.

11.4   Precedent in Relation to the Judicial Committee of the Privy Council

The Privy Council does not bind any other court, but the fact that it is almost entirely constituted of Law Lords means that its decisions may be very strongly persuasive. It does not bind itself (*Bakhshuwen* v. *Bakhshuwen* [1952] AC 1), nor is it bound by the House of Lords (*Australian Consolidated Press Ltd* v. *Uren* [1967] 3 All ER 523). In practice, however, it will normally follow both its own decisions and those of the House of Lords.

Summary

1 The proposition that all courts bind all lower courts can be described as the *vertical dimension* of precedent. The proposition that some courts bind themselves can be described as the *horizontal dimension* of precedent.

2 The Court of Appeal almost always accepts that it is bound by the House of Lords, but in wholly exceptional cases it may refuse to follow the House of Lords if it thinks the interests of justice require it to do so.

3 The Court of Appeal binds Divisional Courts.

4 There is authority to the effect that Divisional Courts do not bind the Crown Court, but this authority is suspect.

5 The Judicial Committee of the Privy Council binds neither itself nor any other court. It is not bound by decisions of the House of Lords. However, in practice, its decisions are usually treated as being very strongly persuasive, and it will also usually follow decisions of the House of Lords.

Exercises

1 What is meant by (a) the *vertical* and (b) the *horizontal* dimension of precedent?

2 Why may it be said that the authority which holds that Divisional Courts do not bind the Crown Court is suspect?

12 Does the House of Lords Bind Itself?

12.1 Introduction

This chapter discusses the extent to which the House of Lords is bound to follow its own previous decisions, and the extent to which it ought to be bound to do so. We will see that the House of Lords itself has changed its own position on this question over the years, and that even now there is some uncertainty as to whether civil and criminal cases are to be treated in the same way. It is useful to begin with a brief consideration of the historical perspective.

12.2 The Historical Perspective

Until the mid-nineteenth century the House of Lords took the view that it was not bound by its own previous decisions (*Bright* v. *Hutton* (1852) 3 HLC 341). However, shortly after that decision, in *Beamish* v. *Beamish* (1861) 11 ER 735, the House changed its mind, although the definitive statement of the position at that stage of its evolution is usually taken from the speech of Lord Halsbury LC, nearly 50 years later, in *London Street Tramways Ltd* v. *London County Council* [1898] AC 375:

> 'Of course I do not deny that cases of individual hardship may arise, and that there may be a current of opinion in the profession that such and such a judgment was erroneous; but what is that occasional interference with what is perhaps abstract justice as compared with the inconvenience – the disastrous inconvenience – of having each question subject to being re-argued and the dealings of mankind rendered doubtful by reason of different decisions, so that in truth and in fact there would be no real final court of appeal? My Lords, *interest rei publicae* [i.e. it is in the public interest] that there should be *finis litium* [i.e. an end to litigation] at some time, and there could be no *finis litium* if it were possible to suggest in each case that it might be re-

argued, because it is not "an ordinary case", whatever that may mean. Under these circumstances I am of the opinion that we ought not to allow this question to be re-argued.'

There seems to have been an element of confusion in Lord Halsbury's thinking, since it is the doctrine of *res judicata*, and not the doctrine of precedent, which provides *finis litium*. (The distinction between the two doctrines is explained at pp. 127–9.) However, the matter is of no real consequence since it is abundantly clear that Lord Halsbury's view no longer represents the current position of the House of Lords in relation to its own self-bindingness.

12.3   The Current Position

The Practice Statement of 1966

The Content and Status of the Practice Statement

In 1966, Lord Gardiner LC, with the concurrence of all the other Law Lords, issued a practice statement to the effect that the House was changing its practice in relation to the self-bindingness of its own decisions. The full text of the statement, which is reported under the heading *Practice Statement (Judicial Precedent)* at [1966] 3 All ER 77, is as follows:

'Their Lordships regard the use of precedent as an indispensable foundation upon which to decide what the law is and its application to individual cases. It provides at least some degree of certainty upon which individuals can rely in the conduct of their affairs, as well as a basis for orderly development of legal rules.

'Their Lordships nevertheless recognise that too rigid adherence to precedent may lead to injustice in a particular case and also unduly restrict proper development of the law. They propose therefore to modify their present practice and, while treating former decisions of this House as normally binding, to depart from a previous decision when it appears right to do so.

'In this connection they will bear in mind the danger of disturbing retrospectively the basis on which contracts, settlements of property and fiscal arrangements have been entered into, and also the especial need for certainty as to the criminal law.

'This announcement is not intended to affect the use of precedent elsewhere than in this House.'

A Press Release issued in connection with the Practice Statement said that the new power to depart would be exercised only rarely. By way of an example, it was said that the House might wish to depart where there were changed conditions. The Press Release also pointed out that one of the advantages of the new power was that it would enable the House to take account of the decisions of other superior courts elsewhere in the Commonwealth.

Perhaps the most startling aspect of the contrast between the attitude which the House of Lords developed in the nineteenth century and the 1966 revision of that attitude is that a single factor – the position of the House of Lords as the highest court of appeal – is used to justify diametrically opposed conclusions, namely that it should not, or conversely should, have power to depart from its own previous decisions.

Before turning to the operation of the Practice Statement, there is at least an academic point to be taken in relation to its status and effect. The problem is that, by their very nature, Practice Statements deal with matters of practice rather than law. The use of a Practice Statement to amend the doctrine would seem, therefore, to assume that no more than practice is involved, although, as we shall see (at pp. 186–9) when we consider the self-bindingness of the Court of Appeal, the House of Lords sometimes prefers to regard the content of the doctrine of precedent as being a matter of law.

The Practice Statement in operation

Turning to the way in which the Practice Statement has been put into operation, there is the purely practical point that the *Practice Direction (House of Lords: Preparation of Case)* [1971] 2 All ER 159 requires a party who intends to invite the House to depart from one of its own previous decisions to draw attention to this intention in the appeal documents. The normal practice will then be for a seven-member court to be convened, although five-member courts are not unknown, as evidenced by the decision in *The Johanna Oldendorff*, which is discussed at p. 169. Two other preliminary points of a more conceptual nature also arise.

First, the Practice Statement itself makes no mention of *overruling*, but merely of *departing from*, earlier decisions. This may simply have been natural timidity arising from the constitutional context of what the House was doing, but from the academic perspective, at least, the distinction between *overruling* and *departing from* earlier decisions is not without significance. If a decision is *overruled*, its ratio ceases to have any binding effect whereas, if it is merely *departed from*, the result is that thereafter there are two mutually inconsistent decisions. In this situation, therefore, theoretically at least, a future court may choose between the two decisions. Admittedly, a subsequent court would normally be very reluctant to follow a decision from which the House of Lords had expressly departed. However, this would not necessarily be so if the departure has been on the grounds of changed circumstances, and the circumstances then change back to those which prevailed at the date of the earlier decision. It would seem that, if this situation were to arise, *any* court could choose to follow the earlier decision if it had merely been departed from.

The point appears never to have arisen in practice, but the potential difficulty may be illustrated by speculating on the case of *Yorke Motors v. Edwards* [1982] 1 All ER 1024, where the House of Lords departed from its own decision in *Jacobs v. Booth's Distillery Co* (1901) 85 LT 262. The cases involved the exercise of judicial discretion on a point of High Court procedure, and the House of Lords said that changed circumstances, namely high inflation and high interest rates, which made it more attractive to a creditor to pay late rather than on time, justified departing from the earlier case. The House made it clear that this was not a matter of overruling the earlier decision. It would follow that, if the national economy were to return to a situation in which low inflation and low interest rates prevailed, the earlier decision could in turn be resurrected without overruling the later one.

Although departing from decisions rather than overruling them may, therefore, be an identifiable and legitimate technique, in *Miliangos v. George Frank (Textiles) Ltd* [1975] 3 All ER 801, Lord Simon criticized his colleagues' reluctance to speak of overruling their own decisions: 'I say "overrule" expressly. It is better to avoid euphemisms like "depart from". A wise decision is more likely to be achieved if the reality is faced.' It should also be noted that law reporters have not generally shared whatever qualms the House may have experienced, with the result that headnotes often speak of earlier decisions being *overruled* where the speeches themselves refer only to *departure from* them.

The second preliminary point involves the well-known logical fallacy of *post hoc ergo propter hoc*, which may be translated as 'after this, therefore because of this'. The fallacious nature of the apparent logic is immediately apparent when the phrase is stated baldly, but it is surprisingly easy to lose sight of the fallacy when it is submerged within a complex context. To illustrate the fallacy, however, it is necessary only to take a single, simple example. If I place a bet on a horse which then proceeds to lose miserably, no-one could seriously argue that the placing of the bet had caused the poor performance, and the fact that many a paranoid punter may be tempted to see such a connection does not mean that it is real. Therefore, although it is tempting to think that the Practice Statement must have been the direct causal factor in every House of Lords case since 1966 which has resulted in an earlier decision being not followed, it is in fact perfectly possible to conclude that, even if the Practice Statement had never been issued, the established techniques of handling precedents – especially distinguishing earlier cases – could have resulted in a number of post-1966 cases being decided as they were.

Nevertheless, it is probably true to say that the Practice Statement created a new atmosphere in which the House of Lords was prepared to be more critical of some of its earlier decisions. This explains the apparent discrepancy between the research findings of Paterson and those of Harris. Paterson, in his book *The Law Lords*, published in 1982, concluded that by 1980 there were eight cases in which the House had used the Practice Statement. Harris, in an article entitled *Towards Principles of Overruling – When Should a Final Court of Appeal Second Guess?* (1990) 10 OJLS 135, found only seven instances, despite the fact that his work was undertaken significantly later than Paterson's. Harris explains the discrepancy thus:

'[Paterson] includes cases in which, although in their opinions Law Lords did not indicate that they were overruling, they have, after the event, told him in personal interviews that they consider that that was what they were really doing. Such anecdotal information is of value to the role-analysis in which Paterson is engaged, since it throws light on the psychological significance of the Practice Statement. It cannot be used in the present enquiry, since we are concerned with principles which underlie the reasons actually given in announced instances of the exercise of the power.' ((1990) 10 OJLS, p. 140, n.27.)

Since the Practice Statement itself spoke of the 'especial need for certainty as to the criminal law', it may be useful to consider civil and criminal cases separately.

The leading civil cases

The first case to consider is *Conway* v. *Rimmer* [1967] 2 All ER 1260, where the House of Lords departed from its decision in *Duncan* v. *Cammell Laird & Co Ltd* [1942] 1 All ER 587. In the earlier case the company built a submarine, the *Thetis*, which foundered while undergoing sea trials, with the loss of 99 lives. In the ensuing litigation, the widow of one of the men wanted to have access to the plans and technical specifications of the submarine. The First Lord of the Admiralty objected to their production on the grounds of Crown Privilege (a concept which has since been redefined as Public Interest Immunity). The House of Lords held that in a case like this the relevant Minister should see the documents himself and form a personal opinion. If he did this, the opinion could relate either to a specific document, on the basis that disclosure would injure national defence or good diplomatic relations, or to a class of documents, on the basis that all documents of that class should be protected from disclosure in the interests of the proper functioning of the public service. The mere fact that the Minister did not wish the documents to be disclosed was not sufficient, but, provided he made a decision on the correct basis, the court would not entertain any challenge.

In *Conway* v. *Rimmer*, Conway was a probationary police constable in Cheshire, and Rimmer was a Superintendent. Conway was charged with the theft of a torch and was acquitted. Nevertheless, he was dismissed, whereupon he sued Rimmer for malicious prosecution. Various reports had been prepared on Conway during his time with the police force, and he wanted them to be produced in evidence. The Home Secretary objected to their production on the ground that they were within a class of documents which should be withheld in the interests of the proper functioning of the public service. The House of Lords held that the Home Secretary's claim would be conclusive only if the documents were such that it would obviously be in the public interest that they should be withheld, and on the present facts this was not so. Therefore the court itself should look at the documents and decide whether or not they should be withheld.

Clearly viewing the case as involving departure from the earlier decision, Lord Morris echoed the text of the Practice Statement itself when he said:

'Though precedent is an indispensable foundation upon which to decide what is the law, there may be times when a departure from precedent is in the interests of justice and the proper development of the law.'

However, it is quite clear that, even without the Practice Statement, the House of Lords could have distinguished on the facts between a warship in time of war and a probationary police constable in time of peace, had it wished to do so.

Jones v. *Secretary of State for Social Services* [1972] 1 All ER 145 is of greater significance than *Conway* v. *Rimmer* in terms of the principles of precedent. Under the industrial injuries legislation in force at the time, claims for long-term benefit were determined in two stages, by two different tribunals. In the first place the question was whether an injury had been caused by an accident arising out of employment. If this question were answered in the affirmative, the second stage was to decide the extent of the disablement, and therefore the amount of benefit payable. The legislation stated that the answer to the first question was to be 'final'. In *Re Dowling* [1967] AC 725, the House of Lords had held that the tribunal determining the second question could not re-open consideration of the first question.

In *Jones*, on legislation which was substantially the same as that which was before the court in Dowling, the majority of a seven-member House of Lords decided to follow *Dowling*. On the face of it this decision may appear to be unexceptionable. However, the fact that four Law Lords thought that *Dowling* was wrongly decided, but only three were willing to depart, seems rather odd, and therefore the case requires some closer analysis. Four significant points emerge. First, the House made it clear that the power to depart from earlier decisions should be exercised very sparingly. In other words, the advantage of finality should not be thrown away lightly. Second, it had not been shown that the rule in *Dowling* was causing administrative inconvenience. The other two points are neatly encapsulated in a short passage from Lord Reid's speech:

'I would not seek to categorize cases in which [the Practice Statement] should or cases in which it should not be used. As time passes experience will provide some guide. But I would venture the opinion that the typical case for reconsidering an old decision is where some broad issue is involved, and that it should only be in rare cases that we should reconsider questions of construction of statute or other documents . . . Holding these views, I am firmly of opinion that *Dowling's* case ought not to be reconsidered. No broad issue of justice or public policy is involved nor is any question of legal principle. The issue is simply the proper construction of complicated provisions in a statute. There must be a large number of decisions of this House of this character.'

However, Lord Reid did acknowledge that overruling could actually promote certainty rather than undermining it:

'It is notorious that where an existing decision is disapproved but cannot be overruled courts tend to distinguish it on inadequate grounds. I do not think that they act wrongly in so doing: they are adopting the less bad of the only alternatives open to them. But this is bound to lead to uncertainty for no-one can say in advance whether in a particular case the court will or will not feel bound to follow the old unsatisfactory decision. On balance it seems to me that overruling such a decision will promote and not impair the certainty of the law.'

Returning to the actual decision in *Jones*, it may seem odd that the House of Lords was prepared to follow an earlier decision which it thought was wrong, but a moment's thought indicates the consequences which would flow from the opposite conclusion. As Lord Pearson put it in that case:

> 'If a tenable view taken . . . in the first appeal could be overruled by . . . another tenable view in a second appeal, then the original tenable view could be restored by . . . a third appeal. Finality of decision would be utterly lost.'

The true weight of the second sentence becomes apparent if we envisage a situation in which inconsistencies such as those described in the first sentence can be justified by reference to such a subjective criterion as the rightness or wrongness of the decision in question. In particular, as we shall see in Part III, subjective impressions are often the determinative factors in questions of statutory interpretation, although this comment must not be taken to imply that they are not also important in the field of common law.

Of course, you may wish to argue that, in reality, the degree of uncertainty which is present within the legal system is such that 'finality of decision' has already been lost to a large extent, if not quite 'utterly'. However, even if you do wish to argue this, you may still be willing to concede that there is a distinction between, on the one hand, uncertainty arising from factors such as the varying skills of the lawyers who prepare and present cases, coupled with inevitable variations of judicial psychology on the part of those who decide those cases, and on the other hand, the institutionalization of such uncertainty by the formal adoption of principles of precedent which justify decision-making on the basis of purely subjective criteria.

Fitzleet Estates Ltd v. *Cherry* [1977] 3 All ER 996 is another case involving statutory interpretation. The case involved some complex aspects of liability to income tax. The House of Lords declined to depart from its earlier decision in *Chancery Lane Safe Deposit Co Ltd* v. *I.R.C.* [1966] 1 All ER 1. More particularly, Lord Wilberforce said:

> 'There is therefore nothing left to the appellant but to contend - as he frankly does – that the 1965 decision is wrong. This contention means, when interpreted, that three or more of your Lordships ought to take the view which appealed then to the minority. My Lords, in my firm opinion, the Practice Statement of 1966 was never intended to allow and should not be considered to allow such a course. Nothing could be more undesirable, in fact, than to permit litigants, after a decision has been given by this House with all appearance of finality, to return to this House in the hope that a differently constituted committee might be persuaded to take the view which its predecessors rejected. True that the

earlier decision was by a majority: I say nothing as to its correctness or as to the validity of the reasoning by which it was supported. That there were two eminently possible views is shown by the support for each by at least two members of the House. But doubtful issues have to be resolved and the law knows no better way of resolving them than by the considered majority opinion of the ultimate tribunal. It requires much more than doubts as to the correctness of such opinion to justify departing from it.'

Emphasizing that mere wrongness is not enough, Viscount Dilhorne said: 'If the decision in the *Chancery Lane* case was wrong, it certainly was *not so clearly wrong and productive of injustice as to make it right for the House to depart from it*' (emphasis added).

Although Lord Wilberforce regarded the smallness of the majority in the earlier decision as being irrelevant, it can in fact be argued that this is a factor against overruling or departing from the decision. As Harris says: 'Where dissenting speeches have been delivered, it is more likely that all pertinent reasons were considered than where unanimity prevailed' ((1990) 10 OJLS 135).

The fact that *Jones* and *Fitzleet Estates* both involved statutory interpretation must not be taken to indicate that there is always an absolute prohibition on overruling, or departing from, all earlier decisions in such cases. Thus, in another income tax case, *Vestey* v. *I.R.C. (Nos 1 & 2)* [1979] 3 All ER 976, the House of Lords overruled its own decision in *Congreve* v. *Inland Revenue Commissioners* [1948] 1 All ER 948, on the basis that the earlier court had not envisaged a set of facts such as the present, with the result that the law established by the earlier case gave rise to what Lord Edmund-Davies described as 'startling and unacceptable consequences'. He was also deeply concerned that the only way to achieve justice within the law as established in the earlier case was to allow the Inland Revenue to exercise an unappealable discretion to an extent which he characterized as being 'unconstitutional'. The final point worth noticing in relation to *Vestey* is that Lord Edmund-Davies also said: 'There can be no absolute veto against overruling decisions turning on the construction of statutes or other documents – or indeed any other type of decision.'

The first case in which the House of Lords appears to have relied unequivocally on the Practice Statement is *British Railways Board* v. *Herrington* [1972] 1 All ER 749. The Board knew not only that there was a defective fence alongside one of its electrified railway lines, but also that people habitually took a short-cut across the line and that children frequently played on it. Using the line for the purposes of a short-cut and as a playground were both activities which, in law, amounted to trespass.

The question of the Board's liability to trespassers arose when Herrington, a six-year-old boy, was burnt while playing on the live rail. The difficulty facing Herrington's claim for damages was the decision of the House of Lords in *Addie (Robert) & Sons (Collieries) Ltd* v. *Dumbreck* [1929] AC 358, where a four-year-old boy, who was trespassing at the time, was killed by being crushed in the terminal wheel of a haulage system belonging to the company. The company knew that the equipment was attractive to children. The company's officials had warned the children from time to time, but their warnings were ignored. The accident happened when the machinery was started without taking any precautions to protect any trespassers who might be present. The House of Lords held that the company was not liable because there was no general duty of care to trespassers. The only duty which an occupier of land owed to trespassers was to avoid inflicting harm on them wilfully.

In *Herrington*, the House of Lords was undeterred by *Addie*, and held the Board liable because the presence of a child trespasser on the line was reasonably foreseeable. Nevertheless, the Law Lords showed some equivocation. Lord Wilberforce said: 'The law as stated in *Addie's Case* is developed but not denied: not, I venture to think, developed beyond what is permissible and indeed required of this House in its judicial capacity.' Lord Pearson was a little more forthright, saying that the rule in *Addie* had been rendered obsolete by changed physical and social conditions. As the proportion of the population living in towns increased, so there was a tendency for children to become short of playing space, with a correspondingly increased temptation to trespass. At the same time, technological developments made it ever more likely that trespassing children would encounter dangerous articles. Similarly, Lord Diplock accepted that the present decision meant rejecting the earlier case, but insisted: 'It takes account, as this House as the final expositor of the Common Law should always do, of changes in social attitudes, circumstances and general public sentiment.'

In *The Johanna Oldendorff* [1974] AC 479, the House, by a majority of four to one, overruled its own previous decision in *The Aello* [1960] 2 All ER 578. Both cases turned on the question of when a ship which is let on a charterparty is to be considered to have arrived at a given port, and thus to have become 'an arrived ship'. The earlier case had decided that a ship had not arrived until it was at a place where it could be loaded or unloaded, but in the later case the House preferred to substitute the view that merely being in a position where ships customarily lie while awaiting an available berth is sufficient. This change was thought to create additional certainty which would make it easier for members of the shipping community to know where they stood in individual cases. The dissenting voice was that of Lord Morris, who had been one of the majority in *The Aello*.

One aspect of *The Johanna Oldendorff* which is worthy of comment is that the House took the view that, once it was decided that the earlier case had been wrongly decided, a decision to overrule it would promote certainty rather than undermining it. This was based on Lord Reid's proposition, in his dissenting speech in *Jones* (see p. 166), that, where a case which is acknowledged to be wrong is nevertheless allowed to stand, subsequent courts may well yield to the temptation to distinguish it, even if only on artificial grounds (as indeed Lord Denning MR had done at the Court of Appeal stage of the present case).

In *The Hannah Blumenthal* [1983] 1 All ER 34, the House of Lords refused to depart from its own decision in *The Bremer Vulkan* [1981] AC 909, which had decided that an arbitration agreement could not be treated as having been repudiated even though one of the parties was guilty of inordinate and inexcusable delay. As far as the principles of precedent are concerned, Lord Brandon said:

'It was contended . . . that this was a case in which it would be right . . . to exercise the freedom conferred . . . by the Practice Statement . . . to depart from . . . *Bremer Vulkan* . . . In support of this contention four main points were put forward. The first point was the obvious regret of the two lower courts at the decision, and the consequent efforts of the trial judge and the majority of the Court of Appeal in the present case to find a way round it if they could possibly do so. The second point concerned the observations of Griffiths LJ in his judgement . . . He . . . said that, if he had not had the advantage of reading Lord Diplock's speech in *Bremer Vulkan*, he would have fallen into the same error as the judge of first instance, the Court of Appeal, and the two of their Lordships who dissented in this House in that case . . . The third point was that the decision, if carried to its logical conclusion, would lead to situations arising in which, although a satisfactory trial of a reference was no longer possible, that reference must nevertheless still proceed to trial. The fourth point was that, since actions and arbitrations were alike adversarial in character the same principles with regard to inordinate and inexcusable delay were expected by commercial men to apply, and should as a matter of justice and common sense apply, equally to both.'

Having cited with approval the view which Lord Wilberforce expressed in *Fitzleet Estates* (see p. 167), Lord Brandon continued:

'I express no opinion one way or another as to the conclusion which I might have reached if I had been a member of the Committee which decided the *Bremer Vulkan* case. It is sufficient to say that that decision was reached by what Lord Wilberforce described as the best way of resolving doubtful issues known to the law, and that no special or unusual circumstances have been put forward as justifying a departure from it.

'Dealing specifically with the four points put forward . . . above, I would say this. With regard to the first point, the fact that a decision of your Lordships' House is so unpopular with members of courts below that they are led to seek a way to get round it if they can, reflects greater credit on their independence of mind than on their loyalty to the established and indispensable principle of judicial precedent. With regard to the second point, it is not difficult to understand the reaction of Griffiths LJ, and of solicitors and others engaged in arbitrations, that it seems hard on a party against whom a claim is being made, to oblige himself to ensure that his opponent proceeds with it with proper dispatch. Against that, it is to be remembered that the primary object sought to be achieved by parties who have agreed to refer a dispute between them to arbitration, is that the dispute should be decided on its merits by the arbitral process which they have chosen with reasonable speed, and not that it shall end up, after inordinate and inexcusable delay, by not being decided on its merits by that process at all. With regard to the third point, I do not consider that the consequence flows from the premise. If a claimant is guilty of inordinate and inexcusable delay in the prosecution of a reference to arbitration, the respondent can and should apply to the arbitrator to give peremptory directions to the claimant to end the delay . . . With regard to the fourth point, that illustrates very well the situation described by Lord Wilberforce . . . in *Fitzleet Estates* . . . where two eminently possible views of a question may be taken; where a decision between them has to be made by the best method known to the law; and where, once such a decision has been made, it must for the future be followed and acted upon without the risk of its being later held to have been wrong and departed from on that account. In this connection I would lay stress on what is generally accepted to be the special need for certainty, consistency and continuity in the field of commercial law.'

The case of *Miliangos* v. *George Frank (Textiles) Ltd* [1975] 3 All ER 801, dealing with the earlier case of *Re United Railways of Havana and Regla Warehouses Ltd* [1960] 2 All ER 332, which is discussed at p. 149, becomes relevant again. In the later case the House of Lords decided that an English court can give judgement expressed in terms of foreign currency, notwithstanding the decision to the contrary in the earlier case.

The facts were that the defendant, an English company, agreed to buy a quantity of yarn from the plaintiff, a Swiss national. The contract price was expressed in Swiss francs. The defendant did not pay in accordance with the terms of the contract and the plaintiff sued, claiming the sterling equivalent of the contract price at the date when payment should have been made in accordance with the contract. Before the date of the hearing, however, the value of sterling fell against the Swiss franc, so that conversion of the contract price into sterling would leave the plaintiff significantly worse off in terms of Swiss francs. The question therefore was whether, at the hearing, the plaintiff should be allowed to amend his claim so that it was expressed in Swiss francs.

The crucial argument advanced on behalf of the plaintiff was that sterling was no longer a stable currency, and that therefore justice required that compensation for loss should be expressed in the terms of the currency in which the loss had been incurred. The plaintiff also argued that a technical objection which had previously prevented judgement being expressed in foreign currency and which had been based on the standard wording of the form of English judgements, was no longer valid because the form of judgement had recently been changed. The House of Lords agreed that, as a result of the changed circumstances, judgement could be expressed in foreign currency.

In *R* v. *Secretary of State for the Home Department ex parte Zamir* [1980] 2 All ER 768, the House of Lords held that when an immigration officer has decided that a person is an illegal immigrant, a court which is dealing with a challenge to this decision is limited to considering whether there was evidence on which the immigration officer could reasonably have come to his decision, and could decide whether the decision was actually correct. However, in *R* v. *Secretary of State for the Home Department ex parte Khawaja* [1983] 1 All ER 765, the House – including two members who had decided the earlier case – decided that it had erred in *Zamir*, and that the courts should approach such cases by asking themselves whether the person concerned actually was an illegal immigrant. Lord Scarman said:

> 'My Lords, in most cases I would defer to a recent decision of your Lordships' House on a question of construction, even if I thought it wrong. I do not do so in this context because . . . I am convinced that the *Zamir* reasoning gave insufficient weight to the important – I would say fundamental – consideration that we are here concerned with the scope of judicial review of a power which inevitably infringes the liberty of those subjected to it. This consideration, if it be good, outweighs, in my judgment, any difficulties in the administration of immigration control to which the application of the principle might give rise.'

At a general level, Lord Scarman also considered the effect of that part of the Practice Statement which states that former decisions are 'normally binding', but that there is scope for departing from them 'when it appears right to do so', saying:

'This formula indicates that the House must be satisfied not only that adherence to the precedent would involve the risk of injustice and obstruct the proper development of the law, but also that a judicial departure by the House from the precedent is the safe and appropriate way of remedying the injustice and developing the law. The possibility that legislation may be the better course is one which, though not mentioned in the Practice Statement, the House will not overlook.'

The possibility that legislation may be the better course can be illustrated by *Pirelli General Cable Works Ltd* v. *Oscar Faber and Partners* [1983] 1 All ER 65, which concerned the length of limitation periods after which action in the courts will be time-barred. The general principle is that limitation periods run from the date when the cause of action accrues. The question in the present case was whether an action in tort accrues at the date when damage is done, even though at that date the damage is not discoverable, or only at the subsequent date when the damage was, or could reasonably have been, discovered. The problem is particularly acute in cases involving building works, where defects in construction may not manifest themselves for several years. In following its own previous decision in *Cartledge* v. *Jopling and Sons Ltd* [1963] 1 All ER 341, the House opted for the first alternative, even though it acknowledged that this produced a result which was unreasonable and contrary to principle, because a plaintiff could be time-barred even before any defects became apparent. Despite the fact that the House had not been invited to exercise its powers under the Practice Statement anyway, Lord Fraser, delivering the leading speech, made it plain that this was a situation in which Parliamentary action was more appropriate than judicial law reform. Any change in the law would have to recognize that fairness does not operate only one way, and that potential defendants should be entitled to the benefit of a long-stop provision to provide an absolute cut-off date after which no action could be brought even if the defect had not manifested itself by then. Moreover, he felt it was inappropriate for the courts to seek to introduce this kind of reform.

In *Woolwich Equitable Building Society* v. *Inland Revenue Commissioners* [1992] 3 All ER 737, the building society had paid money by way of tax. When the court subsequently held that the demand for the tax was unlawful, the building society received a refund, together with interest from the date of the judgement establishing the unlawfulness. Not unnaturally, the building society wished to receive interest for the whole of the time it had been out of its money, and not simply for the period following the judgement.

The pre-existing law was against the building society, but the majority of the House of Lords agreed to overturn that law on the basis that common justice required the payment of interest in full, unless the facts of a particular case revealed some overriding issue of policy which justified a contrary result. Any other conclusion would mean that a public authority would have had the benefit of an interest-free loan as the fruit of its unlawful action. On the other hand, the minority view was that reform should be left to Parliament, on the grounds that the matter should be governed by a detailed scheme of a sort which the courts cannot devise and implement.

The point may be further illustrated by *President of India* v. *La Pintada Compania Navigacion SA* [1984] 2 All ER 773, where the House refused to depart from its own decision in *London, Chatham and Dover Railway Co* v. *South Eastern Railway Co* [1893] AC 429, to the effect that a creditor who receives late payment is not entitled to recover interest by way of general damages, even though it felt that the earlier decision was unjust. The basis of the refusal to interfere with the earlier decision was that Parliament had created a statutory regime dealing with the whole topic of interest on damages, and an alteration of the common law would not be coherent with this regime.

The decision in *Murphy* v. *Brentwood District Council* [1990] 2 All ER 908 suggests that the House may be more easily persuaded to depart if the earlier decision was made on a preliminary point of law. The House decided that *Anns* v. *Merton London Borough Council* [1977] 2 All ER 492 was wrongly decided and should be departed from. Lord Mackay LC pointed out:

'[*Anns*] was taken as a preliminary issue of law and . . . the facts had not . . . been examined in detail . . . When one attempts to apply the proposition established by the decision to detailed factual situations, difficulties arise.'

This is, of course, wholly consistent with the explanation of the distinction between ratio and dictum which was given at p. 138.

The proposition, which we first encountered in Chapter 1, that the courts will not allow themselves to become involved in disputes which are academic, in the sense that there is no real issue between the parties, becomes relevant again in the context of the Practice Statement.

In the arbitration case of *Food Corporation of India* v. *Anticlizo Shipping Corporation* [1988] 2 All ER 513, the House refused to overrule *The*

Bremer Vulkan, even though it accepted that the reasoning in the earlier decision was defective, and had led to harmful consequences. The basis of the refusal was that, on the findings of fact which had already been made, the case had only one possible outcome. Lord Goff, having referred *inter alia* to their Lordships' refusal to consider academic points in cases such as *Sun Life Assurance Co of Canada* v. *Jervis* [1944] 1 All ER 469 (see p. 24), went on: '*A fortiori* they should not do so where the inquiry involves a review of a previous decision of your Lordships' House, because it cannot be right to hold, *obiter*, that such a previous decision was wrong'.

The leading criminal cases

At this stage it is appropriate to recall that the Practice Statement itself spoke of the 'especial need for certainty as to the criminal law'. Common sense is sufficient to indicate that the underlying reasoning here is that it is unfair to create criminal liability on a retrospective basis. Unfortunately, however, the House has not always recognized this point, and has even on some occasions argued that, where the law has been incorrectly stated by the House, with the result that some people have been 'wrongly' convicted, the interests of certainty require that such convictions should continue in the future.

In *Shaw* v. *Director of Public Prosecutions* [1961] 2 All ER 446, Shaw had published a booklet which he called *The Ladies' Directory*. This consisted of advertisements which prostitutes inserted and paid for, giving details of the services which were available and the relevant charges. Shaw was convicted of conspiracy to corrupt public morals and the House of Lords upheld the conviction. There was a great deal of academic argument over whether this offence actually existed or whether it had been invented for the occasion, and many people felt that, if given the opportunity to do so, the House would overrule the decision. This opportunity arose in *R* v. *Knuller* [1972] 3 WLR 143, where a journal entitled *International Times* carried advertizements which were intended to bring homosexual men together. In the event, a seven-member House decided to follow *Shaw*.

Four Law Lords said that the 'especial need for certainty' in the criminal law meant that the House must be satisfied that there is a very good reason for departing from an earlier decision, with three of the four also saying that the need for certainty overrides any consideration of how wrong in principle the previous decision may have been. Incredible though it may seem, three Law Lords also said it would be wrong to upset the earlier decision if many convictions have resulted from it. The House gave effect to the principle of comity with Parliament when three of its members said that it is not for the House to abolish a common law offence through the use of the Practice Statement when Parliament has recognized the existence of the offence through a subsequent statute, even if this recognition is only oblique (the reference here being to the Theatres Act 1968, which recognizes the offence of conspiracy to corrupt public morals). It was also relevant that there was controversy over whether the conduct which constituted the offence should be criminal at all. Nevertheless, the House did acknowledge that it would be right to reconsider a decision which has created real uncertainty as to whether an offence exists, but this situation has to be carefully distinguished from the situation where the offence clearly exists and the uncertainty arises merely on the evidence in each case as to whether a particular defendant is guilty.

One of the most unsatisfactory elements of *Knuller* was taken to an extreme by Lord Hailsham LC in *R* v. *Cunningham* [1981] 2 All ER 863. The facts involved the elements of murder. As it happens, the Lord Chancellor accepted the correctness of the earlier, relevant decisions and therefore did not have to consider the operation of the Practice Statement, but he did nevertheless speculate on what he might have thought if he had reached a different conclusion on the merits. Having said he was impressed by the 'wrong conviction' argument in *Knuller*, he went on to say:

'Nor can I disregard the fact that had I reached a different conclusion I should have been saying that between 1957 [the date of a relevant earlier decision] and the abolition of capital punishment for murder, a number of persons . . . would have been executed when they ought only to have been convicted at common law of manslaughter had the trial judge anticipated my putative decision.'

This sounds suspiciously close to saying that once people have been wrongly hanged it is better to continue hanging people wrongly than to admit the error and change the law. If this is so, it would be taking the idea of certainty in the criminal law to depths of inanity which cannot have been in the minds of the framers of the Practice Statement.

In *Anderton* v. *Ryan* [1985] 2 All ER 355, Ryan dishonestly handled a video recorder, genuinely but mistakenly believing it to be stolen. Obviously she could not be convicted of handling stolen goods, because the goods were not stolen, but could she be convicted of attempting to do so? Answering this question in the negative, the House held that, if the goods were not stolen, there could be no offence of handling them, and therefore there could be no attempt to do so. It was, however, widely believed that this decision resulted from the House's failure properly to understand s.1 of the Criminal Attempts Act 1981.

In *R* v. *Shivpuri* [1986] 2 All ER 334, Shivpuri genuinely believed that a certain substance with which he was concerned was a controlled drug, although in fact it was harmless. The question arose as to whether he could be convicted of attempting to be knowingly concerned in dealing with and harbouring a controlled drug. The House of Lords unanimously decided that *Anderton* v. *Ryan* had been wrongly decided. Lord Bridge said: 'If a serious error embodied in a decision of this House has distorted the law, the sooner it is corrected the better'. One of the factors which the House felt to be relevant in justifying the overruling of *Anderton* v. *Ryan* was that

'in the very nature of the case, [no-one] could have acted in reliance on . . . *Anderton* v. *Ryan* in the belief that he was acting innocently and now find that, after all, he is to be held to have committed a criminal offence.' (Lord Bridge.)

In *R* v. *Howe* [1987] 1 All ER 771, the House held that duress is never available as a defence to a charge of murder. This involved overruling the case of *Lynch* v. *Director of Public Prosecutions for Northern Ireland* [1975] 1 All ER 913, and even Lord Hailsham LC agreed that this was appropriate. The main basis of the decision was that *Lynch* had not been justified by authority in the first place, but Lord Mackay LC also said that the reasoning which prevailed in *Shivpuri* should be applied equally in the instant case.

Although it is clear that the House of Lords is prepared to change the law in criminal cases, it is also clear that it is unhappy about *ex post facto* criminalization. This problem is discussed at pp. 129–31, with particular reference to the decision of the European Court of Human Rights in the marital rape cases of *R* v. *R* and *R* v. *W*.

12.4 Is the Use of the Practice Statement Predictable?

Even when the House of Lords was still proclaiming self-bindingness as the established orthodoxy, A.P. Herbert suggested that the decisions of the House of Lords were so unpredictable that they should be regarded as being Acts of God (*Uncommon Law*, 1935, p. 414). Nevertheless, some 20 years later Megarry felt that matters could still get worse. He began by pointing out that within a period of six years the United States' Supreme Court had 'fourteen times reversed one or more earlier decisions of its own, many of them recent' and proceeded to quote the view of the American judge, Roberts J, that such decisions tended 'to bring adjudications of this tribunal into the same class as a restricted railroad ticket, good for this day and train only', before concluding that if the House of Lords were free from the doctrine of precedent 'the variations in the composition of the House when hearing appeals (unlike the fixed composition of the United States' Supreme Court) would doubtless make uncertainty more unsure' (*Miscellany-at-Law*, 1955, revised impression 1958, pp. 321–32.)

In fact, as we have seen, more than a quarter of a century's experience of the Practice Statement in operation indicates that the House of Lords exercises its power to depart from its own decisions with an abundance of caution. Nevertheless, the question remains whether we can predict when departure will occur. Two matters seem to be clear.

First, the House will require the presence of some factor over and above mere wrongness before it will depart from its own previous decisions. Typical examples of such factors are changed circumstances and the recognition of errors of constitutional principle.

Second, among the factors militating against, but not absolutely preventing, departure, the Practice Statement's own emphasis on 'the especial need for certainty as to the criminal law' is now less important than it once was, and may be no more than a specific variant of the general principle that the House will be particularly reluctant to innovate in situations where it thinks many people may have relied on the law as previously understood. However, *Khawaja* (see p. 172) seems to indicate that even this general principle applies only where the reliance has been on the part of the subject, and does not operate where it is the state which has relied on the earlier statement of the law.

12.5   Departure from Previous Decisions without Relying on the Practice Statement

It is obvious that the principles contained in the Practice Statement, as subsequently developed, are usually central to any argument as to whether the House of Lords should depart from one of its own previous decisions. Nevertheless, in *Moodie* v. *Inland Revenue Commissioners* [1993] 2 All ER 49, where the House of Lords departed from its own previous decision in *Inland Revenue Commissioners* v. *Plummer* [1979] 3 All ER 775, Lord Templeman, giving the only substantial speech, expressly renounced reliance on the Practice Statement.

The circumstances were that in *Plummer* the House had upheld the effectiveness of a particular tax avoidance scheme. Subsequently, in *Ramsay (W. T.) Ltd* v. *Inland Revenue Commissioners* [1981] 1 All ER 865, the House took a stricter line, to the effect that schemes consisting of a series of transactions which cancelled each other out, so that they simply generated tax deductible losses on paper without having any substantial effect in the real world, were not effective for tax avoidance purposes. Lord Templeman expressed the position thus:

'If *Plummer's* case had been decided after *Ramsay*, the Crown would have succeeded, though not on any of the grounds advanced in *Plummer*. The present appeals are heard after *Ramsay* and this House is bound to give effect to the principle of *Ramsay*. I do not consider that it is necessary to invoke the 1966 Practice Statement which allows the House "to depart from a previous decision when it appears right to do so" . . . The result in *Plummer's* case (which is a decision of this House) is inconsistent with the later decision in *Ramsay* (which is also a decision of this House). Faced with conflicting decisions, the courts are entitled and bound to follow *Ramsay* because in *Plummer's* case this House was never asked to consider the effect of a self-cancelling scheme and because the *Ramsay* principle restores justice between individual taxpayers and the general body of taxpayers'.

Summary

1   Consideration of the historical perspective is a useful introduction to a discussion of the self-bindingness of the House of Lords.
2   From the mid-nineteenth century until 1966 the House regarded itself as being bound by its own decisions. The Practice Statement of 1966 reaffirmed the importance of the doctrine of binding precedent generally, but indicated that the House would nevertheless be willing to depart from its own decision where it appeared to be right to do so.
3   The House has been restrained in its use of the Practice Statement. In civil cases it is clear that mere wrongness is not enough, and that some additional factor, such as changed circumstances or an issue of principle, is also necessary. In criminal cases the House began by being particularly reluctant to use the Practice Statement, but subsequently it relaxed this attitude to some extent.
4   Experience has shown that the House uses the Practice Statement relatively infrequently, and with a reasonably high degree of predictability.
5   The House may depart from one of its own previous decisions, without relying on the Practice Statement, where it has to choose between earlier, inconsistent decisions of its own.

Exercises

1   What is the gist of the 1966 Practice Statement? Which types of case did it identify as requiring special consideration? Which other types of case (if any) have since been added to the list?
2   Why is mere wrongness not sufficient to justify departure from a previous decision?
3   What, if anything, is the difference between the House of Lords' approach to departing from their own decisions in civil and criminal cases?

13 Does the Court of Appeal Bind Itself?

13.1 Introduction

Having considered the self-bindingness of the House of Lords at some length in the previous chapter, we must now turn to the Court of Appeal. Our primary concern will be to identify the extent to which the court binds itself, but some cases also raise the question of how, if at all, the principles of self-bindingness at this level in the judicial hierarchy differ from those which operate in House of Lords. The bulk of the material in relation to the House of Lords was divided into a consideration of civil cases followed by criminal cases, and the same distinction is also appropriate here.

13.2 The Position in Civil Cases

The leading statement of principle in relation to the self-bindingness of the Court of Appeal in civil cases is found in *Young* v. *Bristol Aeroplane Co Ltd* [1944] 2 All ER 293, where the Court of Appeal held that the court is generally bound by its own previous decisions in civil cases, but went on to say that this proposition is subject to three exceptions, with the possibility of further exceptions being added from time to time.

The first exception arises where the court encounters two conflicting decisions of its own. In this situation the court clearly cannot follow both decisions, and therefore it must choose to follow one and not the other.

The second exception arises where the House of Lords makes a subsequent decision, which does not expressly overrule a decision of the Court of Appeal but which the Court of Appeal nevertheless feels is of such a nature that the two cases cannot stand alongside each other. In such cases the Court of Appeal will decline to follow its own decision. The position is less clear where the inconsistent House of Lords decision precedes the Court of Appeal decision. In this situation it may be possible simply to conclude that the Court of Appeal decision is *per incuriam*. (The *per incuriam* doctrine is discussed at p. 147, and forms the basis of the third exception, which is discussed in the next paragraph.) Certainly, in *R* v. *Terry* [1983] RTR 321, the *Criminal Division* of the Court of Appeal held that in these circumstances it should follow its own decision. (The position in criminal cases generally is discussed at pp. 184–6.)

The third exception is that the court is not bound to follow one of its own decisions if it is satisfied that that decision was given *per incuriam*. It is significant that in *Young* the court felt that for these purposes the doctrine of *per incuriam* should be interpreted liberally, and this was accepted by Lord Evershed MR in *Morelle* v. *Wakeling* [1955] 1 All ER 708, but both cases also expressed the view that liberal interpretations of the doctrine would nevertheless be extremely unusual in practice. In other words, it seems that the version of the doctrine which is discussed at pp. 147–8 will not always be applicable in this context.

For example, in *Williams* v. *Fawcett* [1985] 1 All ER 787, Sir John Donaldson MR indicated that, where the court has made a 'manifest slip or error', the resulting decision may be treated as being *per incuriam* provided that the growth of the error can be clearly detected in earlier cases; the subject-matter involves the liberty of the subject; and the cases are such that they are unlikely to progress to the House of Lords which will, therefore, be denied the opportunity to correct the error.

In *Rickards* v. *Rickards* [1989] 3 All ER 193, the facts were that an ex-husband was aggrieved by a County Court Registrar's order for financial provision in favour of his ex-wife. Having allowed time for an appeal to expire, the ex-husband applied unsuccessfully to a County Court judge for an extension of time. He then appealed to the Court of Appeal, although there were two previous decisions of that court which indicated that the court had no jurisdiction to hear an appeal in the present circumstances. The first case was *Podbery* v. *Peake* [1981] 1 All ER 699, which had been reluctantly treated as being binding in *Bokhari* v. *Mahmood* (unreported). The court held that, despite the earlier decisions, it did have jurisdiction to hear the appeal. The court said that *Podbery* v. *Peake* had taken the well-established principle that the grant or refusal of leave to appeal is itself unappealable, and wrongly applied it to the refusal of an extension of time for appealing. All the judges pointed out that even *Young* itself envisaged further rare exceptions based on unusual applications of the *per incuriam* principle, and Lord Donaldson MR and Balcombe LJ went on to say that *Podbery* v. *Peake* was such a case.

Nicholls LJ, who had been a party to the *Bokhari* decision, said that in that case the court had felt bound by *Podbery*, but had granted leave to appeal to the House of Lords in the hope that their Lordships would correct the error. In the event, the appeal did not proceed, apparently on financial grounds. He went on, forthrightly, to ask:

'[Is] the Court of Appeal . . . bound to go on indefinitely refusing to entertain a particular class of appeals, even though in practice the House of Lords is unlikely to have the opportunity to consider the decision in *Podbery* v. *Peake*? I am so oppressed by the injustice which this might well cause that I cannot think that this is the law today. This would indeed bring the law into disrepute. For the reasons given by Lord Donaldson MR, I think that this case is in a very special category. Both Lord Greene MR (in *Young* v. *Bristol Aeroplane Co Ltd* . . . and Evershed MR (in *Morelle* v. *Wakeling* . . .) envisaged that there might be rare and exceptional cases where the Court of Appeal could properly consider itself entitled not to follow an earlier decision of its own even though the earlier decision did not fall strictly within the normal definition of a decision reached *per incuriam*. This is such a case. In the instant case there are the two features that (a) the point concerns the jurisdiction of the court and (b) the remedy which the system of judicial precedent assumes will be available to review the earlier decision is, for practical reasons, not so available.'

Although the practical reasons for not proceeding with an appeal to the House of Lords will often be financial, this is not always the case. In *Rickards*, the Court of Appeal dismissed the ex-husband's appeal on the merits, on the basis that the County Court judge had made a proper decision to refuse an extension of time in view of the lack of merit in the appeal itself. This led Lord Donaldson MR to say: 'In the light of our decision on the merits of the husband's appeal, he has no incentive to appeal; and the wife, having succeeded, cannot do so.'

The court in *Young* acknowledged that the list of exceptions was capable of extension, and some extensions have undoubtedly occurred. In *Boys* v. *Chaplin* [1968] 1 All ER 283, the court held that a two-judge court dealing with an interlocutory matter does not bind a three-judge court. The precise status of this proposition is open to question as a result of *Langley* v. *North West Water Authority* [1991] 3 All ER 610, where there are dicta to the effect that it is the interlocutory nature of the proceedings rather than the number of judges which is significant. (This is, of course, consistent with the view discussed at p. 138 that judicial observations which are made before the facts have been established are worth less than those made in the light of the facts.)

In *R* v. *Secretary of State for the Home Department ex parte Al-Medhawi* [1989] 1 All ER 777, the Court of Appeal held that, where a case progresses from the Court of Appeal to the House of Lords, and the House of Lords decision proceeds on a basis which renders it unnecessary to decide an issue on which the Court of Appeal made a decision, but without expressing an opinion on the correctness or otherwise of the Court of Appeal's decision on that issue, a subsequent Court of Appeal is not bound by the earlier one in relation to that issue. Assessing the status of this exception is complicated by the fact that, in due course, this case went to the House of Lords, where it is reported at [1989] 3 All ER 843. The House decided the appeal on its merits in such a way that it was unnecessary to comment on the precedent issue which had been before the Court of Appeal, and indeed the House specifically declined to do so. Nevertheless, it is at least arguable that where the House of Lords could have endorsed a statement made in the Court of Appeal but declined to do so, there is a degree of implicit criticism of that statement. On the other hand, this situation may simply provide additional support for the proposition that the principles of precedent are matters of practice, and it is for each court to determine its own practice in this as in other matters. (The question of whether precedent is a matter of law or practice is discussed at pp. 187–9.)

Further evidence of increasing flexibility on the civil side may be found in *R. v. Parole Board and Another ex parte Wilson* (1992) 4 Admin LR 525, where the question was whether a prisoner who was serving a discretionary life sentence (i.e. a sentence which the court had chosen to impose, rather than one which was dictated by law) was entitled to see the reports on him which the Parole Board had considered when deciding not to recommend that he should be released on licence. The background was that *R. v. Secretary of State for the Home Department ex parte Gunnell* (1984, unreported) had established that the common law was against the prisoner, but the European Court of Human Rights had found in favour of Gunnell, and accordingly provisions had been inserted into the Criminal Justice Act 1991 to bring English law into line with the European Convention on Human Rights. Unfortunately for Wilson, however, these provisions were not yet in force. Taking a robust attitude, Taylor LJ, giving the only substantial judgement in the Court of Appeal, held that although the present case could not be distinguished from *Gunnell*, the liberty of the subject and the requirements of natural justice entitled the court not to follow the earlier case, because it would be unjust to the prisoner to make him wait until the relevant provisions of the 1991 Act were brought into force.

Wilson is, of course, a relatively rare example of a civil case in which the liberty of the subject was at stake, although many cases concerning prisoners and immigrants also fall into that category. On the criminal side, however, the liberty of the subject is often said to be the factor which governs the operation of precedent. It is appropriate, therefore, to turn our attention to criminal cases.

13.3   The Position in Criminal Cases

There is authority to the effect that greater flexibility is appropriate on the criminal side of the Court of Appeal than on the civil side, and this is said to be justified by the fact that the liberty of the subject is at stake in criminal cases. For example, in *R* v. *Taylor* [1950] 2 All ER 170, where the court had to consider the earlier decision of *R* v. *Treanor* [1939] 1 All ER 330, Lord Goddard CJ, contrasting the position of the civil and criminal sides of the Court of Appeal, said:

'This court, however, has to deal with . . . the liberty of the subject, and if it finds, on reconsideration, that in the opinion of a full court assembled for that purpose, the law has either been misapplied or misunderstood in a decision which it had previously given, and that on the strength of that decision, an accused person has been sentenced and imprisoned, it is the bounden duty of the court to reconsider the earlier decision with a view to seeing whether that person has been properly convicted. The exceptions which apply in civil cases ought not to be the only ones applied in such a case as the present, and in this particular instance the full court of seven judges is unanimously of the opinion that the decision in *R* v. *Treanor* was wrong.'

In passing, it is interesting to note that the convening of a seven judge court in this case (rather than the usual bench of three judges) appears to reflect the same thinking which manifested itself in the *Practice Direction (House of Lords: Preparation of Case)* [1971] 2 All ER 159, which is discussed at p. 162.

Further evidence of increased flexibility in criminal cases may be found in *R* v. *Gould* [1968] 1 All ER 849, Diplock LJ said that it was proper to overrule where the law had been 'either misapplied or misunderstood in an earlier decision' even though none of the exceptions in *Young* was applicable.

There is similar evidence in relation to sentencing decisions, as evidenced by *R* v. *Newsome* and *R* v. *Browne* [1970] 3 All ER 455, where a five-judge court refused to follow *R* v. *Corr* [1970] *The Times*, 16 January, on a matter concerning suspended sentences.

Unfortunately, there is also authority to the effect that there should generally be no distinction between the criminal and civil sides. It is best to begin with *R* v. *Spencer* [1985] 1 All ER 673, where May LJ said:

'As a matter of principle we respectfully find it difficult to see why there should in general be any difference in the application of the principle of *stare decisis* between the Civil and Criminal Divisions of this court, save that we must remember that in the latter we may be dealing with the liberty of the subject and if a departure from authority is necessary in the interests of justice to an appellant, then this court should not shrink from so acting. In our opinion, *R* v. *Gould* must be read in this sense and subject to this the principles laid down in *Young* v. *Bristol Aeroplane Co Ltd* should apply.'

Although it seems clear that May LJ thought he was redefining the approach which the court should adopt, the precise meaning of what he said is less clear, since the second part of his comment largely detracts from the first part.

In *R* v. *Leaney* [1995] *The Times*, April 11, the Court of Apeal considered *R* v. *Spencer*. The point at issue in *R* v. *Leaney* was whether an appeal lay against a judge's recommendation as to the minimum period which a convicted murderer should spend in prison. The answer depended on whether or not the recommendation was technically part of the sentence, because it was only if it were part of the sentence that it would be appealable. Lord Taylor LCJ, giving the judgement of the court, pointed out that there were three authorities, delivered by three successive Lord Chief Justices from 1966 onwards, all of which were to the effect that the recommendation was not part of the sentence. Additionally Parliament had amended the relevant statutory provision four times, without having created a right of appeal against such a recommendation. Remaining unmoved by *R* v. *Spencer*, the Lord Chief Justice, who acknowledged that the minimum recommendation in the instant case was excessive, said:

'We do not think we should depart from the authorities in the present case having regard not only to the strength and consistency of judicial decisions on the issue over an extended period of time but also to the attitude of the legislature towards those decisions.'

In other words, the court regarded the specified factors as being sufficient to override the interests of doing justice to the individual prisoner. While this was not necessarily wrong (since as we saw at pp. 22–3 the doing of justice to individuals is only one of the considerations with which the law concerns itself) it does cast doubt on the truth of the proposition that the Court of Appeal prefers flexibility in criminal cases because they involve the liberty of the subject.

It is also worth noticing *R* v. *Shoult* [1996] *The Times*, January 23, where the court, headed by the Lord Chief Justice, expressly repudiated a certain observation of the court in *R* v. *Cook* August 17, 1995 (unreported). In *R* v. *Cook* the Court of Appeal had substituted a fine of £500 for a sentence of two months' imprisonment which the Crown Court had imposed for driving when a breath test showed the defendant had 140 micrograms of alcohol per 100 millilitres of blood, as against the legal limit of 35 micrograms per 100 millilitres. Sachs J, giving the judgement of the court, had said:

> 'It can never be appropriate to send a man for this criminality, at the lower end of the scale as it is, to prison. There are other perfectly appropriate ways of dealing with people who drive with excess alcohol.'

In *Shoult*, however, the Lord Chief Justice said that, having consulted the judges who decided the earlier case, 'it was clear that there had been a misunderstanding about the effect of the figure as to the alcohol content of the breath sample', and that whatever may have been the appropriate sentence in the light of the strong mitigation which had been present in that case, the offence had not in reality been at the lower end of the scale. (In fact, the alcohol level was off the top of the Magistrates' Association's *Suggestions for Road Traffic Offence Penalties*.) The result was that the court's statement to the effect that it could never be appropriate to imprison defendants in such cases was only *obiter* and should not be followed.

Dealing with the case before it, the court declined to interfere with a sentence of three-and-a-half years for causing death by careless driving when analysis showed 147 micrograms per 100 millilitres of blood some two hours after the accident. Admittedly, the court in *Shoult* purported to justify its repudiation of the offending observation in the earlier case by classifying it as *obiter*, rather than on any intrinsic flexibility, but analysis of Court of Appeal decisions on sentencing into *ratio decidendi* and *obiter dictum* is unusual, and in any event it is fairly clear from the tone of the judgement that the court regarded the earlier decision as being simply wrong. *R* v. *Shoult* can, therefore, be seen as falling within the tradition of increased flexibility, but not for the traditional reason, since the flexibility was used *against* the interests of the liberty of the subject.

The only safe conclusion is that the position on the criminal side is less than clear.

13.4   Should the Court of Appeal and the House of Lords Apply the Same Principles?

Although the House of Lords' Practice Statement of 1966, which is discussed at length in Chapter 12, clearly stated that 'this announcement is not intended to affect the use of precedent elsewhere than in this House',

Lord Denning MR was quick to argue that the freedom which the House of Lords had assumed for itself was also appropriate for the Court of Appeal. Although, as we have seen, this view has not taken root, it is nevertheless instructive to consider three cases in which the Court of Appeal considered the question of revising the principles of precedent in the Court of Appeal in the light of the Practice Statement.

At the Court of Appeal stage of *Conway* v. *Rimmer* (which is discussed at pp. 164–5), Lord Denning MR said:

> 'My brethren today feel that we are still bound by the observations of the House of Lords in *Duncan* v. *Cammell Laird & Co Ltd* . . . I do not agree. The doctrine of precedent has been transformed by the recent statement of Lord Gardiner LC. This is the very case in which to throw off the fetters.'

In *Gallie* v. *Lee* [1969] 1 All ER 1062, Lord Denning MR, speaking of the Court of Appeal's self-bindingness, said: 'It was a self-imposed limitation: and we who imposed it can also remove it.' But Salmon LJ, albeit with a clearly detectable lack of enthusiasm, took the more traditional view:

> 'I must accept the *law* as stated in the authorities . . . in spite of the fact that it results too often in inconsistency, injustice and an affront to commonsense. The dicta . . . that this court is absolutely bound by its own decisions are very strong . . . It is . . . only by a pronouncement of the whole court that we could effectively alter a *practice* which is so deeply rooted.' (Emphasis added.)

In passing, it is interesting to note that Salmon LJ seems to be confused as to whether the principles of precedent are matters of law or matters of practice.

In *Davis* v. *Johnson* [1978] 1 All ER 1132, Lord Denning MR was more successful in persuading some of his colleagues in the Court of Appeal that precedent should be relaxed. The issue was whether an injunction could be granted under the Domestic Violence and Matrimonial Proceedings Act 1976, where the effect would be to exclude someone from property in which they have a proprietary interest. In two earlier cases the court had said that injunctions were not available in such cases, but in the instant case a majority refused to follow those cases. Lord Denning MR said:

> 'On principle, it seems to me that, while this court should regard itself as normally bound by a previous decision of the court, nevertheless it should be at liberty to depart from it if it is convinced that the previous decision was wrong. What is the argument to the contrary? It is said

that, if an error has been made, this court has no option but to continue the error and leave it to be corrected by the House of Lords. The answer is this: the House of Lords may never have an opportunity to correct the error; and thus it may be perpetuated indefinitely, perhaps for ever.'

He went on to say:

'To my mind, this court should apply similar guidelines to those adopted by the House of Lords in 1966. Whenever it appears to this court that a previous decision was wrong, we should be at liberty to depart from it if we think it right to do so . . . Alternatively, in my opinion, we should extend the principles in *Young* v. *Bristol Aeroplane Co Ltd* when it appears to be a proper case to do so.'

Sir George Baker P agreed that the court should not be bound, but expressed the principle rather more restrictively:

'The court is not bound to follow a previous decision of its own if satisfied that the decision was clearly wrong and cannot stand in the face of the will and intention of Parliament expressed in simple language in a recent Act passed to remedy a serious mischief or abuse, and further adherence to the previous decision must lead to injustice in the particular case and unduly restrict proper development of the law with injustice to others.'

Shaw LJ formulated an even more restrictive principle:

'The principle of *stare decisis* should be relaxed where its application would have the effect of depriving actual and potential victims of violence of a vital protection which an Act of Parliament was plainly designed to afford them, especially where, as in the context of domestic violence, that deprivation must inevitably give rise to an irremediable detriment to such victims and create in regard to them an injustice irreversible by a later decision of the House of Lords.'

Even if we assume that statements such as these are matters of law, and are therefore capable of forming part of the ratio of the case, (and Salmon LJ's use of the term 'dicta' in *Gallie* v. *Lee* supports this assumption) the principles governing the identification of the ratio of a case in which different judges articulate different ratios (see p. 142) make it plain that the very narrow comments of Shaw LJ would be the ratio of this case.

The House of Lords agreed with the Court of Appeal that an injunction could be granted, but disagreed emphatically on the precedent point, saying that the Court of Appeal had been wrong to deviate from the exceptions laid down in *Young*. Lord Diplock accepted that there was a need to balance certainty against undue restriction on development of the law, but he thought that the Court of Appeal should look after certainty, leaving the House of Lords to deal with development. Viscount Dilhorne also thought the two courts were essentially different, and spoke of 'the unique character of the House of Lords sitting judicially'. Lord Salmon offered perhaps the most perceptive comment:

> 'In the nature of things . . . the point [that is, whether the Court of Appeal is bound by *Young*] could never come before your Lordships' House for decision or form part of its *ratio decidendi* . . . I sympathize with the views expressed . . . by Lord Denning MR, but until such time, if ever, as all his colleagues in the Court of Appeal agree with those views, *stare decisis* must still hold the field. I think this may be no bad thing.'

The reason Lord Salmon said the issue could never form part of the ratio in the House of Lords is, of course, quite simply that it can never be strictly necessary for a decision of the House of Lords to deal with the precedent position in the Court of Appeal. However, as we saw in Chapter 10, the reality of the distinction between those parts of a judgement which are binding and those which are not is rather more sophisticated than Lord Salmon seems to imply. (In passing, it is interesting to note that Lord Salmon appears to be assuming here, contrary to his judgement in *Gallie* v. *Lee*, that the principles of precedent are matters of law rather than practice.)

On balance, therefore, it seems that, apart from the decision in *Davis* v. *Johnson* which is of very limited application anyway, the Practice Statement of 1966 did nothing *directly* to change the way in which precedent operates in the Court of Appeal. However, several cases support the proposition that there is a trend towards increased flexibility on the civil side. Furthermore, the decision in *R.* v. *Spencer* notwithstanding, the pre-existing preference for flexibility on the criminal side has remained undiminished. Whether the Practice Statement has contributed indirectly to the current climate of opinion in the Court of Appeal, or whether that climate is simply the product of more fundamental changes in the way the judiciary perceives its role, must remain a matter for speculation.

13.5 The Relevance of the Leapfrog Procedure

Section 12 of the Administration of Justice Act 1969 introduced a procedure, commonly known as *the leapfrog*, enabling certain appeals from the High Court to go directly to the House of Lords, thus bypassing the Court of Appeal altogether. The purpose of the leapfrog is to save time and money.

A leapfrog appeal will be available only where the trial judge certifies that a point of law of general public importance is involved, and either that it arises out of a point of statutory interpretation which was dealt with fully at the trial, or that the point is one on which the trial judge was bound by a decision of the Court of Appeal or the House of Lords, and that the point was dealt with fully in the report of the decision in the Court of Appeal or House of Lords. The certificate of the trial judge is only a preliminary: it is still necessary for either the trial judge or the House of Lords to grant leave to appeal.

The only justification for applying the leapfrog procedure to cases where the trial judge is bound by a decision of the Court of Appeal is that in these cases the Court of Appeal would also be bound by the same decision, and therefore an appeal to that court would be pointless. It is clear, therefore, that Parliament thinks that the Court of Appeal is bound by its own decisions.

Since appeals in criminal cases go straight from the High Court to the House of Lords anyway (see p. 58), the leapfrog procedure is clearly irrelevant in that context.

Summary

1   When discussing the principles governing the self-bindingness of the Court of Appeal it is interesting not only to examine the principles themselves but also the way in which they differ from those governing the House of Lords.

2   In civil cases the Court of Appeal usually considers itself to be bound by its own decisions, in accordance with the principles contained in *Young* v. *Bristol Aeroplane Co Ltd.*

3   Although the House of Lords' Practice Statement does not apply to the Court of Appeal, it may have created a change of atmosphere generally, and there is some evidence of increasing flexibility in the Court of Appeal, although overall *Young* remains the leading authority.

4   It is unclear whether there is greater flexibility on the criminal side than on the civil side.

5   The existence of the leapfrog procedure, which enables some cases to go straight from the High Court to the House of Lords, supports the suggestion that the Court of Appeal binds itself.

Exercise

Identify the extent to which the Court of Appeal binds itself in (a) civil cases; and (b) criminal cases.

14 Does the High Court Bind Itself?

14.1 Introduction

As we saw in Chapter 3, the High Court has three types of jurisdiction, namely first instance, appellate and supervisory. This classification becomes relevant again in the context of the doctrine of precedent because the High Court's attitude to its own decisions will depend to some extent on the jurisdiction which is being exercised. The various jurisdictions will now be considered in turn.

14.2 The First Instance Jurisdiction

Generally

There is a tendency for the High Court, when exercising its jurisdiction at first instance, to follow its own previous decision. For example, in *Poole Borough Council* v. *B. & Q. (Retail) Ltd* [1983] *The Times*, 29 January, Goulding J said that, as a matter of judicial comity, he would follow another High Court decision, even though he was not bound to do so, and even though he seriously doubted its correctness. However, judicial comity is likely to be a less rigid constraint than bindingness, and therefore it is not surprising that conflicting decisions arise from time to time. Obviously, the existence of conflicting decisions will complicate the task of later judges, who will have to choose which one to follow. When this situation arose in *Colchester Estates (Cardiff) Ltd* v. *Carlton Industries plc* [1984] 2 All ER 601, Nourse J took the view that the interests of certainty required that the second decision should normally be regarded as being correct, provided that it had been made after full consideration of the first. At the hearing of the third case, therefore, the judge should refuse to hear argument as to which case should be preferred, and should simply give judgement in accordance with the second decision. The parties would then be left to argue the point fully on appeal. The only exception to this, and it would be rare, would be if the third judge was convinced that the second judge had been wrong in not following the first: for example where some binding or persuasive authority had not been cited in either of the first two cases.

14.3   The Appellate Jurisdiction

The leading case on the self-bindingness of the High Court when exercising its appellate jurisdiction is *Police Authority for Huddersfield* v. *Watson* [1947] 1 KB 842, where it was said that the principles articulated by the Court of Appeal in *Young* v. *Bristol Aeroplane Co Ltd* [1944] 2 All ER 293, which are discussed at p. 180, are equally applicable in the High Court. However, the most basic principle of precedent is that any case must be read in the context within which it was decided, and in *Young* that context was a court whose sole jurisdiction was appellate. Accordingly, the decision in *Watson* leaves open the question of whether the same principles apply when the High Court is exercising its supervisory jurisdiction. (Although appellate and supervisory jurisdictions may look much the same as each other to the untutored eye, there is, in fact, a clear conceptual distinction between them, as we saw at p. 55.)

The question of the High Court's self-bindingness in the context of its supervisory jurisdiction must, therefore, be considered.

14.4   The Supervisory Jurisdiction

The leading case of *R* v. *Greater Manchester Coroner ex parte Tal* [1984] 3 All ER 240 established that the principles formulated in *Young* v. *Bristol Aeroplane Co Ltd* do not apply to a Divisional Court when it is exercising its supervisory jurisdiction, or to put it another way, when it is dealing with an application for judicial review. *A fortiori*, therefore, those principles do not apply to a single judge exercising that jurisdiction. (The concept of a Divisional Court, and the possibility of a single judge exercising the High Court's supervisory jurisdiction are both discussed at p. 53.) The basis of the decision in *Tal* is that the supervisory jurisdiction is effectively at first instance, because it is the legality of the decision-making process which is before the court, rather than the correctness of the decision itself, and it will be the first time that this issue has been considered.

The proposition that the supervisory jurisdiction is effectively at first instance may also be supported, albeit only on a persuasive basis, from certain case law relating to the award of costs against the legal aid fund. The general principle in civil litigation is that the court will order unsuccessful parties to pay the legal costs of their successful opponents.

Obviously this could create difficulty in the case of legally aided parties, who lack the resources to pay their own legal costs, and who cannot therefore be realistically expected to pay anyone else's. Consequently, the Legal Aid Act 1964 introduced the principle, which was re-enacted in the Legal Aid Act 1988, that, where cases brought by legally aided parties fail, the legal aid fund itself could be ordered to pay the costs of successful parties who had not been legally aided. Under the statute, the test to be satisfied before the court can make such an order depends on the nature of the proceedings in respect of which the order is sought. Where the proceedings are at first instance, successful parties must show that they would suffer 'severe financial hardship' if left to bear their own costs; but where the costs relate to proceedings on an appeal the court need be satisfied merely that it would be 'just and equitable' to make the order.

In the case of *R* v. *Leeds County Court ex parte Morris and Another* [1990] 1 All ER 550, where the court was exercising its supervisory jurisdiction, Watkins LJ said that, in the circumstances of the case, the Divisional Court could make such an order. More particularly, the terms 'court of appeal' and 'court of first instance' were not mutually exclusive, and the correct approach was to regard the supervisory jurisdiction as being in a category of its own. He specifically said, of the court exercising such jurisdiction: 'What I am confident it can never, in any circumstances, be called is a court of first instance.' Taking this comment literally, the basis of *Tal* appears to have vanished. However, in *R* v. *Greenwich London Borough Council ex parte Lovelace and Fay* [1991] 3 All ER 511, the Court of Appeal held that, for the purposes of the Legal Aid Act 1988, the supervisory jurisdiction is at first instance, at least in cases dealing with applications for judicial review of decisions of bodies other than courts and tribunals. The court left open the question of whether the same conclusion would be reached in a case where the decision in question had been made by a court, or by a tribunal which is to be regarded as a court under s.18(9) of the Legal Aid Act 1988.

Strictly speaking, of course, the binding authority of *Greenwich* is limited to the statutory context within which it was decided, and this had nothing to do with the doctrine of precedent. Additionally, the suggestion that the identity of the original decision-maker may be relevant seems to be inappropriate in the context of the doctrine of precedent. Nevertheless, the decision may be regarded as having some persuasive value in the present context.

However, even if *Tal* is correct, the High Court has shown no great enthusiasm for using it as a means of changing the law by wholesale departures from previous decisions. In *Hornigold* v. *Chief Constable of Lancashire* [1985] Crim LR 792, the court said that *Tal* had been intended to provide a sensible basis on which the High Court should approach its own previous decisions, and had not been intended to provide a charter under which parties were free to take points which had previously been argued before another court and then re-argue them, simply in the hope that the second court might be persuaded to reach a different conclusion. The court was anxious that allowing such arguments to be advanced would undermine the legal stability which the doctrine of precedent was said to be designed to maintain. The court went on to say that departure from one of its own previous decisions could be justified only if that decision was plainly wrong. Additionally, advocates seeking to persuade the court to undertake such departures must be able, at the outset of their arguments, to indicate how they intend to persuade the court of the wrongness of the earlier decision.

The decision in *R* v. *Secretary of State for the Home Department ex parte Bagga and Others* [1989] *The Times*, 24 May, also shows an unwillingness to entertain the flexibility conferred by *Tal*. Woolf LJ, having regard to a number of earlier Divisional Court decisions, proceeded to grant applications for judicial review on the basis of those decisions, without hearing argument as to their correctness. Counsel for the Home Secretary agreed to reserve his arguments for the Court of Appeal.

However, it must be noted that the tendency of the High Court to follow its own previous decisions in judicial review is a matter of judicial comity (with perhaps a dash of pragmatism) rather than self-bindingness, and need not, therefore, be followed in all cases. For example, in *R* v. *Newcastle-upon-Tyne City Council ex parte Dixon* (1994) 158 LG Rev 441, Auld J dismissed an application for judicial review, holding that disputes between local authorities and care home proprietors as to the terms on which the former would place elderly residents in establishments run by the latter, were essentially contractual and were therefore matters of private law which were not susceptible to judicial review. However, in the substantially similar case of *R* v. *Cleveland County Council ex parte Cleveland Care Homes Association* (1994) 158 LG Rev 641, Potts J came to the opposite conclusion, although he did acknowledge that the argument persented to him had proceeded on a different basis from that which had been presented to Auld J in the previous case.

Summary

1 The High Court's attitude to self-bingingness depends on the type of jurisdiction which is involved.
2 When exercising its first instance jurisdiction the High Court is not bound by its own decisions but will usually follow them out of judicial comity.

3 When exercising its appellate jurisdiction, the High Court follows the principles laid down by the Court of Appeal in *Young* v. *Bristol Aeroplane Co Ltd.* When exercising its supervisory jurisdiction, the position is less clear. However, it appears that this jurisdiction is probably best regarded as being at first instance, in which case there will be no self-bindingness, but judicial comity will usually produce the same result.

Exercise

Identify the factors which determine whether the High Court binds itself.

15 Precedent as a Vehicle for Law Reform

15.1 Introduction

The previous chapters in this Part have all contained material describing and assessing the basic concepts which operate within the doctrine of precedent and the ways in which the courts use, or refuse to use, the doctrine to develop the law. At this stage, however, it will be useful to discuss the practice of judicial law reform as a whole. It is convenient to do so by surveying, in turn, a number of its perceived strengths and weaknesses, before concluding with a consideration of its constitutional limitations.

15.2 Perceived Strengths of Judicial Law Reform

Speed

The first, and most obvious, argument for the doctrine of binding precedent is speed. Subject to the technical and hierarchical aspects of the doctrine, and provided that a suitable case arises, a court may undertake development of the law as soon as the need to do so is identified. As Lord Wilberforce said, in *Miliangos* v. *George Frank (Textiles) Ltd* [1975] 3 All ER 801: 'I am led to doubt whether legislative reform, at least prompt and comprehensive legislative reform . . . is practicable.' Obvious though this argument for the doctrine of binding precedent is, it must not be thought that Parliamentary action is always and necessarily tardy. For example, in *Oxfam* v. *Birmingham City Council* [1975] 2 All ER 289, the House of Lords held that a charity shop was not occupied wholly or mainly for charitable purposes, and therefore was not eligible for the relief from the payment of rates conferred by s.40 of the General Rate Act 1967. The decision rests on the distinction between raising funds for a charity on the one hand, and spending those funds on the purposes of the charity on the other. This decision was clearly correct on a purely technical basis, but nevertheless it was generally regarded as being unfortunate. Almost immediately, Parliament passed the Rating (Charity Shops) Act 1976, which specified certain conditions, subject to which charity shops became eligible for the relief which the House of Lords had denied them.

Similarly, and still within the area of rating law, in *Cresswell* v. *British Oxygen Co Ltd* [1980] 3 All ER 164, the Court of Appeal held that a fish farm was not within the scope of the agricultural exemption from rates conferred by s.25 of the General Rate Act 1967, as amended by the Rating Act 1971. The crux of the matter for the present purposes is that 'livestock' was defined as including 'any mammal or bird kept for the production of food or wool or for the purpose of its use in the farming of land'. Even if the decision was correct on a technical level, it was scarcely defensible at a policy level. Very shortly after the decision, therefore, its effect was negatived by s.31 of the Local Government, Planning and Land Act 1980, which inserted a new provision, s.26A, into the 1967 Act.

In *Prescott* v. *Birmingham Corporation* [1954] 3 All ER 698, the Court of Appeal held that a local authority had no power to give free bus travel to state retirement pensioners. Parliament promptly passed the Public Service Vehicles (Travel Concessions) Act 1955 legalizing such schemes. The consequence of *Fisher* v. *Bell*, which is discussed at p. 258, is also worth noticing as an example of swift Parliamentary action following a judicial decision which was widely perceived to be unfortunate if not actually wrong.

The speedy introduction of amending legislation is nothing new. The Acts of Parliament (Commencement) Act 1793, abolished the pre-existing rule that all the Acts passed in one Parliamentary session were deemed to have come into force at the beginning of that session unless they contained specific provisions to the contrary, and introduced the current presumption that, in the absence of specific provision to the contrary, an Act comes into force at the beginning of the day on which it receives the Royal Assent (see p. 289). The swift passage of the Act of 1793 was prompted by the decision in *Latless* v. *Holmes* (1792) 100 ER 1230, where a statute which made annuities void if they were not registered within 28 days of being granted was held to apply to an annuity granted earlier in the Parliamentary session, even though the 28-day period had expired before the Act was passed.

The fact remains, however, despite the examples which have just been given and a number of other similar cases which could have been mentioned, that law reform undertaken through judicial process will often be swifter than Parliamentary action would be.

Judicial decisions deal with real situations

As the discussion of the concepts of ratio and dictum in Chapter 10 showed, the facts which give rise to a case also provide the basis for the legal essence of the decision. In the present context, this fact-based aspect of precedent is sometimes advanced as an argument for judicial law reform. As Lord Wilberforce said in *Miliangos* v. *George Frank (Textiles) Ltd* [1975] 3 All ER 801: 'Questions as to the recovery of debts or of damages depend so much on individual mixtures of facts and merits as to make them more suitable for progressive solutions in the courts.' Here again, however, the argument is not quite as clear-cut as it may seem, since its corollary is that the courts may decide that the judicial process is not an appropriate vehicle for certain types of reform. The differences of judicial opinion which emerged from the *Pirelli* and *Woolwich* cases, (see p. 173) are instructive in this context. Furthermore, the pitfalls which may await the courts when they make decisions other than on the basis of established facts have already been illustrated by *Murphy* v. *Brentwood District Council* [1990] 2 All ER 908 (see p. 138).

Precedent operates outside the party-political arena

The fact that the doctrine of precedent undoubtedly operates outside the party-political arena is sometimes advanced as an argument in support of the doctrine, since it means that the law can be reformed without the need to find either the party-political will, or the Parliamentary time, which would otherwise be necessary. However, this argument is less clearly in favour of the doctrine of binding precedent than might at first sight appear to be the case, since it is, in effect, the other side of the coin of the constitutional limitations of judicial reform, which are discussed at p. 206.

15.3   Perceived Weaknesses of Judicial Law Reform

The process is haphazard

Whatever strengths the doctrine of precedent may possess, there can be no doubt that one of its weaknesses is that it is haphazard in its operation. There are three main elements in this, namely the need for cases to arise; the way in which cases are argued and decided; and the fact that one party may 'buy off' another. We will now consider these elements in turn.

The need for cases to arise

Law reform through precedent requires not only that an appropriate set of facts must arise, but also that the parties must be willing and able to litigate to a sufficiently elevated point in the hierarchy of the courts to ensure that any existing authorities can be either overruled or at least departed from. As Lord Diplock said, in *Gouriet* v. *Union of Post Office Workers* [1977] 3 All ER 70: 'Courts of justice do not act of their own motion. In our legal system it is their function to stand idly by until their aid is invoked . . .'

The way in which cases are argued and decided

One of the limitations of the adversarial system is that the quality of the decision is to a large extent dependent upon the quality of the argument which is presented to the court. As Lord Wilberforce said, in *Air Canada* v. *Secretary of State for Trade (No 2)* [1983] 1 All ER 910:

'In a contest purely between one litigant and another . . . the task of the court is to do . . . justice between the parties . . . There is no higher or additional duty to ascertain some independent truth. It often happens, from the imperfection of evidence, or the withholding of it, sometimes by the party in whose favour it would tell if presented, that an adjudication has to be made which is not and is known not to be, the whole truth of the matter; yet if the decision has been in accordance with the available evidence, and with the law, justice will have been fairly done.'

The point may be illustrated by *Aswan Engineering Establishment Co* v. *Lupdine Ltd (Thurgar Bolle Ltd, Third Party)* [1987] 1 All ER 135, which raised the question of the extent to which the court can consult extrinsic material when seeking to identify the meaning of a statute. This is considered in more detail at pp. 290–9, but for the present purposes it is sufficient to note that Lloyd LJ said:

'We invited [counsel for Thurgar Bolle] to refer us to the Law Commission Report on Exemption Clauses in Contracts . . . which preceded [the Act in question] and also to the Law Commission Working Paper on the Sale and Supply of Goods . . . But [counsel for the appellants] objected. I can see no conceiveable reason why we should not have been referred to the Law Commission papers, and good reason why we should . . . In my judgement it is not only legitimate but also highly desirable to refer to Law Commission reports on which legislation has been based. But since [counsel for Thurgar Bolle] concurred in [counsel for the appellants'] objection, I can say no more about it.'

Bennion gives this view short shrift:

> 'This dictum reflects the still-lingering idea that civil litigation is a kind
> of joust between the parties, where the court does little more than hold
> the ring. It is surely wrong that any court, as an emanation of the
> judicial power of the Crown, should apply what may not be the law just
> because the parties' counsel acquiesce in this. To find out what the law
> is, the court is not merely entitled but under a duty to have recourse to
> all legitimate sources. If it hands down a judgment based on anything
> but what it believes is truly the law, a court denies its function.
> Moreover the judge or judges involved contravene the judicial oath or
> affirmation requiring them to apply in their judgments "the law and
> usages of this realm".' (*Statutory Interpretation*, 2nd edn, 1991,
> pp. 467–8.)

Unfortunately, this comment assumes that pre-Parliamentary reports are
'legitimate sources', which was, of course, precisely the point at issue.

Despite Bennion's adverse comment, it is clear that Lloyd LJ was merely
reflecting judicial orthodoxy. Speaking of the House of Lords, although
there is no reason in principle why the position should be different in other
courts, Paterson says: '[There is] a shared expectation that a Law Lord in
giving his reasons for deciding for or against the appeal ought to confine
his propositions of law to matters covered by the arguments of counsel'
(*The Law Lords*, 1982, p. 38). However, two further points arise.

First, Paterson's 'shared expectation' falls somewhat short of total
unanimity. For example, Lord Simon was prepared to countenance a
court undertaking its own researches, but felt that, having done so, it
should 'proceed with special caution' (Paterson, *The Law Lords*, 1982,
p. 40). More particularly, it seems that, in an exceptional case where a
judge does undertake his own researches, he must then inform the
advocates of the opinion which he has formed in consequence. In *Hadmor
Productions Ltd* v. *Hamilton* [1982] 1 All ER 1042, Lord Denning MR
consulted *Hansard* (the official record of proceedings in Parliament)
without telling the advocates that he had done so. In due course, Lord
Diplock, giving the judgement of the House of Lords, rebuked Lord
Denning on the basis that he had breached a fundamental principle of
natural justice, namely 'the right of each party to be informed of any point
adverse to him that is going to be relied on by the judge, and to be given an
opportunity of stating what his answer to it is'. Since the decision in
Hadmor the House of Lords has reconsidered the use of *Hansard* (see
p. 293), but this does not affect the validity of Lord Diplock's comment in
principle.

Second, a court which is considering a case has a residual power to ensure that there is an argument. In *R* v. *McFarlane* [1994] 2 WLR 494, the issue was whether the term 'prostitute' is appropriate to describe a woman who takes money by purporting to offer sexual services for payment, when in fact she does not intend to fulfil her side of the bargain and does not do so. The defendant submitted that this made her a clipper rather than a prostitute. Counsel for the prosecution in the crown court agreed with this submission, but the judge did not and a trial ensued. In his summing up to the jury, the trial judge said:

'There are not two categories – a clipper and a prostitute. There are prostitutes who are honest and prostitutes who are dishonest. [The defendant] tells you that she is a dishonest prostitute.'

When an appeal against conviction came before the Court of Appeal, once again counsel on both sides agreed that the defendant's argument was correct, but once again the court disagreed, saying that there was a 'substantial argument' in favour of the trial judge's view. Accordingly, the case was adjourned to be argued by different counsel for the Crown, and eventually the Court of Appeal upheld the conviction.

Quite apart from the way in which cases are argued, their potential as vehicles for law reform may be restricted by the way in which they are decided. More particularly, all the issues raised by a case may not need to be decided, and those which are left undecided may nevertheless involve important issues of principle. *R* v. *Kuxhaus and Others* [1988] 2 All ER 75 involved ss.87 and 88 of the Town and Country Planning Act 1971, which dealt with the powers of local planning authorities to enforce planning control. The basic mechanism was the issue of an enforcement notice; and failure to comply with an enforcement notice was an offence. However, there was a right of appeal against an enforcement notice to the Secretary of State for the Environment, and under s.246 of the Act there was the further possibility of an appeal against the Secretary of State's decision, on a point of law, to the High Court.

Section 88(10) of the Act provided that, 'where an appeal is brought under this section, the enforcement notice shall be of no effect pending the final determination or the withdrawal of the appeal'. In other words, the offence of non-compliance could not be committed until determination or withdrawal of the appeal. On the facts of the case, two issues arose. First, did s.88(10) refer only to the determination or withdrawal of the s.88 appeal, or did it include the s.246 appeal? Second, was the offence of non-compliance one of strict liability, or was *mens rea* required? (The concept of strict liability offences is discussed at pp. 306–11.) Having decided the first point in favour of the defendants, the court did not have to decide – and indeed expressly declined to decide – the strict liability point, which therefore remained open to doubt.

One party may 'buy off' another

The rather cryptic comment that one party may 'buy off' another requires explanation. Briefly, it may well be that the facts of a case involve a small amount of money to one party, but the principle of the case may involve a much larger amount of money to the other party. Suppose, for example, that the holder of an insurance policy is in dispute with the insurance company as to whether a claim for £50 is covered by the policy. The most the policyholder stands to lose, leaving aside the question of costs, is £50. But multiplied out across all the similar policies which the company has issued, the potential cost to the company in terms of other, similar claims may be very considerable indeed.

Against this background, suppose that the policyholder with the £50 claim wins in the County Court but loses in the Court of Appeal. While he is contemplating an appeal to the House of Lords, the company comes to him and says: 'As a gesture of goodwill, and without accepting any legal liability, we will now pay you the £50 you are claiming – on condition that you do not go to the Lords.' The temptation for the policyholder to accept this is obvious, since £50 is all he will get anyway, assuming he wins in the Lords. But if he does accept, the company have had to lay out only £50, and in return they have ensured that the development of the law is arrested at a stage which suits their commercial interests. In reality, the company may also agree to pay the policyholder's legal costs, and they will also have their own legal costs, so the deal may not be quite so attractive to them as the summary given above might indicate. Nevertheless, even when all things are considered, the principle of 'buying off' may be very attractive to one party, and the prospect of being 'bought off' may not be unattractive to the other.

It is difficult to know how widespread the practice is, because in the nature of things there is no official record of the reasons why people decide not to appeal. An additional obstacle to full public knowledge becoming available is that settlements may not only deal with compensation and costs, but may also contain confidence clauses to the effect that the party accepting the settlement must not disclose its terms to third parties. Despite lack of knowledge as to the extent of the practice, however, there is no doubt that it exists, or that it can result in the proper development of the law being stultified in order to serve the best interests of large organizations.

Judicial law reform causes injustice in individual cases

There are two ways in which judicial law reform causes injustice in individual cases. First, it puts the cost of law reform onto the shoulders of individual litigants, with the added twist that it will usually be the loser who pays for having had the law changed in favour of the winner. The principles of costs generally were outlined at p. 30. In the present context the cost point may be self-evident, but it is nevertheless worth identifying explicitly. For example, even if the House of Lords' reform of the law in favour of child trespassers, as introduced by the House of Lords in *British Railways Board* v. *Herrington* [1972] 1 All ER 749 (see p. 168) was a thoroughly good idea, why should the individual landowner be liable for the legal costs involved in securing this reform, as well as the damages?

The solution to this problem is simple enough in principle. The courts could be given power to order that costs should be paid out of public funds in cases involving the development of the law in the general public interest. As it is, however, no such power exists in civil cases, although criminal courts, even down to the level of the magistrates' courts, do have power to award costs out of public funds, and this is not limited to cases involving development of the law. Indeed, leaving aside the possibility of disposing of a case after an art.177 reference to the European Court of Justice (see p. 81), it is difficult to see how a magistrates' court could conceivably be involved in developing the law.

Where one party is effectively the state, in one guise or another, an *ad hoc* solution to the problem could be achieved by that party giving an undertaking to pay all the legal costs of both sides, irrespective of the outcome of the case. This practice has already been adopted by the Inland Revenue in some cases, but even here there is no entitlement to such an undertaking.

The second element of unfairness in individual cases is that precedent operates retrospectively. This point has already been made (see p. 129), but it does raise the question of whether the courts should adopt the practice of prospective overruling, which has found some favour in the American legal system. (See, for example, *Linkletter* v. *Walker* (1965) 381 US 618.) The practice of prospective overruling means that the court decides the present case on the basis of the pre-existing authority, but announces that for the future that authority is overruled and will not be followed again. Such a power would have been useful, for example, in *Prudential Assurance Co Ltd* v. *London Residuary Body and Others* [1992] 3 All ER 504, which was discussed at p. 131.

Although prospective overruling avoids the unfairness of retrospectivity, it may have the practical consequence of deterring some people from litigating in pursuit of law reform, since even if they win the argument in principle they will still lose the case. Admittedly this would apply only to certain types of litigant. Large organizations involved in much litigation of a repetitive nature may find it worth pursuing a point in one case because of the future value of a reforming judgement, but such pursuit of law reform would make unrealistic demands on the altruism of ordinary individuals.

There are other objections to the introduction of prospective overruling. First, at the purely technical level of precedent, any judicial statement that the pre-existing authority was being overruled would necessarily be *obiter*, on the basis that it could not be necessary to the actual decision on the dispute between the parties. It must, however, be conceded that this argument is purely technical, since subsequent courts would doubtless disregard cases which had been prospectively overruled. Second, prospective overruling may be said to be constitutionally objectionable, because it confers naked legislative power upon the courts. Whether or not you find this latter point convincing depends on your assessment of the degree of legislative power which the courts already have, and whether you think it matters if that power is naked or interstitial in nature. The introduction of prospective overruling into the English legal system was canvassed by Lord Simon in both *Jones* v. *Secretary of State for Social Services* [1972] 1 All ER 145 and *Miliangos* v. *George Frank (Textiles) Ltd* [1975] 3 All ER 801 (discussed in their respective contexts at pp. 165 and 171) and supported in principle by Lord Diplock in *Jones*. However, it must be emphasized that the seed sown in these cases has not germinated, and the practice of prospective overruling is quite definitely not part of the English legal system. (The position in the European Court of Justice is noted at p. 215.)

Judges are ill-equipped for the work of law reform

There are at least two elements here, namely lack of training and lack of information.

Lack of training

Judges are promoted from the ranks of practising lawyers who have spent their working lives advising clients and arguing cases on their behalf. It is not surprising that a lifetime of strictly limited horizons tends to produce a similarly limited outlook. As Lord Simon said, in *Miliangos* v. *George Frank (Textiles) Ltd* [1975] 3 All ER 801:

'The training and qualification of a judge is to elucidate the problem immediately before him, so that its features stand out in stereoscopic clarity. But the beam of light which so illuminates the immediate scene seems to throw surrounding areas into greater obscurity; the whole landscape is distorted to the view . . . The very qualifications for the judicial process thus impose limitations on its use. This is why judicial advance should be gradual. "I am not trained to see the distant scene: one step enough for me" should be the motto on the wall opposite the judge's desk. It is, I concede, a less spectacular method of progression than somersaults and cartwheels; but it is the one best suited to the capacity and resources of a judge.'

Lack of information

In *Morgans* v. *Launchbury* [1972] 2 All ER 606, the House of Lords was invited to hold that the owner of a car, which was being driven by someone else at the request of the owner's husband, was liable to passengers injured as a result of the driver's negligence. Lord Wilberforce said:

'Liability and insurance are so intermixed that judicially to alter the basis of liability without adequate knowledge (*which we have not the means to obtain*) as to the impact which this might make on the insurance system would be dangerous and . . . irresponsible.' (Emphasis added.)

By way of contrast, in the American legal system the appellate courts commonly receive arguments in the form of long, written documents known as briefs. These may contain a great deal of argument based on social and economic factors, rather than on propositions of law. In one case early in the twentieth century, concerning statutory restrictions on the hours which women could work, an attorney by the name of Brandeis delivered a lengthy brief of this nature. The Supreme Court commented favourably on its utility, and such documents have come to be known as 'Brandeis briefs'.

For the time being, however, the English courts remain firmly wedded to the tradition of oral argument. In *Yorke Motors* v. *Edwards* [1982] 1 All ER 1024 the House of Lords expressly rejected the idea of the submission of written argument, saying that the only acceptable form of written submission is a written skeleton, containing the outline of the argument, together with case names and references and short quotations from the key judgements. 'The purpose of a skeleton argument is to identify and summarize the points, not to argue them fully on paper'. (*Practice Direction (Court of Appeal: Procedure)* [1995] 1 WLR 1197, para.37).

However, in *R* v. *Admiralty Board of the Defence Council ex parte Lustig-Prean and Another* (1996) 8 Admin LR 29, Henry LJ suggested that if the European Convention on Human Rights were to be incorporated into English law, 'the court might well ask for more material than the adversarial system normally provides, such as Brandeis briefs'.

Furthermore, there is some evidence that written argument may be acceptable in the House of Lords. In *Chief Adjudication Officer* v. *Foster* [1993] 1 All ER 705, the House had heard oral argument and was considering its judgement when *Pepper* v. *Hart* [1993] 1 All ER 42, which permitted the courts to refer to *Hansard*, was decided. (*Pepper* v. *Hart* is discussed at pp. 293–9.) The respondent invited the House to receive written representations from both parties on the relevance of *Hansard* to the point at issue in the case, and those representations were in fact received and considered before judgement was given.

In *Bolton Metropolitan District Council* v. *Secretary of State for the Environment* [1995] 1 WLR 1176, the question of costs raised issues of general importance, quite apart from the substantive issue in the appeal. At the conclusion of oral argument on the substantive issue, the House of Lords invited the parties to make written submissions in relation to costs. In due course, the House gave judgement on the costs point, and apart from the fact that Lord Lloyd explained what had happened, there is nothing to show that oral argument was not received.

Of course, both these examples arose in somewhat unusual circumstances, but it may not be altogether fanciful to see them as straws in the wind.

15.4   The Constitutional Limitations of Judicial Law Reform

It is not surprising that judges who work under a constitution which is largely dominated by the doctrine of the legislative supremacy of Parliament, should be aware that their own lack of electoral accountability means that their activities in the field of law reform should be limited. Admittedly, there is room for some debate as to exactly where the line should be drawn, beyond which only Parliament should reform the law, and the line itself may be rather fuzzy, but there would be general acceptance that, in any particular case, a line of some sort does exist somewhere.

There would, for example, be general agreement that the judges should not take sides in matters of party politics. As Lord Scarman said, in

Duport Steels Ltd v. *Sirs* [1980] 1 All ER 529, when the House of Lords was dealing with the interpretation of politically contentious trades' union legislation:

'Within . . . limits . . . judges . . . have a genuine creative role . . . But the constitution's separation of powers, or more accurately functions, must be observed if judicial independence is not to be put at risk. For if people and Parliament come to think that the judicial power is to be confined by nothing other than the judge's sense of what is right . . . confidence in the judicial system will be replaced by fear of it becoming uncertain and arbitrary in its application. Society will then be ready for Parliament to cut the power of the judges. Their power to do justice will become more restricted by law than it need be, or is today.'

One of the most balanced statements of the judges' role may be found in *Malone* v. *Metropolitan Police Commissioner* [1979] 1 All ER 256. Malone had been prosecuted for dishonestly handling stolen goods. During the police investigation which preceded the prosecution his telephone had been tapped. He sought a number of declarations, which required the court to decided whether the telephone tap infringed his rights. Deciding the issue against Malone, Sir Robert Megarry v-c said:

'I am not unduly troubled by the absence of English authority: there has to be a first time for everything, and if the principles of English law, and not least analogies from the existing rules, together with the requirements of justice and commonsense, pointed firmly to such a right existing, then I think the court should not be deterred from recognizing the right.

'On the other hand, it is no function of the courts to legislate in a new field. The extension of the existing laws and principles is one thing, the creation of an altogether new right is another. At times judges must, and do, legislate; but as Holmes J once said, they do so only interstitially and with molecular rather than molar motions: see *Southern Pacific Co* v. *Jensen* (1917) 244 US 205, in a dissenting judgment. Anything beyond that must be left for legislation. No new right in the law, fully-fledged with all the appropriate safeguards, can spring from the head of a judge deciding a particular case: only Parliament can create such a right . . . Where there is some major gap in the law, no doubt a judge would be capable of framing what he considered to be a proper code to fill it; and sometimes he may be tempted. But he has to remember that his function is judicial, not legislative, and that he ought not to use his office to legislate in the guise of exercising his judicial powers.

'One of the factors that must be relevant in such a case is the degree of particularity in the right that is claimed. The wider and more indefinite the right claimed, the greater the undesirability of holding that such a right exists . . . To create a right for one person, you have to impose a corresponding duty on another.'

Further support for the proposition that the formulation of public policy is a matter for Parliament may be derived from *R* v. *Cunningham* (see p. 176), where Lord Hailsham LC said:

' "Public policy" [and] "concepts of what is right and what is wrong that command general acceptance in contemporary society" are difficult horses for the judiciary to ride, and, where possible, are arguably best left to the legislature to decide.'

Similarly, in *C (A Minor)* v. *DPP* [1995] 2 All ER 43, a unanimous House of Lords was distinctly unhappy with the rule of English criminal law which states that a child between the ages of 10 and 14 cannot be convicted of a criminal offence unless the prosecution proves that the child in question knows the difference between right and wrong. Nevertheless, the House reversed a decision of the High Court, which had held that the rule was no longer part of the law. Lord Lowry said, towards the end of the only substantial speech:

'The distinction between the treatment and the punishment of child "offenders" has popular and political overtones, a fact which shows that we have been discussing not so much a legal as a social problem, with a dash of politics thrown in, and emphasizes that it should be within the exclusive remit of Parliament.'

The House of Lords was similarly conscious of its limited law-making role in *R* v. *Clegg* [1995] 1 All ER 374, where a soldier on duty in Northern Ireland had been convicted of murder. The legal issue was whether someone who caused death by using excessive force, either in self-defence or while trying to prevent the commission of an offence by another person, could be convicted of the lesser offence of manslaughter rather than murder, and whether it was relevant that the defendant was a police officer or a member of the armed forces. The practical consequence of the distinction between conviction for murder and manslaughter was that life imprisonment was mandatory for the the former, but discretionary for the latter.

The House was clearly unhappy with the existing state of the law, but nevertheless refused to change it. Lord Lloyd, in the only substantial speech, acknowledged that the power of the House to change the law was not necessarily excluded simply because the facts raise an issue of social policy, but nevertheless concluded:

'In the present case I am in no doubt that your Lordships should abstain from law-making. The reduction of what would otherwise be murder to manslaughter in a particular class of case seems to me essentially a matter for decision by the legislature, and not by this House in its judicial capacity. For the point in issue is, in truth, part of the wider issue whether the mandatory life sentence for murder should still be maintained. That wider issue can only be decided by Parliament. I would say the same for the point at issue in this case.'

Judicial reluctance to intervene may be particularly noticeable in cases arising from areas of law in which Parliament has been active on a selective basis, since there may be a natural assumption that Parliament has impliedly approved those aspects of the law which it has not changed. The case of *Re Brightlife* [1986] 3 All ER 673, involved floating charges, which originated at common law, but have been subject to some statutory provisions. Floating charges are a type of secured loan and are widely used in commercial circles. In the event of insolvency, secured creditors are, of course, in a better position than unsecured creditors, but the question of how the balance should be struck between the two groups is ultimately a matter of public policy. The commercial community needs to be able to raise capital, but investors need some degree of protection. Against this background, Hoffman J said:

'The limited and pragmatic interventions by the legislature make it, in my judgment, wholly inappropriate for the courts to impose additional restrictive rules on grounds of public policy. It is certainly not for a judge of first instance to proclaim a new head of public policy which no appellate court has even hinted at before.'

Similarly, the courts may decline to intervene where Parliament has, quite self-conciously, been totally inactive. As Lord Bridge said in *Brind* v. *Secretary of State for the Home Department* [1991] 1 All ER 720, when upholding the established view that the European Convention on Human Rights is not part of English law:

'When Parliament has been content for so long to leave those who complain that their Convention rights have been infringed to seek their remedy in Strasbourg [i.e. in the European Court of Human Rights], it would be surprising suddenly to find that the judiciary had, without

Parliament's aid, the means to incorporate the Convention into such an important area of domestic law and I cannot escape the conclusion that this would be a judicial usurpation of the legislative function.'

15.5   Conclusion

It is clear that there are both advantages and disadvantages to the common law tradition of developing the law on a case-by-case basis. However, what is clear, not only from this chapter but from the whole of this Part of this book, is that although it is conventional to speak of a doctrine of *binding* precedent, a substantial degree of flexibility is available to the courts in practice. It is now appropriate, in the next chapter, to consider how the civil law tradition operates, as evidenced by the workings of the European Court of Justice.

Summary

1   Having considered how precedent works in different courts, it is appropriate to consider some of the doctrine's perceived strengths and weaknesses as a vehicle for law reform, as well as the constitutional limitations on the role of the judges.

2   The perceived strengths are that it is speedy; is based on real facts situations; and is outside the party-political arena.

3   The perceived weaknesses are that it is haphazard in operation; it causes injustice in individual cases; and the judges are ill-equipped for the task of law reform.

4   Judges are conscious that, because they operate outside the field of electoral accountability, there are limits to the kind of law reform they should undertake.

Exercise

Assess the adequacy of the doctrine of binding precedent as a vehicle for law reform.

16 Precedent in the European Court of Justice and the Court of First Instance

16.1 Introduction

Although the doctrine of binding precedent is distinctive of Common law jurisdictions, there is clearly a tendency in all developed legal systems – including those of the European countries who were the founder and formative members of the Communities – for previous cases to be used as guidance in deciding current ones. In the case of the European Court of Justice itself, however, the lack of any concept of strict bindingness in the legal traditions from which Community law sprang was compounded by the fact that the early years of a new legal order are likely to put a premium on the kind of creativity which might seem to be diametrically opposed to the atavistic tendencies inherent in a system of bindingness. (Since there is no distinction between the European Court of Justice and the Court of First Instance for the present purposes, this chapter will adopt the expedient of referring to both courts by the name of the former.)

Before proceeding with any further analysis of the way the European Court of Justice perceives and performs its judicial role, it may be useful to make some comment on some of the ways in which its judgements differ from the traditional English model.

16.2 Reading European Court of Justice Reports

Anyone who is used to reading reports of cases decided by the English courts is likely to find certain unfamiliar elements in the style of reports of decisions in the European Court of Justice. First, although the judges of the court will, of course, always be lawyers, you will recall from pp. 79–80 that there is no requirement that they must have been practitioners: academic lawyers are perfectly acceptable. Second, the working language of the court is French. Combining these two points, Rudden says:

'Thus the student will almost always be reading a translation . . . which will inevitably not stand comparison with the vigour of original native speech. This last word points to another contrast: the characteristic tone of the common-law judgment is that of the speaking voice of an individual who was once an advocate. European Court decisions are invariably written, and are the work of a committee, not all of whose members practised at a bar . . . Not only is French the language of the draft judgment, the French judicial style is also the model. The keynote of this style is austerity . . . a great deal is written as one sentence with facts, procedural steps, arguments, and reasons, all drafted as subordinate clauses leading with an air of cold inevitability to the ruling . . . In later years the style becomes slightly more relaxed, but the court never attempts to achieve verbal bite or pungency.' (*Basic Community Law Cases*, 1987, pp. 3–4.)

Second, developing the theme that the court's decisions are made by a committee, Rudden says:

'There is never a concurring, much less a dissenting, opinion and, as to the court's own deliberations, the judges are - literally – sworn to secrecy . . . To a common lawyer, the result of this technique of anonymity and unanimity is to present a chain of reasoning which is compelling only in syntax, while in terms of judicial reasoning, what is framed as deduction sometimes reads like mere assertion. The position taken may well be satisfactory . . . but readers must often supply for themselves the "policy" reasons.' (*Basic Community Law Cases*, 1987, p. 5.)

16.3   Principles and Precedents

The factors which explain the existence of judicial precedent in a broad sense apply, of course, to the European Court of Justice, and the court will commonly follow its own previous decisions. Theoretically, however, there is no element of bindingness in this practice, so it follows that some other basis is necessary for developing an understanding of the judicial formulation and development of Community law.

As we have seen, at pp. 132–6, common lawyers may argue whether the decisions of the courts actually are the law or are merely evidence of what the law is. Lawyers from the continental tradition would tend much more readily to accept the latter proposition. In other words, an accumulated body of coherent cases is good evidence of the existence of the law stated in the judgements. Perhaps not surprisingly, in formulating the principles which apply across the spectrum of Community law, the Court has drawn on material from the legal systems of individual member states. Perhaps more surprisingly – at least to a mind nurtured in the common law tradition which tends to respect robust pragmatism and to suspect abstract theorizing – is the fact that material is presented to, and by, the Court of Justice in terms of *principles of law* rather than precedents. Hartley sees the matter as being essentially a question of judicial psychology:

'In no legal system is it possible for legislation or other written sources of law to provide an answer to every question which comes before the courts. The judges are therefore obliged to create rules of law to decide the issues before them; but if their law-creating role becomes too apparent, the judges may be accused of going beyond their proper function and trespassing on the domain of the legislature. How are they to resolve this dilemma? In England the courts have traditionally resorted to the myth of the common law, the age-old tradition of customary law which, by a fiction, was regarded as being both immemorial and within the special cognizance of the judges. The European Court, on the other hand, has utilized general principles of law to cloak the nakedness of judicial law-making: the idea is that, if a ruling can be shown to be derived from a principle of sufficient generality as to command common assent, a firm legal foundation for the judgment will be provided.' (*The Foundations of European Community Law*, 3rd edn, 1994, p. 137.)

It is appropriate, therefore, to approach the topic which may loosely be termed *precedent in the Court of Justice* by way of examining some of the more important of these principles.

There is no universally agreed body of doctrine which can be neatly labelled 'the principles of Community law', but the following headings would all be familiar to, and generally accepted by, Community lawyers: *proportionality, legal certainty* and the closely related concept of *legitimate expectation, equality, fundamental rights* and *procedural propriety*. We will consider these in turn, before commenting on the principle of *subsidiarity*, and concluding with a discussion of the extent to which the practice of the European Court of Justice differs from that of the English courts.

16.4 Proportionality

The idea of proportionality is as old as Aristotle's principle of distributive justice. In essence it simply means that social burdens should be distributed in a fair manner, with fairness being assessed by reference to the capacity of members of society to bear the burdens in question. As legal systems develop, of course, their use of some of the basic ideas of justice becomes more sophisticated. For example, in its Community manifestation, the principle of proportionality can be used to decide whether a Regulation is valid.

The case of *Atalanta* [1979] ECR 2137, arose from a situation in which the law required a party to a contract to give security to ensure the performance of the contract. Where there was non-performance, a Regulation required forfeiture of the whole of the security irrespective of whether the non-performance was major or minor. The Court of Justice held that the lack of any relationship between the extent of the non-performance on the one hand, and the amount of the penalty on the other, amounted to a breach of the principle of proportionality.

16.5   Legal Certainty and Legitimate Expectation

The Community law principles of legal certainty and legitimate expectation are very closely related to each other. Taking them in turn, the principle of legal certainty simply requires that people who are subject to the law should be able to ascertain their rights and obligations. Thus, for example, in *Goudrand Frères* [1981] ECR 1931, the Court of Justice said that in the field of financial liability, the principle of legal certainty requires that: 'Rules imposing charges on the taxpayer must be clear and precise so that he may know without ambiguity what are his rights and obligations and may take steps accordingly.' Where this principle is breached, any ambiguity should be resolved in favour of the individual.

The Community principle of legitimate expectation may be illustrated by the case of *Deuka* [1975] 2 CMLR 28. The essence of the case was that the Commission, faced with a surplus of wheat, adopted a policy of making payments in order to encourage the processing of wheat in such a way as to render it unfit for human consumption, provided that the processors obtained authorization before they embarked on the process. The amount of the payment varied from time to time. *Deuka* bought some wheat before 1 June 1970 with a view to processing it, and obtained the appropriate authorization. However, the processing itself did not actually occur until June and July, by which time a new Regulation reducing the amount of the payment had been introduced, with effect from 1 June. The Court of Justice held that the new Regulation was valid, but that it must be interpreted in such a way as not to disentitle Deuka to the higher payment which had been envisaged when the authorization had been obtained, because Deuka had clearly had a legitimate expectation of receiving payment at the higher rate.

Before leaving the principles of legal certainty and legitimate expectation, it is worth noticing that, as a matter of first impression, both principles may appear to require that judgements of the Court of Justice should have only prospective effect, in the sense that they should not affect existing rights and obligations.

The case of *Amministratzione delle Finanze dell Stato* [1981] ECR 2735 is sometimes treated as containing a sound statement of principle:

> 'Although procedural rules are generally held to apply to all proceedings pending at the time when they enter into force, this is not the case with substantive rules. On the contrary, the latter are usually interpreted as applying to situations existing before their entry into force only in so far as it clearly follows from their terms, objectives or general scheme that such an effect must be given to them.
>
> 'This interpretation ensures respect for the principles of legal certainty and the protection of legitimate expectation, by virtue of which the effect of Community legislation must be clear and predictable for those who are subject to it.'

This judgement, which reflects the position which obtained in English law before the decision in *Secretary of State for Social Services* v. *Tunnicliffe* [1991] 2 All ER 712 (see p. 302), seems to be clear enough, but in practice the position is rather less certain. More particularly, the Court will generally require good reason to be shown before it will say that its judgement in any particular case should not operate retrospectively. For a case where such good reason was shown, it is necessary to do no more than recall *Defrenne* v. *Sabena (No 2)* [1976] 2 CMLR 98, which is discussed at p. 90 in the context of the direct effect of Community law. The Court said that its decision that art.119 of the EC Treaty was directly effective, could not generally be used to support future claims in respect of the time before the judgement was given, because

> 'in view of the large number of people concerned, such claims, *which undertakings could not have foreseen*, might seriously affect the financial situation of such undertakings and even drive some of them to bankruptcy.' (Emphasis added.)

However, even here the Court was willing to allow a limited degree of retrospectivity, but only in cases where proceedings had already been instituted at the date of that judgement.

On the other hand, the Court imposed no temporal limitation on the effects of its judgements in *Francovich* or *Marshall (No 2)*, which are discussed at pp. 92 and 93, even though they both gave rise to potentially massive financial liabilities.

16.6 Equality

The importance of the principle of equality before the law is a fundamental part of any developed system of justice which should require no justification. However, in the context of Community law, the principle of equality has an additional and rather more specific meaning, namely that 'comparable situations must not be treated differently and different situations must not be treated in the same way unless such treatment is objectively justified' (Wyatt and Dashwood, *European Community Law*, 3rd edn, 1993, p. 96). The following cases illustrate the need for objective justification.

First, in *Royal Scholten-Honig Holdings Ltd* [1979] 1 CMLR 675 the facts were that glucose producers were in competition with sugar producers. Regulations were then made, introducing a system of subsidies whereby the production of sugar was, in part, financed by levies on glucose producers. The Court of Justice held that the Regulations were invalid because they breached the principle of equality.

Second, however, and by way of contrast, in *Walter Rau* [1987] ECR 2289, margarine producers challenged the legality of a Community policy which aimed to reduce surplus stocks of butter by selling it cheaply to certain categories of the population. Although it may seem to be obvious that the producers of butter and margarine were competing with each other, and that therefore this case was on all fours with *Royal Scholten-Honig Holdings Ltd*, the Court decided that there were differences between the general objectives of the organization of the Community butter market on the one hand and the oil and fats market on the other hand, and that these differences, viewed objectively, justified the discrimination. It will be apparent that Community lawyers are just as adept as Common lawyers at drawing fine distinctions between cases.

16.7 Fundamental Rights

On 5 April 1977, the European Parliament, the Council and the Commission issued a Joint Declaration stressing that all three institutions attach 'prime importance to the protection of fundamental rights, as derived in particular from the constitutions of the Member States and the European

Convention for the Protection of Human Rights and Fundamental Freedoms' and that 'in exercise of their powers and in pursuance of the aims of the European Communities they respect and will continue to respect these rights'. Valuable though this Declaration is as a declaration of intent, it must be said that it does not belong to any of the formally recognized types of Community legislation, and cannot, therefore, be accurately described as a statement of Community law. However, art.F.2 of the Treaty on European Union, which is clearly a source of law, is to similar effect:

> 'The Union shall respect fundamental rights, as guaranteed by the European Convention for the Protection of Human Rights and Fundamental Freedoms signed in Rome on 4 November 1950 and as they result from the constitutional traditions common to the member states, as general principles of Community Law.'

In practice, there is no doubt that the Court of Justice clearly pays great attention to the principles embodied in the Convention, and indeed did so even before the Treaty on European Union.

For example, in *Stauder* v. *City of Ulm* [1969] ECR 419, the facts arose from the Community's plan to reduce surplus stocks of butter by selling it cheaply to certain groups within the population. One individual objected that the German authorities implemented the scheme in such a way that he had to disclose his name to the retailer of the butter, which meant that he was also revealing the fact that he was in receipt of certain state benefits. The Court of Justice acknowledged that this would be a breach of the individual's fundamental rights, because it would infringe the principle of equality. In the event, however, the Court avoided the problem by saying that the Commission's decision, which formed the basis of the scheme, should be interpreted so that such disclosure by individuals was not a precondition to their obtaining cheap butter.

16.8 Procedural Propriety

The concept of procedural propriety is, by its nature, open-ended, but two examples may be usefully given. First, in *Transocean Marine Paint Association* v. *Commission* [1979] 2 CMLR 459, the Court of Justice held that people whose interests would be significantly affected by a decision of a public authority must be given an opportunity to make their views known. Second, the court has held several times that a person who is subject to an adverse decision is entitled to be given the reasons for the decision. (See, for example, *UNECTEF* v. *Heylens* [1987] ECR 4097.)

16.9   Subsidiary

The principle of subsidiarity gives effect to the proposition that action should be taken at the most local level at which it will be effective. The legal source of this principle in Community law is art.3(b) of the EC Treaty, which was inserted by the Treaty on European Union:

> 'The Community shall act within the limits of the powers conferred upon it by the Treaty and of the objectives assigned to it therein.
>
> 'In areas which do not fall within its exclusive competence, the Community shall take action, in accordance with the principle of subsidiarity, only if and insofar as the objectives of the proposed action cannot be sufficiently achieved by the member states and can therefore, by reason of the scale or effects of the proposed action, be better achieved by the Community.
>
> 'Any action by the Community shall not go beyond what is necessary to achieve the objectives of the Community.'

The wording of art.3b creates a problem. Does an area fall within the exclusive competence of the Community as soon as the member states have transferred power to the Community in respect of it, or must the Community also have exercised that power?

Even when this question is resolved, the fact will remain that the whole concept of subsidiarity will necessarily require the Court to 'resolve difficult political disputes over the proper sphere of competence of the Community as against the member states' (Craig and de Burca, *EC Law: Text Cases and Materials*, 1995, p. 87).

16.10   To what Extent does the Court of Justice Differ in Practical Terms from the English Courts with Regard to Precedent?

As we have seen throughout this Part, the English doctrine of precedent is a great deal less binding and a great deal more flexible than it might at first appear to be. Similarly, despite the lack of any formal doctrine of bindingness, the Court of Justice's insistence on the development and maintenance of legal principles means that its decisions exhibit a very substantial degree of coherence, and in later years it has become common for the Court to refer to earlier decisions by name as the bases for decisions in instant cases. In Rudden's words: 'Thus there has grown up a settled body of case-law which, for all practical purposes, has as much normative authority as the Treaty' (*Basic Community Law Cases*, 1987, p. 5).

Perhaps the major difference between the Court of Justice and the English courts, at a purely practical level, is that it is impossible to conceive of the Court of Justice treating itself as being compelled to reach a particular decision, against its better judgement, simply because there was a single prior decision of its own supporting that decision. On the other hand, it may very plausibly be argued that even this is scarcely a point of distinction between the two systems, because, as we have seen throughout this Part, most modern English judges would be willing and able to find a way round a decision if they genuinely felt that they did not want to be bound by it.

Summary

1 The Court of Justice spent its formative years without being exposed to the common law tradition and the doctrine of binding precedent.

2 Judgements in the Court of Justice are presented in a style which is different from, and in particular less closely reasoned than, those in the English courts.

3 The Court of Justice proceeds by applying generally accepted principles of law rather than by following decisions in individual cases.

4 The principle of proportionality requires that consequences should be in proportion to their causes.

5 The principles of legal certainty and legitimate expectation require that people who are subject to the law should be able to ascertain their rights and obligations; and that, where a public authority creates a legitimate expectation on the part of an individual, that expectation should be fulfilled.

6 Despite the requirements of the principle of legal certainty, in practice the Court of Justice will require good reason to be shown before it will say that a particular judgement should not be given retrospective effect.

7 The principle of equality provides a ground for challenging administrative or legislative action which differentiates arbitrarily between persons in comparable circumstances.

8 The Community attaches prime importance to the protection of fundamental rights.

9 The principle of procedural propriety is, by its nature, open-ended, but in general terms it requires that procedural fairness should be observed.

10 The principle of subsidiarity requires that the Community should take action only where the desired objective cannot be achieved by the member states.

11 Given the degree of flexibility inherent in the English doctrine of binding precedent, and the tendency of the European Court of Justice to apply accepted principles, the difference between the English law and Com-

munity law in terms of the predictability of judicial outcomes in practice is less than might be thought, bearing in mind the two different legal traditions which are involved.

Exercises

1   How does the European Court of Justice seek to achieve a reasonable degree of consistency in its decisions?
2   Identify and explain any two principles of Community law.
3   What is the Court of Justice's attitude towards the retrospectivity of its own decisions?
4   In practical terms, to what extent does the European Court of Justice differ from the English courts with regard to following previous decisions?

Part III

Statute Law and Statutory Interpretation

Having read this Part you should understand the processes of legislative drafting, enactment and interpretation. More particularly, you should understand the ways in which drafting and interpretation reflect problems of communication generally, and the ways in which specific problems arise from their technical nature.

17 An Introduction to Statute Law and Statutory Interpretation

17.1 Introduction

This chapter deals with a variety of matters by way of introduction to the study of statute law and statutory interpretation. It will also help to put the doctrine of the legislative supremacy of Parliament into a practical context.

17.2 Drafting, Interpretation and Communication

At one level the complementary processes of statutory drafting and interpretation can be seen simply as the two constituent parts of an exercise in communication, and we should never lose sight of the fact that many of the so-called 'principles of statutory interpretation' are no more than the ordinary principles of linguistic communication. However, it is also important to identify the constitutional nature of the context of statutory drafting and interpretation, because this context creates complications which are additional to those ordinarily encountered in other processes of communication.

The short point is that the English doctrine of the legislative supremacy of Parliament, as currently understood, was created by the courts (see p. 68) and both its scope and continued existence are largely in their hands, as the *Factortame* litigation and other similar cases so clearly show (see pp. 103–5). More particularly, just as different judges have different perceptions of the judicial role in relation to precedent (see Part II generally and Chapter 15 in particular), so there are various views as to the proper role of the judiciary when interpreting statutes.

Interpretation and Construction

The terms *interpretation* and *construction* are almost always used interchangeably in the present context, but it may occasionally be possible to discern a distinction between them. The starting point is that the courts certainly distinguish between the ordinary meaning of an ordinary word of the English language and the legal meaning of a statute. In *Brutus* v. *Cozens* [1972] 2 All ER 1297, the facts were that anti-apartheid activists disrupted the Wimbledon tennis tournament with a political demonstration. The magistrates acquitted them of 'insulting behaviour whereby a breach of the peace was likely to be occasioned'. The House of Lords took the view that the question of whether specific conduct was 'insulting' was a matter of fact to be determined by the tribunal of fact, and was not a question of law to be taken on appeal. Lord Reid said: 'The meaning of an ordinary word of the English language is not a question of law. The proper construction of a statute is a question of law.' On the other side of the line, in the patents case of *Energy Conversion Devices Incorporated's Applications* [1982] FSR 544, Lord Diplock expressed the following opinion on behalf of a unanimous House of Lords:

'Your Lordships should, however, in my view take this opportunity of stating once again the important constitutional principle that questions of construction of all legislation, primary or secondary, are questions of law to be determined authoritatively by courts of law; that errors in construing primary or secondary legislation made by inferior tribunals that are not courts of law, however specialized and prestigious they may be, are subject to correction by judicial review; no tribunal and no court of law has any discretion to vary the meaning of the words of primary or secondary legislation from case to case in order to meet what the tribunal or court happens to think is the justice of the particular case. Tempting though it might sound, to do so is the negation of the rule of law. If there are cases in which the application of the Patents Rules leads to injustice, the cure is for the Secretary of State to amend the Rules. If what is thought to be the injustice results from the terms of the Act itself, the remedy is for Parliament to amend the Act.'

It may be suggested that judicial observations such as these support a distinction between the concepts of interpretation and construction, on the basis that the former applies to identifying the meaning of individual words, while the latter applies to the process of identifying the enacted meaning of a provision as a whole. Whether or not this distinction is sensible, there is no doubt that it is seldom observed: practically everyone, practically all the time, uses the terms interchangeably. This book will, therefore, proceed on the basis of interchangeability, with each term being used according to the most natural usage in context.

17.3 The Classification of Acts of Parliament

Acts of Parliament may be classified as either *public* on the one hand or *private and personal* on the other. Public Acts, which are sometimes known as *Public and General Acts* are intended to change the general law, and they constitute the vast bulk of Parliament's legislative output. Private and personal Acts relate either to particular places or to particular people. Examples of personal Acts include those which authorize the marriage of people who would otherwise be within the prohibited degrees, and examples of private Acts include those promoted by local authorities who wish to acquire powers which they would not have under the general law.

The doctrine of the supremacy of Parliament, which was discussed at p. 68, applies equally to all Acts (*British Railways Board* v. *Pickin* [1974] 1 All ER 609), but it does not necessarily follow that the same principles of interpretation apply equally in all cases. More particularly, the courts have sometimes argued that the promoters of private Acts have gained for themselves some additional legal advantage which is denied to other people, and that therefore private Acts should be construed strictly.

In *South Staffordshire Waterworks Co* v. *Barrow* (1896–97) 13 TLR 549, two waterworks companies had been operating in adjoining areas. The basis on which they calculated their charges varied, with the result that consumers in one of the areas paid more than consumers in the other. Under the authority of a private Act of Parliament, the two companies merged and extended the area of their operation. Clearly the question then arose as to the basis of charging for those consumers who were in the area which had previously been served by neither company. The court held that they should be charged on the lower basis.

It seems, however, that there may be scope for an exception where the private Act is intended to operate for the public good rather than for commercial advantage. *Pyx Granite Co Ltd* v. *Ministry of Housing and Local Government* [1959] 3 All ER 1, involved the interpretation of the Malvern Hills Act 1924, a private Act giving certain powers to the Malvern Hills Conservators, to enable them to conserve the Malvern Hills for the benefit of the public at large. A question arose as to the meaning of the phrase 'all lands common or waste'. Viscount Simonds said:

'The meaning of the expression "all lands common or waste" has been debated, and it has been urged that, since common and waste are themselves a kind of land, these words must be read as adjectivally qualifying "lands", and the expression must be read as if it were "common or waste lands". The result of this would be to exclude from the conservators' jurisdiction any land in which they might have or acquire any right or interest other than common or waste land. So strange a consequence must be avoided if any other interpretation is possible. I think that it is, for I do not regard it as extravagant to suppose that the draftsman . . . if only *ex majore cautela*, thought it proper to add "common or waste" in case it should be supposed that they were not "lands". It is legitimate to add that, if common or waste lands only were intended, the transposition to "lands common or waste" is one that requires explanation, which is not forthcoming.'

Although the distinction which Viscount Simonds was making may seem both technical and obscure, it is perfectly clear that his interpretation gave the statute a wider meaning rather than a narrower one, in the sense that it applied to all land in the area, rather than merely to some of it.

17.4 Precedent in Relation to Decisions on Statutory Interpretation

When considering the doctrine of precedent in cases involving statutory interpretation, we must return to the distinction which the House of Lords was making in *Brutus* v. *Cozens* [1972] 2 All ER 1297 and *Energy Conversion Devices Incorporated's Applications* [1982] FSR 544 (see pp. 37–8), namely that the meaning of an ordinary word of the English language is a question of fact, while the construction of legislation is a question of law. The distinction between *law* and *fact* is discussed more generally at pp. 37–45, but for the present purposes two closely related consequences flow from the distinction.

First, decisions on the meanings of ordinary words are not subject to the doctrine of binding precedent, because it is the nature of that doctrine to deal with issues of law as distinct from issues of fact. Second, although decisions on the construction of statutes, being matters of law, may constitute binding precedents, it does not necessarily follow that they must do so in every case. This cautionary note flows logically from the most elementary principle of statutory interpretation, namely that the essential task is to find the meaning of the words *for the purposes of the Act in which those words are used.*

In *Quillotex Co Ltd* v. *Minister of Housing and Local Government* [1965] 2 All ER 913, stating the proposition at the level of general principle, Salmon LJ said:

'No real help can be gained as to the meaning of a word in statute A by reference to its meaning in statutes B, C, or D. *All one can derive from the cases are the relevant principles of construction to be applied.'* (Emphasis added.)

Putting this another way, decisions on the interpretation of one statute are no more than *persuasive* authorities in relation to other statutes, or as Lord Diplock said, in *Carter* v. *Bradbeer* [1975] 3 All ER 158:

'a question of statutory construction is one in which the strict doctrine of precedent can only be of narrow application. The *ratio decidendi* of a judgement as to the meaning of particular words or combinations of words used in a particular statutory provision can have no more than a persuasive influence on a court which is called upon to interpret the same word or combination of words appearing in some other statutory provision.'

The cases of *Newman* v. *Lipman* [1950] 2 All ER 832 and *Burgess* v. *McCracken* (1986) 150 JP 529 provide good examples of the significance of the precise statutory context, and therefore of the need for extreme caution when dealing with precedent in relation to statutory interpretation. In *Newman* v. *Lipman*, the High Court held that a professional photographer, who wandered round taking photographs of tourists against the backdrop of famous landmarks, in the hope that the tourists would buy the photographs, was not trading, and therefore was not contravening a prohibition on trading in the street. In *Burgess* v. *McCracken*, a photographer was conducting his business in a precisely similar way, except that he was operating in a public park rather than in the street.

The High Court held that the prohibition on trading in the street was distinguishable from the prohibition on trading in public parks, because the purpose of the former is to prevent obstruction of the highway, whereas the purpose of the latter is wider, and includes protecting people, who are using the park for relaxation, from being annoyed by traders. Therefore, in a borderline case on the meaning of 'trading', an activity which is lawful on the highway may be prohibited in a park, because annoyance can occur without obstruction.

It would appear, at this stage, therefore, that a case which decides the meaning of a specific form of statutory words cannot bind a subsequent court unless it is considering the same form of words *in the same statute*. However, there is one, strictly limited, exception. A decision in relation to one statute may be binding in relation to another, provided that both statutes deal with the same subject-matter or, to use the Latin tag, they are *in pari materia* with each other. The classic statement of the principle is from *R* v. *Palmer* (1785) 168 ER 279: 'If there are several Acts *upon the same subject*, they are to be taken together as forming one system and as interpreting and enforcing each other' (emphasis added).

The courts take a strict approach to the question of whether statutes are *in pari materia* with each other. In *Crosley* v. *Arkwright* (1788) 100 ER 325, statutes relating to stamp duties were held to be *in pari materia* with each other, but in *Powell* v. *Cleland* [1947] 2 All ER 672 the Rent and Mortgage Interest Restrictions (Amendment) Act 1933 was held to be not *in pari materia* with the 1925 property legislation.

On the other hand, the courts are less strict when it comes to identifying the type of instrument to which the *in pari materia* principle can apply. *R* v. *Newcastle-upon-Tyne Justices ex parte Skinner* [1987] 1 All ER 349 indicates that the principle is not limited to statutes, but can be extended to enable statutory instruments to be used when interpreting earlier statutes, even where the statutory instrument was not made under the statute in question. The facts of the case were that s.114 of the Magistrates' Courts Act 1980 provided that magistrates need not state a case for the High Court unless the appellant entered into a recognizance to proceed with the appeal. The Act said nothing as to how the amount of the recognizance was to be fixed, but r.26 of the Crown Court Rules 1982 provided that, in appeals by way of case stated from the Crown Court, a recognizance was to be 'such sum as the Crown Court thinks proper, having regard to the means of the applicant'. In the Divisional Court, Glidewell LJ said: 'In our view, although the same phrase is not to be found in s.114 of the 1980 Act, the same principle must necessarily apply to magistrates'.

Summary

1   A detailed consideration of statute law and statutory interpretation shows the doctrine of the legislative suremacy of Parliament in its practical context.

2   The processes of statutory drafting and interpretation share many of the problems which are raised by communication generally, but their specifically legal context also raises special problems of a constitutional nature.

3   The doctrine of the legislative supremacy of Parliament applies equally to all statutes, but for the purposes of interpretation it may be possible to distinguish between *public and general* statutes on the one hand and *private and personal* statutes on the other.

4   Decisions on the meaning of statutory words are always made in the context of the statute in question, and therefore they do not constitute binding precedents where the same wording is used in other statutes.

Exercises

1 In the present context, what (if anything) is the significance of the distinction between *public and general* statutes and *private and personal* statutes?

2 How does the doctrine of binding precedent apply to cases involving statutory interpretation?

18 Legislative Drafting

18.1 Introduction

The origins of Parliament

According to Radcliffe and Cross, 'few matters in English history are more controverted than the origins of Parliament', although it seems to be reasonably clear that it was initially 'some sort of special and formal gathering about the King . . . an occasion . . . rather than a body or an institution' (*The English Legal System*, 6th edn, 1977, p. 53). Additionally, at least two further things are reasonably clear. First, Parliament dates from very shortly after Magna Carta. Second, as the French origins of the term itself clearly denote, Parliament began life as a talking-shop.

In the early stages of Parliament's development, the business of legislating, or enacting statutes, was still in the hands of the King, who acted with the advice of the *Curia Regis*, which was the forerunner of the modern Privy Council. Originally statutes were drafted in either Latin or Norman French. The first Commons Bill in English appeared in 1414, which was, of course, only fourteen years after the death of Geoffrey Chaucer, whose poetry had established the status of the English language as a proper medium for serious writing. The process by which the legislative function was transferred to Parliament may be traced in any of the standard works on legal history. However, one natural result of this transfer was that statutes – a term which basically means simply decrees which have been set up or established – became known as Acts of Parliament.

Securing the enactment of legislation by the King in Council involved the submission of a petition or Bill asking for a particular legal remedy to be made available, in response to which a committee of judges, royal advisers and other officials would draft a statute. The fifteenth century saw the origin of the modern practice of drafting Bills in the form of the statute which was itself the desired result of the legislative process.

Although very few of these early statutes are likely to be encountered by the modern lawyer, it is interesting to note that the history of statutory drafting shows that there is nothing new in the complaint that statutes are unnecessarily obscure:

'From the laconic and often obscure terseness of our earliest statutes, especially when in Latin, we swung in the sixteenth, seventeenth and eighteenth centuries to a verbosity which succeeded only in concealing the real matter of the law under a welter of superfluous synonyms.' (Allen, *Law in the Making*, 7th edn, 1964, p. 482.)

Commentators on the law are not, of course, alone in noting the potential conflict between a multiplicity of words and clarity of meaning. As Alexander Pope said, albeit in another context:

> 'Words are like leaves, and where they most abound
> Much fruit of sense beneath is seldom found.'
> *(An Essay on Criticism.)*

Jonathan Swift noted one possible solution, albeit from a fictitious legal system:

> 'No law [in Brobdingnag] must exceed in words the number of letters in their alphabet, which consists only in two and twenty. But indeed few of them extend even to that length. They are expressed in the most plain and simple terms, wherein those people are not mercurial enough to discover above one interpretation; and to write a comment upon any law is a capital crime.' *(Gulliver's Travels: A Voyage to Brobdingnag,* 1726, ch.7.)

Many students, faced with the vast literature on English law might sympathize with the view that writing about the law should be a capital crime. On the other hand, no-one could pretend that the Brobdingnagian restriction on the length of laws would be practical in a modern legal system, unless it had the obvious result of causing an immediate extension of the alphabet by several thousand characters, which would in turn produce its own difficulties.

The origins of the Office of the Parliamentary Counsel

The modern English orthodoxy that legislative drafting is a highly specialized skill is not shared by all other legal systems. For example, the American practice is for legislation to be prepared not only by the Offices of Legislative Counsel of the House of Representatives and the Senate, but also by the legal staffs of committees of Congress and individual government departments. According to Reed Dickerson, a distinguished American commentator who gave evidence to the *Committee*

on the Preparation of Legislation, under the chairmanship of Sir David
Renton:

> 'Most legislation in the United States is drafted by people who, however
> good they may be in their substantive specialities, have only fleeting
> acquaintance with the expertise required for good drafting. This is
> perhaps the main reason why so much of American legislation is
> inadequate . . . [the British] are light years ahead of us in this respect.'
> (Para.8.18 of the Committee's Report, 1975, Cmnd 6053.)

Even in England, the practice of specialized legislative drafting has been
established for less than 150 years. In the early nineteenth century, the
drafting of government Bills was still allocated either to drafters attached
to individual government departments or to lawyers in private practice.
The latter undertook the work of legislative drafting for the Government
just as they would undertake any other work for any other client.

18.2 The Modern Office of the Parliamentary Counsel

In 1869 Henry Thring – later Lord Thring – was appointed to the newly-
created office of Parliamentary Counsel to the Treasury. The last three
words are no longer part of the title, and the office is now part of the
Cabinet Office. It seems the removal of the limiting words, which dates
from the creation of the Civil Service Department in 1969, was simply an
expedient to avoid having to change the name of the office whenever
internal reorganizations of the Civil Service occur. Although counsel have
a close working relationship with the Law Officers, they are not responsible to them in a departmental sense.

Thring was not a complete newcomer to legislative drafting, having
been engaged in such work initially while in private practice at the bar, and
subsequently as a drafter attached to the Home Office. His department
consisted originally of himself and a single assistant. Nevertheless, on the
basis that even the longest journey begins with a single step, Thring's
appointment was probably one of the most important individual events in
the history of English legislative drafting, introducing as it did the idea
that it was desirable for legislative drafters to be full-time specialists.

Although dissenting views are heard from time to time (see, for
example, p. 329 for Dale's view of the continental experience), there is
no doubt that the currently prevailing – indeed entrenched – view is that
such specialization in drafting is not merely desirable but virtually
essential. For example, in 1985 a very distinguished group of academic
lawyers presented a report to the Law Commission, concerning the

codification of the general principles of criminal liability. The group drafted a proposed code, but acknowledged that their code 'would require the expert attention of Parliamentary Counsel' (Law Com 143, para.0.5).

In short, therefore, the orthodox English view supports Pope's assertion:

> 'True ease in writing comes from art not chance,
> As those move easiest who have learn'd to dance.'
>
> (*An Essay on Criticism.*)

The Office of the Parliamentary Counsel has developed from its tiny origins with Thring and his single assistant into a group of approximately 30 lawyers, with both solicitors and barristers being eligible for appointment. The head of the Office has the style of First Parliamentary Counsel.

The principal task of Parliamentary Counsel is the drafting of all government legislation, except that relating exclusively to Scotland and Northern Ireland, each of which has its own legislative drafters. Additionally, Parliamentary Counsel may draft delegated legislation if asked to do so by the responsible department, but usually each department's own lawyers will undertake such work themselves. Additionally, where delegated legislation drafted by departmental lawyers amends primary legislation (which is particularly likely to be the case where English law is being amended in response to a Community obligation) the practice is for Parliamentary Counsel to settle the draft of the proposals.

Before looking more closely at the work of Parliamentary Counsel it may be instructive to consider the kind of personal qualities which are thought to be necessary in a good drafter. In 1951, the then First Parliamentary Counsel explained that the standard of entry was high because 'only men or women of first class ability can do the work' (Sir Granville Ram, *The Improvement of the Statute Book* [1947–51] JSPTL, p. 442). More recently, recruitment literature issued by the Civil Service Commission in 1988 expressed the qualities considered to be necessary:

> 'Drafting Bills calls ideally for an analytical mind, imagination, mental toughness, physical endurance, practical as well as intellectual ability and (a quality which may be acquired by practice) the power to express oneself on paper. Many Bills are prepared under pressure, generated either by the need to adhere to a pre-determined Parliamentary programme or by the immediate urgency of the particular Bill. This pressure is sometimes intense, and the hours of work are not always predictable. The intrinsic interest of the work and the difficulties of the problems to be solved make the life stimulating and, when the pressure is great, arduous.'

The working methods of the Parliamentary Counsel Office were described by Sir George Engle, the then First Parliamentary Counsel, in a paper presented to a Franco-British Round Table on Legislative Drafting in 1986, the transactions of which were published by London University's Institute of Advanced Legal Studies as *British and French Statutory Drafting* (1987). Engle's account is worth considering at some length, in view of both the authoritative nature of its source and the central importance of the subject-matter.

'Every government Bill is drafted by Parliamentary Counsel upon the instructions of the Government Department concerned. These drafting instructions are normally in writing – I say 'normally' because there can be some form of instant legislation required in which case it may be necessary for somebody to rush around and speak – and are prepared by one of the Department's legal advisers in consultation with its administrators ... Before they are sent to Parliamentary Counsel, drafting instructions are usually cleared with any other government department likely to be affected by the proposed legislation.

'Drafting instructions are expected to give, in plain language, a full explanation of the purpose and background of the Bill, and to state what existing legislation affects the subject ... [They] do not take the form of a draft of a Bill ... though they sometimes ask for provisions similar to those which appear in an existing Act ...

'On receipt of drafting instructions for a Bill, the First Parliamentary Counsel allocates the Bill to one of the senior Counsel, who from then on has full responsibility for it. Counsel usually work in pairs, so the senior Counsel (whom I will refer to as 'the draftsman') will normally be assisted by a less experienced junior Counsel ... The draftsman is responsible for the actual wording of the Bill; and his functions include, to a greater or lesser extent, the clarification and detailed working out, in concert with the lawyers and administrators in the Department, of the policy to be given effect to by the Bill and of the conceptual and legislative structure appropriate for the purpose.

'When ... the draftsman fully understands the instructions and has cleared up any difficulties which they present, he produces a first draft of the Bill and sends it to the Department concerned, where it is examined both by the legal advisers and by the administrators ... Copies are also sent to other interested departments for comment. On the basis of the comments received, the draftsman produces a revised draft – and this process continues until the Bill is considered ready for presentation to Parliament ... A large Bill may take nine months or more to draft ... and could go through ten or more drafts ... When a draft Bill is ready, it is circulated to all Government Departments, and its presentation to Parliament is finally authorized by a small committee of Ministers whose members include the Lord Chancellor and the Law Officers . . .

'. . . a Bill can be amended at various stages during its passage through each House of Parliament. Amendments propose the insertion, omission or substitution of words in the text of the Bill under consideration . . . All amendments therefore need to be drafted with as much skill as the Bill itself. All amendments proposed by the Government are drafted by the draftsman of the Bill on instructions from the Department. Other proposed amendments are drafted by the Member proposing them or are supplied to him by organizations or pressure groups outside Parliament. Their drafting is nearly always unsatisfactory; so if the government is willing to accept a badly drafted amendment in principle, the Minister will ask the proposer to withdraw it . . . in return for an undertaking by the Government to propose a properly drafted Government amendment at the next stage of the Bill . . . Similarly if, as sometimes happens, an unsatisfactorily drafted amendment is passed against the wishes of the Government, then unless this defeat can be reversed at a later stage, the draftsman will be instructed to prepare whatever further amendments are needed to remedy the defective drafting.' (*British and French Statutory Drafting*, 1987, pp. 19–22.)

In passing, it is worth noticing that Engle's opening comment ('every government Bill is drafted by Parliamentary Counsel') has recently become subject to a very minor qualification. By way of an experiment, approximately 10 per cent of the Bill which became the Finance Act 1996 was drafted by private sector drafters, who were chosen following an open competition. The experiment will be evaluated in due course.

The existence of the Office of the Parliamentary Counsel as a specialized unit does not detract from its essential nature as a provider of technical services. The Office is consulted as and when government departments wish to introduce legislation, and the Office is expected to act on instructions, just as any other professional adviser is expected to act on behalf of his client. Kent, a former Parliamentary Counsel, considered that the Office was governed by two rules:

'The first was that nothing was undraftable, if the conception was clear. The second was that whenever the Government demanded a Bill by a certain time, which might be twenty four hours later, that Bill would be delivered. It might be wrong, indeed it was bound to be wrong, but it would be there.' (*In on the Act: Memoirs of a Law Maker*, 1979, p. 19.)

One beneficial consequence of the existence of a specialist Office is that it helps to guarantee the integrity of the legislative process. The point can be made by way of contrast with the American practice whereby departmental lawyers draft many Bills. Commenting on this, Dickerson said:

'Some Bill drafters in the executive branch intentionally use fuzzy or misleading language to get the legislature unwittingly to enact policies that come to light only when the agency sponsoring the legislation is given a chance to administer it.' (*Legislative Drafting in London and Washington* [1959] CLJ, p. 49.)

The calculated use of 'fuzzy or misleading language' by the drafter, as distinct from the politicians who are responsible for the formulation of the legislative policy, contrasts strongly with the British tradition. When one administrator commented that a particular provision in a draft Bill was 'nice and vague', Kent's response was that this was 'a dubious compliment' (*In on the Act: Memoirs of a Law Maker*, 1979, p. 45).

It is important to maintain a sense of perspective. The drafter must bear in mind the fact that the authority of those instructing him – or at any rate the authority of their political masters – ultimately derives its legitimacy from the electoral process: 'He operates only as a technician, but the democratic process requires that he does so as an ardent democrat. He needs to be fired by a sense of the public importance of his function' (Bennion, *Statute Law*, 3rd edn, 1990, p. 21). Similarly, insight may be derived from the following comment of the Renton Committee: 'Between the taking of policy decisions and the start of the drafting process, and shading into that process, is what First Parliamentary Counsel has called "the grey area"' (*The Preparation of Legislation*, 1975, para.8.5). It is easy to discern here an echo of the inevitability, if not the despair, which T. S. Eliot noted in *The Hollow Men*:

'Between the idea
And the reality
. . .
Falls the Shadow.'

One aspect of the existence of a separate Office which should not be underestimated is the very considerable influence of its members in terms of promoting or resisting change. Thus on one occasion Bennion was able to secure the use the modern phrase 'tried his best' in place of the more conventional 'used his best endeavours' (*Statute Law*, 3rd edn, 1990, p. 35), although some Members of Parliament were less than enthusiastic and the more traditional usage might well have prevailed if a General

Election had not supervened. On the other hand, as Lord Cross of Chelsea said, of the long-running argument over whether the detailed British style of drafting is preferable to the more generalized but economical Continental style: 'But in truth the debate as to the respective merits of the two systems is somewhat academic because . . . there is not the remotest likelihood of Parliamentary Counsel voluntarily abandoning their system of drafting' ([1981] Stat LR, p. 123).

18.3 The Drafting Process

Introduction

According to Kent:

'There are two main objects that the draftsman aims at, and they are not easy to reconcile. First and foremost, to get the Bill right. The test is that when it is passed, and a trained lawyer or judge has mastered its intricacies, the meaning is clear (in the sense of unambiguous) and the intention carried out. Subject to this, the second object is to make the Bill as intelligible as possible to Parliament and the general public.' (*In on the Act: Memoirs of a Law Maker*, 1979, p. 97.)

Leaving aside the presumably unintentional implication that judges are not trained lawyers, the most interesting aspect of this comment is the use of the phrase 'clear (in the sense of unambiguous)'. This concept of clarity is further illuminated by an examination of, and a comment on, the provision which eventually became s.89(8) of the Civil Defence Act 1939:

'For the purposes of this Act, the number of persons who work in or about a mine shall be deemed to be a number ascertained as follows, that is to say –
(a) by having regard to all the people employed in or about the mine and ascertaining how many of them are from time to time simultaneously present in or about the mine otherwise than below the surface, and
(b) if the numbers so ascertained fluctuate, by ascertaining the highest figure below which throughout any consecutive period of fifteen minutes the numbers do not fall.'

When the responsible Minister, Sir John Anderson, was told that the drafter was trying to simplify the provision, he replied that there was no need to change the wording because 'it's perfectly clear, when you understand it'. Kent acknowledged that 'this seemed to draw the proper distinction between clarity (intelligibility) and clarity (unambiguity)' (*In on the Act: Memoirs of a Law Maker*, 1979, p. 118). This distinction, although easily overlooked, is also useful in perceiving the real meaning of a famous dictum coined by another eminent Parliamentary Counsel, Sir John Rowlatt: 'The intelligibility of a Bill is in inverse proportion to its chance of being right' (quoted by Kent, *In on the Act: Memoirs of a Law Maker*, 1979, p. 97).

No matter how successful the drafter may appear to have been in achieving clarity, there will always be lawyers who wish to dispute the meaning of whatever words are used. There is perhaps more than a grain of truth in Jonathan Swift's description of lawyers as 'a society of men . . . bred up from their youth in the art of proving by words multiplied for the purpose, that white is black, and black is white, according as they are paid' (*Gulliver's Travels: A Voyage to the Country of the Houyhnhnms*, 1726, ch. 5). One consequence of this argumentative propensity on the part of the legal profession, is that, in the words of Stephen J,

'it is not enough [for the drafter] to attain to a degree of precision which a person reading in good faith can understand, but it is necessary to attain if possible to a degree of precision which a person reading in bad faith cannot misunderstand. It is all the better if he cannot pretend to misunderstand it'. (*In re Castioni* [1891] 1 QB 149.)

The next question to be considered, therefore, is: how does the drafter set about achieving this degree of precision?

Thornton's *Five Stages* of Statutory Drafting

G. C. Thornton, whose authority as a commentator on legislative drafting derives from his experience as Parliamentary Counsel in Western Australia and Solicitor-General in Hong Kong, identified five stages of the drafting process, which he labelled *understanding, analysis, design, composition* and *scrutiny* (*Legislative Drafting*, 3rd edn, 1987, p. 112). Before looking at each of these in turn, it is worth noticing that, although the drafter may hope to progress logically through this scheme, the reality of drafting is usually different:

'These five stages cannot be regarded as consisting of five watertight compartments; they are better regarded as recognizable areas of the process as a whole. Progress from stage 1 to stage 5 is usually neither smooth nor regular, and frequently it is necessary to return to an earlier stage and try again.' (Thornton, ibid.)

Understanding

The importance of beginning from a clear understanding of the legislative proposal is emphasised by Kent: 'When you are drafting a big Bill you must get it all in your mind; the multifarious ramifications of the Bill, the background of law and practice, the political issues' (*In on the Act: Memoirs of a Law Maker*, 1979, p. 96).

As we have already seen, from the drafter's point of view, the starting place will usually be the receipt of drafting instructions, although those issuing the instructions may occasionally consult the drafter at a preliminary stage. It is instructive at this point to note that Elmer Driedger, the doyen of Canadian legislative drafters, has been quoted as saying that the Canadian practice of involving drafters at an early stage is thought to 'contribute something to the form and clarity of the statute' (*The Preparation of Legislation*, 1975, para.8.7). According to Thornton, drafting instructions 'should contain sufficient background information to enable the draftsman to see in perspective and in context the facts and problems which the legislative proposal is intended to meet' (*Legislative Drafting*, 3rd edn, 1987, p. 113). More particularly, where the proposals originate from a report of a Royal Commission or some similar advisory body, the report embodying the recommendations should be given to the drafter. Similarly, if the proposal results from a judicial decision, the drafter should be given a copy of the judgement, or at least a reference to it in the law reports.

Second, the instructions should state the principal objects of the legislation clearly and fully, together with the intended means of achieving those objects. They should also refer to all known implications and difficulties, including those of a social or administrative nature, as well as matters of purely legal import.

Analysis

Having understood the legislative proposal itself, the drafter should proceed to analyse it not only in relation to the existing law, but also in relation to both its own intrinsic practicability and to certain 'potential danger areas' in respect of which the drafter has a special responsibility (see Thornton, *Legislative Drafting*, 3rd edn, 1987, p. 115).

The relevance of the existing law is self-evident. The question of the proposal's practicability may, however, seem to be no concern of the drafter, whose role is to be – in Bennion's phrase – 'an ardent democrat'. After all, the decision as to what must be done is essentially a political one which will have been taken before his instructions were prepared. Nevertheless, to take a single example, at a technical level the drafter should take particular care when creating criminal offences to ensure that all the elements justifying conviction are clear, and that, in practical terms, it will be possible to adduce evidence to prove them. More fundamentally, everyone involved in the legislative process, at whatever stage and in whatever role, should constantly remind themselves of Thornton's words:

> 'Experience confirms the widespread existence of an illusion that to legislate in respect of a problem is of itself in some way to meet that problem, as if legislation amounted in some mystical way to action instead of amounting only to a legal framework for action.' (*Legislative Drafting*, 3rd edn, 1987, p. 120.)

Turning to the topic of the drafter's special responsibilities, once again, of course, it would be possible simply to say that the merits and demerits of the proposal are not the drafter's concern. However, Thornton puts the drafter's position into perspective:

> 'His independence from the instructing officer or department and his familiarity with law as a whole enables him to see a legislative proposal in a wider and more balanced context than is possible for those who instruct him. It is the ability to see the legislative proposals against the background of the whole structure of the law which gives the draftsman both an advantage and a special responsibility.'

One particular aspect of this special responsibility requires closer attention. It is well established that the courts may apply a variety of presumptions in statutory interpretation in situations where the wording of the statute is capable of bearing more than one meaning (see pp. 300–18). By their very nature, presumptions deal with matters which are not explicit. Accordingly, the drafter must bear them constantly in mind, so that either the statute can be drafted in terms which avoid the possibility of the courts employing a particular presumption which the drafter did not consider to be relevant, or the intention that the courts should rely on a presumption is genuinely implicit, as distinct from not having been given any consideration at all.

The existence of presumptions emphasizes the significance of many of Thornton's 'potential danger areas', which may be briefly summarized as including proposals which:

(a)   affect personal rights;
(b)   affect private property rights;
(c)   would be retrospective in effect;

(d) are inconsistent with international obligations;
(e) are of doubtful constitutional propriety;
(f) are unnecessarily bureaucratic;
(g) affect the interests of other government departments or public bodies; and
(h) affect prerogative powers.

(See *Legislative Drafting*, 3rd edn, 1987, pp. 116–20.)

Design

Obviously the drafter should observe the established conventions as to the layout of a statute. For example, the reader expects to find the short title, and provisions dealing with definitions, commencement and territorial extent towards the end of an Act.

At a more general level it is important to bear in mind the political realities, such as presenting the material in an order which will facilitate debate in Parliament. Political factors may, of course, conflict with the principles of good drafting, in which case the problem will be solved according to the relative importance of the competing points of politics and drafting, and the personalities involved. In this situation, however, the drafter should recall one of the recommendations of the *Renton Report*:

'In principle the interests of the ultimate users should always have priority over those of the legislators: a Bill, which serves a merely temporary purpose, should always be regarded primarily as a future Act, and should be drafted and arranged with this object in view.' (*The Preparation of Legislation*, 1975, para.10.3.)

Engle expands on three constraints on Parliamentary drafting in an article entitled *Bills Are Made To Pass As Razors Are Made To Sell* ([1983] Stat LR, p. 7). This curious title is, in fact, a much-quoted aphorism of Thring, first published in 1875 in a pamphlet on *Simplification of the Law*. It is an allusion to an eighteenth-century poem by the pseudonymous Peter Pindar. The poem concerns a street-trader who sells razors very cheaply. When a disgruntled customer called Hodge returns to complain that the razors are useless for shaving, the poet says:

'"Friend", quoth the razor-man, "I am no knave:
As for the razors you have bought,
Upon my soul, I never thought
That they would *shave*".
"Not think they'd shave!" quoth Hodge with wondering eyes

And voice not much unlike an Indian yell;
"What were they made for then, you dog?" he cries –
"Made!" quoth the fellow with a smile, – "to sell".'
(Quoted at [1983] Stat LR, p. 9.)

Although concluding that Thring's aphorism was intended light-heartedly, Engle does say: 'Just as . . . razors must indeed sell before they get a chance to shave, so . . . Bills must pass before they can become law and do their work' (ibid). Engle's three constraints on Parliamentary drafting are, first, that statutes are legal documents; second, that time is always short; and third that it is impracticable continuously to redesign the fundamental structure of a Bill even when repeated amendments have distorted the original conception.

Taking these in turn, Engle cited Sir Bruce Fraser's 1973 revision of Sir Ernest Gowers' *The Complete Plain Words* in order to illuminate the significance of the status of legal documents:

'The legal draftsman . . . has to ensure to the best of his ability that what he says will be found to mean precisely what he intended, even after it has been subjected to detailed and possibly hostile scrutiny by acute legal minds . . . What matters most to him is that no-one will succeed in persuading a court of law that his words bear a meaning which he did not intend, and, if possible, that no-one will think it worthwhile to try.'

So far as shortage of time is concerned, Engle explained the practical reality thus:

'The process of settling the legislative programme for a given session of Parliament may take . . . anything up to five months; and the fact that it only starts around Christmas, after the preceding session has got under way, means that the final details will probably not be decided until some time in May – though it may be clear before then that certain Bills will almost certainly be included. This period of uncertainty coincides with the main period of Parliamentary activity on the current session's Bills, when departmental lawyers and administrators may have little or no time to spare for new work. So until a sponsoring department knows for certain that a particular Bill . . . has obtained a firm place in the next session's programme, it will in the nature of things be reluctant to devote too much of the time of its hard-pressed officials to the detailed working out of the policy, let alone to the all-important but onerous task of preparing draft instructions – something which, in any case, cannot be taken very far until the details of the policy have been settled.

'The result of this is that, for too many Bills, the time left for serious work on their preparation is less, and for large and difficult Bills often far less, than the minimum needed to do the job satisfactorily. Instructions may have to be sent before the policy is finally settled. Drafting too often has to begin on the basis of partial or incomplete instructions.' ([1983] Stat LR, pp. 13–14.)

Of course, Engle is not the first drafter to bemoan the lack of time. For example, Kent explained how political developments resulted in only about 48 hours being available for the drafting of a four-and-a-half-page clause dealing with the treatment of the endowment funds of voluntary hospitals when the National Health Service was created. With evident feeling, he comments that this clause 'caused me as much anxiety, one way and another, as anything I ever drafted' (*In on the Act: Memoirs of a Law Maker*, 1979, p. 168).

However, as Sir Noel Hutton, another former First Parliamentary Counsel, pointed out, constraints of time may benefit drafters in one way, because 'they are always striving after the perfection which . . . is usually in fact unattainable; and the last bell, even if it comes too soon, does at least release them from that vain endeavour' (*The Mechanics of Law Reform* (1961) 24 MLR, p. 18). There can be few drafters who, whether with relief or frustration, have never concluded that Bills, like poems, are never finished but merely abandoned.

Engle explained his third constraint, namely the impracticability of continuous redesign, thus:

'In the case of nearly all complex or controversial Bills, the process of amendment goes relentlessly on; and though the draftsman can sometimes achieve a measure of redesign in the course of preparing government amendments to the Bill, his ability to do anything radical in this line is limited by the fact that it is usually not until the Bill is nearing the end of its course that its ultimate content becomes settled in substance . . .' ([1983] Stat LR, p. 15.)

Composition

Although all drafters will develop their own methods of composition, it is common to find that the first draft is composed with the creation of overall structure and the establishment of basic principles uppermost in the drafter's mind, while the elaboration of detail may be reserved for subsequent drafts.

Drafters may, of course, quite properly use precedents from previous statutes. In some cases, precedents from other jurisdictions may be particularly useful in this respect, since the different solutions which different drafters have adopted in respect of similar problems are likely to provide much food for thought.

Scrutiny

Although all drafters will try to detect errors in their own work, there may come a point where scrutiny by a colleague who has no previous knowledge of the Bill may be useful.

18.4   Parliamentary Supervision of Legislative Drafting

It is tempting, though erroneous, to think that the progress of a Bill through Parliament necessarily provides a sufficiently fine filter to ensure the elimination of infelicitous drafting. Once again pressure of time is at the heart of the problem.

Engle analysed the 30 Parliamentary sessions from 1952–3 to 1980–81 ([1983] Stat LR, pp. 13–14). He found 20 of them to be of normal length, that is to say the House of Commons sat for between 160 and 180 days in each of them. After deducting time to take account of Consolidation and Statute Law Revision Bills, and the inevitable Finance and Consolidated Fund Bills and associated matters, there were only, on average, 62 days per session left for optional, or 'programme' Bills. Some indication of the amount of consideration which each one received may be gleaned from the fact that on average 42 programme Bills were passed in each session. The result is that:

'Into the sixty-odd days available for programme Bills there have to be fitted all those proceedings on these Bills which fall to be taken on the floor of the House, namely Second Reading, Committee of the whole House, Report, Third Reading and, for Bills amended by the Lords after they have left the Commons, Consideration of Lords' Amendments. In practice the Committee stage of nearly all programme Bills takes place "upstairs" in one of the standing committees rather than on the floor of the House; and since 1965 it has been possible for the government, with the agreement of the Opposition, to arrange for the Second Readings of a number of non-controversial government Bills to be taken upstairs in a Second Reading Committee, thus saving some time in the House itself. Even so, when it comes to deciding how many Bills can sensibly be included in the legislative programme for a given session, the primary constraint is the number of days on the floor of the House that they may be expected to occupy.' ([1983] Stat LR, p. 12.)

18.5 Consolidation and Statute Law Revision

So far we have been considering what might be called 'new' law. It is appropriate to conclude, however, by mentioning the concepts of consolidation and statute law revision. Taking these concepts in turn:

> 'A consolidation statute . . . is an expedient of convenience to assemble and re-enact a number of antecedent statutory provisions. It often happens that a long course of legislation on a particular subject, involving many repeals, amendments, and supplements, is scattered in unwieldy fashion over the so-called statute book, until the time comes when it is necessary to "tidy it up".' (Allen, *Law in the Making*, 7th edn, 1964, p. 477.)

It follows that, basically, consolidation does not change the law, but merely reorganizes it so as to improve its accessibility. Such Bills are usually called 'pure' consolidation. However, since the Consolidation of Enactments (Procedure) Act 1949, it has been possible to consolidate with the addition of 'corrections and minor improvements'. This phrase is defined by s.2 of the Act as:

> 'Amendments of which the effect is confined to resolving ambiguities, removing doubts, bringing obsolete provisions into conformity with modern practice, or removing unnecessary provisions or anomalies which are not of substantial importance, and amendments designed to facilitate improvements in the form or manner in which the law is stated, and includes any transitional provisions which may be necessary in consequence of such amendments.'

Since the creation of the Law Commissions, however, this procedure has largely fallen into disuse, having been replaced by the practice of drafting consolidating Bills which incorporate amendments reflecting Law Commission recommendations. The two Law Commissions – one for Scotland and one for England and Wales – were created by the Law Commissions Act 1965. By s.3(1) of the Act, the task of each Commission is:

> 'To take and keep under review all the law with which [it is] concerned with a view to its systematic development and reform, including in particular . . . the elimination of anomalies, the repeal of obsolete and unnecessary enactments, the reduction of the number of separate enactments and generally the simplification and modernisation of the law.'

Statute law revision is the name often given to the process whereby a statute is enacted to repeal earlier statutes, or parts of statutes, which have become obsolete for one reason or another. Unlike Scots Law, which has a limited doctrine of desuetude extending to Acts of the Scots Parliament which existed before the Act of Union 1707, English Law has no doctrine, even of a limited nature, which could reduce the need for such revision.

The significance of the concepts of consolidation and statute law revision is that Bills of both kinds qualify for a specially expedited Parliamentary procedure, at the heart of which is the Joint Committee on Consolidation etc. Bills, composed of members from both the Commons and the Lords. The expedited Parliamentary procedure consists of the Bills being automatically referred to the Joint Committee after a formal Second Reading in the House into which they are first introduced, which in practice is the House of Lords. The procedure therefore is intended to provide sufficient Parliamentary scrutiny to satisfy constitutional propriety, whilst ensuring that the Bills entrusted to it occupy a bare minimum of time on the floor of each House.

The drafting of consolidation and statute law revision Bills is undertaken principally by Parliamentary Counsel on secondment to the Law Commission, although there has been some limited use of external expertise – for example, by using retired members of the Office (*The Preparation of Legislation*, 1975, para.14.16). Although the drafting of consolidation Bills may sound a simple and straightforward process, the reality is rather different:

> 'Consolidation . . . is really a matter very often of extreme difficulty, more than the Committee would imagine . . . There is very great difficulty in getting it done; it is a task requiring exceedingly skilled and rare labour, and the labour of months . . . skilled labour of a character which I cannot always get; it is not altogether a question of money.' (Lord Thring, quoted in the Renton Report on *The Preparation of Legislation*, 1975, para.14.15, where the view was accepted as having continuing validity.)

18.6   Tilling's Rules for the Drafting of Legislation

The identity of Mr Tilling is a matter of some uncertainty, but he was clearly a civil service administrator. Although he obviously wrote his 'rules' in light-hearted vein, they may not be wholly without a grain of truth, and they will at least provide a measure of light relief. Tilling's Rules reflect a tripartite relationship between an administrator from the instructing department, a solicitor from the instructing department and parliamentary counsel. This still represents the normal practice in most contexts, except that it is usual for administrators in the Inland Revenue to instruct Parliamentary Counsel directly.

Tilling's Rules

'1. Your first step in drafting your Bill consists in disclosing to the public the day on which the Bill will come into force.

'2. Immediately after that, your solicitor will tell you exactly what to do next. Insofar as the consent of any other adult is needed, he will have obtained it.

'3. You will then instruct your solicitor – i.e. you will disclose in writing that you do not know what the law is now or how you would like it altered.

'4. Your solicitor will then instruct your counsel – i.e. disclose to him in writing that he (the solicitor) does not know what the law is now or what it will be if his proposals for altering it are implemented.

'5. You will then be invited to take part in a discussion with your solicitor and your counsel. Remember that, before and during the event, the discussion is called "a conference". Not until afterwards may you call it "a shambles".

'6. Your solicitor will then send you drafts of sections which, to confuse you, he will call "clauses".

'7. Read them carefully. If in your opinion they accurately and intelligibly reflect your intentions, they will need correcting.

'8. Beware of the common error of telling your counsel how to draft. You must tell your solicitor why the results of the drafting will be disastrous. He will not agree with you but will explain that, for reasons which you have failed to see, the results will be disastrous in a way you will not comprehend.

'9. Action will follow as in 4 and 5 above. Do not be distressed if your solicitor hesitates to tell your counsel to "belt up and get on with it". Solicitors do not address counsel in this way, as both are descended from a common stock, known in English folklore as "the fiddlers three". You yourself may tell counsel to "belt up": but see 15 below.

'10. If your Bill is a hybrid Bill – i.e. bad only in parts – the third fiddler, called "an agent", will join the party. He will explain that it is now too late. Nobody else will believe this, so you must keep on with it.

'11. Eventually you will have either a General Election, a change of policy, a coronary, or a Bill. The last two may occur simultaneously.

'12. From now on it is vital that you consistently misinterpret the Bill. Your solicitor will claim to understand it, and – as the only available man who does – he will have to write the Clause Notes himself.

'13. You will then explain the Bill to your Minister. Do not waste too much time on this: it is unlikely that he will pay attention.

'14. Your Bill will then have two Readings, during which nobody will read it.

'15. After that it will go into Committee. At this stage people will put down amendments. There will be so many that only some can be selected for discussion. Nobody knows how amendments are selected, but if you have needled your counsel hitherto, Heaven help you now.

'16. Your Bill will then have a third Reading, which will resemble the Committee stage, but the accommodation provided for you will be even more uncomfortable.

'17. Your Bill may need "resolutions" and even "Queen's Consent". Do not ask about these complications. Tell your solicitor and your counsel what you have decided: they will enjoy putting you right.

'18. Your Bill will then go to the Lords, if they are still there. Do not worry about this: they are unlikely to commit suicide for your sake.

'19. You will then get the Royal Assent.

'20. All that remains is to disclose to the public the day on which will come into force the Bill putting right what you have just finished doing.'

Summary

1 For several centuries the English legal system had no specialist statutory drafters. However, from 1869 onwards, there has been an office of the parliamentary counsel.

2 The drafting process is complicated by a number of factors, including pressure of time and the possibility of *ad hoc* amendments which may distort the original conception of the Bill as a whole.

3 Parliamentary supervision of the legislative process does not ensure the quality of legislation which is enacted.

4 Special legislative procedures are available for measures embodying consolidation and statute law revision.

5 *Tilling's Rules* provide a light-hearted view of the drafting process as seen from the perspective of a civil service administrator.

Exercises

1 What did Engle identify as the constraints on statutory drafting?
2 What two meanings did Kent ascribe to *clarity*?
3 Read *Tilling's Rules* again. Humour is good for you!

19 Plain Meanings, Mischiefs and Purposes

19.1 Introduction

It is tempting to assume that the process of statutory interpretation simply requires the identification and application of the *literal* (or *plain*) meaning of the enacted words. In fact, however, such simple literalism is fundamentally defective, because it proceeds on the false assumption that a word, or a group of words, will always have a plain meaning. The truth of the matter is that many words have a variety of meanings, and the only way of identifying their meaning on a particular occasion is by reference to the context within which they are used. This proposition is not limited to statutory interpretation, as the examples at p. 12 illustrate. However, a useful judicial statement of the proposition may be found in the case of *Bourne* v. *Norwich Crematorium Ltd* [1967] 1 All ER 576, which is discussed at pp. 8–9, Stamp J said:

'Parliament cannot, so the argument as I understand it runs, have intended to exclude from the definition a process whereby refuse or waste material is destroyed or consumed by fire and, putting it crudely, for it can only be put crudely, the consumption by fire of the human body is a process. I protest against subjecting the English language, and more particularly a simple English phrase, to this kind of process of philology and semasiology. English words derive colour from those which surround them. Sentences are not mere collections of words to be taken out of the sentence, defined separately by reference to the dictionary or decided cases, and then put back again into the sentence with the meaning which one has assigned to them as separate words so as to give the sentence or phrase a meaning which as a sentence or phrase it cannot bear without distortion of the English language. That one must construe a word or phrase in a section of an Act of Parliament with all the assistance one can from decided cases and, if you will, from the dictionary, is not in doubt; but having obtained all that assistance, one must not at the end of the day distort that which has to be construed and give it a meaning which in its context one would not think it can possibly bear.'

Similarly, in *Attorney-General* v. *Prince Ernest Augustus of Hanover* [1957] 1 All ER 49, Viscount Simonds said: 'Words, and particularly general words, cannot be read in isolation, their colour and content are derived from their context.' It follows that the principal task in any exercise in interpretation is to identify the correct context, and much of this Part of the book will be devoted to an examination of the way this is done in practice. Nevertheless, there are two reasons why we cannot simply disregard simple literalism. First, since simple literalism was the basis of statutory interpretation for much of the nineteenth and twentieth centuries, and since its inadequacies gave rise to the modern approach to interpretation, it follows that our understanding of what happens now will be enhanced by an appreciation of the inadequacies of the older technique. Second, some judges may, albeit rarely, still make decisions on the basis of simple literalism, and therefore we need to be able to understand what is happening on those occasions. Pausing only to emphasize that, until we come to *the purposive approach to interpretation* (p. 258), the following discussion does not represent the mainstream of modern judicial technique, we must move on to consider the workings of simple literalism.

19.2 Simple Literalism in Practice

One classic statement of the so-called literal rule is in the *Sussex Peerage Case* (1884) 8 ER 1034, where Lord Tindal CJ said: 'If the words of the statute are in themselves precise and unambiguous, then no more can be necessary than to expound those words in their natural and ordinary sense. The words themselves alone do, in such a case, best declare the intention of the lawgiver.'

The case of *Whiteley* v. *Chappell* (1868–69) LR 4 QB 147 is commonly cited in the context of the literal rule. It was a statutory offence to impersonate 'any person entitled to vote' at an election. The defendant, who had impersonated someone who had been entitled to vote but who had died before the date of the election, was convicted. The defendant's appeal was allowed on the basis that dead men are not 'entitled to vote', and therefore he was not guilty. Although the court came to this decision reluctantly, and the result of the case is commonly regarded as being contrary to common sense, the decision is capable of being supported on grounds other than simple literalism. As with all questions of statutory interpretation, the first question is, or should be: why was the provision enacted? In this case there seem to be two possibilities.

First, if A votes in B's name, B will not subsequently be allowed to vote because the records will show that B has already voted. Therefore the purpose of the enactment may be to prevent A from 'stealing' B's vote. However, a voter who has died can no longer suffer this kind of loss, and therefore, arguably, A should not be convicted of an offence. This argument is strengthened if A, never having had any intention of casting his own vote but knowing how B would have voted, then votes in B's name and in the same way as B would have voted if he were still alive. It is even more arguable in such a case that no harm has been done, and that therefore there should be no criminal liability.

Alternatively, of course, the position may be different, and A might vote twice. This would clearly undermine the integrity of the democratic process, and therefore A should be guilty of an offence. However, if the purpose of the enactment is the prevention of such double voting, it is difficult to see why Parliament did not say so more directly.

The fact that *Whiteley* v. *Chappell* is not as self-evidently absurd as it may appear to be at first sight does not detract from the fact that simple literalism can produce results which are plainly unsustainable. It is not surprising, therefore, that even some nineteenth century judges tried to provide themselves with an escape-route by introducing a qualification which was often described as 'the golden rule'. In *River Wear Commissioners* v. *Anderson* (1877) 2 App Cas 743, Lord Blackburn said:

'The golden rule is . . . that we are to take the whole of the statute together, and construe it all together, giving the words their ordinary signification, unless when so applied they produce an *inconsistency*, or an *absurdity* or *inconvenience* so great as to convince the court that the intention could not have been to use them in their ordinary signification, and to justify the court in putting on them some other signification, which, though less proper, is one which the court thinks the words will bear.' (Emphasis added.)

Ruther v. *Harris* (1876) 1 ExD 97 shows how the golden rule worked in practice. The Salmon Fishery Act 1861 prohibited net fishing for salmon at certain times, and also provided that contravention of the Act could result in forfeiture of 'all fish taken . . . and any net . . . used . . . in taking the same'. The question which arose was whether the nets could be forfeited even though the poachers had been caught before they had taken any fish. Grove J, holding that the nets could be forfeited under these circumstances, said:

'It is no doubt a rule of interpretation that the grammatical construction of a sentence must be followed, but this is not to be adopted when it leads to *difficulty*. I think it is plain that the language of the section is not strictly accurate and grammatical; and it is my opinion that it was intended that the net should be forfeited . . . whenever persons were unlawfully using it in fishing, although no salmon might be caught.' (Emphasis added.)

It is apparent that although the operation of the golden rule did temper the rigour of the literal rule somewhat, the extent to which it did so was uncertain. This was partly due to the fact that the meanings of the terms which were used in order to justify the application of the rule (*inconsistency, absurdity, inconvenience, difficulty*) are all intrinsically vague, but was also partly due to the fact that the very existence of the rule was denied by some judges.

For example, in *R* v. *Judge of the City of London Court* [1892] 1 QB 273, Lord Esher MR said: 'If the words of an Act are clear, you must follow them, even though they lead to a manifest absurdity. The court has nothing to do with the question whether the legislature has committed an absurdity.' Similarly, in *Hill* v. *East & West India Dock Co* (1884) 9 App Cas 448, Lord Bramwell said: 'I should like to have a good definition of what is such an absurdity that you are to disregard the plain words of an Act of Parliament. It is to be remembered that what seems absurd to one man does not seem absurd to another.'

Although the history of statutory interpretation in the English courts during the second half of the twentieth century may be summarized as a retreat from simple literalism and the advance of purposivism, the fact remains that the idea of simple literalism did spring from the basic constitutional concepts of the legislative supremacy of Parliament, the separation of powers and the rule of law. Emphasizing the constitutional nature of statutory interpretation is useful because it stresses that the problems we are addressing are concerned with the allocation of power within the state, rather than being simply a sophisticated form of wordplay. However, as we saw in Part II, the judges are by no means unanimous as to the scope of their proper role in developing the law through the doctrine of precedent, and therefore it is not surprising that they should be similarly inconsistent when considering the nature and extent of their power to manipulate the words which the supreme legislature has enacted.

One of the most famous differences of judicial opinion arose between Denning LJ and the House of Lords in *Magor & St. Mellons Rural District Council* v. *Newport Corporation* [1951] 2 All ER 839. This case cannot be fully understood without some background knowledge of local government finance. Briefly, a large part of any local authority's income came from a sort of local taxation known as the rates. Generally, rates were paid by the occupiers of all land, but it had long been a matter of national policy that agricultural land was not rated. This meant that local authorities with densely populated urban areas generated more rate income in relation to their geographical area than those with sparsely populated agricultural areas. Therefore, in the common situation where a rural area included a dormitory village which functioned as a satellite to an adjoining urban authority, the rate income from the village would be very welcome to the rural authority. Equally naturally, the adjoining urban authority would prefer to see its boundaries redrawn so that the village became part of its area.

Where boundary disputes between local authorities result in the redrawing of boundaries, with a consequent increase in the burden on one authority, the other authority can be liable to pay compensation to its neighbour. In the instant case such a redrawing of boundaries occurred, in a situation where there had been one urban authority and two adjoining rural authorities. However, there was the added complication that, at the same time, the two rural authorities were merged into one new rural authority.

The urban authority argued, on a literal basis, that it had no liability to compensate either the old rural authorities (because they no longer existed), or the new rural authority (because it had just come into existence and therefore it could not be said to have lost anything). Both the Court of Appeal and the House of Lords accepted this argument, but for the present purposes the real interest of the case centres on the dissenting judgement of Denning LJ in the Court of Appeal: 'We sit here to find out the intention of Parliament and of Ministers and carry it out, and we do this better by filling in the gaps and making sense of the enactment than by opening it up to destructive analysis.' This was roundly rejected by the House of Lords, where Lord Simonds said:

> 'The general proposition that it is the duty of the court to find out the intention of Parliament – and not only of Parliament but of Ministers also – cannot by any means be supported. The duty of the court is to interpret the words that the legislature has used. Those words may be ambiguous, but, even if they are, the power and duty of the court to travel outside them on a voyage of discovery are strictly limited.'

He went on to describe the approach which Denning LJ had adopted as: 'A naked usurpation of the legislative function under the thin disguise of interpretation.'

However, Lord Radcliffe was able to reach the same conclusion as Denning LJ, but by more conventional means. Lord Radcliffe's argument had two stages. First, if the amount of compensation had been quantified before the reorganization had taken place, there could be no doubt that both the burden of paying it and the benefit of receiving it would have passed to the successor local authorities, in common with all the other liabilities and assets of the former authorities. Second, there could be no significance in the fact that the sum had not yet been quantified. (Before leaving this case, it is worth noting that the question of the relevance of Ministerial intention will arise again at p. 296, in the context of the use of *Hansard* as an aid to interpretation.)

Another case which is often cited as a classic illustration of the inadequacy of simple literalism is *Inland Revenue Commissioners* v. *Hinchy* [1960] 1 All ER 505, which turned on the interpretation of s.25 of the Income Tax Act 1952. The section provided:

'A person who neglects or refuses to deliver . . . or wilfully makes delay in delivering, a true and correct . . . return . . . shall . . . forfeit the sum of £20 and *treble the tax which ought to have been charged under this Act* . . .' (Emphasis added.)

The taxpayer under-declared interest on a savings account by about £33, thereby evading about £14 in tax. The Inland Revenue claimed the fixed sum of £20 plus treble the taxpayer's total tax bill for the year, which produced a total penalty of over £400. The Court of Appeal held that this was wrong, and that the true liability was the fixed sum of £20, plus treble the tax which had been evaded. This calculation produced a total of about £62.

However, the House of Lords held that the Inland Revenue had been right in the first place, on the basis that 'treble the tax which ought to have been charged' meant what it said, namely treble the total tax liability for the year. One line of reasoning which influenced the House of Lords was that the provision in the 1952 Act could be traced back about 150 years, to a time when methods of collection of taxes were much less efficient. It followed that, in those days, tax evasion was much easier, and therefore it made sense to have Draconian penalties by way of deterrence. The trouble with this is that in other cases the courts have held that the meaning of a statutory provision can change over the years (see p. 318) and that the bindingness of previous precedents may evaporate when the circumstances which gave rise to them no longer exist (see p. 148), so the argument is not as self-evident as it may appear to be.

On the other hand, there is a perfectly good argument in favour of the House of Lords' conclusion. Careful reading of the section shows that there was a single penalty (that is, £20 plus treble another figure), which could arise in a variety of ways (that is, *neglecting* or *refusing* to deliver a full and accurate return, or *delaying* in so doing). In a case where there was merely *delay*, the penalty would have to be calculated on the basis of the total tax liability, because there would be no other figure which could be trebled. Therefore, if the Court of Appeal was right, a taxpayer who dishonestly concealed part of his income would be liable to a smaller penalty than a taxpayer with the same total income who was merely late in making his return. This conclusion seems contrary to common sense.

19.3   The Mischief Rule

The mischief rule itself

The House of Lords' argument in *Inland Revenue Commissioners* v. *Hinchy*, which was based on examining the original purpose of the provision, is an example of the rule of interpretation known variously as the *mischief rule*, and the *rule in Heydon's Case* (1584) 76 ER 637. The facts of that case concerned the intricacies of land law and are irrelevant for our purposes. What matters is the following statement of principle:

'For the sure and true interpretation of all statutes . . . four things are to be discerned and considered:

1st   What was the Common Law before the making of the Act?

2nd   What was the mischief and defect for which the Common Law did not provide?

3rd   What remedy the Parliament hath resolved and appointed to cure the disease of the Commonwealth?

4th   The true reason of the remedy; and then the office of all the judges is always to make such construction as shall suppress the mischief and advance the remedy, and to suppress continuance of the mischief . . . according to the true intent of the makers of the Act.'

How the mischief rule is applied

There was sometimes an element of doubt as to whether the rule in *Heydon's Case* should be regarded as the basic rule, to be applied before seeking a literal meaning, or whether it was a subsidiary rule which became relevant only where literalism had failed to provide a solution. To a large extent, the fact that we are rejecting the notion of simple literalism may seem to indicate that this question is scarcely worth either asking or answering. In fact, however, the question is worth some consideration, because the mischief-based approach to interpretation has developed into the modern basis of statutory interpretation, namely the purposive approach, and anything which enhances our understanding of that approach will be useful.

The leading case is *Maunsell* v. *Olins* [1975] 1 All ER 16, where Lord Simon said:

'The first task of a court of construction is to put itself in the shoes of the draftsman – to consider what knowledge he had and, importantly, what statutory objective he had – if only as a guide to the linguistic register. Here is the first consideration of the "mischief". Being thus placed in the shoes of the draftsman, the court proceeds to ascertain the meaning of the statutory language. In this task "the first and most elementary rule of construction" is to consider the plain and primary meaning, in their appropriate register, of the words used. If there is no such plain meaning (i.e. if there is an ambiguity), a number of secondary canons are available to resolve it. Of these, one of the most important is the rule in *Heydon's Case*. Here, then, may be a second consideration of the "mischief".'

In passing, it is worth noticing that, when Lord Simon speaks of 'linguistic register', he is referring to one specific aspect of the general proposition that meaning depends on context, namely the fact that words may have different meanings when used in ordinary as opposed to technical ways, or in formal as opposed to vernacular ways. For example, the phrase 'black tie' may simply indicate an ordinary tie which is black, and which might therefore be worn at a funeral by a male mourner. On the other hand, in the context of certain types of social events, the phrase 'black tie' is commonly understood to mean that men who are attending should wear dinner jackets, and that women should dress with a corresponding degree of formality.

One practical difficulty with the mischief-based approach to interpretation is that the mischief is only one consideration which the court will take into account, and therefore it may not always be treated as being determinative of the issue. For example, in *Smith* v. *Hughes* [1960] 1 WLR 830, it was an offence under s.1 of the Street Offences Act 1959, for a prostitute 'to solicit in a street . . . for the purpose of prostitution'. The facts were that prostitutes, who were either behind the windows or on the balconies of buildings overlooking the street, were soliciting men who were in the street. The section can, of course, be read in two ways. If the court takes the view that the section should be interpreted strictly in favour of the defendant, it could conclude that a prostitute cannot commit the offence of soliciting unless she is in a street. Alternatively, the court may interpret the Act as meaning simply that it is an offence to solicit men who are in the street. The High Court upheld the second contention, with Lord Parker CJ saying:

> 'Everybody knows that this was an Act intended to clean up the streets, to enable people to walk along the streets without being molested or solicited by common prostitutes . . . For my part, I am content to base my decision on that ground and that ground alone.'

A useful contrast to *Smith* v. *Hughes* may be found in *Fisher* v. *Bell* [1960] 3 All ER 731. It was an offence under the Restriction of Offensive Weapons Act 1959 to 'sell, hire, offer for sale or hire, or lend or give to any person' a flick knife. The High Court held that a defendant who displayed a flick knife in a shop window should be acquitted of offering it for sale, because technically, according to the law of contract, a shop-keeper does not make an offer to sell his goods: the customer makes an offer to buy, which the shopkeeper then accepts. Although this may be regarded as a perfectly legitimate application of the principle of strict interpretation of penal provisions (see p. 306), the fact remains that it frustrates, rather than promotes, the suppression of the mischief at which the Act was clearly aimed. Incidentally, it is interesting to note that this case prompted the enactment of s.1 of the Restriction of Offensive Weapons Act 1961, which extended the offence under the 1959 Act to include anyone who 'exposes or has in his possession for the purpose of sale or hire' an offensive weapon.

Although it is practically impossible to reconcile *Smith* v. *Hughes* with *Fisher* v. *Bell* at the level of legal doctrine, it may not be altogether fanciful to discern the operation of differing inarticulate major premises in terms of the judges' attitudes towards shopkeepers and prostitutes. (See p. 14 for an explanation of the concept of the inarticulate major premise.)

19.4   The Purposive Approach to Interpretation

General recognition of the inadequacies of simple literalism means that modern judges have had to look elsewhere for a guiding principle. More particularly, the judges have been increasingly willing to accept that the purpose underlying the words which they are considering is an important part of the context within which those words are used. This has led them to adapt the idea of the mischief rule into what is now commonly called the purposive approach. As Lord Diplock said in *Carter* v. *Bradbeer* [1975] 3 All ER 158:

'If one looks back to the actual decisions of this House . . . over the last thirty years one cannot fail to be struck by the evidence of a trend away from the purely literal towards the purposive construction of statutory provisions.'

The closeness of the link between purposivism and the rule in *Heydon's Case* is underlined by the fact that it is quite common for the courts still to speak in terms of mischiefs. Strictly speaking, however, there are three points of distinction between the mischief rule and purposivism. First, as *Heydon's Case* itself makes clear, the mischief rule applies only where there is a gap in the common law, whereas purposivism clearly applies whether the area covered by the enactment was previously within the domain of common law or statute law. Second, and more importantly, purposivism is merely one aspect of the modern emphasis on the importance of context, and therefore can be regarded as a refinement of literalism, in contradistinction to *Heydon's Case*, which pre-dated literalism. Third, according to Lord Diplock in *Black-Clawson International Ltd* v. *Papierwerke Waldhof-Aschaffenburg AG* [1975] 1 All ER 810, the rule in *Heydon's Case* was originally intended to restrict the scope of the court's inquiry to the four corners of the Act itself, whereas purposivism as currently practised clearly allows reference to pre-parliamentary materials, and may even allow reference to *Hansard*. (See pp. 293–9.)

The power of the purposive approach to interpretation can be illustrated by three widely different cases, dealing with the law relating to landlord and tenant, the law relating to majority verdicts in Crown Court trials, and the law relating to adoption.

Kammins Ballrooms Co Ltd v. *Zenith Investments Ltd* [1970] 2 All ER 871 involved the scheme of security of tenure for business premises under Part II of the Landlord and Tenant Act 1954. Briefly, the statutory scheme requires that a tenant who wishes to retain the tenancy of premises on the expiry of the existing tenancy should ask the landlord to grant him a new one. If the landlord refuses to comply, the tenant can then apply to the court where the matter will be resolved. In the context of this procedure, s.29(3) of the Act provides that 'no application . . . shall be entertained unless it is made not less than two nor more than four months after . . . the making of the tenant's request for a new tenancy'. In *Kammins* the tenant's application to the court was made outside the statutory period, but the

House of Lords held that this did not necessarily invalidate it. Lord Diplock acknowledged that:

> 'Semantics and the rules of syntax alone could never justify the conclusion that the words "*No* application . . . *shall be* entertained *unless*" meant that some applications should be entertained notwithstanding that neither of the conditions which follow the word "unless" was fulfilled.' (Original emphasis.)

Nevertheless, this seemingly strange conclusion could be reached by way of the purposive approach. Lord Diplock pointed out that the purpose of the Act was to persuade landlords and tenants to proceed by agreement wherever possible, and that the time limit in question had been enacted for the protection of landlords. It followed that landlords should be entitled to waive compliance with the time limit if they so wished. (The fact that, in the event, this particular landlord was held not to have waived compliance is irrelevant to the principle of interpretation.)

The purposive approach may prevail even over the conventional willingness of the court to give the benefit of the doubt to defendants in criminal cases by construing statutes strictly in their favour, as illustrated by *R* v. *Pigg* [1983] 1 All ER 56. The point in issue was the validity of a conviction for rape. Under s.17(2) of the Juries Act 1974 a majority verdict shall not be accepted unless: 'The foreman of the jury has stated in open court the number of the jurors who respectively agreed to and dissented from the verdict.' In *Pigg* the foreman indicated that ten jurors had agreed to convict, and the clerk of the court then said 'Ten agreed to two of you.' The foreman did not say anything in reply, therefore there had been a contravention of the plain words of the statute. Lord Brandon approached the matter thus:

> 'If the foreman of the jury states no more than that the number agreeing to the verdict is ten, it is nevertheless a necessary and inevitable inference, obvious to any ordinary person, that the number dissenting from the verdict is two. True it is that the foreman of the jury has not said so in terms as the 1974 Act, interpreted literally, requires. In my opinion, however, it is the substance of the requirement . . . which has to be complied with, and the precise form of words by which such compliance is achieved, so long as the effect is clear, is not material.'

It is interesting to note that in *Pigg* the Court of Appeal had felt bound by its own decision in *R* v. *Reynolds* [1981] 3 All ER 849, where the charge involved the less emotive offence of shoplifting. It seems reasonably clear that the peculiarly abhorrent nature of the offence in *Pigg* brought an inarticulate major premise into play in the House of Lords, and that that premise was sufficient to induce the House to depart from the plainest of plain statutory words.

In *Re X (A Minor) (Adoption Details: Disclosure)* [1994] 3 All ER 372, the Court of Appeal was considering the Adoption Act 1976, which, together with regulations made under the Act, requires the Registrar-General to maintain the Adopted Children Register which is open to public inspection and includes, *inter alia*, the names, addresses and occupations of adopting parents. The case involved a child whose natural mother suffered from a personality disorder which made her prone to aggressive and violent behaviour, such that there was reason to fear for the safety of both the social workers in the case and the child itself. The Registrar-General's duty to maintain, and allow inspection of, the register was expressed in absolute terms. Nevertheless, the court concluded that it would be proper to make an order requiring that, until the child became an adult, the Registrar-General must obtain the leave of the court before disclosing any of the registered details relating to that adoption. This conclusion was justified on the basis that the paramount consideration in adoption cases is always the welfare of the child.

On the evidence of cases such as *Kammins*, *Pigg* and *Re X*, you may think that purposivism is objectionable on the constitutional ground that it transfers to the courts a degree of power which ought properly to reside in Parliament. However, there are two reasons why this objection appears to be misconceived. First, a modern understanding of the relationship between Parliament and the courts (see Chapter 20) reveals a functional partnership which is inconsistent with the simplistic notion that Parliament is supreme and the courts are simply subordinate. Second, in *R v. Broadcasting Complaints Commission ex parte Owen* [1985] 2 All ER 522 May LJ said:

'Whilst . . . it is clearly legitimate to adopt a purposive approach and hold that a statutory provision does apply to a given situation when it was clearly intended to do so, even though it may not apply on its strict literal interpretation, nevertheless I do not think that the converse is correct and that it is legitimate to adopt a purposive construction so as to preclude the application of a statute to a situation to which on its purely literal construction it would apply.'

In other words, purposivism is a technique for extending the application of statutory principles rather than restricting them, and so may be seen as a technique for promoting the efficacy of the rules which Parliament has enacted, rather than for frustrating them.

Identifying the purpose

The modern practice of preferring interpretations which promote statutory purposes over those which do not do so requires that the statutory purpose should be identifiable, although there is clearly nothing new in this, since the same point arises whether we speak in terms of *mischiefs* or *purposes*. The traditional view was that in many cases the intention was contained in the words which Parliament had used. As we have already seen (at p. 251) Lord Tindall CJ said, in the *Sussex Peerage Case* (1844) 8 ER 1034: 'If the words of the statute are in themselves precise and unambiguous, then no more can be necessary than to expound those words in their natural and ordinary sense. *The words themselves alone do, in such a case, best declare the intention [or purpose] of the lawgiver*' (emphasis added). However, where the purpose is not clear from the words of the statute there is the makings of a problem, since, as Lord Halsbury LC said in a contract case of similar vintage: 'It appears to me to be arguing in a vicious circle to begin by assuming an intention apart from the language of the instrument itself, and having made that fallacious assumption to bend the language in favour of the assumption so made' (*Leader* v. *Duffy* (1888) 13 App Cas 294).

Two points arise. First, the same comment could be made with equal validity in respect of any instrument, including a statute. Second, although Lord Halsbury's assertion that the assumption as to intention will be fallacious may not always be true, his essential point about circularity remains sound.

There is some authority, discussed at p. 287, to suggest that marginal notes may be used as indicators of the legislative purpose, but you may well wonder why Parliament does not make explicit statements of purpose within statutes themselves. The matter is usefully discussed in the report of the Renton Committee on *The Preparation of Legislation* (1975). This report (commonly referred to as the *Renton Report*) is also considered in Chapter 22, but for the moment we need consider only the following extracts:

'11.7 Among the advocates of statements of purpose are those whose task it is to pronounce or advise on the effects of legislation: members of the judiciary, practising lawyers, and teachers of law. The draftsmen themselves are less enthusiastic. First Parliamentary Counsel takes the view that "in many cases the aims in the legislation cannot usefully or safely be summarized or condensed", and that "there may be a temptation to call for something which is no more than a manifesto, and which may obscure something which is otherwise precise and exact". He also points out that "detailed amendments to a Bill after introduction may not merely falsify the accompanying proposition but may even make it impracticable to retain any broad proposition". The Parliamentary Draftsman for Scotland adopts the same view: apart from certain special circumstances, he says "the Act should in general explain itself". New Zealand's Chief Parliamentary Counsel told us that preambles were rare in public Acts in New Zealand; purpose clauses, forming part of the text of the Act, were sometimes used, but were not thought to aid comprehension. Professor Reed Dickerson thinks that "most purpose clauses are quite unnecessary"; that general purpose clauses tend to degenerate into pious incantations . . . such as . . . the one in a recent ecology Bill, which in substance said "Hurray for Nature!", but that "in prefatory language in individual sentences such as *For the purpose of this*, or *For the purpose of that*, or *In order to do this*, you may have an economic, focussed purpose statement that is of some use".

'11.8 We agree that statements of purpose can be useful . . . A distinction should, however, be drawn between a statement of purpose which is designed to delimit and illuminate the legal effects of the Bill and a statement of purpose which is a mere manifesto . . . the latter kind should in our view be firmly discouraged . . . and we should not like to see a reversion to the archaic use of preambles as a means of declaring or justifying the objectives of public Bills. The preamble can be valuable as a means of reciting facts, such as the terms of a relevant treaty. But when a general statement of purpose is appropriate, we think it should be contained in a clause in the Bill. This has advantages at the Parliamentary stage, since a purpose clause can be amended (or omitted) exactly like any other clause. Preambles are subject to special rules. For the reasons we have given, we think that purpose clauses can be helpful, but that they should be used selectively and with caution.'

It must be said that, on the whole, this aspect of the *Renton Report* has had little effect on the practice of English statutory drafting, although there are notable exceptions, such as s.17 of the Courts and Legal Services Act 1990, which introduces Part II of the Act. The first subsection of the section provides:

'The general objective of this Part is the development of legal services in England and Wales (and in particular the development of advocacy, litigation, conveyancing and probate services) by making provision for new or better ways of providing such services and a wider choice of persons providing them, while maintaining the proper and efficient administration of justice.'

In *Making the Law* (1992), the Hansard Society adopted a different approach to statements of purpose, suggesting that

> 'notes on sections, explaining the purpose and intended effect of each section (and Schedule) should be prepared by Government departments, with the assistance of Parliamentary Counsel, by up-dating the notes on clauses (and notes on amendments) prepared for Ministers; these notes on sections should be approved by Ministers and laid before Parliament, but should not require formal parliamentary approval; and notes on sections should be published at the same time as Acts.' (*Conclusions and Recommendations*, para.36.)

At the level of practical politics, it is worth remembering that excluding statements of purpose from the body of the Act may in some cases facilitate its enactment, by allowing individual members of Parliament to persuade themselves that the Act means what they want it to mean (see also p. 236).

19.5   The Problem of Statutory Nonsense

Although there are cases in which simple literalism and purposivism may produce diametrically opposed results, both techniques will always have at least one thing in common: they will both assume that the enacted words do have some meaning. However, from time to time situations arise where the enacted words are meaningless.

In *Lyde* v. *Barnard* [1835–42] All ER Rep 690, the provision under consideration was s.6 of the Statute of Frauds Amendment Act 1828. The section dealt with certain situations where one person made a 'representation or assurance . . . to the intent or purpose that . . . [an]other person may obtain credit, money, or goods upon'. Although something had clearly gone adrift with the drafting of this provision, the judges disagreed as to what had gone wrong, and what had been intended. Gurney B had no doubt that the word 'credit' should be inserted after 'upon'. Lord Abinger CB, on the other hand, thought that 'upon' should be deleted, on the basis that the draftsman had probably written 'thereupon' and then crossed it out in a careless fashion, so that the typesetter thought only the first syllable was to be omitted.

Some examples of statutory nonsense appear never to have received the benefit of judicial comment. Section 11(5) of the Landlord and Tenant (Rent Control) Act 1949 referred to s.6 of the Furnished Houses (Rent Control) Act 1946, whereas the content of the 1946 Act made it obvious that the reference should have been to s.7 of the Act. The Queen's Printer simply altered the text of subsequent printings of the 1949 Act.

Similarly, s.22(3) of the Artizans and Labourers Dwellings Act (1868) Amendment Act 1879 required that, where mortgage loans were made in accordance with the Act, the mortgage document should be 'in the form set forth in the Third Schedule hereto'. There was no Third Schedule to the Act, nor was there any form of mortgage anywhere else within the Act. Parliament corrected the error with an amending Act the following year.

Now that the courts are much less literalistic, express corrections may not be felt to be necessary unless additional enacted material is required. Section 10(2) of the House of Commons Disqualification Act 1975 provided for the repeal of the enactments 'specified in Schedule 4 to this Act'. The Act contained no Schedule 4, but Schedule 3 was headed 'Repeals' and is plainly what the drafter of s.10(2) intended. This particular embarrassment was removed from the statute book when the Statute Law (Repeals) Act 1977 repealed, *inter alia*, both s.10(2) of, and Schedule 3 to, the 1975 Act.

The examples discussed above may be interesting, but they are not particularly amusing. This deficiency may be remedied by referring to the original version of the Canadian Marriage Act (c.M50: Revised Statutes of Manitoba 1970), dealing with the publication of the banns of marriage, which made provision for the situation where the parties were 'in the habit of attending whorship at different churches' (quoted by Megarry, *A Second Miscellany-at-Law*, 1973, p. 183).

19.6 Are There Any 'Rules' of Interpretation?

Having concluded our survey of meanings, mischiefs and purposes, it is appropriate to ask whether it is sensible to speak of 'rules' of interpretation at all. You may well conclude that the word 'rules' implies a degree of rigidity and precision, and therefore a predictability of outcome, which is simply not present in practice. As Lord Reid said in *Maunsell* v. *Olins* [1975] 1 All ER 16:

'They are not rules in the ordinary sense of having some binding force. They are our servants, not our masters. They are aids to construction: presumptions or pointers. Not infrequently one "rule" points in one direction, another in a different direction. In each case we must look at all relevant circumstances and decide as a matter of judgment what weight to attach to any particular "rule".'

This comment provides a valuable reminder that problems of interpretation, in common with other tasks in legal method, will often involve balancing competing arguments, and deciding which one is to be preferred in the context of the instant case. It may also prompt you to develop the habit of thinking about interpretation in terms of *techniques*, or *principles*, or *approaches*, rather than *rules*.

Summary

1   It is wrong to assume that words always have plain meanings.
2   Nevertheless, the practice of statutory interpretation in the nineteenth century developed largely along the lines of simple literalism.
3   However, the pre-nineteenth-century technique of interpreting statutes in the light of the mischief which they were intended to cure did not die out entirely, and was sometimes used to mitigate the worst excesses of simple literalism.
4   The mischief-based approach has developed into the modern approach known as *purposivism*, under which the starting-point is to consider the purpose of the statute in question.
5   Where statutes literally do not make sense, either Parliament will correct the error or the courts will do their best with the defective text if called upon to do so.
6   Strictly speaking, there are no rules of statutory interpretation. It is more helpful to think in terms of techniques, principles and approaches.

Exercises

1   Why is it wrong to assume that words have plain meanings?
2   What is the relationship between the *mischief rule* and the *purposive approach* to statutory interpretation?

20 The Idea of Legislative Intention

20.1 Introduction

The courts and commentators often use phrases such as 'the intention (or will) of Parliament'. Indeed, for many years *Maxwell on the Interpretation of Statutes* defined 'statutes' as being simply 'the will of the legislature' (see, for example, 11th edn, 1962, p. 1). Similarly, in *Ealing London Borough Council* v. *Race Relations Board* [1972] 1 All ER 105, Lord Simon said: 'It is the duty of a court so to interpret an Act of Parliament as to give effect to its intention.' On the other hand, it is not difficult to find statements, from both academic and judicial sources, which are sceptical about both the existence of 'the intention of Parliament' and its relevance to the process of statutory interpretation. Bell and Engle, for example, say that the phrase is 'not so much a description as a linguistic convenience' (*Cross, Statutory Interpretation*, 3rd edn, 1995, p. 28), while, according to Lord Reid, in *Black-Clawson International Ltd* v. *Papierwerke Waldhof-Aschaffenburg AG* [1975] 1 All ER 810: 'We often say that we are looking for the intention of Parliament, but that is not quite accurate. We are seeking not what Parliament meant but the true meaning of what they said.' Support for Lord Reid's point may be found in *Hilder* v. *Dexter* [1902] AC 474, where Lord Halsbury declined to give judgement as to the meaning of Companies Act 1900, on the ground that he had drafted the Act:

'I have more than once had occasion to say that in construing a statute I believe the worst person to construe it is the person who is responsible for its drafting. He is very much disposed to confuse what he intended to do with the effect of the language which in fact has been employed. At the time he drafted the statute, at all events, he may have been under the impression that he had given full effect to what was intended, but he may be mistaken in construing it afterwards just because what was in his mind was what was intended, though perhaps it was not done. For that reason I abstain from giving any judgment in this case myself.'

In short, it is impossible to imagine a modern English court adopting the view expressed by Hengham CJ in 1305, when he rebuked counsel thus: 'Do not gloss the Statute; we understand it better than you do, for we made it.'

Nevertheless, despite the problems which are inherent in the concept of the intention of Parliament, it can be said to serve a constitutional role, as Lord Simon emphasized in *Stock* v. *Frank Jones (Tipton) Ltd* [1978] 1 All ER 948, when he said:

> 'In a society living under the rule of law, citizens are entitled to regulate their conduct according to what a statute has said, rather than by what it was meant to say, or by what it would have otherwise have said if a newly considered situation had been envisaged.'

Similarly, an American commentator has said:

> 'Of course we use a fiction if we speak of the legislature as if it were a being of one mind. But so durable a fiction endures because it has a use validated by experience. This formula reminds all who deal with a statute that they are operating in a field of law in which they are not free to define public policy simply according to their own judgement.' (Hurst, *Dealing With Statutes*, 1982, New York, p. 33, quoted in Bell and Engle, *Cross, Statutory Interpretation*, 3rd edn, 1995, p. 29.)

The variety of reactions provoked by the idea of the intention of Parliament provides a clear indication that it is a topic deserving close consideration. However, bearing in mind Lord Watson's comment that 'the intention of the legislature' is a 'very slippery phrase' (*Saloman* v. *Saloman & Co Ltd* [1897] AC 22), it may be as well to approach the concept cautiously by recognizing that there are different types of intention, not only in legislation but also more generally.

20.2 Different Types of Intention

Direct and indirect intentions

It is clearly not always realistic to assume that all intentions, even when they are of a single person, are of the same type. For example, I may have both a *direct intention* and an *indirect intention* (or *motive*). The difficulty is that, even if the direct intention is readily apparent, it may well be that the indirect intention is not. For example, a husband and wife may share a direct intention to save a specific sum of money, but one of them may be thinking of spending it on a new car while the other is thinking of spending it on a holiday.

Particular and general intentions

In the context of legislative drafting and interpretation, it is possible to draw a corresponding distinction between *particular intention* and *general intention* (see, Harris, *Legal Philosophies*, 1980, p. 149, adopting the terminology used by the Law Commissions in *The Interpretation of Statutes*, 1969, Law Com No 21). According to this usage, *particular intention* applies to the meaning of the words enacted in a statute, while *general intention* applies to the purpose underlying the enactment of those words. Bearing in mind the fact that in complex societies legislation will typically be produced by multi-member legislatures, it is obvious that the problem of multiple intentions is likely to arise. This may be at the level of either general or particular intention. For example, a shared particular intention to increase taxation may well reflect varying general intentions, such as a desire to curtail the level of activity in the domestic economy, and a desire to increase the level of public spending. Moreover, even particular intentions may vary, since parliamentarians, in common with judges, must sometimes disagree on the meanings of words.

Additionally, in terms of practical politics, the intention of the individual member of the legislature may have other dimensions beyond the narrowly legislative context. In a democratic system, for example, securing re-election may be the prevailing general intention motivating everything which the individual member does. This may lead to voting on legislative proposals according to the member's perception of public opinion, without any intention whatsoever as to the legislative effect of that vote. Alternatively, the member may have no intention beyond toeing the party line, as a matter either of political commitment, intellectual indolence or as a means of currying favour with the party leaders. W. S. Gilbert's account of how Sir Joseph Porter became First Lord of the Admiralty illustrates a combination of the second and third possibilities:

> 'I always voted at my party's call,
> And I never thought of thinking for myself at all.
> I thought so little they rewarded me,
> By making me the Ruler of the Queen's Navee!'
>
> (*HMS Pinafore*, Act I.)

The fact that individual members of a legislature may have different general intentions leads us on to a crucial problem. How can a body such as Parliament be said to have an intention when, not being a natural person, it cannot have a mind? Harris's proposition that 'it is not necessary to assume that the intention of a body of persons is the same sort of thing as the intention of a single person' (*Legal Philosophies*, 1980, pp. 148–9) is clearly correct, but, equally clearly, it gives no indication of what sort of thing the intention of a body of persons actually is.

It is tempting to think we might make progress if we changed our angle of investigation, and concentrated on what words are *understood* to mean, rather than what they are *intended* to mean. This leads on to a consideration of *the speaker's meaning* theory of interpretation.

20.3   The Speaker's Meaning Theory

According to the speaker's meaning theory, legislation is an act of communication in which the legislature transmits its meaning to the judges and to anyone else who uses statutes. Superficially attractive though this theory sounds, it is difficult, if not impossible, to sustain in the face of the problems which it generates. The starting-point is that, in a corporate sense, there can be no speaker. An individual may choose his own words, albeit with greater or lesser felicity according to his degree of linguistic sophistication. In this context the choice of words is part and parcel of the thought process itself: 'Having a thought and choosing words to represent that thought are not two separate activities' (Dworkin, *Law's Empire*, 1986, p. 315).

However, where legislative bodies are concerned, individual members cannot honestly say that the legislative product consists of them expressing themselves in their own words. In reality, individual members are limited to adopting, or rejecting, the words of someone else, who will typically be an apolitical drafter:

> '[The member] is . . . not like someone choosing to communicate some thought or idea or wish. He occupies a position intermediate between speaker and hearer. He must decide what thought the words on the paper before him are likely to be taken to express and then decide whether he wishes that message to be sent . . . given the only realistic alternative of sending no message at all . . . he treats the document, not himself or any other person, as the author of the message he agrees to send'. (Dworkin, *Law's Empire*, 1986, p. 322.)

Even if we resort to the artificial device of deeming the legislature to be the speaker for the present purposes, there remains the difficulty of identifying its collective membership. To be logical, in many cases this would have to be done not only as at the date of the statute's enactment, but also for the duration of each succeeding legislature which allows the statute to continue in force without amendment.

For example, the Offences Against the Person Act 1861 remains, well over a century later, as the major statute defining crimes of violence. In a sense, therefore, every Parliament since the one which enacted it can be taken as having tacitly approved its continuation in force. Therefore the membership of those Parliaments is relevant, if the speaker's meaning theory of interpretation is to be taken seriously. You may respond that the argument about the continued existence of a statute being evidence of a continuing legislative intention is thoroughly artificial, because in reality many statutes continue in existence without successive Parliaments giving them any thought whatsoever. However, it is inconceivable that a statute like the 1861 Act, which is interpreted by the courts on a daily basis, could have been allowed to remain in force unless successive Parliaments had been substantially satisfied with its operation.

The task of identifying the speaker is, therefore, certainly formidable, and probably impossible. In view of the difficulties relating to the concept of general legislative intention, one way forward may be to reject – provisionally at least – theories which depend on Parliamentary majorities and the idea that Parliament is a speaker with a meaning. It may be better to approach the problem of general intention through the concept of *delegation*. Fortunately, this concept is also useful with regard to particular intention.

20.4 Particular Intention

Since Parliament itself cannot speak, it must necessarily delegate to drafters the task of formulating the words to be enacted. It goes without saying that drafters may, and indeed as responsible and effective technicians should, have coherent intentions at least at the level of what they intend their words to mean. It also goes without saying that delegation to the drafter is not absolute and uncontrolled, since the legislature may amend or reject Bills which are submitted to it. Nevertheless the basic fact of delegation to the drafter remains.

At this stage it will be instructive to consider whether the idea of delegation may not also be applicable to explain the functional relationship between the legislature and the courts.

20.5 Delegation to the Judges

The basis of this model of the relationship between the legislature and the judiciary is that when Parliament enacts a statute it realizes that it cannot hope to foresee all possible eventualities. As Payne says:

'The proper office of a judge in statutory interpretation is . . . that of a junior partner in the legislative process, a partner empowered and expected within certain limits to exercise a proper discretion as to what the detailed law should be.' (*The Intention of the Legislature in the Interpretation of Statutes* [1956] *Current Legal Problems*, p. 96.)

Even this model of partnership is too weak for some commentators. For example, Mac Callum says:

'The judgment of . . . persons . . . authorized by the legislature may stand for the judgment of the legislature . . . Thus our discovery of what these persons intended in attempting to . . . interpret the language . . . so as, in their judgment to achieve what the legislature wanted to achieve, is a discovery of intentions that the legislature stood behind, wished us to attend to, wished us to regard as authoritative as their own – indeed wished us to regard as their own. These intentions may therefore be taken as, and in fact are, the intentions of the legislature.' (*Legislative Intent* (1966) 75 Yale LJ 754, reprinted in *Essays in Legal Philosophy*, 1968, ed. Summers.)

The argument so far has not dealt with one fundamental difficulty: given that Parliament allows the judges a discretion, how are the judges to decide how they should exercise that discretion, unless it is by reference to the concept of the general intention of Parliament?

In a simple case, of course, where the language of the statute is clear and explicit, the problem can be glossed over for, as Lord Tindal cj said in *Warburton* v. *Loveland* (1832) 2 D & Cl 480, 'in that case the words of the statute speak the intention of the Legislature'. For more difficult cases it will be useful to consider Dworkin's solution based on the idea of political integrity.

The idea of political integrity

If it is self-evident that the state as a political entity ought to act consistently through the formulation, adoption and application of a coherent body of principle, there is no difficulty in accepting Dworkin's proposition:

'We have two principles of political integrity: a legislative principle which asks lawmakers to try to make the total set of laws morally coherent, and an adjudicative principle, which instructs that the law be seen as coherent in that way, so far as possible.' (*Law's Empire*, 1986, p. 176.)

It follows that, when exercising judicial discretion, judges should look to the coherence of the legal system as a whole: a decision which promotes that integrity is, in a real sense of the word, 'better' than one which detracts from it. If there are disputes as to what the promotion of coherence actually requires in terms of a decision in a specific case, judges must, in the final analysis, simply make up their own minds. A judge

'must rely on his own judgment . . . not because he thinks his opinions are automatically right, but because no one can properly answer any question except by relying at the deepest level on what he himself believes.' (Dworkin, *Law's Empire*, 1986, pp. 313–14.)

Three points must immediately be made. First, the judge's personal beliefs will by no means always be objectively reasoned:

'Any judge will develop . . . a fairly individualised working conception of law on which he will rely . . . in making . . . judgments . . . and the judgments will then be, for him, a matter of feel or instinct rather than analysis.' (Dworkin, *Law's Empire*, 1986, p. 256.)

Admittedly, as Dworkin's second point makes clear, judges' beliefs are unlikely to be highly idiosyncratic because 'most judges will be like other people in their community'. (Ibid.)

Nevertheless, as his third point, Dworkin acknowledges that it is possible, even though unlikely, that a judge with unusually eccentric or radical opinions may emerge. In this eventuality the judge should adopt the solution which will 'show the community's record in the best light', rather than pursuing his own idiosyncrasies. (Ibid.)

As an aside, it is worth commenting that we may accept Dworkin's argument based on political integrity without necessarily also accepting his much more contentious proposition (see p. 11) that judges do not make law at all, but merely declare what the law already is.

Political integrity in operation

The case of *Harrogate Borough Council* v. *Simpson* (1986) 2 FLR 91 illustrates how a decision may be justified on the basis of political integrity. Miss Simpson and Mrs Rodrigo were a lesbian couple who regarded themselves as husband and wife. Mrs Rodrigo was the masculine partner while Miss Simpson was the feminine counterpart. The couple lived in a house owned by Harrogate Borough Council. The tenancy, which was in the sole name of Mrs Rodrigo, was a periodic one and was what is technically known as a 'secure tenancy'. The cohabitation lasted approximately two-and-a-half years, until it was terminated by Mrs Rodrigo's death. The council sought to recover possession of the house from Miss Simpson, and obtained judgement in the county court accordingly. Miss Simpson appealed unsuccessfully to the Court of Appeal.

The relevant parts of s.30 of the Housing Act 1980 stated:

'(1) Where a secure tenancy is a periodic tenancy and, on the death of the tenant, there is a person qualified to succeed him, the tenancy vests by virtue of this section in that person . . .

'(2) A person is qualified to succeed a tenant under a secure tenancy if he occupied the dwelling-house as his only or principal home at the time of the tenant's death and either (a) he is the tenant's spouse; or (b) he is another member of the tenant's family and has resided with the tenant throughout the period of twelve months ending with the tenant's death.'

The relevant part of the definition of 'family' was to be found in s.50(3): 'A person is a member of another's family . . . if she is his spouse . . . or if they live together as husband and wife'. Although the argument for Miss Simpson referred to a line of apparently similar cases decided under the succession provisions contained in the Rent Act 1977 and its precursors (which are discussed at p. 319) her appeal failed. Watkins LJ felt that the Rent Act cases were clearly distinguishable because they all involved heterosexual couples:

'If Parliament had wished homosexual relationships to be brought into the realm of the lawfully recognised state of a living together of man and wife for the purpose of the relevant legislation, it would plainly have so stated in that legislation, and it has not done so . . . It would be surprising in the extreme to learn that public opinion is such today that it would recognise a homosexual union as being akin to a state of living as husband and wife. The ordinary man and woman . . . would in my opinion not think even remotely of there being a true resemblance between those two very different states of affairs.'

Why did Watkins LJ not conclude, instinctively or otherwise, that adjudicative integrity requires homosexual and heterosexual couples to be treated in the same way in relation to security of tenure? The answer may appear to lie in his appeal to the views of the 'ordinary [i.e. heterosexual] man and woman'. In other words, even if ordinary people might feel initially that all couples should be treated equally in terms of security of tenure, they would give even greater weight to the cultural preference for heterosexuality over homosexuality. The decision can also be justified on the basis of adjudicative integrity, by saying that society promotes heterosexuality over homosexuality because the former is the basis of the family unit and thus reinforces cultural stability and traditional values.

Against the view of delegation of legislative power which is here being advanced, it may be argued that such a process places excessive power in the hands of judges. Certainly some judges feel that public confidence in the independence of the judiciary can be put at risk if the courts effectively amend statutes which they feel to be injurious to the public interest. In *Duport Steels Ltd* v. *Sirs* [1980] 1 All ER 529, this unease moved Lord Scarman to complain about the use of open-ended expressions (such as conduct 'in contemplation or furtherance of a trade dispute') in politically sensitive statutes such as the Trade Union and Labour Relations Act 1974: ' "Open-ended expressions" will bring the judges inevitably into the industrial arena exercising a discretion which may well be misunderstood by many and which can damage confidence in the administration of justice.'

Although it is possible to sympathize with Lord Scarman as to the practical consequences, it is important to emphasize his point that the danger arises from a misunderstanding, since in English law delegation consists of a sharing, rather than a transfer, of power. In *Huth* v. *Clarke* (1890) 25 QBD 39, a local authority appointed an executive committee, which in turn appointed local sub-committees to deal with diseases of animals. When the sub-committees took no action under the Rabies Order 1887, the executive committee itself made appropriate regulations. Following a conviction for an offence against the regulations, the question arose as to whether the executive committee had retained the power to make the regulations. The High Court held that the power had been retained, and that giving the delegate authority to act on behalf of the delegator did not involve a transfer of all the delegator's powers.

Moreover, delegation can be revoked. In *Manton* v. *Brighton Corporation* [1951] 2 All ER 101, a councillor had been appointed to three committees of the local authority. Following allegations of misconduct by the councillor, the local authority decided he should no longer serve on any of the committees. The High Court held that a local authority can revoke the authority of any of its committees as a whole, and therefore it could revoke the authority of individual committee members.

In the present context, the idea of delegation explains how the courts acquire the extensive discretion which they undoubtedly possess in cases of statutory interpretation. On the other hand, the doctrine of the legislative supremacy of Parliament is always there as a long-stop, ensuring that the courts acknowledge the possibility that sufficiently plain words may compel them to a particular conclusion. The case of *R* v. *Secretary of State for the Environment ex parte Merton London Borough Council* (1990) 154 LG Rev 655 (see p. 301) illustrates the point. Additionally, as the cases discussed at pp. 196–7 show, Parliament can enact legislation to annul the effect of judicial decisions which offend Parliament's view of what the law either is or ought to be.

Once we have adopted and applied Dworkin's concept of political integrity, it may be argued that our provisional rejection of the concept of a general intention of Parliament can be revoked. This argument would depend on the proposition that the concept of *adjudicative integrity* can be reconciled with the traditional view of the general intention of Parliament on the basis that Parliament either intends, or may at least be deemed to intend, that judges should adjudicate in accordance with the promotion of coherence within the legal system. We may concede that this argument is useful, even though it either resurrects the problem of collective intention or depends on the fiction of deeming. Furthermore, we can see how this argument may well appeal to those judges who crave the comfort of feeling that their actions are, however remotely, justified by the electoral system.

Summary

1   It is commonplace to encounter references to phrases such as *the intention of Parliament*, but there is doubt as to what (if anything) such phrases mean, and in any event the rule of law requires that the courts apply the meaning of what Parliament said, rather than giving effect to what Parliament meant to say.
2   Individuals' intentions may be classified as *direct* and *indirect*. A single individual may have multiple intentions, and in the case of multi-member legislatures this possibility is even more obvious. However, in legislative terms some people find it more helpful to think in terms of *particular* and *general* intentions, but even these concepts cause difficulties.
3   The superficially attractive idea of regarding the legislature as a speaker which communicates its meaning to an audience does not survive critical analysis.
4   In terms of the problems caused by the concept of *particular intention*, the most useful analysis lies in the model of *delegation by Parliament to the drafters*.
5   In terms of the problems caused by the concept of general intention, the most useful analysis lies in the model of *delegation by Parliament to the judges*.

Exercises

1   Distinguish between *particular intention* and *general intention* in the context of legislation.
2   How (if at all) can the model of *delegation to the judges* be reconciled with the constitutional requirement that Parliament should retain control of the legislative process?

21 Modern Interpretation in Practice

21.1 Introduction

As we saw in Chapter 19, the technique which we labelled *simple literalism* is seriously defective and no longer characterizes the judicial approach to statutory interpretation. As we also saw, there is a greatly increased perception of the significance of the context within which words are used, and more particularly, of the purpose underlying the enactment. The contemporary approach is, therefore, sometimes called either *contextualism*, or, more usually, *purposivism*, but the alternative label of *enlightened literalism* is also useful, because it recognizes the evolutionary development of the modern approach, whilst at the same time clearly differentiating it from its predecessor.

21.2 Contextualism or Purposivism or Enlightened Literalism

Freeman suggests the following:

'There seems now to be just one "rule" of interpretation, a revamped version of the literal rule which requires the general context and the purpose to be taken into consideration before any decision is reached concerning the ordinary (or, where appropriate, the technical) meaning of statutory words.' (*Lloyd's Introduction to Jurisprudence*, 6th edn, 1994, pp. 1291–2.)

Although this statement recognizes a distinction between ordinary and technical meanings, it gives no indication as to how that distinction is to be drawn. Some case-law will clarify the matter by illustrating the problem and indicating how the courts may make the choice between ordinary and technical meanings.

21.3   Ordinary and Technical Meanings

The basic proposition that the meaning of an ordinary word of the English language is a question of fact for the tribunal of fact has already been discussed (see p. 37). However, there remains the possibility that the court may give a technical meaning to an apparently ordinary word or phrase, as in *Fisher* v. *Bell* [1960] 3 All ER 731, where the contract lawyer's understanding of the phrase 'offer for sale' was preferred to the ordinary meaning. Similarly, in *Knocker* v. *Youle* [1986] 2 All ER 914, the court held that the term 'interest' in s.1(1) of the Variation of Trusts Act 1958, which deals with interests 'whether vested or contingent', must be given its technical, legal meaning, otherwise the words 'whether vested or contingent' would not make sense. The technical context which gives special meanings to words need not be legal. In *Prophett* v. *Platt Brothers & Co Ltd* [1961] 2 All ER 644 the wording in question was 'fettling of metal castings'.

Clearly, therefore, the question arises as to how ordinary and technical meanings are to be distinguished from each other. The truth of the matter is that there is no acid test, and the courts are quite happy to preserve an element of uncertainty in order to give themselves a degree of flexibility. Nevertheless, some guidance was offered by Lord Simon in *Maunsell* v. *Olins* [1975] 1 All ER 16:

> 'Statutory language, like all language, is capable of an almost infinite gradation of "register" – i.e. it will be used at the semantic level appropriate to the subject matter and to the audience addressed (the man in the street, lawyers, merchants, etc.). It is the duty of a court of construction to tune into such register and so to interpret the statutory language as to give it the primary meaning which is appropriate in that register (unless it is clear that some other meaning must be given in order to carry out the statutory purpose or to avoid injustice, anomaly, absurdity or contradiction). In other words, *statutory language must always be given presumptively the most natural and ordinary meaning which is appropriate in the circumstances.* (Emphasis added. See p. 257 for an explanation of the concept of *linguistic register.*)

Since modern interpretation emphasizes the meaning of the words in the context within which they are used, it is obviously of the first importance that we should be able to identify the elements which make up that context. It is convenient to consider this topic under two headings: *matters of language*, which apply to all linguistic communication, and *matters of law*, which take account of the specific problems of interpretation which arise from the technical nature of statutes.

21.4   Analysing the Context: Matters of Language

Dictionaries

It may seem obvious that the courts should rely heavily on dictionaries for guidance as to the meanings of words, but in fact they are seldom much use in statutory interpretation. In *Attorney-General's Reference (No 1 of 1988)* [1989] 1 AC 971, the House of Lords had to decide whether a person who came into possession of certain information, without making any effort to do so, could be said to have 'obtained' that information for the purposes of the Company Securities (Insider Dealing) Act 1985. The House of Lords answered this question in the affirmative, on the basis that within the statutory context under consideration, Parliament must have intended the word 'obtained' to be given a wide meaning which was, in effect, synonymous with 'received'. Lord Templeman cited with approval the following passage from the speech of Lord Upjohn in *Customs and Excise Commissioners* v. *Top Ten Promotions Ltd* [1969] 1 WLR 1163:

> 'It is highly dangerous, if not impossible, to attempt to place an accurate definition upon a word in common use; you can look up examples of its many uses if you want to in the *Oxford Dictionary* but that does not help on definition. The task of the court in construing statutory language such as that which is before your Lordships is to look at the mischief at which the Act is directed and then, in that light, to consider whether as a matter of common sense and everyday usage the known, proved or admitted or properly inferred facts of the particular case bring the case within the ordinary meaning of the words used by Parliament.'

Even more forthrightly, Lord Wilberforce once told Bennion that he 'never used dictionaries and shut his ears if they were referred to in court' (Bennion, *Statutory Interpretation*, 2nd edn, 1992, p. 849, n.8). It seems that the best occasion for using dictionaries arises when the court is seeking the meaning of a word at the time the Act was passed, in which case it may be worth consulting a contemporary dictionary.

The *noscitur a sociis* principle

Turning to some legal illustrations of the principles of language generally, but without yet entering the realm of specifically legal principles, the Latin phrase *noscitur a sociis* – a literal translation of which might be 'a thing is known by its associates' – embodies the single fundamental principle that the context of a word governs its meaning.

In *Foster* v. *Diphwys Casson Slate Co* (1887) 18 QBD 428, the relevant statute provided that explosives could be taken into a mine only if they were contained in a 'case or canister'. The question for the court was whether a cloth bag was sufficient. The court held that, in context, what was covered were containers of the same strength and solidity as 'canisters', and that therefore a cloth bag did not comply with the statute.

The *ejusdem generis* principle

Although the courts often talk of this principle as if it were uniquely legal, it is, basically at least, only a specific illustration of *noscitur a sociis*, and therefore it may be regarded as being one of the rules of language generally. Despite its affinity with the *noscitur a sociis* principle, however, it is customary to discuss the *ejusdem generis* principle separately.

Ejusdem generis may be literally translated as meaning *of the same class*, and the principle may be stated thus: where general words follow particular words, the general words are to be restricted to things of the same class as those which are specified. The reasoning underlying the principle is explained in *Brownsea Haven Properties Ltd* v. *Poole Corporation* [1958] 1 All ER 205, where Romer LJ said: 'The doctrine of *ejusdem generis* is only part of a wider principle of construction, namely that, where reasonably possible, some significance and meaning should be attributed to each and every word and phrase.'

More specifically, Odgers says it is assumed that 'the general words were only intended to guard against some accidental omission in the objects of the kind mentioned and were not intended to extend to objects of a wholly different kind' (*Construction of Deeds and Statutes*, 5th edn, 1967, p. 184).

The leading statement on how to apply the principle was given by McCardie J in *Magnhild S. S.* v. *McIntyre Bros & Co* [1921] 2 KB 97: 'The only test seems to be whether the specified things which precede the general words can be placed under some common category. By this I understand that the specified things must possess some common and dominant feature.' In other words, it is not sufficient that the unspecified thing is like one, or other, or even all of the specified things: they must all possess a common characteristic which is sufficiently basic to justify classifying them together as a class (or *genus*).

Thus, for example, in *Re Stockport Ragged, Industrial and Reformatory Schools* [1898] 2 Ch 687 the phrase 'cathedral, collegiate, chapter or other schools' in the Charitable Trusts Act 1853 was held to be limited to schools associated with the Church of England. Similarly, in *Wood* v. *Commissioner of Police for the Metropolis* [1986] 2 All ER 570, the statutory definition of 'offensive weapon', namely 'any gun, pistol, hanger, cutlass, bludgeon, or other offensive weapon' was held not to apply to a piece of broken glass which had just fallen out of the defendant's front door. The court said the definition was to be confined to articles made or adapted for use for causing injury to the person, therefore the fact that a particular object merely had the potential for such use was not sufficient to bring it within the scope of the statutory definition. Consideration of these examples leads to the conclusion that there are least two other situations, namely those cases where the specific words do not create a *genus*, and those cases where the specific words are as wide as the general words. It may be that the specific words are such that the general words cannot include anything which is not included anyway. For example, in *NALGO* v. *Bolton Corporation* [1943] AC 166 a provision related to 'a contract with an employer', whether for 'manual work', 'clerical work', 'or otherwise'. Lord Wright took the view that the provision applied to any 'contract with an employer'.

Where only one specific word precedes general words, it is logical to say that the *ejusdem generis* principle, as such, cannot apply. As Scott LJ said in *Alexander* v. *Tredegar Iron & Coal Co Ltd* [1944] KB 390, when dealing with the Coal Mines Act 1911, which required haulage roads to be kept clear as far as possible of pieces of coal and other obstructions: 'If one tries to apply [the *ejusdem generis* principle], one is at once met with the difficulty that, there being only one species, viz. pieces of coal, there is no basis for formulating a *genus*.' In such cases it may well be that the court will fall back on the *noscitur a sociis* principle. However, in *Quazi* v. *Quazi* [1979] 3 All ER 897, the House of Lords concluded that the second part of the phrase 'judicial or other proceedings' in the Recognition of Divorces and Legal Separations Act 1971 simply meant 'other proceedings which were not judicial', rejecting a submission that it meant 'quasi-judicial proceedings'.

The *ejusdem generis* principle may apply where the general words are surrounded by the particular words, rather than following them. *Shaw* v. *Ruddin* (1858) 9 Ir CLR 214 involved the Dublin Carriages Act 1853, which required a licence to be held before a person could lawfully 'use or let to hire any hackney carriage, job carriage, stage carriage, cart or job horse'. The court held that all the terms except 'cart' referred specifically to things which were let on hire, and therefore the provision applied only to carts which were let on hire. In passing, it may be noted that this case also shows that the principle can apply to a single general word, as well as to the more common situation where there are two or more general words. However, the principle appears not to apply where the general words precede the specific words. In *Ambatielos* v. *Anton Jurgens Margarine Works* [1923] AC 175 Lord Cave LC said: 'I know of no authority for applying the rule to . . . a case where, to begin with, the whole clause is governed by the initial general words.' In this situation, of course, a court which wished to do so could fall back on the *noscitur a sociis* principle.

Perhaps the best summary of the functioning of the *ejusdem generis* principle is to be found in the words of the great Canadian drafter, Elmer Driedger:

> 'The result of the decisions appears to be as follows: if no class can be found, the rule cannot apply and a broad construction may be favoured; if a class can be found but the specific words exhaust the class, then rejection of the rule may be favoured because its adoption would make the general words unnecessary; if, however, the specific words do not exhaust the class, then adoption of the rule may be favoured because rejection would make the specific words unnecessary.' (*The Construction of Statutes*, 2nd edn, p. 119, quoted in Bennion, *Statutory Interpretation*, 2nd edn, 1992, p. 860.)

The *expressio unius exclusio alterius* principle

This principle, which also comes in the form *inclusio unius, exclusio alterius*, may be translated as 'the expression [or the inclusion] of one thing implies the exclusion of another'. As with the *ejusdem generis* principle, *expressio unius* is clearly no more than a sub-category of the *noscitur a sociis* maxim. A classic example can be found in the well-known case of *Shylock* v. *Antonio* (reported by William Shakespeare in *The Merchant of Venice*, Act IV, Sc. 1). Shylock was seeking to enforce a bond given by Antonio, under which if Antonio defaulted he was to forfeit 'a pound of flesh'. In argument before the court, Antonio's advocate says:

> 'This bond doth give thee here no jot of blood;
> The words expressly are "a pound of flesh":
> Then take thy bond, take thou thy pound of flesh;
> But, in the cutting it, if thou dost shed
> One drop of Christian blood, thy land and goods
> Are, by the laws of Venice, confiscate
> Unto the state of Venice.'

R v. *Cuthbertson* [1980] 2 All ER 401 provides a more recent (and authoritative) example. Under the Misuse of Drugs Act 1971, forfeiture of property could be ordered by the court by which a person 'is convicted of an offence under this Act'. The defendant was convicted of conspiracy to contravene the 1971 Act. Although this was undoubtedly an offence, the offence of conspiracy was not created by the 1971 Act, and therefore he had not been 'convicted of an offence under this Act'. The House of Lords held that there was no power to order forfeiture of his property.

The rank principle

Bennion states the rank principle thus: 'Where a string of items of a certain rank is followed by residuary words, it is presumed that the residuary words are not intended to include items of a different rank.' As with the *ejusdem generis* and *expressio unius* principles, the rank principle is clearly no more than a sub-category of the *noscitur a sociis* maxim.

Casher v. *Holmes* (1831) 109 ER 1263 provides an illustration of the principle, in that a provision imposing excise duties on 'copper, brass, pewter, and tin, and all other metals not enumerated' was said not to apply to gold and silver. In more modern times, the phrase 'an officer or examiner of the court or some other person' in RSC Ord.39, r.4(a) was said not to apply to a judge (*Re Brickman's Settlement* [1982] 1 All ER 336).

21.5   Reading an Act as a Whole

The statement that an Act should be read as a whole may, when expressed in this form, appear to be a specifically legal proposition. However, in reality, an exactly similar proposition could be made with equal force in the context of any other document, and therefore the proposition may legitimately be discussed as a matter of language.

In *Courtauld* v. *Legh* (1869) LR 4 Exch 126 Cleasby J said: 'It is a sound rule of construction to give the same meaning to the same words occurring in different parts of an Act.' Despite the undoubted soundness of this statement in general terms, it is nevertheless sometimes apparent that the same word may have different meanings even within a single section, let alone within a single Act. Section 57 of the Offences Against the Person Act 1861 provides: 'Whosoever being married shall marry any other person during the life of the former husband or wife . . . shall be guilty of felony.' In *R* v. *Allen* (1872) LR 1 CCR 367, the court held that if you are already married you cannot marry anyone else, and therefore the section must mean 'whosoever being validly married shall go through a ceremony of marriage . . .'

The value of reading an Act as a whole may be illustrated by *R* v. *Millward* [1985] 1 All ER 859, which concerned s.1(1) and (6) of the Perjury Act 1916. Subsection 1 stated: 'If any person lawfully sworn as a witness . . . in a judicial proceeding wilfully makes a statement material in that proceeding, which he knows to be false or does not believe to be true, he shall be guilty of perjury.' Subsection (6) provided that the materiality or otherwise of a statement was a matter of law to be determined by the judge. A police officer made statements during a trial which he subsequently admitted he knew to have been untrue. He pleaded not guilty to perjury on the basis that he did not think they were material, but when the judge ruled against him on this point the defendant changed his plea. On appeal the defendant was held to have been rightly convicted. One ground of the decision was that, if the defendant's argument was right, subs.(6) had no function.

Quite apart from matters of interpretation, there may be other reasons for reading an Act as a whole. *Lloyd* v. *McMahon* [1987] 1 All ER 1118 involved an action by the District Auditor against certain members of Liverpool City Council who delayed making a rate until well after the start of the relevant financial year, thus causing substantial financial loss to the council. (The rates were a form of local taxation raised by local authorities.) There was no statutory provision prescribing any cut-off date by which a rate had to be made, but the court, having read the Act as a whole, identified the right of domestic ratepayers to pay their rates by ten monthly instalments. The court concluded, therefore, that at the very latest the rate must be made in time to enable this right to be exercised.

A particular problem with reading an Act as a whole arises where the Act has been amended. Is the court to look at the whole Act as originally passed, or at the whole Act in its amended form? In *Attorney-General* v. *Lamplough* (1878) 3 ExD 214, the Court of Appeal held that the appropriate context was the Act as originally passed. In the High Court case of *R* v. *Greater Manchester North District Coroner ex parte Worch* [1987] 3 All ER 661, where *Lamplough* was not cited, Slade LJ nevertheless came to the same conclusion:

'The original s.21(2) [of the Coroners (Amendment) Act 1926] is no longer law, since it has been replaced by s.23(3) of the Births and Deaths Registration Act 1953. Nevertheless, the original subsection is admissible in construing the section as a whole and, in our judgement, throws light on its construction.'

21.6   Analysing the Context: Matters of Law

Having considered some matters which arise in the use of language generally, as well as in statutory interpretation, we can now turn to some more specifically legal matters. Bearing in mind the fact that we are constantly looking for the meaning of the words in the context within which they are used, it will be useful to begin by analysing the structure of statutes, since this will establish the most immediate context, and then to consider a variety of other matters beyond the physical limits of the statutes themselves.

The anatomy of a statute

Preambles

Where there is a preamble to a statute it will recite the reasons why the statute was passed. However, modern drafting practice in relation to Public Bills has almost entirely dispensed with the use of preambles, although they still appear in Private Bills, and therefore in Private Acts. It follows that their status for the purposes of interpretation is relatively insignificant in quantitative terms. Nevertheless, preambles are encountered from time to time, and their status is quite clear. According to Lord Normand in *Attorney-General* v. *Prince Ernest Augustus of Hanover* [1957] 1 All ER 49: 'It is only when it conveys a clear and definite meaning in comparison with relatively obscure or indefinite enacting words that the preamble may legitimately prevail.'

The case of *Siu Yin Kwan* v. *Eastern Insurance Co Ltd* [1994] 1 All ER 213 arose from a complex factual background involving insurance, agency and insolvency, coupled with the Life Assurance Act 1774 which states that life policies are unlawful unless they name the people whose lives are covered. The Privy Council said that the Act was irrelevant, because its preamble states that its provisions are aimed at 'a mischievous kind of gaming', and, on its facts, the instant case did clearly not arise from that sort of background.

The idea that something may resolve an ambiguity but not create one occurs elsewhere within statutory interpretation. Additionally, however, it carries echoes of certain techniques which the courts use when handling precedents. For example, as we saw at p. 148, there may be situations in which the changed circumstances principle may justify the exercise of the power to distinguish earlier cases, although that power clearly exists independently of that principle.

Long titles

Long titles have the same status as preambles, but they are much more important in practice because all statutes have them. In *R* v . *Galvin* [1987] 2 All ER 851, Lord Lane CJ, speaking of the Official Secrets Act 1911, and its predecessor of 1889, said:

'One can have regard to the title of a statute to help resolve an ambiguity in the body of it, but it is not, we consider, open to a court to use the title to restrict what is otherwise the plain meaning of the words of the statute simply because they seem to be unduly wide.'

It is fortunate that the same principle applies to preambles and long titles, because some judges have difficulty in distinguishing one from the other. In *Ward* v. *Holman* [1964] 2 All ER 729, Lord Parker CJ, while stating the principle, spoke of the preamble to the Public Order Act 1936, although even the most cursory glance at the first page of that Act reveals that there is no preamble.

However, long titles are not necessarily infallible. The Bill which became the Rating and Valuation Act 1928 contained a clause empowering the Minister of Health to refer to the High Court any 'substantial question of law' concerning valuations of property for rating purposes, in order to remedy 'want of uniformity or inequality in valuation'. While the Bill was making its legislative progress through the House of Lords, several Law Lords objected to this provision in principle, on the ground that it would require the courts to express opinions on abstract points rather than on hard facts. The clause was withdrawn, but no corresponding alteration of the long title was made. The long title of the Act as passed included a declaration that it was an Act 'to provide for obtaining decisions on points of law with a view to securing uniformity of valuation'.

Short titles

The short title is almost always found towards the end of the statute. The leading case is *R* v. *Boaler* [1915] 1 KB 21, where it was acknowledged that the short title is part of the Act, and as such the court can and should consider it. However, it is by definition a *short* title and therefore, as Scrutton LJ said, 'accuracy may be sacrificed to brevity'. Moreover, particular care should be taken when dealing with the short titles of old Acts. Before 1896 it was not the practice for Acts to have short titles, but the Short Titles Act of that year conferred short titles on many older Acts. However, all the short titles were not necessarily appropriate, so that, for example, the short title of the Criminal Procedure Act was given to one statute passed in 1865 which dealt with both criminal and civil procedure.

Headings, marginal notes and punctuation

A glance at any substantial statute will reveal a collection of *headings* (also known as *cross-headings*) between groups of sections, and *marginal notes* (also known as *side-notes* or *shoulder notes*) in the margin. These are both inserted by the drafter and are never subject to debate by Parliament. Where the text of a Bill is amended during its passage through Parliament, it is a matter for the drafter to amend these headings and notes appropriately. The best drafting practice, where this would cause problems, is to replace the original text with a whole new section, complete with a new heading or marginal note, as appropriate. It follows that where this has not be done, the original marginal notes and headings should be treated with a great deal of caution. However, leaving aside such special cases and returning to the mainstream, there is a reasonably clear judicial consensus that marginal notes and headings are relevant to the process of interpretation, 'provided that we realise that they cannot have equal weight with the words of the Act' (Lord Reid in *Director of Public Prosecutions* v. *Schildkamp* [1969] 3 All ER 1640).

More particularly, marginal notes may be used to identify the mischief at which the section is aimed, as Upjohn LJ explained in *Stephens* v. *Cuckfield RDC* [1960] 2 QB 373:

'While the marginal note to a section cannot control the language used in the section, it is at least permissible to approach a consideration of its general purpose and the mischief at which it is aimed *with the note in mind*.' (Emphasis added.)

In *R.* v. *Hare* [1934] 1 KB 354, the heading 'Unnatural Offences' preceded a section containing the offence of indecent assault on a male under the age of 16. According to traditional usage, the phrase 'unnatural offences' clearly has homosexual connotations, but the Act specified the sex of the victim only, being silent as to the sex of the offender. The facts were that a woman was charged with indecent assault on a male under the age of 16. The court held that a woman could commit the offence, on the basis that the statutory wording was plain anyway, but the court also indicated that if there had been ambiguity the heading could have been used to resolve it.

There is specific authority on the status of headings within schedules, but this is best considered within the topic of schedules as a whole.

Schedules

Bennion explains the nature of schedules:

'It is often convenient to incorporate part of the operative provisions of an Act in the form of a schedule. The schedule is often used to hive off provisions which are too long or detailed to be put in the body of the Act. This does not mean they are unimportant.' (*Statutory Interpretation*, 2nd edn., 1992, p. 490.)

As Brett LJ said in *Attorney-General* v. *Lamplough* (1878) 3 ExD 214: 'A schedule in an Act is a mere question of drafting, a mere question of words. The schedule is as much part of the statute, and is as much an enactment, as any other part.'

In *Re Baines* (1840) 41 ER 401 Lord Cottenham LC held that where there is inconsistency between the body of the Act and a schedule, the body of the Act should prevail. This proposition is, of course, not only contrary to the maxim *posteriora derogant prioribus* (i.e. there is a presumption that later provisions derogate from – or prevail over – earlier ones), but also seems to be wrong in principle. Issues of this type are best resolved by recalling the fundamental principle that an Act should be construed as a whole, and attempting to give the best possible meaning to the words which have been used, having regard to the statutory purpose. In any event, there can be no doubt that Part I of Schedule 16 to the Environmental Protection Act 1990, which repeals part of s.79(10) of the same Act, must prevail, otherwise it would have no effect whatsoever.

As far as headings within schedules are concerned, the leading case is *Inland Revenue Commissioners* v. *Gittus* [1920] 1 KB 563, where Lord Sterndale MR said:

'If the Act says that the schedule is to be used for a certain purpose and the heading of the part of the schedule in question shows that it is *prima facie* at any rate devoted to that purpose, then you must read the Act and the schedule as though the schedule were operating for that purpose, and if you can satisfy the language of the section without extending it beyond that purpose you ought to do it. But if in spite of that you find in the language of the schedule words and terms that go clearly outside that purpose, then you must give effect to them and you must not consider them as limited by the heading of that part of the schedule or by the purpose mentioned in the Act for which the schedule is *prima facie* to be used. You cannot refuse to give effect to clear words simply because *prima facie* they seem to be limited by the heading of the schedule and the definition of the purpose of the schedule contained in the Act.'

Definition sections

Definition sections, which are commonly found towards the end of statutes but towards the beginning of statutory instruments, contain provisions of two types. First there are those which simply state that the defined terms shall 'mean' whatever the provision states them to mean. Second, there are those which state that the defined terms shall 'include' whatever the provision states them to include. In cases falling within the latter category the words will have not only their special statutory meaning but, according to Lord Selborne LC in *Robinson* v. *Barton-Eccles Local Board* (1883) 8 App Cas 798, they will also possess their 'ordinary, popular and natural sense whenever that would be applicable'. In other words, this category does not enact definitions in the strict sense of the term, since it is in the nature of a definition to restrict, rather than simply to illustrate, the meaning of a word.

Definition sections generally include a form of words to the effect that the definitions they contain shall yield to a contrary intention within the main part of the Act, although some drafters omit these words on the basis that they are no more than a statement of the obvious. In addition to specific definition sections, the Interpretation Act 1978 will often be relevant. The most commonly relied upon provisions of that Act are reproduced in Appendix 2.

Commencement sections

Commencement sections are commonly found towards the end of statutes. Section 4 of the Interpretation Act 1978, whose ancestry can be traced to the Acts of Parliament (Commencement) Act 1793, states that, where provision is made for an Act or part of an Act to come into force on a particular day, it comes into force at the beginning of that day; and that, where no such provision is made, an Act comes into force at the beginning of the day on which it receives the Royal Assent. The limited degree of retrospectivity inherent in this provision appears to cause no injustice in practice, and is in any event a marked improvement over the pre-1793 position, when Acts took effect from the beginning of the Parliamentary session in which they were passed (see *Latless* v. *Holmes*, which is discussed at p. 197).

In practice it is common for statutes to state that they will come into force either on a particular future date, or on the expiry of a stated period (commonly two months) after they receive the Royal Assent, but a degree of flexibility is often preserved by enacting a provision to the effect that the Act will come into force on whatever day may be appointed by the appropriate Secretary of State, who will usually be empowered to make a commencement order by way of a statutory instrument. Appointed days and commencement orders are frequently used when the successful implementation of an Act depends on things such as setting up administrative machinery, appointing staff, making delegated legislation, and so on. In *R* v. *Secretary of State for the Home Department ex parte Fire Brigades Union and Others* (1995) 7 Admin LR 473, the House of Lords decided that a power to make appointed day and commencement orders puts the relevant Secretary of State under a continuing obligation to consider whether the time is ripe for a relevant order to be made, and therefore it is unlawful for a Secretary of State to make a decision which will effectively preclude the making of such an order.

It is common for different parts of the same Act to come into force on different days, and it is not unknown for provisions which are not yet in force to be amended, or even repealed.

Reference to extrinsic materials

Having surveyed the anatomy of a statute, we must now consider how far beyond the actual text a court may go when seeking to establish the context within which the statutory words are to be understood. In other words, what use can the court make of extrinsic materials? The answer to this question depends on analysing extrinsic materials into three different categories: pre-Parliamentary materials, Parliamentary materials and post-Parliamentary materials.

Pre-parliamentary materials

The explanatory memorandum which, in practice, accompanies every government Bill cannot be referred to when interpreting the ensuing Act (*Escoigne Properties Ltd* v. *Inland Revenue Commissioners* [1958] 1 All ER 406).

Pre-Parliamentary materials, such as reports of Royal Commissions and committees of various kinds, are useful because, according to Lord Halsbury, in *Eastman Photographic Materials Co Ltd* v. *Comptroller of Patents* [1898] AC 571, there is 'no more accurate source of information' as to the mischief at which the Act was aimed. In *Assam Railways and Trading Co* v. *Commissioners of Inland Revenue* [1935] AC 445, Lord Wright emphasized that in the *Eastman* case Lord Halsbury had been speaking only about the mischief, not the meaning, and in *Letang* v. *Cooper* [1964] 2 All ER 929, Lord Denning MR pointed out that identifying the mischief 'does not help very much, for the simple reason that Parliament may, and often does, decide to do something different to cure the mischief'.

The case of *Black-Clawson International Ltd* v. *Papierwerke Waldhof-Aschaffenburg AG* [1975] 1 All ER 810 requires careful consideration. The Foreign Judgments (Reciprocal Enforcement) Act 1933 resulted from the report of a committee under the chairmanship of Greer LJ. The House of Lords disagreed as to the use to which the committee's report could be put. Lord Reid and Lord Wilberforce took the established line that the report could be used only for identifying the mischief, but Lord Simon and Viscount Dilhorne thought it could also be used in relation to identifying the meaning of the statutory words. In this situation, the views of the fifth member of the House, Lord Diplock, are particularly important, even though he thought that the meaning of the provision in question was plain anyway, and therefore he did not need to consider the report for any purpose. Nevertheless, he did deliver the following dictum:

> 'Parliament, under our constitution, is sovereign only in respect of what it expresses by the words used in the legislation it has passed.
>
> 'This is not to say that, where those words are not clear and unambiguous in themselves but are fairly susceptible of more than one meaning, the court, for the purpose of resolving – though not of inventing – an ambiguity may not pay regard to authoritative statements that were matters of public knowledge at the time the Act was passed, as to what were regarded as deficiencies in that branch of the existing law with which the Act deals. Where such statements are made in official reports commissioned by government, laid before Parliament and published, they clearly fall within this category and may be used to resolve the ambiguity in favour of a meaning which will result in correcting those deficiencies in preference to some alternative meaning that will leave the deficiencies uncorrected. The justification of this use of such reports as an aid to the construction of the words used in the statute is that knowledge of their contents may be taken to be shared by those whose conduct the statute regulates and would influence their understanding of the meaning of the ambiguous enacting words.'

Although this dictum appears to give a majority in favour of using reports as an aid to identifying meanings, at least in cases where there is ambiguity, this is not the general understanding of the courts. In *R* v. *Allen* [1985] 2 All ER 641, where the Court of Appeal had declined to look at a report of the Criminal Law Revision Committee, Lord Hailsham LC described the use of reports for identifying the mischief only as being 'the present practice'. Similarly, in *R* v. *Broadcasting Complaints Commission ex parte British Broadcasting Corporation* (1995) 7 Admin LR 575, Brooke J cited *Black-Clawson* in support of the view that he was entitled to consult the pre-parliamentary history of a statute 'to help [him] identify the mischief', while *Pepper* v. *Hart* (which is discussed at p. 296) meant that *Hansard* was available 'to assist [him] in interpreting any ambiguity in the Act, particularly in relation to the parliamentary intention behind' the section under consideration.

In *British Leyland Corporation* v. *Armstrong Patents Co Ltd* [1986] 1 All ER 850, the House of Lords referred to the report of the Gregory Committee on Copyright, which had preceded the Copyright Act 1956. Lord Templeman took the traditional line when he said: 'Thus s.9(8) of the

Copyright Act 1956 was defective to achieve the intended purpose.' Similarly, Lord Edmund-Davies said:

> 'I do not know what Parliament intended to do. Assume, as one reasonably may, that the Gregory Report was available to the legislators in 1956, and one will still have no knowledge of how far they intended to implement any of its recommendations when legislating as expansively as they did. We may think they could, and should, have done better, but that is by the way.'

However, the restriction on using pre-parliamentary materials to identify only the mischief is subject to an exception where the court is considering reports of the Law Commissions. These may be used even to interpret the meaning of a statute. *R* v. *Horseferry Road Metropolitan Stipendiary Magistrate ex parte Siadatan* [1991] 1 All ER 324 dealt with the concluding words of s.4(1) of the Public Order Act 1986, which creates an offence where certain things are done

> 'with intent to cause [a] person to believe that immediate unlawful violence will be used against him or another by any person, or to provoke the immediate use of unlawful violence by that person or another, or whereby that person is likely to believe that such violence will be used or it is likely that such violence will be provoked.'

The issue was whether 'such violence' in the last line of the provision meant *any* unlawful violence, or only *immediate* unlawful violence. Watkins LJ quoted the Law Commission report (Law Com No 123 (1983)) which had preceded the Act:

> '*Fear of violence and provoking violence*
> 5.43 The offence requires that each defendant use threatening etc, words or behaviour which is intended or is likely (a) to cause another person to fear immediate unlawful violence, or (b) to provoke the immediate use of unlawful violence by another person.'

Deciding the case on the basis that the report made it plain that only immediate unlawful violence was meant, Watkins LJ said: 'That the parliamentary draftsman, when drafting the last part of s.4(1), did not achieve the same clarity and precision is, we think, most regrettable.'

The question of whether the court can compel counsel to cite pre-Parliamentary reports is considered at pp. 199–200. The use of international conventions as pre-parliamentary materials is considered at p. 312, in the context of the presumption of compliance with international law.

Finally, quite apart from their use in statutory interpretation, pre-parliamentary reports which set out the pre-existing law may be cited in the same way as any other commentary on the law. The use of textbooks and other scholarly publications is discussed generally at pp. 107–11, but in the present context the point may be illustrated by reference to *R* v. *Mayor and Commonalty and Citizens of the City of London ex parte Matson* (1996) 8 Admin LR 49, where the Court of Appeal referred to the *Report of the Royal Commission on Local Government in Greater London* (1960) to help it to understand the role of aldermen of the City of London.

Parliamentary materials: the use of Hansard

As a matter of first impression it may seem obvious that *Hansard*, as the official record of Parliamentary proceedings, should be available to the courts when interpreting statutes, on the basis that the Parliamentarians who debated a Bill before it became an Act may well have said what they intended it to mean. However, two bundles of arguments have tradition-ally been deployed against this proposition. One bundle of arguments is constitutional, the other purely practical.

One of the constitutional arguments for saying that the courts should interpret statutes without reference to *Hansard* relies on the doctrine of the separation of powers (see p. 71). This argument proceeds on the basis that it is the function of the legislature to make the law, and the function of the courts to intepret and apply it. As we have already noted (p. 267), in *Black-Clawson International Ltd* v. *Papierwerke Waldhof-Aschaffenburg AG* [1975] 1 All ER 810, Lord Reid said: 'We often say that we are looking for the intention of Parliament, but that is not quite accurate. We are seeking not what Parliament meant but the true meaning of what they said.'

For nearly two centuries the House of Commons itself raised an additional constitutional argument, to the effect that using *Hansard* could, at least potentially, constitute a breach of art.9 of the Bill of Rights 1689, which provides, in modernized spelling, 'that the freedom of speech and debates or proceedings in Parliament ought not to be impeached or questioned in any court or place out of Parliament'.

Admittedly, in practice the Commons were often willing to give permission for the use of *Hansard* when specifically asked to do so, and on 31 October 1980 the Commons passed a resolution giving general leave for reference to be made to *Hansard* to be used in court, without any specific request being made. Obviously, however, this resolution did nothing to invalidate Lord Reid's point in *Black-Clawson*, nor did it address the other bundle of traditional arguments, namely those based on considerations of sheer practicality.

Turning, therefore, to the practical arguments, the views of Lord Reid are once again significant. In *Beswick* v. *Beswick* [1967] 2 All ER 1197, his Lordship pointed out that *Hansard* is not always easily available, and therefore allowing its use would be expensive in terms of both time and money. Furthermore, in many cases *Hansard* would not help, containing as it does a multiplicity of views as to what a Bill may, or should, mean or not mean. However, in *R* v. *Warner* [1968] 2 All ER 356, which turned on whether a particular offence was one of strict liability or whether *mens rea* was required, Lord Reid was prepared to acknowledge the possibility of an exception to the exclusionary principle if the case were such that referring to *Hansard* would almost certainly solve the problem of interpretation which was before the court.

Certainly the House of Lords did not consider the Commons' resolution of 1980 to be of overriding significance. When Lord Denning MR admitted that he had referred to *Hansard* while formulating his judgement in the Court of Appeal, five Law Lords unanimously declared that he had been wrong to do so and that neither advocates nor judges should refer to *Hansard* (*Hadmor Productions Ltd* v. *Hamilton* [1982] 1 All ER 1042).

However, the 1980 resolution does appear to have had some effect, at least to the extent of creating a more relaxed atmosphere. The starting-point is *R* v. *Secretary of State for Trade and Industry ex parte Anderson Strathclyde plc* [1983] 2 All ER 233, where Dunn LJ acknowledged that, whilst the courts could use *Hansard*, both the extent of that use, and the weight to be given to it, were 'entirely at large'. In *Brind* v. *Secretary of State for the Home Department* [1991] 1 All ER 720, the House of Lords referred to *Hansard* in order to identify the Home Secretary's reasons for preventing the BBC and the IBA from broadcasting certain types of material relating to Northern Ireland. Furthermore, their Lordships appear to have seen nothing odd in what they were doing, since the use of *Hansard* was accompanied by neither apology nor explanation.

Perhaps more startling, from the traditional point of view, was the case of *Pierce* v. *Bemis* [1986] 1 All ER 1011. When deciding whether the sunken ship *The Lusitania* was 'derelict', Sheen J not only allowed counsel to cite, but also himself cited, *Hansard* in order to explain how the provision which became s.72 of the Merchant Shipping Act 1906 came to be enacted. On the other hand, in *Church of Scientology* v. *Johnson-Smith* [1972] 1 All ER 378, Browne J said that a plaintiff, who was suing a Member of Parliament for libel in respect of comments made in a television interview, could not refer to *Hansard* in order to prove malice on the part of the defendant.

In addition to the cases involving purely domestic law, it seems that special considerations may arise where Community Law is involved. The case of *Pickstone* v. *Freemans plc* [1988] 2 All ER 803 involved the construction of a statutory instrument which was introduced as a consequence of a decision by the European Court of Justice to the effect that the United Kingdom had failed to comply with a specific requirement of Community Law. The House decided to read the instrument as if it contained certain words which were not actually there. By way of justification, Lord Templeman said:

> 'The draft of the 1983 regulations was not subject to any process of amendment by Parliament. In these circumstances the explanations of the government and the criticisms voiced by members of Parliament in the debates which led to approval of the draft regulations provide some indications of the intentions of Parliament.'

His Lordship's speech continued, and included a passage from *Hansard*. Lord Oliver acknowledged that the decision involved

> 'a departure from a number of well-established rules of construction. The intention of Parliament has, it is said, to be ascertained from the words which it has used and those words are to be construed according to their plain and ordinary meaning. The fact that a statute is passed to give effect to an international treaty does not, of itself, enable the treaty to be referred to in order to construe the words used in other than their plain and unambiguous sense. Moreover, even in the case of ambiguity, what is said in Parliament in the course of the passage of a Bill cannot ordinarily be referred to to assist in construction. I think, however, that it has also to be recognised that a statute which is passed in order to give effect to the United Kingdom's obligations under the E.E.C. Treaty falls into a special category and it does so because, unlike other treaty obligations, those obligations have, in effect, been incorporated into English Law by the European Communities Act 1972.'

Given that the courts have in fact been referring to *Hansard* for several years, albeit normally for purposes other than those of statutory interpretation, the case of *R* v. *Governors of Haberdasher Aske's Hatcham Schools ex parte Inner London Education Authority* (1989) 153 LG Rev 809, is instructive on the approach which they should take towards the words which they find. The case involved the High Court in considering, *inter alia*, a Parliamentary answer given by a junior Education Minister. Glidewell LJ indicated that the courts should assume that people meant what they said:

> 'I cannot accept that we should interpret the Parliamentary answer as being in some sort of code: in other words that we should interpret the

Ministers who say they have not yet made up their minds . . . as meaning that they have made up their minds.'

The use of *Hansard* in the specific context of statutory interpretation came before the House of Lords in *Pepper* v. *Hart* [1993] 1 All ER 42, which is now the leading case. The facts concerned the quantification of the liability of certain income tax payers in respect of benefits which were to be treated as part of their emoluments. The taxpayers were schoolmasters at an independent school, and their children were being educated at the school under a concessionary fee scheme which resulted in them paying some 20 per cent of the normal fees. At all relevant times the school had spare capacity, and therefore the question arose as to whether the taxpayers' liability should be based on the difference between the amount which the taxpayers paid and the marginal cost which the school actually incurred in educating the taxpayers' children, or on the difference between the amount which the taxpayers paid and the full cost which the school incurred in educating the taxpayers' children, including an apportionment of overheads. Section 63 of the Finance Act 1976 was capable of bearing either meaning but, when the provision was going through Parliament, the Financial Secretary to the Treasury had made it plain that the government intended the words to bear the meaning which was favourable to the taxpayers. Delivering the leading speech, Lord Browne-Wilkinson, having canvassed all the relevant arguments and authorities, said:

'I therefore reach the conclusion, subject to any question of Parliamentary privilege, that the exclusionary rule should be relaxed so as to permit reference to Parliamentary materials where (a) legislation is ambiguous or obscure, or leads to an absurdity; (b) the material relied upon consists of one or more statements by a minister or other promoter of the Bill together if necessary with such other Parliamentary material as is necessary to understand such statements and their effect; (c) the statements relied upon are clear.'

The echo of Lord Reid in *Warner* (see p. 294) is clear. Expressing his conclusion on the Parliamentary privilege aspect of the matter, Lord Browne-Wilkinson said:

'I trust when the House of Commons comes to consider the decision in this case, it will be appreciated that there is no desire to impeach its privileges in any way. Your Lordships are motivated by a desire to carry out the intentions of Parliament in enacting legislation and have no intention or desire to question the processes by which such legislation was enacted or of criticizing anything said by anyone in Parliament in the course of enacting it. The purpose is to give effect to, not thwart, the intentions of Parliament.'

Although the decision in *Pepper* v. *Hart* is clear, it is worth noticing that Lord Mackay LC dissented in principle on the *Hansard* point, although he was able to concur on the substantive point by using conventional means of interpretation. Lord Mackay accepted that using *Hansard* would not breach the Bill of Rights, but based his dissent simply on the practical issue that reference to *Hansard* would be time-consuming and therefore expensive, and it would not be until the time and the money had been spent that the parties would know whether it had been worthwhile. Bearing in mind, therefore, the public interest in containing the cost of litigation, the Lord Chancellor declined to be a party to a decision which could substantially increase those costs. (In passing, it is worth noticing that the Lord Chancellor is the government minister with responsibility for legal aid, so his participation in this decision was questionable in terms of the constitutional doctrine of the separation of powers.)

Lord Oliver was unimpressed with the argument based on increased costs, saying: 'I do not, for my part, consider that the relaxation of the rule . . . will lead to any significant increase in the cost of litigation or in the burden of research required to be undertaken by legal advisers.'

Since the decision in *Pepper* v. *Hart*, there has been a steady stream of cases in which the courts have referred to *Hansard* as an aid to statutory interpretation, beginning with *R* v. *Warwickshire County Council ex parte Johnson* [1993] 1 All ER 299, where the manager of an electrical shop who displayed a misleading price notice was prosecuted under the Consumer Protection Act 1987. Having consulted *Hansard* the House held that he should be acquitted on the basis that Parliament had not intended individual employees to be prosecuted, and therefore the manager had not been acting 'in the course of any business of his' within the meaning of the Act.

The concept of ambiguity is fundamental to the *Pepper* v. *Hart* criteria, therefore it is necessary to consider how the courts decide whether an ambiguity exists in a particular case. Although a judge may take a robust view of the matter, as Millett LJ did when he declared that the meaning of s.56(4) of the Taxes Management Act 1970 was 'too plain for argument' (*Petch* v. *Gurney* [1994] 3 All ER 731), it is clear that the individual judge's opinion is not decisive of the matter. In *Restick* v. *Crickmore* [1994] 2 All ER 112, Stuart-Smith LJ considered there was no ambiguity in the relevant provision, but nevertheless said:

'Perhaps it may be said that the difference of judicial opinion between the judges in the courts below and this court shows that there is an ambiguity (see *Chief Adjudication Officer* v. *Foster* [1993] 1 All ER 705 at 717 *per* Lord Bridge of Harwich).'

When applying *Pepper* v. *Hart*, the courts will not go behind the statement which is reported in *Hansard*. In *R* v. *Secretary of State for Foreign and Commonwealth Affairs ex parte Rees-Mogg* [1994] 1 All ER 457, the court was invited to disregard a ministerial statement which had been made on the advice of the Attorney-General and that advice was demonstrably wrong. Lloyd ʟᴊ said that this argument:

'would, if correct, undermine the utility of *Pepper* v. *Hart* in every case in which it would otherwise apply. Ministers act on advice. It cannot make any difference whether the source of the advice is made explicit.'

The courts have even referred to *Hansard* as an aid to statutory interpretation without mentioning *Pepper* v. *Hart* as the empowering authority. For example, in *Doody* v. *Secretary of State for the Home Department* [1993] 3 All ER 92, Lord Mustill referred at length to a speech of the Minister of State at the Home Office, relating to the Bill which became the Criminal Justice Act 1991.

However, there is some evidence that the House of Lords is beginning to see the danger which only Lord Mackay ʟᴄ perceived in *Pepper* v. *Hart* itself, namely that references to *Hansard* may cost more than they are worth. More particularly, in *Melluish* v. *BMI (No 3) Ltd* [1995] 4 All ER 453, Lord Browne-Wilkinson, giving the only substantial speech, emphasized that only statements specifically related to the provision in question could be brought within *Pepper* v. *Hart*, and that where attempts were made to introduce other material:

'judges should be astute to check such misuse of the new rule by making appropriate orders as to costs wasted. In the present case, if it were otherwise appropriate to order the taxpayers to pay the costs of this issue, I would advise your Lordships to disallow any costs incurred by the Crown in the improper attempt to introduce this irrelevant parliamentary material.'

Pausing only to comment that the possibility of wasted costs orders is discussed at p. 30, it will be apparent that Lord Browne-Wilkinson's comment could easily be applied more widely to cases where the material in *Hansard* was relevant to the provision before the court, but nevertheless did not assist in the process of interpretation.

By way of comment on the desirability of the rule in *Pepper* v. *Hart*, it must be conceded that the traditional argument based on the Bill of Rights is unconvincing, but this still leaves the other constitutional arguments, as well as the practical ones. More particularly, the decision seems to be taking the legal system down a road which leads to government according to the intentions of the executive as understood by the executive, rather than government according to the enactments of the legislature as interpreted by the courts. As such, it is a significant step away from constitutional orthodoxy, and towards what may be termed, in Lord Hailsham's memorable phrase, 'elective dictatorship'.

Finally, and at a purely practical level, it is worth noticing that a *Practice Note* [1995] 1 All ER 234, requires parties who intend to introduce *Hansard* into their arguments, whether in reliance on *Pickstone* v. *Freemans plc* or *Pepper* v. *Hart*, to provide the court and the other parties with advance notice, in the form of copies of the extracts on which they propose to rely and a summary of the arguments they propose to raise.

Post-parliamentary materials

It is commonplace to find that government departments who bear responsibility for administering, or supervising the administration of, particular areas of law will issue guidance to their own officials and to the public. This raises the question of whether such guidance can be used for the purposes of statutory interpretation.

In *London County Council* v. *Central Land Board* [1958] 3 All ER 676, the court took a strict view, saying that such guidance should not even be cited by counsel, let alone relied on by the judge, because, once the court knows the official view of the statutory meaning, it will be practically impossible for the court to ignore this information. However, this view seems to be not only unduly insulting to the judges' powers of rational analysis, but also unrealistic in the light of the complexity of some statutory schemes. Perhaps it is not surprising that it does not represent current practice.

For example, in *R* v. *West Dorset District Council ex parte Poupard* (1987) 19 HLR 254 (and, on appeal, (1988) 20 HLR 295), which is discussed at p. 9 in the context of inarticulate major premises, the question was whether people living on an overdraft were receiving 'income' which would disqualify them from receiving Housing Benefit. The relevant government department published a Guidance Manual, which explicitly disclaimed any pretensions to be legally authoritative, but which was nevertheless intended to help people who had to administer the scheme. Balcombe LJ referred to the Manual without giving any indication that he was aware of any reason why he should not do so.

21.7   Presumptions

The courts have regard to a number of principles which they call presumptions. Although there is no universally accepted list of these principles, nor of the way in which each one should be formulated, there is a large measure of agreement as to most of them, and the major ones can be dealt with relatively easily. As a preliminary, though, it is important to note that all the presumptions will always give way to a clear contrary intention, and also that they can conflict not only with each other but also with the other principles of interpretation. Such conflicts clearly give the courts considerable leeway in interpretation.

Presumption against injustice

The presumption against injustice is the most basic presumption and all the others can be regarded as sub-formulations of it. It is exemplified by *West Midland Baptist (Trust) Association (Inc)* v. *Birmingham City Corporation* [1969] 3 All ER 172, which involved the principles of compensation where land has been compulsorily purchased. The normal basis of compensation is the market value of the land, including the buildings on it, but the law recognizes that some uses of land are so specialized that there is effectively no market, and therefore there is no market value. In these cases the acquiring authority can pay compensation on the basis of the cost of re-establishing the use elsewhere, which is technically known as 'equivalent reinstatement'. In the instant case, for example, equivalent reinstatement compensation was being paid in respect of a church.

One stage in the compulsory purchase procedure involves the service of a document called a notice to treat. In *Penny* v. *Penny* (1868) 18 LT 13, the House of Lords, decided that the date of the notice to treat was the date at which the compensation was to be assessed, even though in practice there would inevitably be at least some delay before the money was paid to the dispossessed landowner on completion of the conveyancing side of the transaction. In the *Birmingham* case, notice to treat was served in 1947 but substantial delay followed and it was not until 1961 that rebuilding elsewhere could reasonably begin. The cost of rebuilding at 1947 values was about £50 000, but at 1961 values it was about £90 000. The House of Lords held that, despite *Penny*, it would be unjust to make the landowner accept 1947 values, so the higher figure was appropriate.

The case of *Coltman* v. *Bibby Tankers Ltd* [1987] 3 All ER 1068 is also instructive. Section 1(3) of the Employer's Liability (Defective Equipment) Act 1969 provides that 'equipment' 'includes any plant and machinery, vehicles, aircraft and clothing'. In the High Court, Sheen J held that a worker injured in a ship had a remedy under the Act even though ships are not mentioned in the definition, because it would be unjust to differentiate between accidents in, say, aircraft and ships. A majority of the Court of Appeal reversed the decision, but Sheen J's conclusion was unanimously reinstated by the House of Lords, where Lord Oliver said:

> 'The purpose of the Act was manifestly to saddle the employer with liability for defective plant of every sort with which the employee is compelled to work in the course of his employment, and I can see no ground for excluding particular types of chattel merely on the ground of their size or the element on which they are designed to operate.'

However powerful the presumption against injustice may be, it can, of course, in common with all the other presumptions, be rebutted by plain language. In *R* v. *Secretary of State for the Environment ex parte Merton London Borough Council* (1990) 154 LG Rev 655, an error in the estimate of a local authority's total expenditure in relation to the financial year 1985–6 had been discovered after the estimate had been submitted to the Secretary of State for the Environment as part of the process of allocating central government grant to the local authority. The scale of the error was such that an additional burden of £65 would be placed on each of the local authority's community charge payers if no corrective measures were taken. The High Court held that it was powerless to remedy the obvious injustice of the situation, because the wording of paragraph 1 of Schedule 1 to the Rate Support Grants Act 1988 was unambiguous and was clearly designed to ensure finality in the financial arrangements between central and local government.

Presumption against absurdity

The presumption against absurdity may be illustrated by *Jones* v. *Conway & Colwyn Bay Joint Water Supply Board* [1893] 2 Ch 603, which concerned the statutory right of a company which was supplying water to lay mains through other people's land. The court held that this right could be exercised before the water was supplied, because it would be absurd to say that water had to be supplied before the necessary mains had been laid.

Presumption against retrospectivity

Although the doctrine of precedent operates retrospectively (see Part II generally, and pp. 203–4 in particular) there is a strong presumption that statutes are not retrospective.

At one time the courts drew a distinction between matters of procedure and matters of substance, with the presumption against retrospectivity applying only to the latter. However, this changed with the decision of the Privy Council in *Yew Bon Tew* v. *Kenderaan Bas Mara* [1982] 3 All ER 833, where the facts involved the limitation period in respect of a personal injuries claim. (Limitation periods are regarded as being procedural, not substantive, because they only affect the exercise of the right to bring proceedings, and not the existence of the right in the first place.) Under a law enacted in 1948 the limitation period was 12 months. An accident happened in April 1972, and therefore the limitation period expired in April 1973. However, in June 1974 the 1948 law was amended so that the limitation period became three years. In the instant case, proceedings were begun in March 1975, so the action was clearly statute-barred if the original limitation period applied, but not if the new one did. The procedural nature of the provision did not prevent the Privy Council from holding that the action was statute-barred, on the basis that the purpose of the amendment was to extend limitation periods which had not yet expired, and to extend those which would arise in the future. Putting it the other way round, the purpose of the provision was not to deprive potential defendants of defences which they already had, because to do so would be unfair.

For many years, the decision in *Re A Solicitor's Clerk* [1957] 3 All ER 617 was commonly cited as a classic example of the way in which the presumption against retrospectivity operates. Under the Solicitors Act 1941, the Law Society could prohibit solicitors from employing clerks who had been convicted of theft of property belonging either to their employer or to their employer's clients. The Solicitors (Amendment) Act 1956 changed this so that the ownership of the property became irrelevant. In 1953 a clerk was convicted of theft in respect of property which belonged neither to his employer nor to his employer's clients, and therefore at that stage his employment could not be prohibited. In 1957 the Law Society prohibited the clerk's employment. The court held that this would not be giving retrospective effect to the 1956 Act because although the prohibition referred to something done in the past it did not affect what had been done in the past. Despite the court's argument, you may find it difficult to avoid feeling that the conclusion of the case really was retrospective.

However, in *Secretary of State for Social Services* v. *Tunnicliffe* [1991] 2 All ER 712, the Court of Appeal doubted the correctness of *Re A Solicitor's Clerk*. The facts were that the Secretary of State had power to recover welfare benefits which had been paid in error. Until 6 April 1987, the exercise of the power was subject to different tests according to whether the benefit in question was means-tested or not, with repayment of non-means-tested benefits being subject to a test of due care and diligence on the part of the claimant, and means-tested cases being subject to a test of misrepresentation and non-disclosure by the claimant. From that date the two systems were reconciled by making the test of misrepresentation and non-disclosure common to both types of benefit. The question arose as to which test should be applied after 6 April 1987, in respect of overpayments occurring before that date. The Court of Appeal held that the test which had become universal should be applied. From the point of view of the presumption against retrospectivity, the significance of the case lies in the judgement of Staughton LJ:

'A good illustration of the difficulty is afforded by *Re A Solicitor's Clerk* . . . From the point of view of the clerk, that was in my view plainly retrospective legislation if he was caught by it: a new disability was imposed in respect of his sins in the past. So far as any employer was concerned, however, I would not say that the legislation was retrospective. It regulated whom he might employ in the future . . . it will be apparent that I have doubts about the decision.

'In my judgment the true principle is that *Parliament is presumed not to have intended to alter the law applicable to past events and transactions in a manner which is unfair to those concerned in them, unless a contrary intention appears.* It is not simply a question of classifying an enactment as retrospective or not retrospective. Rather it may well be a matter of degree – the greater the unfairness, the more it is to be expected that Parliament will make it clear if that is intended.

'Applying that principle to the present case . . . the new rule as to misrepresentation or non-disclosure will not in all cases be harder on the recipients of benefit than the old test of due care and diligence. That was common ground before us. Nevertheless it is likely that in many cases the new rule will prove disadvantageous to recipients and correspondingly advantageous to the Secretary of State.

'On the other hand [the new Act] did no more than apply to benefits which are not means tested the test which had previously been applied to means-tested benefits. It would be convenient for adjudicators and tribunals, and for those who advise on social security law, if only one test could arise for consideration. In a case where overpayment of benefit straddled the commencement date of April 6, 1987, there would be some degree of inconvenience if liability to repay had in a subsequent determination to be decided in part by each of two different tests. But any change in the law is liable to produce some degree of inconvenience for lawyers and administrators.

'On the whole I reach the conclusion that the retrospective aspect of [the new Act] is *not so unfair* to recipients of benefit, or some of them, as to require greater clarity than Parliament has used.' (Emphasis added.)

The House of Lords approved this approach in *L'Office Cherifien des Phosphates and Another* v. *Yamashita-Shinnihon Steamship Co Ltd: The Boucraa* [1994] 1 All ER 20, where the facts involved a dispute over damage to a ship. The dispute had been referred to arbitration in 1985, but no steps beyond an initial claim and defence were taken. On January 1, 1992, s.13A of the Arbitration Act 1950 (as inserted by the Courts and Legal Services Act 1990) came into force, conferring upon an arbitrator the power to dismiss a claim for want of prosecution where the claimant had been guilty of inordinate and inexcusable delay in pursuing his claim. The respondent in the arbitration in the present case then applied for the claim to be dismissed. The respondent succeeded before the arbitrator, but the High Court and a majority of the Court of Appeal, both applying their understanding of the presumption against retrospectivity, held in favour of the claimant. The House of Lords rejected the reasoning on which the arbitrator had based his decision in favour of the respondent (namely that he must regard s.13A as having been part of the statute since its original enactment in 1950) but upheld the actual decision. More particularly, Lord Mustill, delivering the principal speech, approved the approach which Staughton LJ had formulated in *Tunnicliffe*:

'Precisely how the single question of fairness will be answered in respect of a particular statute will depend on the interaction of several factors, each of them capable of varying from case to case. Thus, the degree to which the statute has retrospective effect is not a constant. Nor is the value of the rights which the statute affects, or the extent to which that value is diminished or extinguished by the retrospective effect of the statute. Again, the unfairness of adversely affecting the rights, and hence the degree of unlikelihood that this is what Parliament intended, will vary from case to case. So also will the clarity of the language used by Parliament, and the light shed on it by consideration of the circumstances in which the legislation was enacted. All these factors must be weighed together to provide a direct answer to the question whether the consequences of reading the statute with the suggested degree of retrospectivity is so unfair that the words used by Parliament cannot have been intended to mean what they might appear to say.'

The power of the presumption is illustrated by the case of *Re Barretto* [1994] 1 All ER 447. The Drug Trafficking Offences Act 1986 gave the court power to make a confiscation order in respect of the proceeds of drug trafficking, and in January 1990 such an order was made against Barretto, who was also sentenced to 20 years' imprisonment. The court found that Barretto had benefited to the extent of approximately £600 000 from drug trafficking, but that only about £287 000 was realisable, and therefore the order was made in the latter figure, with three years' imprisonment in default of payment. In 1991 the Criminal Justice (International Co-operation) Act 1990 came into effect. One purpose of the Act was to allow the amount specified in confiscation orders to be increased where additional assets subsequently came to light. In the present case substantial subsequent assets did come to light after the 1990 Act had come into force, and therefore the question arose as to whether the sum specified in the original order could be increased. The Court of Appeal held that the application of the presumption against retrospectivity meant that no increase was possible. Sir Thomas Bingham MR aknowledged that:

'Many would think that on the present facts there would be nothing unfair in stripping Mr Barretto of the fruits of his criminal activity which he did not disclose in January 1990 even if this means relying on a law enacted later. But the court is here concerned with fairness in a more particular sense. A defendant is not to be substantially prejudiced by laws construed as having retroactive effect unless Parliament's intention that they should have that effect is plain. The blackest malefactor is as much entitled to the benefit of that presumption as anyone else. Parliament has not displaced the presumption in this case and it would not be fair to treat it as having done so however strong one's disapproval of Mr Barretto's conduct.'

One crucial consideration was that the 1986 Act had been made expressly retrospective, and it would have been easy for the 1990 Act to have been expressed in similar terms if retrospectivity had been intended. Clearly, however, the result would have been different if the court had given primacy to the presumption against gaining advantage from wrongdoing, which is discussed at p. 316.

In common with all other presumptions, the presumption against retrospectivity may, of course, be rebutted by plain words. *Chebaro* v. *Chebaro* [1987] 1 All ER 999 dealt with s.12 of the Matrimonial and Family Proceedings Act 1984, which provided that where

'a marriage *has* been dissolved . . . by . . . judicial . . . proceedings in an overseas country . . . and . . . the divorce . . . *is* entitled to be recognised as valid in England and Wales, either party . . . may apply to the court . . . for financial relief.' (Emphasis added.)

The parties' marriage had been dissolved in the Lebanon in April 1985, and the provision had come into force in September 1985. Balcombe LJ said:

'The meaning of the words used is plain and unequivocal. The use of the past tense, "where a marriage has been dissolved", in contradistinction to the present tense . . . "and the divorce . . . is entitled to be recognised," makes it clear that the section is intended to apply to a decree of divorce whenever pronounced.'

Presumption of strict interpretation of penal provisions

Generally

A convenient statement of the presumption that penal provisions should be construed strictly in favour of the person who is liable to be penalized is contained in the judgement of Brett J in *Dickenson* v. *Fletcher* (1873) LR 9 CP 1:

'Those who contend that a penalty may be inflicted must show that the words of the Act distinctly enact that it shall be incurred under the present circumstances. They must fail if the words are merely equally capable of a construction that would, and one that would not, inflict the penalty.'

A common source of difficulty arising from this principle is the presumption that *mens rea* is a necessary ingredient of statutory offences.

The presumption that mens rea is a necessary ingredient of statutory offences

The common law requires two elements to be present before a defendant may be convicted of a crime, namely an *actus reus* and *mens rea*. The *actus reus* is the guilty act, and the *mens rea* is the guilty mind or intention. Many statutes also require both elements to be essential preconditions to the imposition of criminal liability. For example, the offence of theft under the Theft Acts 1968–78 requires both the appropriation of property belonging to someone else (the *actus reus*) and the dishonest intention that that person should be permanently deprived of the property (the *mens rea*). However, a problem arises where a statute which creates an offence is silent as to the need for *mens rea*. Is the silence to be explained on the ground that no *mens rea* is necessary? Or is it to be explained on the ground that the requirement of *mens rea* is so basic that Parliament was confident that the courts would imply the need for it to be proved, without any express provision being necessary?

The short answer is that the courts will normally presume that Parliament expected *mens rea* to be a precondition of guilt, and accordingly they will refuse to convict in its absence. However, it is important to remember that this is only a presumption, and the possibility of rebuttal must always be borne in mind.

Before examining the operation of the presumption more closely, we must distinguish the concept of *mens rea* from the principle that ignorance of the law is no excuse. The distinction may be illustrated by returning to the Theft Acts 1968–78, which, as we have already seen makes dishonesty an essential ingredient of the offence of theft. It follows that if I appropriate property belonging to you, I commit the *actus reus*, but if I genuinely believe that the property is mine and therefore that I am entitled to take it, I will not be acting dishonestly, so there will be no *mens rea*, and I am not guilty. On the other hand, if I appropriate your property, being dishonest and intending to deprive you of it permanently, I am guilty even if I know nothing of the criminal law and do not know that what I am doing is an offence.

Returning to the topic of strict liability, the classic starting-point is *Sherras* v. *de Rutzen* [1895] 1 QB 918, where Wright J said:

'There is a presumption that *mens rea*, or evil intention, or knowledge of the wrongfulness of the act, is an essential ingredient in every offence; but that presumption is liable to be displaced either by the words of the statute creating the offence or by the subject-matter with which it deals, and both must be considered.'

According to Lord Diplock in *Sweet* v. *Parsley* [1969] 1 All ER 347, the explanation of the presumption is that

'it is contrary to a rational and civilized criminal code . . . to penalize one who has performed his duty as a citizen to ascertain what acts are prohibited by law . . . and has taken all proper care to inform himself of any facts which would make his conduct unlawful.'

Even more succinctly, in *Lim Chin Aik* v. *R* [1963] 1 All ER 223, the Privy Council said: 'It cannot be inferred that the legislature imposed strict liability merely in order to find a luckless victim.' However, it must be remembered that, in common with all other presumptions in statutory interpretation, the presumption that *mens rea* is a necessary ingredient of statutory offences may be rebutted. It is useful to approach the topic of rebuttal by applying the two-fold classification which we have already encountered (in Wright J's judgement in *Sherras* v. *de Rutzen*) to the effect that rebuttal may arise from either the words or the subject-matter of the statute, although it will be necessary to add a gloss to the first of these two possibilities .

Express words showing that no *mens rea* is necessary will genuinely rebut the presumption, but it is more common to find the enactment of a specific formula expressing what the *mens rea* is to be, in which case it is more accurate to say that the presumption has become redundant, rather than that it has been rebutted. The example of the Theft Acts illustrates a specific formula, namely 'dishonestly . . . with the intention of permanently depriving'. Innumerable other provisions incorporate words such as 'knowingly', 'intentionally', and 'wilfully' to indicate the need for *mens rea*, but even these can cause difficulty.

In *Arrowsmith* v. *Jenkins* [1963] 2 QB 561, a campaigner for nuclear disarmament found a crowd had assembled round her while she held a public meeting on the highway. Upholding her conviction for *wilfully* obstructing the highway without lawful authority or excuse, Lord Parker CJ said:

'If a person, without lawful authority or excuse, intentionally as opposed to accidentally, that is, by an exercise of his or her free will, does something or omits to do something which will cause an obstruction or the continuance of an obstruction, he or she is guilty of an offence.'

In other words, once the defendant had wilfully done the act of holding the meeting, her liability for the ensuing obstruction was strict.

Similarly, in *Cotterill* v. *Penn* [1936] 1 KB 53, a defendant was convicted of wilfully killing a house pigeon even though he believed that the bird which he shot was a wild pigeon. His act of shooting was wilful. This particular difficulty could be avoided if the courts were to give full weight to Lord Diplock's opinion that in order to give the word 'wilfully' any effect beyond excluding mere accidents, it ought to be understood as implying a requirement of proof of knowledge of something beyond the mere doing of the act itself. (*R* v. *Sheppard* [1980] 3 All ER 899.)

Turning to Wright J's second basis for displacing the presumption, namely the subject-matter of the offence, the leading case is *Gammon (Hong Kong) Ltd* v. *Attorney-General for Hong Kong* [1984] 2 All ER 503. The issue was whether it was an offence of strict liability to contravene the Hong Kong equivalent of the English Building Regulations, which prescribe standards aimed at ensuring the quality and safety of buildings. Holding that contravention was an offence of strict liability, the Privy Council said:

'(1) There is a presumption of law that *mens rea* is required before a person can be guilty of a criminal offence; (2) the presumption is particularly strong where the offence is "truly criminal" in character;

(3) the presumption applies to statutory offences, and can be displaced only if this is clearly or by necessary implication the effect of the statute; (4) the only situation in which the presumption can be displaced is where the statute is concerned with an issue of social concern, and public safety is such an issue; (5) even where a statute is concerned with such an issue, the presumption of *mens rea* stands unless it can also be shown that the creation of strict liability will be effective to promote the objects of the statute by encouraging greater vigilance to prevent the commission of the prohibited act.'

The reference in *Gammon* to offences which are 'truly criminal' in character is intended to distinguish between offences involving turpitude, conviction in respect of which therefore involves some moral stigma, and offences which are sometimes referred to as being merely 'regulatory'. Regulatory offences are said to be those where a statutory prohibition is imposed in the public interest, and is enforced by means of a penalty imposed on conviction. (The Trade Descriptions Act 1968 was regarded as being within this category in *Wings Ltd* v. *Ellis* [1984] 3 All ER 577, where the House of Lords was concerned with an inaccurate holiday brochure.) In practice, however, this distinction is seldom very satisfactory, because enforcement by means of a penalty imposed on conviction is usually a sign that the prohibition involves a matter of social concern. It can be argued, therefore, that contraventions of such prohibitions must involve turpitude, and that as a result they can properly be stigmatized as being genuinely criminal.

Nevertheless, it is clear that the courts are influenced by their perception of the seriousness of the conduct which constitutes the *actus reus*, even though the degree of seriousness may not always be immediately apparent to the untutored eye. For example, in *R* v. *St. Margaret's Trust Ltd* [1958] 2 All ER 289, the defendant finance company unknowingly contravened a Hire Purchase Order which required substantial minimum deposits where goods were bought on hire purchase. Holding the offence to be one of strict liability, Donovan J said:

'The object of the order was to help to defend the currency against the peril of inflation which, if unchecked, would bring disaster on the country. There is no need to elaborate this. The present generation has witnessed the collapse of the currency in other countries and the consequent chaos, misery and widespread ruin. It would not be at all surprising if Parliament, determined to prevent similar calamities here, enacted measures which it intended to be absolute prohibitions of acts which might increase the risk in however small a degree. Indeed, that would be the natural expectation. There would be little point in enacting that no one should breach the defences against a flood, and at the same time excusing anyone who did it innocently.'

Strict liability was also held to exist in *R* v. *Wells Street Magistrate ex parte Westminster City Council* [1986] 3 All ER 4. Section 55 of the Town and Country Planning Act 1971 created an offence of doing certain works to buildings which were listed as being of special architectural or historic interest. The court held that the defendant could be convicted even without knowing that the building was listed, because protection of the national heritage is a serious matter. On the other hand, in *Sweet* v. *Parsley* the House of Lords held that the owner of a house could not be convicted of being concerned in the management of premises used for drug-taking when she did not know that her tenants were taking drugs. In other words, her lack of *mens rea* was vital.

However, by way of further contrast, it is useful to consider the House of Lords' decision in *Pharmaceutical Society of Great Britain* v. *Storkwain Ltd* [1986] 2 All ER 635. Under s.58(2) of the Medicines Act 1968 it was an offence to dispense certain drugs on a forged prescription. The House held that a pharmacist committed the offence even without knowing, and without reason to believe, that the prescription was forged. Lord Goff, with whom the other four Law Lords agreed, laid heavy emphasis on the fact that various other provisions of the Act created offences which expressly required *mens rea*, and therefore it was reasonable to suppose that the absence of any requirement of *mens rea* from s.58(2) was intentional. The logical force of this is clear, and thus it is probably safe to assume that *Storkwain* has overruled that part of *Sweet* v. *Parsley* in which Lord Reid said: 'It is . . . firmly established that the fact that other sections of the Act expressly require *mens rea* . . . is not in itself sufficient to justify a decision that a section which is silent as to *mens rea* creates an absolute offence.' Furthermore, Lord Reid's use of the expression 'absolute offence' must be treated with caution. The topic we are discussing is *strict* liability, not *absolute* liability. The distinction is important because in all the cases we have considered the defendant intended to do something – such as shooting a pigeon, undertaking building works, lending money on hire purchase, allowing a tenant to occupy premises, or dispensing drugs – even though in each case the intention was accompanied by a degree of ignorance as to at least some element of the surrounding circumstances.

Finally, the courts may be less ready to find strict liability in cases where members of the general public are liable to be convicted than in cases where it is only members of some defined, and self-selected, group who are at risk. As Lord Diplock said in *Sweet* v. *Parsley*:

'Where penal provisions are of general application to the conduct of ordinary citizens in the course of their everyday life, the presumption is that the standard of care required of them in informing themselves of facts which would make their conduct unlawful is that of the familiar common law duty of care. But where the subject-matter of a statute is the regulation of a particular activity involving potential danger to public health, safety or morals, in which citizens have a choice whether they participate or not, the court may feel driven to infer an intention of Parliament to impose, by penal actions, a higher duty of care on those who choose to participate and to place on them an obligation to take whatever measures may be necessary to prevent the prohibited act, without regard to those considerations of cost or business practicability which play a part in the determination of what would be required of them in order to fulfil the ordinary common law duty of care. But such an inference is not lightly to be drawn, nor is there any room for it unless there is something that the person on whom the obligation is imposed can do directly or indirectly, by supervision or inspection, by improvement of his business methods or by exhorting those whom he may be expected to influence or control, which will promote the observance of the obligation.'

Presumptions relating to consolidating and codifying statutes

Before looking at the presumptions relating to consolidating and codifying statutes it is necessary to distinguish *consolidation* from *codification*. *Consolidation* is the process whereby all the existing statute law on a particular subject is brought together into one Act, or into a small group of Acts. It is a technical matter, designed to make the law more accessible, and is generally not intended to change the law, although, as we saw at p. 245, some minor changes are permitted.

Codification must be approached with a little more caution, because the term has two distinct usages. In English Law (as opposed to the civil law systems of mainland Europe) the term 'code' is used to mean a statute, or a small group of statutes, containing all the law (and not merely all the statute law) on a particular subject. This is quite distinct from the concept of codification in civil law jurisdictions, where a code is a basic but comprehensive statement of basic principles of law embodied in the legal system. Of course, we are concerned with the English usage.

While codifying statutes will, in common with consolidating ones, improve the accessibility of the law, they will also introduce changes. This distinction underlies the difference in approach to the interpretation of the two types of statute. In *Beswick* v. *Beswick* (see p. 294) Lord Reid pointed out that, when a consolidation Bill is presented to Parliament, those who are responsible for it must certify that it contains no substantial changes in the law, and that a Committee checks the Bill to see that this is so. It follows from this that the courts are entitled to apply a presumption that a consolidating Act does not change the law. It also follows that previously decided cases can be good authority in relation to the meaning of a subsequent consolidation Act, although in *Farrell* v. *Alexander* [1976] 2 All ER 721, Lord Wilberforce, Lord Simon and Lord Edmund-Davies all said that, if the meaning of a consolidation Act was clear, there was no need to refer to decisions on the previous statutes. In passing, it is also interesting to note that neither Lord Wilberforce nor Lord Simon was particularly attracted to the idea that, when Parliament re-enacted a form of words which had previously been interpreted by the courts, it necessarily followed that Parliament was endorsing the correctness of the courts' interpretation.

In *Bank of England* v. *Vagliano Brothers* [1891] AC 107, Lord Herschell LC, speaking of a codifying statute, said:

'I think the proper course is, in the first instance, to examine the language of the statute, and to ask what is its natural meaning, uninfluenced by any considerations derived from the previous state of the law, and *not* to start with enquiring how the law previously stood, and then, assuming that it is intended to leave it unaltered, to see if the words of the enactment will bear an interpretation in conformity with this view. If . . . treated in this fashion it appears to me that its utility will be almost entirely destroyed and the very object with which it was enacted will be frustrated. *The purpose of such a statute surely was that on any point specifically dealt with by it, the law should be ascertained by interpreting the language used, instead of, as before, by roaming over a vast number of authorities.*' (Emphasis added.)

When reading this quotation, it is important to realize that the italicised *not* governs the whole of the remainder of the first sentence.

Presumption of compliance with international law

The case of *Fothergill* v. *Monarch Airlines Ltd* [1980] 2 All ER 696 is authority for the proposition that Parliament will be presumed to have intended to comply with international law. In many cases this presumption will involve the use of international agreements as aids to statutory interpretation.

Ellerman Lines Ltd v. *Murray* [1930] All ER Rep 503 clearly established that a relevant international convention could be used in order to resolve an ambiguity, even though on the instant facts the House of Lords concluded that the meaning of the enacted words was plain beyond doubt. More recently, however, it has become clear that recourse may be had to treaties as an aid to interpretation without first having to identify an ambiguity. As Lord Denning MR said, in *Salomon* v. *Commissioners of Customs and Excise* [1966] 3 All ER 871: 'I think we are entitled to look at [a convention], because it is an instrument which is binding in international law; and we ought to interpret our statutes so as to be in conformity with international law.'

It is immaterial whether the Act specifically refers to the convention in question, and of course the court may have to read a text in some language other than English. The correct approach was laid down by Lord Wilberforce in *Fothergill* v. *Monarch Airlines Ltd* [1980] 2 All ER 696:

'My Lords, as in *Buchanan (James) & Co Ltd* v. *Babco Forwarding and Shipping (UK) Ltd* [1977] 3 All ER 1048, I am not willing to lay down any precise rule . . . The process of ascertaining the meaning must vary according to the subject-matter. If a judge has some knowledge of the relevant language, there is no reason why he should not use it; this is particularly true of the French or Latin languages, so long languages of our courts. There is no reason why he should not consult a dictionary, if the word is such that a dictionary can reveal its significance; often, of course, it may substitute one doubt for another . . . In all cases he will have in mind that ours is an adversary system: it is for the parties to make good their contentions. So he will inform them of the process he is using, and, if they think fit, they can supplement his resources with other materials, other dictionaries, other books of reference, textbooks and decided cases. They may call evidence of an interpreter, if the language is one unknown to the court, or an expert if the word or expression is such as to require expert interpretation. Between a technical expression in Japanese and a plain word in French there must be a whole spectrum which calls for suitable and individual treatment.'

Fothergill is also authority for the proposition that, in interpreting an international agreement, it is legitimate to consult preliminary documentation, or *travaux préparatoires*, provided: 'First that the material involved is public and accessible, and secondly, that the *travaux préparatoires* clearly and indisputably point to a definite legislative intention' (Lord Wilberforce).

The question of reference to international agreements repeatedly comes before the courts in the context of the European Convention on the Protection of Human Rights and Fundamental Freedoms, to which the United Kingdom is a party, but which it has not incorporated into domestic law.

The position generally is that the courts must have regard to the Convention when seeking to resolve ambiguities within statutes, but public administrators need not do so. As Lord Bridge said, in *Brind* v. *Secretary of State for the Home Department* [1991] 1 All ER 720, which is reported in most other series of reports as *R* v. *Secretary of State for the Home Department ex parte Brind*:

> 'It is accepted, of course, by the appellants that, like any other treaty obligations which have not been embodied in the law by statute, the Convention is not part of the domestic law, that the courts accordingly have no power to enforce Convention rights directly and that, if domestic legislation conflicts with the Convention, the courts must nevertheless enforce it. But it is already well settled that, *in construing any provision in domestic legislation which is ambiguous in the sense that it is capable of a meaning which either conforms to or conflicts with the Convention, the courts will presume that Parliament intended to legislate in conformity with the Convention, not in conflict with it.*' (Emphasis added.)

However, Lord Bridge went on to say that it does not follow that a decision-maker who is interpreting the law which governs the decision-making process must have regard to the Convention:

> 'Where Parliament has conferred on the executive an administrative discretion without indicating the precise limits within which it must be exercised, to presume that it must be exercised within Convention limits would be to go far beyond the resolution of ambiguity. It would be to impute to Parliament an intention not only that the executive should exercise the discretion in conformity with the convention, but also that the domestic courts should enforce that conformity by the importation into domestic administrative law of the text of the Convention and the jurisprudence of the European Court of Human Rights in the interpretation and application of it.'

Although Lord Bridge's comment reflects the general position, a different principle applies where the statute in question has been passed to make English law conform to the Convention. In *R* v. *Secretary of State for the Home Department and Another ex parte Norney and Others* (1995) 7 Admin LR 861, the High Court was considering s.34 of the Criminal Justice Act 1991, which had been passed to bring English law into line with art.5(4) of the Convention. More particularly, the section placed the Home Secretary under a duty to release a particular category of prisoners when directed to do so by the Parole Board. In practice, the Parole Board adopted a procedure which meant that the prisoners' release was delayed by several months beyond the earliest date on which they could properly be released. Holding this conduct to be unlawful, although the prisoners lost on other grounds, Dyson J recognized the general rule, as stated in *Brind*, to the effect that the legality of the exercise of a discretion is not to be determined by asking whether it involves an infringement of rights under the Convention. He nevertheless went on to say that it would be perverse to hold that a court must ignore the relevant provisions of the Convention, where the case involves the legality of the exercise of a discretion which has been conferred by a statute which was passed in order to bring English law into line with the Convention.

The right-recognizing provisions of the Convention are reproduced in Appendix 3.

Presumption of compliance with Community law

As we saw, at p. 99, when considering the need to avoid conflicts between English law and Community law:

> 'It is a principle of construction of United Kingdom statutes . . . that the words of a statute passed after the Treaty has been signed and dealing with the subject matter of the international obligations of the United Kingdom, are to be construed, if they are reasonably capable of bearing such a meaning, as intended to carry out the obligation, and not to be inconsistent with it.' (Lord Diplock, in *Garland* v. *British Rail Engineering Ltd* [1982] 2 All ER 402.)

Subsequently, as we also saw, the *von Colson principle* as clarified in *Marleasing SA* v. *La Comercial Internacional de Alimentacion SA* [1992] 1 CMLR 305, requires national courts to interpret national law in such a way as to accord with Community law whenever possible. In this connexion it is also useful to emphasize that, as we saw at p. 216, the Community is formally committed to the legal protection of fundamental rights.

Sometimes, of course, there will be no need to invoke this presumption, because there is no conflict, or apparent conflict, between English law and Community law. Indeed, the two systems may be indentical, as will happen where the English drafter has used the 'copy-out' method of transposing a Directive into English law. Copy-out is exactly what it says: the drafter may simply copy out the relevant provisions of the Directive and incorporate them into a piece of English legislation. Although copy-out is an obvious way of avoiding conflict, its use is not always appropriate. For example, the Directive may say nothing at all about the means to be adopted in achieving its objective, in which case copy-out will obviously produce a defective result. In other cases, there may already be English provisions governing the subject-matter covered by the Directive, in which case the least disruptive amendment may be achieved by conventional drafting, rather than by copy-out. However, even where the Directive is self-contained and there is no pre-existing English law, it does not follow that copy-out will always be appropriate, because the Directive may deal with concepts and use terminology which require redefinition or translation in order to produce a result which fits into English law.

Presumption against gaining advantage from wrongdoing

Re Sigsworth [1934] All ER Rep 113 provides a classic example of the commonsense presumption that people should not be allowed to profit from their own wrongdoing. Section 46 of the Administration of Estates Act 1925 provides that on an intestacy the deceased's property 'shall be distributed' in accordance with the section. The court held that, where a son had murdered his mother, s.46 did not apply, because otherwise he would inherit her property and therefore profit from his own wrongdoing.

In cases such as *Re Sigsworth* the presumption against gaining advantage from wrongdoing is particularly strong, and indeed the Forfeiture Act 1982 refers to 'the forfeiture rule', which it defines as 'the rule of public policy which in certain circumstances precludes a person who has unlawfully killed another from acquiring a benefit in consequence of the killing'. A rule of public policy is clearly rather more than a mere presumption of interpretation. Nevertheless, the Act gives the court power to modify the effect of the rule where 'the justice of the case' so requires, and gives a Social Security Commissioner a corresponding power in respect of social security benefits. Curiously, the court's power does not apply to cases of murder, but there is no such restriction on the power of a Social Security Commissioner.

Re Sigsworth involved the court looking backward to the actual conduct of an individual, and preventing financial gain on the part of the wrongdoer. It is apparent, however, that neither of these elements is essential. The court may also look forward, on the basis of an intelligent estimation of likely future conduct, and apply the presumption in order to frustrate the illicit attainment of some non-financial goal which is nevertheless subjectively valuable.

Under s.51(1) of the Adoption Act 1976, the Registrar-General is under a duty to give applicants who have been adopted certain information which will enable them to obtain certified copies of their birth certificates, which will in turn, of course, enable them to identify their natural mothers. This duty is stated to be subject to the satisfaction of certain conditions specified in the Act but otherwise it is couched in absolute terms. In *R* v. *Registrar-General ex parte Smith* [1991] 2 All ER 88, Smith had been adopted while he was still a baby. While serving life imprisonment for murder, he killed another prisoner, saying that he believed his victim to be his adoptive mother. He was convicted of manslaughter and sent to Broadmoor. He then applied to the Registrar-General under s.51(1) of the 1976 Act. The Registrar-General took medical advice and refused to issue the information, fearing that Smith would do harm to his natural mother.

The Court of Appeal held as a rule of public policy that, even when Parliament has enacted statutory duties in apparently absolute terms, there is a presumption that there was no intention either to enable people to benefit from serious crimes committed in the past, or to assist them to commit serious crime in the future.

Presumption against binding the Crown

The practical significance of the presumption that statutes do not bind the Crown lies in the fact that for the present purposes 'the Crown' includes all the departments of central government. (*Town Investments Ltd* v. *Department of the Environment* [1977] 1 All ER 813.) The presumption can be rebutted either by clear words to that effect, or by necessary implication.

Where there is a statutory provision to the effect that the Crown is bound, it will usually be found towards the end of the statute, along with provisions containing the short title, and dealing with the commencement and the territorial extent. The case of *Bombay Province* v. *Bombay Municipal Corporation* [1947] AC 58 shows that the doctrine of necessary implication will be applied strictly, and it must be shown that the purpose of the statute would be wholly frustrated if the Crown were not bound. Thus, for example, in *Cooper* v. *Hawkins* [1904] 2 KB 164, it was held that the driver of a Crown vehicle was not bound by a statutory speed limit. (Subsequent Road Traffic Acts have expressly bound the Crown.)

In *Lord Advocate* v. *Dumbarton District Council and Another* [1990] 1 All ER 1, the House of Lords surveyed the authorities dealing with this presumption and categorically reaffirmed the existing doctrine. The Ministry of Defence coned off part of a road to facilitate work on the perimeter fence of a defence installation. A private operator doing this would have needed the consent of the roads authority and the local planning authority, but the Ministry took the view that it did not require these consents. When the authorities took enforcement action, the Ministry applied for judicial review, conceding that it had no right to do what it had done, but nevertheless arguing that it was not bound by the statutes. The issue was stated by Lord Emslie in the First Division (i.e. a Scottish Court):

> 'It is not suggested that the Crown has any right whatever to occupy and erect structures and obstructions upon . . . the public road. It is not contended, accordingly, that the application to the Crown of the provisions . . . would encroach in any prejudicial way upon the Crown's rights, interests or privileges. The question to be answered is whether upon a proper construction of the statute it can be affirmed that the Crown meant to be bound by the particular provisions. In order to answer that question it is essential to determine whether there is . . . a special rule of construction which applies to the construction of all statutory provisions when the issue of Crown immunity has to be resolved, or whether . . . the special rule of construction only applies when the statutory provisions in question would bind the Crown to its prejudice.'

In the House of Lords, Lord Keith, giving the only substantial speech, said: 'It is preferable, in my view, to stick to the simple rule that the Crown is not bound by any statutory provision unless there can somehow be gathered from the terms of the relevant Act an intention to that effect.'

21.8   Change of Meaning with the Passage of Time

The classical doctrine of statutory interpretation is that the meaning of an Act does not change with the passing of time. In the late nineteenth-century case of *The Longford* (1889) 14 PD 34, an Act dating from the time of William IV prohibited the bringing of any 'action' in 'his Majesty's courts of law' against certain shipowners, unless one month's notice had been given. The question was whether a particular kind of case, referred to technically as an Admiralty action *in rem*, was within the prohibition. In the Court of Appeal Lord Esher said:

> 'The first point to be borne in mind is that the Act must be construed as if one were interpreting it the day after it was passed . . . the word "action" . . . was not applicable when the Act was passed to the procedure of the Admiralty Court. Admiralty actions were then called "suits" or "causes"; moreover, the Admiralty Court was not called and was not one of His Majesty's courts of law.'

Simple and straightforward though this appears to be, the reality is rather more complicated, as can be seen from two groups of cases. The first deals with security of tenure legislation and the other deals with technological developments arising after the passing of an Act.

The problem of social change

Since the Increase of Rent and Mortgage Interest (Restrictions) Act 1920, the law has given security of tenure to a member of a tenant's family who was residing with the tenant at the time of the tenant's death. In *Gammans* v. *Ekins* [1950] 2 KB 328, the facts were that a Mr Ekins lived with a Mrs Smith, who was the tenant of the house concerned. On her death in 1939, Mr Ekins claimed to be a member of her family. The Court of Appeal rejected his claim. Asquith LJ said: 'To say of two people masquerading . . . as husband and wife (there being no children to complicate the picture) that they were members of the same family seems to be an abuse of the English language.'

Only a few years later, however, in *Hawes* v. *Evendon* [1953] 1 WLR 1169, the Court of Appeal decided that the survivor of a non-marital relationship was a member of the tenant's family, although in this case there were children, so the comment of Asquith LJ in the previous case was not directly applicable. Subsequently, in *Dyson Holdings Ltd* v. *Fox* [1975] 3 All ER 1031, the Court of Appeal returned to the same problem, but this time without the complicating factor of children. Although their Lordships did so with differing degrees of enthusiasm, all three held that the surviving common law wife was a member of the tenant's family. On the basis that times change and the meanings of words change with them, it was held that *Gammans* v. *Ekins* should not be followed because the word 'family' in 1939 had not borne the same meaning as it did in 1961, which was the date of death in the present case.

Similarly, in *Watson* v. *Lucas* [1980] 3 All ER 647, the Court of Appeal held that a family exists if the relationship looks like a marriage in the old sense of a lifelong union rather than one which is merely temporary or casual. However, as we saw at p. 273, the court has refused to extend this line of case-law to include the survivor of a homosexual relationship.

The problem of technological change

Another group of illustrative cases covers a range of technological advances rather than one single, social change, but from the point of view of statutory interpretation the point is substantially the same.

First, in *Barker* v. *Wilson* [1980] 2 All ER 647, the High Court had to decide whether microfilm was within the meaning of a 'bankers' book' for the purposes of the Bankers' Books Evidence Act 1879. Section 9 of the Act defined 'bankers' books' as including 'ledgers, day books, cash books, account books and all other books used in the ordinary business of the bank'. Holding that microfilm could be a bankers' book, Bridge LJ said:

> 'The Bankers' Books Evidence Act 1879 was enacted with the practice of bankers in 1879 in mind. It must be construed in 1980 in relation to the practice of bankers as we now understand it. So construing the definition of 'bankers' books' and the phrase 'an entry in a banker's book', it seems to me that clearly both phrases are apt to include any form of permanent record kept by the bank of transactions relating to the bank's business, made by any of the methods which modern technology makes available, including, in particular, microfilm.'

Second, in *Re Attorney-General's Reference (No 5 of 1980)* [1980] 3 All ER 816, the Court of Appeal decided that a video cassette was an 'article' within the meaning of s.1(2) of the Obscene Publications Act 1959: 'In this Act 'article' means any description of article containing or embodying matter to be read or looked at or both, any sound record, and any film or other record of a picture or pictures.' In dealing with the submission that, when the Act had been passed, video tapes were scarcely beyond the experimental stage, the court accepted that ordinary words should be construed 'in the ways in which they would have been understood by ordinary literate persons at the material time, namely in 1959'. Despite the traditional tone of this statement, the court was nevertheless able to come to a conclusion which allowed the law to keep pace with technology, because:

> 'If the clear words of the statute are sufficiently wide to cover the kind of electronic device with which we are concerned in this case, the fact that that particular form of electronic device was not in the contemplation of Parliament in 1959 is an immaterial consideration.'

Third, in *Royal College of Nursing* v. *Department of Health and Social Security* [1981] 1 All ER 545, the House of Lords had to decide what s.1(1) of the Abortion Act 1967 meant when it referred to a pregnancy being 'terminated by a registered medical practitioner'. The proceedings began when the Royal College applied for a declaration that a circular issued by the Department was wrong as a matter of law. The circular purported to give advice as to the state of the law on abortion and, in particular, as to the extent to which nurses and midwives could lawfully participate in termination. The legal difficulty arose because when the Act was passed only surgical techniques of abortion were medically accepted in cases where the mother was three months pregnant or more, and therefore there was no question of anyone other than a registered medical practitioner performing the operation. From 1972 onwards, however, a new technique became available, involving two stages. First, a registered medical practitioner introduced a catheter and a cannula into the mother's body. Second, the registered medical practitioner gave instructions to the nursing staff who then introduced abortifacient drugs into the body, through the catheter and cannula. The registered medical practitioner remained available for consultation throughout.

The House of Lords divided three to two, with the minority holding that under these circumstances it was the nursing staff who were terminating the pregnancy because it was they who actually introduced the abortifacient drugs. The majority, however, held that Parliament had envisaged that abortions within the Act would be team efforts, as is the case with most hospital treatment. It followed that, provided a registered medical practitioner prescribes treatment, and remains in charge throughout the time the treatment is being administered, the pregnancy has been 'terminated by a registered medical practitioner'.

Clearly the pragmatic approach which emerges from the cases we have just considered makes it difficult to the point of impossibility to reconcile the *Longford* principle with current judicial reality.

Summary

1   Simple literalism in statutory interpretation has been replaced by the approach known as contextualism or purposivism or enlightened literalism.
2   Freeman's formulation of the basis of modern statutory interpretation is the best short statement of this approach.
3   The court may have to choose between ordinary and technical meanings.
4   Many matters which are commonly regarded as being principles of statutory interpretation are in fact simply matters of language in general.
5   In particular, any statute should be read as a whole in order to establish the context of the words in question.
6   However, in addition to matters of language in general, certain specialized principles are necessary because of the legal and constitutional context of statutory interpretation.
7   There are various presumptions of statutory interpretation. However, these may conflict with each other and with other principles of interpretation.
8   The courts are willing to provide updating constructions to take account of social and technological changes since a statute was passed.

Exercises

1   'The court which interprets a statute has more power than the Parliament which enacted it.'
Discuss.

2   Read the fictitious Act which is set out below, and answer the questions which appear beneath it. You must make the following assumptions:

A: The Act is neither a consolidating nor a codifying measure.

B: There are no other Acts *in pari materia* with the Act, nor are there any relevant provisions of European Community Law.

C: The Act was passed as a result of a Report by a Committee set up by the Department of Trade.

D: The Act was passed two years ago.

TRAVEL AGENTS REGISTRATION ACT

An Act to provide for the registration of travel agents and tour and charter operators.

Be it enacted etc., etc.

Travel Trade Registration Council

1(1)   There shall be established in accordance with this section a Travel Trade Registration Council (hereinafter referred to as 'the Council'), which shall consist of a chairman appointed by the Secretary of State for Trade and Industry (hereinafter referred to as 'the Secretary of State'), and such other members (not exceeding ten) as the Secretary of State may appoint, being persons appearing to him to have knowledge and experience of the requirements of the travelling public and of the interests of travel agents and of tour and charter operators.

(2)   The Council may from time to time fix the quorum required at its meetings and regulate its own procedure.

(3)   The Council may employ such officers and servants as it thinks fit.

Register of Travel Agents and Tour and Charter Operators

2(1)   It shall be the duty of the Council to prepare and maintain in accordance with the provisions of this Act a Register of travel agents and tour and charter operators (hereinafter referred to as 'the Register'), which shall be open to inspection by the public during business hours and on such terms as the Council with the approval of the Secretary of State may determine.

(2)   No person shall carry on business as a travel agent or tour or charter operator unless his name and address are included in the Register, and any person carrying on business in breach of the provisions of this subsection shall be guilty of an offence under this Act; Provided that this subsection shall come into force three months after the passing of this Act.

(3)   A person carrying on business as a travel agent or tour or charter operator at any time before the last foregoing subsection comes into

force, or proposing at any time thereafter to commence such a business, may apply to the Council on the prescribed form; and subject to the conditions of registration mentioned in the next following section, the Council shall cause his name and address to be included in the Register.

(4) A person whose name and address are included in the Register shall notify the Council when he ceases to carry on business as a travel agent or tour or charter operator; and on such notification his name and address shall be removed from the Register.

Conditions of Registration

3(1) The conditions of registration referred to in the last foregoing section are as follows:

(a) that the applicant is able to satisfy such criteria as to his financial solvency as the Secretary of State may from time to time prescribe; and

(b) that the applicant has, and declares himself to have, in force such a policy of insurance as may be approved by the Secretary of State.

(2) If any person makes or signs any declaration under the last foregoing subsection which is untrue in any material particular, he shall be guilty of an offence under this Act.

4(1) It shall be the duty of any person whose name and address are included in the Register to notify the Council forthwith of any change of circumstances such that, if he were to apply again for registration, he would be unable to comply with conditions specified in the first subsection of the last foregoing section.

(2) If any person fails to comply with the requirements of the last foregoing subsection, he shall be guilty of an offence under this Act.

Cancellation of Registration

5(1) Without prejudice to the duty imposed by the last foregoing section upon persons whose names and addresses are included in the Register, the Council may at any time require information from such persons relating to their suitability to be so registered.

(2) If the Council is satisfied that a person whose name and address are included in the Register is no longer able to comply with the conditions specified in s.3(1), the Council may either:

(a) Invite that person to request that his registration shall be cancelled forthwith; or

(b) where such an invitation is either not issued, or is issued and refused, cancel the registration.

Expenses of the Council

6(1) The prescribed form shall require applicants for registration to state their annual turnover to the nearest £1000.

(2) The expenses of the Council shall be met by a levy set by the Secretary of State and expressed as a percentage of the annual

turnover of persons whose names and addresses are included in the Register.

Penalties and Proceedings

7(1) A person guilty of an offence under this Act shall be liable:
   (a) on summary conviction to a fine not exceeding £10 000; or
   (b) on conviction on indictment to a fine not exceeding £100 000.
 (2) No proceedings for an offence under this Act may be initiated except by, or with the consent of, the Director of Public Prosecutions.

Interpretation

8   In this Act the following expressions have the meaning assigned to them respectively, that is to say:-

'charter operator' means a person who arranges or provides travel facilities for sale to organizations, societies, or other groups, but not to individual customers;

'holiday accommodation' means temporary accommodation in hotels, boarding houses, other dwellings or caravans;

'prescribed form' means such form as the Secretary of State shall prescribe;

'tour operator' means a person who arranges, on a large scale, travel or holiday facilities for sale either directly or through travel agents, to individual customers;

'travel agent' means a person who carries on business arranging or providing holiday accommodation for members of the public.

Short Title, Commencement and Territorial Extent

9(1) This Act may be cited as the Travel Agents Registration Act.
 (2) Without prejudice to section 2(2), this Act shall come into force at the expiration of one month after the day on which it is passed.
 (3) This Act does not extend to Scotland or Northern Ireland.

QUESTIONS:

(a) For what purposes, if any, would the courts be able to refer to the Report of the Committee which preceded the Act?
(b) Must each person appointed to the Council have comprehensive 'knowledge and experience of the requirements of the travelling public and of the interests of travel agents and of tour and charter operators', or is it sufficient that the Council as a whole should have such knowledge and experience, with individual members each having only one kind of knowledge and experience?
(c) Jason, who is registered for the purposes of the Act, has an insurance policy which satisfies the Secretary of State. However, as a result of an error by his bank, the annual premium is not paid. The insurance company decides that, in accordance with the terms of the policy,

Jason no longer has insurance cover. When Jason discovers what has happened, he immediately pays the premium and the company re-instates his cover. Naturally, Jason did not initially know of the non-payment of the premium, and accordingly he did not notify the Council under s.4(1). Has Jason committed an offence under s.4(2)?

(d) Would the definition of 'holiday accommodation' include (i) a camp site where holiday-makers pitch their own tents; and (ii) a camp site where permanently pitched tents are let to holiday-makers?

22 Some Studies of Statutory Drafting and Interpretation

22.1 Introduction

Having considered the processes of statutory drafting and interpretation, it may be useful at this stage to look at certain specific criticisms and proposals which have emerged from a number of studies in relatively recent times. The Law Commissions' report, published in 1969, on *The Interpretation of Statutes* (Law Com No 21), was followed in 1975 by the report of a committee appointed by the Lord President of the Council, under the chairmanship of Sir David Renton, on *The Preparation of Legislation*. In 1977, Sir William Dale published a comparative study, *Legislative Drafting: A New Approach*. In 1993, the Hansard Society for Parliamentary Government published a substantial report under the title *Making the Law*.

This chapter outlines some of the major recommendations of the Law Commissions and the Renton Committee, as well as considering Dale's *New Approach*, before concluding with a statement of 'five central principles' which the Hansard Society formulated.

22.2 The Law Commissions' Report

The Law Commissions recommended that *such weight as appropriate* should be given to headings, marginal notes and punctuation; reports laid before Parliament before the Act was passed; relevant treaties and other international agreements which were presented to Parliament before the Act was passed; other relevant documents which were presented to Parliament before the Act was passed; and any documents which the Act itself declared to be relevant.

The report also recommended that *regard should be had* to the legislative purpose, and to international obligations. In accordance with the Law Commissions' common practice, the report included a draft Bill which, if enacted, would implement its recommendations.

22.3 The Renton Report

The *Renton Report* supported the Law Commissions' recommendations relating to headings, marginal notes and punctuation; relevant treaties and other international agreements which were presented to Parliament before the Act was passed; the legislative purpose; and international obligations. However, the report concluded that the Law Commissions' recommendation as to documents which an Act itself declares to be relevant was superfluous. It also concluded that the Law Commissions' recommendations relating to reports laid before Parliament before the Act was passed, and to other relevant documents which were presented to Parliament before the Act was passed, would both be too time-consuming in practice.

The *Renton Report* emphasized the importance of having regard to the interests of the users of statutes. More particularly, an Act is a long-term creation, and therefore the interests of its users should prevail over the interests of Parliament, which is merely the short-term user of the Bill. The *Renton Report* also recognized that the traditional English style of drafting was intended to achieve immediate certainty, but doubted whether this was always necessary, especially with regard to private law topics (such as land law, tort, contract and so on), as opposed to public law topics (such as immigration, town and country planning, public housing law and so on), where the rights of the individual against the state are involved.

In terms of the structure of legislation, the *Renton Report* recommended that, where detail was desirable, there should be a generally recognized framework. The body of an Act should contain general principles; the schedules should contain details which are unlikely to change very often, or at all; and delegated legislation, which can be amended much more easily than a statute, should contain detail which is likely to be changed frequently. The *Renton Report* also recommended that the Interpretation Act 1889 should be updated.

Neither the *Law Commissions' Report*, nor the *Renton Report* thought that *Hansard* should be used.

22.4 Parliament's Responses to the Reports of the Law Commissions and the Renton Committee

The Law Commissions' proposals

Lord Scarman introduced the Law Commissions' draft Bill into the House of Lords but withdrew it at Second Reading in the face of criticism.

The Renton Committee's proposals

The draft Bill, as amended in the light of the proposals contained in the *Renton Report*, was then introduced into the House of Lords in 1981, where it successfully completed all stages. In the Commons, however, it failed to obtain a Second Reading. The provisions of the Bill may be summarized as follows:

Clause 1

In ascertaining the meaning of a statute, the following may be considered, in addition to anything which could be considered under the existing principles, but the weight given to them should be 'no more than is appropriate in the circumstances':

(a) all indications in the Act as printed by authority, including headings, side notes, punctuation;
(b) treaties and other international agreements which are referred to in the Act, or of which copies have been presented to Parliament by command of the Queen, before the Act was passed;
(c) reports of Royal Commissions, committees or other bodies, which had been presented to, or laid before, either House of Parliament before the Act was passed;
(d) provisions of the European Communities' Treaties and Community instruments thereunder, to which the Act was intended to give effect. (This clause was not intended to change the existing principles in relation to the use of *Hansard*.)

Clause 2

Where more than one construction of a provision is reasonably possible, the following are relevant:

(a) the legislative intention;
(b) the international obligations of Her Majesty's Government;
(c) the presumption against retrospectivity.

Clause 3

The same principles apply to delegated legislation.

The *Renton Report's* suggestions for reform of the Interpretation Act 1889 were, however, taken up. The result is the Interpretation Act 1978.

The Interpretation Act 1978

English Interpretation Acts date from 1850, when *Lord Brougham's Act* was passed, with the express purpose of 'shortening the language of Acts of Parliament'. This was achieved then, and is still achieved now, by enacting a number of provisions which are of general application unless they are excluded either expressly or by implication. In other words, despite their titles, English Interpretation Acts have never prescribed principles of interpretation of the kind discussed in the previous chapters of this Part of this book.

The Interpretation Act 1978 updated the Interpretation Act 1889 in a number of detailed ways. For example, s.1 of the 1889 Act provided that words importing the masculine gender included females; and that words in the singular included the plural, and words in the plural included the singular. Thus the singular/plural provision worked both ways, whereas the gender provision worked only one way. Section 6 of the 1978 Act makes the gender provision work both ways.

The provisions of the Interpretation Act 1978 upon which drafters most commonly rely are reproduced in Appendix 2.

22.5 Dale's *New Approach*

Sir William Dale's study was commissioned by the Commonwealth Secretary-General, in order 'to examine means of improving and simplifying legislative drafting techniques, and methods of training draftsmen' in the specific context of the needs of developing countries. However, Dale's comments are of general interest. He noted that:

'In common law countries legislative drafting is regarded as a specialized art. It is endowed with a mystique which it does not possess in civil law countries. There we find neither mystery about it, nor training in it. Competent lawyers, it is assumed, able to express themselves clearly in writing, can pick up legislative drafting without difficulty . . . The prime requirement is to know the facts and the law on the subject – which goes for every legal process'. (*Legislative Drafting: A New Approach*, 1977, p. 339.)

This observation led to the conclusion that:

'The tendency of a system under which the drafting is entrusted to specialist technicians . . . is to produce texts of growing legal technicality, complexity and length; and one cannot see how this tendency can be reversed except by a basic change of style.' (*Legislative Drafting: A New Approach*, 1977, p. 333.)

The change in style which Dale envisaged was towards the 'lucid and often succinct drafting [which] is to be found in the countries on the European continent' (*Legislative Drafting: A New Approach*, 1977, p. 322). More particularly:

'We need at least to reduce the verbal impedimenta; to be less fussy over detail, to be more general and concise; and to situate each rule where it belongs in an orderly and logical development. On this level, the question is largely a matter of style and arrangement. A more profound change is also desirable: a determination to seek the principle, to express it, and to follow up with such detail, illuminating and not obscuring the principle, as the circumstances require.' (*Legislative Drafting: A New Approach*, 1977, p. 335.)

One of Dale's key recommendations was the establishment of a Law Council, which would be independent of government and whose role would be to:

'examine [draft Bills] from the point of view of coherent and orderly presentation, clarity, conciseness, soundness of legal principle, and suitability for attaining the Government's objective. It would report on these matters to the minister responsible, recommending such redrafting as it considered desirable. It would not concern itself with matters of policy; and it would be open to the government to reject the advice . . .

'The Law Council should possess sufficient expertise, and authority, and be sufficiently catholic in its composition, to command attention, respect and confidence.' (*Legislative Drafting: A New Approach*, 1977, p. 336.)

Dale suggested that the Law Council's membership should include not only judges, practitioners and professors of law, but also lay people, including authors and professors of literature.

Perhaps not surprisingly, Dale's suggestions were received with noticeable scepticism on the part of commentators from common law backgrounds. For example, in *Observations on the Proposed New Approach to Legislative Drafting in Common Law Countries* [1980] Stat LR 144, Geoffrey Kolts, the Second Parliamentary Counsel in Canberra, pointed out that Dale's study was based on an analysis of only four English statutes. Kolt's article is also generally sceptical of Dale's basic thesis that significant simplification is possible, bearing in mind the complexity of the schemes which are often implemented by legislation in the modern world.

22.6   The Hansard Society's 'Five Central Principles'

The Hansard Society identified the following five central principles:

'Laws are made for the benefit of the citizens of the state. All citizens directly affected should be involved as fully as possible in the processes by which statute law is prepared.

'Statute law should be as certain as possible and as intelligible and clear as possible, for the benefit of the citizen to whom it applies.

'Statute law must be rooted in the authority of Parliament and thoroughly exposed to open democratic scrutiny by the representatives of the people in Parliament.

'Ignorance of the law is no excuse, therefore the current statute law must be as accessible as possible to all who need to know it.

'The Government needs to be able to secure the passage of its legislation, but to get the law right and intelligible, for the benefit of citizens, is as important as to get it passed quickly.' (*Making the Law*, 1993, para.64.)

Summary

1   The Law Commissions' report, 1969, was followed in 1975 by the report of a committee under the chairmanship of Sir David Renton, on *The Preparation of Legislation*. In 1977, Sir William Dale published a comparative study, *Legislative Drafting: A New Approach*.

2   The Law Commissions made detailed recommendations as to what should and should not be taken into account when interpreting statutes. The report included a draft Bill which, if enacted, would implement its recommendations.

3   The *Renton Report* supported some of the Law Commissions' recommendations, but regarded others as being either superfluous or too time-consuming. The report recognized that the traditional English style of drafting was intended to achieve immediate certainty, but doubted whether this was always necessary. The report recommended that the Interpretation Act 1889 should be updated.

4   None of the major recommendations of the reports issued by the Law Commissions and Renton Committee has been enacted, except that the Interpretation Act 1889 was replaced by the Interpretation Act 1978.

5   Sir William Dale recommended that a simplified style of drafting should be adopted and that a Law Council, which would be independent of government, should be established in order to examine Bills with a view

to improving their presentation. Dale's suggestions were received with noticeable scepticism on the part of commentators from common law backgrounds.

6 The Hansard Society formulated five central principles which emphasized the perspective of people who are affected by statute law.

Exercise

Consider the principles contained in the Bill which the House of Lords passed in 1981, but which failed in the House of Commons. To what extent would the adoption of those principles alter the existing practice of statutory interpretation?

23 The Principles of Interpretation used by the European Court of Justice

23.1 Introduction

Historically it would have been legitimate to characterize the principal distinction between common law and civil law styles of interpretation in terms of the contrast between simple literalism and purposivism. Also historically, the matter was of largely academic interest, since very few practitioners of English law would ever come across laws originating from civil law jurisdictions. However, the reception of Community law into English law has meant that the civil law style of interpretation as practised by the Court of Justice is now of immediately practical importance to English lawyers. As Lord Denning MR said in *Bulmer (HP) Ltd* v. *Bollinger SA* [1974] 2 All ER 1226:

'It is apparent that in very many cases the English courts will interpret the Treaty themselves . . . Beyond doubt the English courts must follow the same principles as the European court. Otherwise there would be differences between [the member states] . . .'

Perhaps fortunately, the English judiciary's widespread conversion to purposive interpretation means that the gap between the two styles of interpretation has narrowed very considerably. Nevertheless, it is worth giving some attention to the Community law style of interpretation, and this chapter will do so. As a preliminary, however, it may be useful to offer some general observations on those characteristics of Community law which have the greatest influence on how it is interpreted.

23.2 Characteristics of Community Law which are Relevant to its Interpretation

First, Community legislation is drafted in several languages, and, since all the texts are equally authentic, all must be taken into account.

'When a single decision is addressed to all the Member States the necessity for uniform application and accordingly for uniform interpretation makes it impossible to consider one version of the text in isolation but requires that it be interpreted on the basis of both the real intention of its author and the aim he seeks to achieve, in the light in particular of the versions in all [the official] languages.' (*Stauder* v. *City of Ulm* [1969] ECR 419.)

Second, Community law has its own terminology and employs its own concepts, and every provision of Community law must be interpreted in the light of Community law as a whole:

'It must . . . be borne in mind, even where the different language versions are entirely in accord with one another, that Community Law uses terminology which is peculiar to it. Furthermore, it must be emphasized that legal concepts do not necessarily have the same meaning in Community Law and in the law of the various Member States.

'Finally . . . every provision of Community Law must be placed in its context and interpreted in the light of the provisions of Community Law as a whole, regard being had to the objectives thereof and to its state of evolution at the date on which the provision in question is to be applied.' (*CILFIT* v. *Ministry of Health* [1982] ECR 3415.)

Third, and in some ways most importantly, although the Treaties contain the fundamental provisions on which the Community's legal order is based, when it comes to Regulations, Directives and Decisions, the Community knows no doctrine of legislative supremacy. For example, the Court may quash Community legislation which contravenes the general principles of Community law (see Chapter 16). By way of further example, art.190 of the EC Treaty provides that 'Regulations, Directives and Decisions of the Council and of the Commission shall state the reasons on which they are based . . .' The Court explained the multi-faceted purpose of this provision in the *Brennwein Case* (*Germany* v. *Commission*) [1963] ECR 63:

'In imposing . . . the obligation to state reasons . . . art.190 is not taking mere formal considerations into account but seeks to give an opportunity to the parties of defending their rights, to the Court of exercising its supervisory functions, and to member states and to all interested nationals of ascertaining the circumstances in which [the Treaty has been applied].'

It follows that when the Court is deciding whether to quash a provision because its statement of reasons is insufficient to comply with art.190, it will ask itself whether the opportunities set out in *Brennwein* have been genuinely made available. However, the stringency of the test which the Court applies will vary with the type of act in question. For example, Regulations are legislative measures of a general character, and therefore will require less specific reasons than Decisions, which are issued to named addressees, and where, therefore, a higher degree of specificity can reasonably be expected.

23.3   The Principles of Interpretation

Teleological interpretation

Although, the practice of statutory interpretation in the English courts has become increasingly purposive since the Second World War, there are nevertheless degrees of purposivism. The English courts have generally moved towards a relatively conservative version in which the court seeks to identify what it calls the intention of the legislature, even though, as we saw in Chapter 20 this apparently simple concept is far from straightforward.

The European Court of Justice, in common with the courts of the Communities' original members, draws on a different legal tradition from that which gave rise to the common law. Within the continental tradition, which traces its origins back to Roman law, a more dynamic form of purposivism, known as the *teleological* approach, has been commonplace. It is not surprising, therefore, that the Court of Justice, faced with the task of turning the Communities' legislative texts into a working legal system, should have embraced the teleological approach.

> 'Rather than adopting a narrower historical-purposive approach, the Court tends to examine the whole context in which a particular provision is situated – which often involves looking at the preamble to the Treaties or the legislation – and it gives the interpretation most likely to further *what the Court considers that provision in its context was aimed to achieve*. Often this is very far from a literal interpretation of the Treaty or legislation in question, even to the extent of flying in the face of the express language . . .' (Craig and de Burca, *EC Law: Text Cases and Materials*, 1995, p. 82. Emphasis added.)

However, without in any way intending to cast doubt on the primacy of the teleological approach to the interpretation of Community law, it would be wrong to suggest that the Court of Justice is entirely free from textual constraints.

Literal meaning, clear meaning and legal meaning

As Advocate-General Mayras explained in *Fellinger* [1980] ECR 535, there may be a distinction between the 'literal meaning' and the 'clear meaning' of a provision:

'Where a literal interpretation of a rule of written law leads to an unreasonable or unjust result is it permissible for the Court to look for another interpretation which avoids that result? In my opinion, one may be guided on this by general principles of interpretation and by the case-law of the Court.

'The distinct roles of the legislator and the judge within a national legal system have been elegantly described by Portalis:

"There is the art of the legislator just as there is the art of the judge, and they are not alike. The art of the legislator lies in seeking for each issue those principles which are most beneficial to the common weal; the art of the judge lies in putting those principles into practice, in developing them and extending them by applying them wisely and rationally to individual cases; in studying the spirit of the law when its letter is lifeless; in not exposing himself to the danger of being in turn both slave and rebel and of transgressing through a spirit of servility."

'In accordance with the distinction drawn by that eminent jurist, this Court may not substitute its discretion for that of the Community legislature; when the meaning of the legislation is clear it has to be applied with that meaning, even if the solution prescribed may be thought to be unsatisfactory. That is not to say, however, that the literal construction of a provision must always be accepted. If such construction were to lead to a nonsensical result in regard to a situation which the Court believed the provision was intended to cover, certain doubts might properly be entertained in regard to it. In other words, the clear meaning and the literal meaning are not synonymous. *There have been many cases in which the Court has rejected a literal interpretation in favour of another which it found more compatible with the objective and the whole scheme of the legislation in question.*' (Emphasis added.)

More particularly, a word is to be given its ordinary legal meaning, unless the context otherwise requires. In *Netherlands* v. *Commission* [1979]

ECR 245, a Regulation dealing with the so-called butter mountain provided for butter which had been in store for more than four months to be sold to the intervention agency, which would then re-sell the butter in the export market. The resale had to be within 30 days of the sale to the agency. An issue arose as to whether the thirty day period ran from the conclusion of the contract of sale to the agency, or from the time the butter left the store. The date of leaving the store was held to be irrelevant, because there was 'no reason why the term "sale" . . . should be given a meaning different to that which it has in ordinary legal language'.

Where a provision has been amended or replaced, the original can be consulted, because a change of wording raises a presumption of a change of meaning. In *Simon* v. *Court of Justice* [1961] ECR 115, employees who lived more than a certain distance from their place of work were eligible for separation allowances. An early Regulation had spoken in terms of living 'within a radius of 25 km', but its successor spoke merely in terms of 'distance'. Simon's journey to work was 26 km by road and 29 km by rail, but less than 25 km as the crow flies.

'If the word "radius" had replaced the word "distance" in the article, the scope of the amendment would have been clear, for the authors of the new provisions would have obviously had the intention of choosing between the two possible interpretations of the former wording that which related to the concept of distance as the crow flies.

'In the present case, however, it is the reverse which has happened.

'The very fact of having replaced in the present case the word "radius" by the word "distance" clearly shows that the authors of the article wished to reject the concept of "as the crow flies" (a concept which was clearly expressed by the word "radius") and that they wished on the other hand to adopt the concept of "journey" by road or railway . . .

'It must also be observed that [the provision] does not prescribe precisely the method of calculating the distance (by road or rail or the shortest of these two ways).

'If the drafting is defective there is nothing to prevent selecting by means of interpretation the most reasonable criterion, that is to say, that of the shortest distance either by road or by rail of a normal journey.'

Retrospectivity

The extent to which the Court's decisions have retrospective effect has already been discussed at pp. 214–16.

Where there is no express statement

In *Meroni & Co* [1957–58] ECR 157, the Court formulated what amounts to a rather restrictive version of the *expressio unius exclusio alterius* principle, which is discussed in the context of English law at p. 282. More particularly, the Court said that what it called 'an argument in reverse' is possible only where 'no other interpretation appears appropriate and compatible with the provision and its context and with the purpose of the same'. In other words, such arguments are available only as a last resort.

Summary

1   Since the English courts have generally moved towards the purposive approach to interpretation, the gap between English and European styles of interpretation has been reduced, and is now more a matter of degree than of kind.
2   Community legislation is drafted in several languages, and all the texts are equally authentic.
3   Community law has its own terminology and employs its own concepts.
4   The Community knows no doctrine of legislative supremacy, and therefore the Court of Justice may quash Community legislation.
5   The Court of Justice may draw a distinction between the clear meaning and the literal meaning of a provision. A word is to be given its ordinary legal meaning, unless the context otherwise requires.
6   Where a provision has been amended or replaced, the original can be consulted, because a change of wording raises a presumption of a change of meaning.
7   An interpretation deduced from the absence of an express statement may be acceptable, but only as a last resort.

Exercises

1   What particular problems of legislative interpretation arise from the nature of the European Community?
2   What (if anything) is the difference between the European Court of Justice and the English courts in their approach to ordinary and legal meanings?

Appendix 1: Law Reports and Journals (Some Useful References)

(A comprehensive listing of current references is included in each monthly part of *Current Law*.)

AC (formerly App Cas) = Appeal Cases (Law Reports)
Admin LR = Administrative Law Reports
All ER = All England Law Reports
All ER (EC) = All England Law Reports (European Cases)
All ER Rep = All England Law Reports Reprint (containing a selection of cases which predate the All England Law Reports themselves).
Anglo-Am = Anglo-American Law Review

BLR = Building Law Reports

CJQ = Civil Justice Quarterly
CLY = Current Law Yearbook
CMLR = Common Market Law Reports
CML Rev = Common Market Law Review
COD = Crown Office Digest
Ch (formerly ChD) = Chancery (Law Reports)
Co Law = Company Lawyer
Con LR = Construction Law Reports
Conv(ns) (or Conv or Conveyancer) = Conveyancer and Property Lawyer (New Series)
Cox CC = Cox's Criminal Cases
Cr App R (or CAR) = Criminal Appeal Reports
Cr App R (S) (or CAR(S)) = Criminal Appeal Reports (Sentencing)
Crim LR = Criminal Law Review
DLR = Dominion Law Reports (a Canadian series)

EBLRev = European Business Law Review
ECR = European Court Reports
EG =Estates Gazette
EGLR = Estates Gazette Law Reports
EHRR = European Human Rights Reports

ELRev = European Law Review
ER = English Reports

FCR = Family Court Reporter
FLR = Family Law Reports
FSR = Fleet Street Reports
FTLR = Financial Times Law Reports
Fam = Family Division (Law Reports)
Fam Law = Family Law

Harv LR = Harvard Law Review
HLR = Housing Law Reports

ICLQ = International and Comparative Law Quarterly
ICR = Industrial Cases Reports
ILJ = Industrial Law Journal
Imm AR = Immigration Appeals Reports
IRLR = Industrial Relations Law Reports
ITR = Industrial Tribunal Reports

JBL = Journal of Business Law
JP = Justice of the Peace Reports
JPL = Journal of Planning and Environment Law (formerly Journal of
    Planning Law)
JPN = Justice of the Peace Journal (Abbreviating 'Journal' to 'N' may
    seem rather odd. The explanation is that this periodical was originally
    known as 'Justice of the Peace Newspaper', and the 'JPN' abbreviation
    has survived even though it is now commonly referred to as 'Justice of
    the Peace Journal' by way of contradistinction to 'Justice of the Peace
    Reports' – see 'JP')
JR = Juridical Review
JSPTL = Journal of the Society of Public Teachers of Law
JSWL = Journal of Social Welfare Law

KB = King's Bench (Law Reports)
KIR = Knight's Industrial Reports

LGR = Local Government Reports
LG Rev = Local Government Review (renamed as Local Government
    Review Reports in November 1993)
LJ = Law Journal
Ll Rep (formerly Lloyd's Rep) = Lloyd's List Reports
LQR = Law Quarterly Review
LS = Legal Studies
LS Gaz = Law Society's Gazette
LT = Law Times

MLR = Modern Law Review
Med LR = Medical Law Reports
NILQ = Northern Ireland Legal Quarterly
NZLR = New Zealand Law Reports
New LJ (or NLJ)= New Law Journal

OJ = Official Journal of the European Communities
OJLS = Oxford Journal of Legal Studies

P (formerly PD) = Probate (Law Reports)
P & CR = Property and Compensation Reports (formerly Planning and Compensation Reports)
PL = Public Law

QB (formerly QBD) = Queen's Bench (Law Reports)

RPC = Reports of Patent, Design and Trade Mark Cases
RTR = Road Traffic Reports

SJ (sometimes given as Sol Jo) = Solicitors' Journal
SLT = Scots Law Times
STC = Simon's Tax Cases
Stat LR = Statute Law Review

TLR = Times Law Reports

US = United States Reports

WLR = Weekly Law Reports

Yale LJ = Yale Law Journal

Appendix 2:   Extracts from the Interpretation Act 1978

The words appearing in **bold type** immediately after the section numbers are the marginal notes of the Queen's Printer's text.

EXTRACTS FROM THE
INTERPRETATION ACT 1978

General provisions as to enactment and operation

3   **Judicial notice** Every Act is a public Act to be judicially noticed as such, unless the contrary is expressly provided by the Act.

4   **Time of commencement** An Act or provision of an Act comes into force –
(a) where provision is made for it to come into force on a particular day, at the beginning of that day;
(b)   where no provision is made for its coming into force, at the beginning of the day on which the Act receives the Royal Assent.

Interpretation and construction

5   **Definitions** In any Act, unless the contrary intention appears, words and expressions listed in Schedule I to this Act are to be construed according to that Schedule.

6   **Gender and number** In any Act, unless the contrary intention appears –
(a) words importing the masculine gender include the feminine;
(b) words importing the feminine gender include the masculine;
(c) words in the singular include the plural and words in the plural include the singular.

7   **References to service by post** Where an Act authorises or requires any document to be served by post (whether the expression 'serve' or the expression 'give' or 'send' or any other expression is used) then, unless the contrary intention appears, the service is deemed to be effected by properly addressing, pre-paying and posting a letter containing the document and,

unless the contrary is proved, to have been effected at the time at which the letter would be delivered in the ordinary course of post.

8 **References to distance** In the measurement of any distance for the purposes of an Act, that distance shall, unless the contrary intention appears, be measured in a straight line on a horizontal plane.

9 **References to time of day** Subject to section 3 of the Summer Time Act 1972 (construction of references to points of time during the period of summer time), whenever an expression of time occurs in an Act, the time referred to shall, unless it is otherwise specifically stated, be held to be Greenwich mean time.

11 **Construction of subordinate legislation** Where an Act confers power to make subordinate legislation, expressions used in that legislation have, unless the contrary intention appears, the meaning which they bear in the Act.

Statutory powers and duties

12 **Continuity of powers and duties** (1) Where an Act confers a power or imposes a duty it is implied, unless the contrary intention appears, that the power may be exercised, or the duty is to be performed, from time to time as occasion requires.

(2) Where an Act confers a power or imposes a duty on the holder of an office as such, it is implied, unless the contrary intention appears, that the power may be exercised, or the duty is to be performed, by the holder for the time being of the office.

13 **Anticipatory exercise of powers** Where an Act which (or any provision of which) does not come into force immediately on its passing confers powers to make subordinate legislation, or to make appointments, give notices, prescribe forms or do any other thing for the purposes of the Act, then, unless the contrary intention appears, the power may be exercised, and any instrument made thereunder may be made so as to come into force, at any time after the passing of the Act so far as may be necessary or expedient for the purpose –

(a) of bringing the Act or any provision of the Act into force; or

(b) of giving full effect to the Act or any such provision at or after the time when it comes into force.

14 **Implied power to amend** Where an Act confers power to make –

(a) rules, regulations or byelaws; or

(b) Orders in Council, orders or other subordinate legislation to be made by statutory instrument,

it implies, unless the contrary intention appears, a power, exercisable in the same manner and subject to the same conditions or limitations, to revoke, amend or re-enact any instrument made under the power.

Repealing enactments

15 Repeal of repeal Where an Act repeals a repealing enactment, the repeal does not revive any enactment previously repealed unless words are added reviving it.

16 General savings (1) Without prejudice to section 15, where an Act repeals an enactment, the repeal does not, unless the contrary intention appears –

(a) revive anything not in force or existing at the time at which the repeal takes effect;

(b) affect the previous operation of the enactment repealed or anything duly done or suffered under that enactment;

(c) affect any right, privilege, obligation or liability acquired, accrued or incurred under that enactment;

(d) affect any penalty, forfeiture or punishment incurred in respect of any offence committed against that enactment;

(e) affect any investigation, legal proceeding or remedy in respect of any such right, privilege, obligation, liability, penalty, forfeiture or punishment;

and any such investigation, legal proceeding or remedy may be instituted, continued or enforced, and any such penalty, forfeiture or punishment may be imposed, as if the repealing Act had not been passed.

(2) This section applies to the expiry of a temporary enactment as if it were repealed by an Act.

17 Repeal and re-enactment (1) Where an Act repeals a previous enactment and substitutes provisions for the enactment repealed, the repealed enactment remains in force until the substituted provisions come into force.

(2) Where an Act repeals and re-enacts, with or without modification, a previous enactment then, unless the contrary intention appears –

(a) any reference in any other enactment to the enactment so repealed shall be construed as a reference to the provision re-enacted;

(b) in so far as any subordinate legislation made or other thing done under the enactment so repealed, or having effect as if so made or done, could have been made or done under the provision re-enacted, it shall have effect as if made or done under that provision.

Miscellaneous

18 Duplicated offences Where an act or omission constitutes an offence under two or more Acts, or both under an Act and at common law, the offender shall, unless the contrary intention appears, be liable to be prosecuted and punished under either or any of those Acts or at common law, but shall not be liable to be punished more than once for the same offence.

Supplementary

21   Interpretation etc (1) In this Act 'Act' includes a local and personal or private Act; and 'subordinate legislation' means Orders in Council, orders, rules, regulations, schemes, warrants, byelaws and other instruments made or to be made under any Act.
(2) This Act binds the Crown.

Schedule I
(extracts)

'Commencement', in relation to an Act or enactment, means the time when the Act or enactment comes into force.

'The Communities', 'the Treaties' or 'the Community Treaties' and other expressions defined by section 1 of and Schedule I to the European Communities Act 1972 have the meanings prescribed by that Act.

'Month' means calendar month.

'Person' includes a body of persons corporate or unincorporate.

'Secretary of State' means one of Her Majesty's Principal Secretaries of State.

'Writing' includes typing, printing, lithography, photography and other modes of representing or reproducing words in a visible form, and expressions referring to writing are to be construed accordingly.

Appendix 3: Extracts from the European Convention for the Protection of Human Rights and Fundamental Freedoms

Article 1

The High Contracting Parties shall secure to everyone within their jurisdiction the rights and freedoms defined in section 1 of this Convention.

SECTION 1

Article 2

1. Everyone's right to life shall be protected by law. No one shall be deprived of his life intentionally save in the execution of a sentence of a court following his conviction of a crime for which this penalty is provided by law.
2. Deprivation of life shall not be regarded as inflicted in contravention of this Article when it results from the use of force which is no more than absolutely necessary:
    (a) in defence of any person from unlawful violence;
    (b) in order to effect a lawful arrest or to prevent the escape of a person lawfully detained;
    (c) in action lawfully taken for the purpose of quelling a riot or insurrection

Article 3

No one shall be subjected to torture or to inhuman or degrading treatment or punishment.

Article 4

1. No one shall be held in slavery or servitude.
2. No one shall be required to perform forced or compulsory labour.

3.   For the purpose of this Article the term 'forced or compulsory labour' shall not include:

(a)   any work required to be done in the ordinary course of detention imposed according to the provisions of Article 5 of this Convention or during conditional release from such detention;

(b)   any service of a military character or, in case of conscientious objectors in countries where they are recognized, service exacted instead of compulsory military service;

(c)   any service exacted in case of an emergency or calamity threatening the life or well-being of the community;

(d)   any work or service which forms part of normal civic obligations.

Article 5

1.   Everyone has the right to liberty and security of person. No one shall be deprived of his liberty save in the following cases and in accordance with a procedure prescribed by law:

(a)   the lawful detention of a person after conviction by a competent court;

(b)   the lawful arrest or detention of a person for non-compliance with the lawful order of a court or in order to secure the fulfilment of any obligation prescribed by law;

(c)   the lawful arrest or detention of a person effected for the purpose of bringing him before the competent legal authority on reasonable suspicion of having committed an offence or when it is reasonably considered necessary to prevent his committing an offence or fleeing after having done so;

(d)   the detention of a minor by lawful order for the purpose of educational supervision or his lawful detention for the purpose of bringing him before the competent legal authority;

(e)   the lawful detention of persons for the prevention of the spreading of infectious diseases, of persons of unsound mind, alcoholics or drug addicts, or vagrants;

(f)   the lawful arrest or detention of a person to prevent his effecting an unauthorized entry into the country or of a person against whom action is being taken with a view to deportation or extradition.

2.   Everyone who is arrested shall be informed promptly, in a language which he understands, of the reasons for his arrest and of any charge against him.

3.   Everyone arrested or detained in accordance with the provisions of paragraph 1(c) of this Article shall be brought promptly before a judge or other officer authorized by law to exercise judicial power and shall be entitled to trial within a reasonable time or to release pending trial. Release may be conditioned by guarantees to appear for trial.

4.   Everyone who is deprived of his liberty by arrest or detention shall be entitled to take proceedings by which the lawfulness of his detention shall be decided speedily by a court and his release ordered if the detention is not lawful.

5.   Everyone who has been the victim of arrest or detention in contravention of the provisions of this Article shall have an enforceable right to compensation.

Article 6

1.   In the determination of his civil rights and obligations or of any criminal charge against him, everyone is entitled to a fair and public hearing within a reasonable time by an independent and impartial tribunal established by law. Judgement shall be pronounced publicly but the press and public may be excluded from all or part of the trial in the interest of morals, public order or national security in a democratic society, where the interest of juveniles or the protection of the private life of the parties so require, or to the extent strictly necessary in the opinion of the court in special circumstances where publicity would prejudice the interests of justice.

2.   Everyone charged with a criminal offence shall be presumed innocent until proved guilty according to law.

3.   Everyone charged with a criminal offence has the following minimum rights:

   (a)   to be informed promptly, in a language which he understands and in detail, of the nature and cause of the accusation against him;

   (b)   to have adequate time and facilities for the preparation of his defence;

   (c)   to defend himself in person or through legal assistance of his own choosing or, if he has not sufficient means to pay for legal assistance, to be given it free when the interests of justice so require;

   (d)   to examine or have examined witnesses against him and to obtain the attendance and examination of witnesses on his behalf under the same conditions as witnesses against him;

   (e)   to have the free assistance of an interpreter if he cannot understand or speak the language used in court.

Article 7

1.   No one shall be held guilty of any criminal offence on account of any act or omission which did not constitute a criminal offence under national or international law at the time when it was committed. Nor shall a heavier penalty be imposed than the one that was applicable at the time the criminal offence was committed.

2.   This Article shall not prejudice the trial and punishment of any person for any act or omission which, at the time when it was committed, was criminal according to the general principles of law recognized by civilized nations.

Article 8

1.   Everyone has the right to respect for his private and family life, his home and his correspondence.
2.   There shall be no interference by a public authority with the exercise of this right except such as is in accordance with the law and is necessary in a democratic society in the interests of national security, public safety or the economic well-being of the country, for the prevention of disorder or crime, for the protection of health or morals, or for the protection of the rights and freedoms of others.

Article 9

1.   Everyone has the right to freedom of thought, conscience and religion; this right includes freedom to change his religion or belief, and freedom, either alone or in community with others and in public or private, to manifest his religion or belief, in worship, teaching, practice and observance.
2.   Freedom to manifest one's religion or beliefs shall be subject only to such limitations as are prescribed by law and are necessary in a democratic society in the interests of public safety, for the protection of public order, health or morals, or for the protection of the rights and freedoms of others.

Article 10

1.   Everyone has the right to freedom of expression. This right shall include freedom to hold opinions and to receive and impart information and ideas without interference by public authority and regardless of frontiers. This Article shall not prevent States from requiring the licensing of broadcasting, television or cinema enterprises.
2.   The exercise of these freedoms, since it carries with it duties and responsibilities, may be subject to such formalities, conditions, restrictions or penalties as are prescribed by law and are necessary in a democratic society in the interests of national security, territorial integrity or public safety, for the prevention of disorder or crime, for the protection of health or morals, for the protection of the reputation or rights of others, for preventing the disclosure of information received in confidence, or for maintaining the authority and impartiality of the judiciary.

Article 11

1. Everyone has the right to freedom of peaceful assembly and to freedom of association with others, including the right to form and to join trade unions for the protection of his interests.
2. No restrictions shall be placed on the exercise of these rights other than such as are prescribed by law and are necessary in a democratic society in the interests of national security or public safety, for the prevention of disorder or crime, for the protection of health or morals or for the protection of the rights and freedoms of others. This Article shall not prevent the imposition of lawful restrictions on the exercise of these rights by members of the armed forces, of the police or of the administration of the State.

Article 12

Men and women of marriageable age have the right to marry and to found a family, according to the national laws governing the exercise of this right.

Article 13

Everyone whose rights and freedoms as set forth in this Convention are violated shall have an effective remedy before a national authority notwithstanding that the violation has been committed by persons acting in an official capacity.

Article 14

The enjoyment of the rights and freedoms set forth in this Convention shall be secured without discrimination on any ground such as sex, race, colour, language, religion, political or other opinion, national or social origin, association with a national minority, property, birth or other status.

Article 15

1. In time of war or other public emergency threatening the life of the nation any High Contracting Party may take measures derogating from its obligations under this Convention to the extent strictly required by the exigencies of the situation, provided that such measures are not inconsistent with its other obligations under international law.
2. No derogation from Article 2, except in respect of deaths resulting from lawful acts of war, or from Articles 3, 4 (paragraph 1) and 7 shall be made under this provision.
3. Any High Contracting Party availing itself of this right of derogation shall keep the Secretary-General of the Council of Europe fully informed

of the measures which it has taken and the reasons therefor. It shall also inform the Secretary-General of the Council of Europe when such measures have ceased to operate and the provisions of the Convention are again being fully executed.

Article 16

Nothing in Articles 10, 11, and 14 shall be regarded as preventing the High Contracting Parties from imposing restrictions on the political activity of aliens.

Article 17

Nothing in this Convention may be interpreted as implying for any State, group or person any right to engage in any activity or perform any act aimed at the destruction of any of the rights and freedoms set forth herein or at their limitation to a greater extent than is provided for in the Convention.

Article 18

The restrictions permitted under this Convention to the said rights and freedoms shall not be applied for any purpose other than those for which they have been prescribed.

PROTOCOL 1 – ENFORCEMENT OF CERTAIN RIGHTS AND FREEDOMS NOT INCLUDED IN SECTION 1 OF THE CONVENTION

Article 1

Every natural or legal person is entitled to the peaceful enjoyment of his possessions. No one shall be deprived of his possessions except in the public interest and subject to the conditions provided for by law and by the general principles of international law. The preceding provisions shall not, however, in any way impair the right of a State to enforce such laws as it deems necessary to control the use of property in accordance with the general interest or to secure the payment of taxes or other contributions or penalties.

Article 2

No person shall be denied the right to education. In the exercise of any functions which it assumes in relation to education and to teaching, the State shall respect the right of parents to ensure such education and teaching in conformity with their own religious and philosophical convictions.

Article 3

The High Contracting Parties undertake to hold free elections at reasonable intervals by secret ballot, under conditions which will ensure the free expression of the opinion of the people in the choice of the legislature.

PROTOCOL 4 – PROTECTING CERTAIN ADDITIONAL RIGHTS

Article 1

No one shall be deprived of his liberty merely on the ground of inability to fulfil a contractual obligation.

Article 2

1.   Everyone lawfully within the territory of a State shall, within that territory, have the right to liberty of movement and freedom to choose his residence.
2.   Everyone shall be free to leave any country, including his own.
3.   No restrictions shall be placed on the exercise of these rights other than such as are in accordance with law and are necessary in a democratic society in the interests of national security or public safety, for the maintenance of 'ordre public', for the prevention of crime or for the protection of the rights and freedoms of others.
4.   The rights set forth in paragraph 1 may also be subject, in particular areas, to restrictions imposed in accordance with law and justified by the public interest in a democratic society.

Article 3

1.   No one shall be expelled, by means either of an individual or of a collective measure, from the territory of the State of which he is a national.
2.   No one shall be deprived of the right to enter the territory of the State of which he is a national.

Article 4

Collective expulsion of aliens is prohibited.

Selected Further Reading

The task of selecting further reading raises two problems. First, this book covers a very wide range of material, and therefore the range of potential further reading is so vast that it would be both impossible and unhelpful to list it all. Second, much of the material which I have tried to make accessible in this book is sometimes discussed elsewhere in more abstruse and theoretical terms, which can make it rather intimidating for readers approaching the study of law for the first time. It follows that the suggestions set out below do not claim to be exhaustive.

Furthermore, the selection is even more subjective than selected reading lists usually are, and therefore readers who are pursuing formal courses of study should pay careful attention to the recommendations of their lecturers, since some people may have a high regard for certain books which I have omitted. In all cases I have specified the editions which were current at the time of writing, but it is important that you use any later editions which may have become available subsequently.

Within each category I have tried to list the books in ascending order of difficulty.

Part I: Ideas and Institutions

For a basic book on thinking logically in any context, see:

Thinking About Thinking, by A. Flew, 1989, Fontana.

For a description of the structure of the English Legal Systems, see:

The English Legal Process, by T. Ingman, 6th edn, 1996, Blackstone Press.

For the constitutional background, see:

Constitutional and Administrative Law, by J. Alder, 2nd edn, 1994, Macmillan.
Constitutional and Administrative Law, by S. de Smith and R. Brazier, 7th edn, 1994, by R. Brazier, Penguin.

For material specifically on the European Community Dimension, see:

Law of the European Union, by J. Shaw, 2nd edn, 1996, Macmillan.
Textbook on EC Law, by J. Steiner and L. Woods, 5th edn, 1996, Blackstone Press.
EC Law: Text, Cases and Materials, by P. Craig and G. du Burca, 1995, Oxford University Press.

For material on jurisprudence, legal theory and legal reasoning, see:

> *The Law Making Process*, by M. Zander, 4th edn, 1994, Butterworths.
> *Learning Legal Skills*, by S. Lee and M. Fox, 2nd edn, 1994, Blackstone Press.
> *Legal Philosophies*, by J. W. Harris, 1980, Butterworths.
> *Jurisprudence*, by J. G. Riddall, 1991, Butterworths.
> *How To Do Things With Rules*, by W. Twining and D. Miers, 3rd edn, 1991, Butterworths.
> *Jurisprudence: Texts and Commentary*, by H. Davies and D. Holdcroft, 1991, Butterworths.
> *Lloyd's Introduction to Jurisprudence*, by M. D. A. Freeman, 6th edn, 1994, Sweet & Maxwell.

Part II: Case-Law and Precedent

In addition to the books already cited on jurisprudence, legal theory and legal reasoning, see:

> *Precedent in English Law*, by Sir Rupert Cross, 4th edn, 1991, by J. W. Harris, Oxford University Press.
> *Precedent and Law*, by J. Stone, 1985, Butterworths.
> *Precedent in Law*, by L. Goldstein, (ed.), 1987, Oxford University Press.

Part III: Statute Law and Statutory Interpretation

In addition to the books already cited on jurisprudence, legal theory and legal reasoning, see:

> *Cross: Statutory Interpretation*, by J. Bell and Sir George Engle, 3rd edn, 1995, Butterworths.
> *Statutory Interpretation*, by J. Evans, 1988, Oxford University Press.
> *Statute Law*, by F. Bennion, 3rd edn, 1990, Longman.
> *Statutory Interpretation*, by F. Bennion, 2nd edn, 1992, with 1995 supplement, Butterworths.

For a standard text on legislative drafting, see:

> *Legislative Drafting*, by G. C. Thornton, 3rd edn, 1987, Butterworths.

And for a more radical approach, see:

> *Legislative Drafting: A New Approach*, by Sir William Dale, 1977, Butterworths.

The Lighter Side

For two books in which a vast amount of learning is not only carried lightly; but also deployed deftly in the simultaneous achievement of entertainment and instruction, see:

> *Miscellany at Law*, by R. E. Megarry, 1955, revised impression 1958, Stevens.
> *A Second Miscellany-at-Law*, by R. E. Megarry, 1973, Stevens.

Index